The Grateful Dead in Concert

THE GRATEFUL DEAD IN CONCERT

Essays on Live Improvisation

Edited by JIM TUEDIO *and* STAN SPECTOR

Foreword by STANLEY KRIPPNER

McFarland & Company, Inc., Publishers
Jefferson, North Carolina, and London

Lyrics to Grateful Dead songs © copyright Ice Nine Publishing Company. Used with permission.

Library of Congress Cataloguing-in-Publication Data

The Grateful Dead in concert : essays on live improvisation / edited by Jim Tuedio and Stan Spector ; foreword by Stanley Krippner.
    p.   cm.
Includes bibliographical references and index.

ISBN 978-0-7864-4357-4
softcover : 50# alkaline paper ∞

1. Grateful Dead (Musical group)   2. Rock music — History and criticism.   3. Improvisation (Music)   I. Tuedio, James Alan.   II. Spector, Stan.
ML421.G72G72   2010
782.42166092'2 — dc22   2009047270

British Library cataloguing data are available

©2010 Jim Tuedio and Stan Spector. All rights reserved

No part of this book may be reproduced or transmitted in any form or by any means, electronic or mechanical, including photocopying or recording, or by any information storage and retrieval system, without permission in writing from the publisher.

On the cover: The Grateful Dead performing at the Greek Theatre on the campus of the University of California at Berkeley (photograph by Susana Millman); cover art from the *Danse Macabre* woodcut by Michael Wolgemut, 1493

Manufactured in the United States of America

McFarland & Company, Inc., Publishers
    Box 611, Jefferson, North Carolina 28640
        www.mcfarlandpub.com

*For Shea,
and
for Avra.*

*For Julie, my patron saint since Winterland 1972,
and
for Sharona, my sweet chaos.*

*With special thanks to
Forrest Williams and Jerry Garcia.*

"...[T]he full Body, the stationary voyage ... experimentation. Where psychoanalysis says, 'Stop, find yourself again,' we should say instead, 'Let's go further still, we haven't found our BwO (body without organs) yet, we haven't sufficiently dismantled our self.' Substitute forgetting for anamnesis, experimentation for interpretation. Find your body without organs. Find out how to make it. It's a question of life and death, youth and old age, sadness and joy. It is where everything is played out."
— Deleuze and Guattari, *A Thousand Plateaus, 151.*

"My way is music. Music is me being me and trying to get higher. I've been into music so long that I'm dripping with it; it's all I ever expect to do. I can't do anything else. Music is a yoga, something you really do when you're doing it. Thinking about what it means comes after the fact and isn't very interesting. Truth is something you stumble into when you think you're going someplace else, like those moments when you're playing and the whole room becomes one being — precious moments, man. But you can't look for them and they can't be repeated. Being alive means to continue to change, never to be where I was before. Music is the timeless experience of constant change."
— Jerry Garcia, 1969 (*Dead Zone interview*).

"Collective Improvisation" means the ability of beings to communicate on a level beyond our normal relationships. When this occurs, those involved are able to not merely anticipate and react, but to lead, follow and affect the "conversation." This can happen in a room full of two without words, and it can happen in a landscape of thousands without sounds. But it can only happen when those involved are open to allowing it to happen and are aware enough to recognize it when it happens. Then it can be ridden like a wave — never the same but nevertheless recognizable.
— Michael Marlitt

Surf the sea of chaos / to find the islands of order.
— Phil Lesh

Meeting space for musical rapture. Buffalo, July 4, 1989 (© Lloyd Wolf/www.lloydwolf.com).

Contents

Tuning Up

Foreword: The Grateful Dead Phenomenon Stanley Krippner	1
Preface: Kaleidoscopic Entry to the Show	7
Introduction: "Shall We Go?"	11

First Set: Musical and Lyrical Elements of Grateful Dead Improvisation

Non-Systematic Thoughts About Improvisation Cristian Amigo	15
Mandalas and the Dead Graeme M. Boone	25
The Eccentric Revolutions of Phil Lesh Brent Wood	43
American Chaos: Charles Ives and the Grateful Dead Shaugn O'Donnell	58
"Mr. Charlie Told Me So": Heidegger and the Dead's Early Assimilation to the Technology of the Blues David Malvinni	71
Dark Star Mandala Graeme M. Boone	85
"Where All the Pages Are My Days": Metacantric Moments in Deadhead Lyrical Experience Revell Carr	107
"Not Just a Change of Style": Reading *Workingman's Dead* as an American Commentary with Americana Roots Erin McCoy	118

Second Set: Some Philosophical Contours of Grateful Dead Improvisation

Improvised Philosophy
    ALAN TRIST   129

"Pouring Its Light Into Ashes": Exploring the Multiplicity of Becoming in Grateful Dead Improvisation
    JIM TUEDIO   133

"Searching for the Sound": Grateful Dead Music and Interpretive Transformation
    JASON KEMP WINFREE   152

Plato's *Pharmakon*: Grateful Dead Concerts and the Politics of Getting High
    ELIZABETH CARROLL   164

When "Reason Tatters": Nietzsche and the Grateful Dead on Living a Healthy Life
    STAN SPECTOR   180

The Other One and the Other: Moral Lessons from a Reluctant Teacher
    STEVEN GIMBEL   191

Innocence and Experience in the Grateful Dead: A Reading of Stuart Hampshire
    NICHOLAS MERIWETHER   200

Third Set: Experiencing Community Through Grateful Dead Improvisation

Modeling Improvisation
    MARY GOODENOUGH   211

"Mysteries Dark and Vast": Grateful Dead Concerts and Initiation into the Sublime
    ERIC K. SILVERMAN   214

Bears and Flags: The Grateful Dead's America and Bohemian Nationalism
    JAY WILLIAMS   232

Improvising Community: A Hermeneutic Analysis of Deadheads and Virtual Communities
    GARY BURNETT   251

Strategic Improvisation: Management Lessons from the Dead
    BARRY BARNES   267

Cultural Communication Codes Among Deadheads:
A Chronological Account of Communicative Improvisation
    NATALIE J. DOLLAR   279

Examining Grateful Dead Improvisation as a Catalyst for
Creating Sustained *Communitas*
    AMANDA DIEDERICH-HIRSH   294

"I Can't Do Anything but Lie": Studying Deadheads While
Wearing Simmelian Lenses
    REBECCA G. ADAMS   310

Encore

The Thing Is the Thing Is the Thing Is the Thing Is
There Is No Thing
    CHRISTIAN CRUMLISH   325

All His Children Grew and Grew (Who Killed Uncle John?)
    DAVID GANS   329

Greensleeves

The Grateful Dead Came to Our House One Day (with
20 People and a Bottle of LSD): A Story About Discovering
the Power of Channeling Healing Energy
    JEAN MILLAY   339

Contributors   345

Index   351

TUNING UP

The sound bubble wasn't just an illusion. Greek Theatre, August 18, 1989 (courtesy Barry Barnes, all rights reserved).

FOREWORD: THE GRATEFUL DEAD PHENOMENON

BY STANLEY KRIPPNER

In the mid–1960s, a gigantic wave of cultural and political change, originating in San Francisco, swept over much of the United States. Because of my interest in contemporary culture and altered states of consciousness, I followed these developments with interest and visited the Haight-Ashbury district during a visit to San Francisco in 1967. My Bay Area friends told about the "First Human Be-In," held earlier that year, and mentioned that the Grateful Dead had been one of the San Francisco bands that played in this Golden Gate Park event. In fact, my friends thought there were three bands that would interest me: The Grateful Dead, Jefferson Airplane, and Big Brother and the Holding Company.

I did not hear the Grateful Dead until they played as the opening act at the Fillmore East in New York City the following year. Serendipitously, I met Mickey Hart a few days after the show at a birthday party for his tabla teacher, Alla Rakha. Later, I would discover that the Grateful Dead had a community of fans and followers, many of whom claimed to have had transcendent experiences during concerts. However, these "Deadheads" did not emerge immediately in New York City. I recall attending Grateful Dead gigs at the Café a Go-Go in Manhattan when its audience could not fill up a 200-seat club.

Such albums as *Anthem of the Sun* (1968) and *Live Dead* (1969) were instrumental in increasing the band's popularity. Indeed, these are among the albums often cited as evoking transcendent experiences, and I even used "Dark Star" from the latter album in an experiment involving altered states of consciousness (Krippner, et al., 1972). Further, the lyrics of the Dead's songs express a code of ethics where "one man gathers what another man spills," and a spirituality you can "believe in if you need it, if you don't just pass it on." The Dead played a composite of folk, rock, country, blues, and jazz, with an occasional

Somewhere off in the space between. Winterland, December 31, 1978 (courtesy Pat and Dena Lee, all rights reserved).

dip into traditional music from India, stimulated by Alla Rakha's tutelage of Mickey Hart.

Through Mickey Hart, I came to know other members of the band: Jerry Garcia, Bill Kreutzmann, Phil Lesh, Ron McKernan, and Bob Weir. Many of them took an interest in the experiments I was supervising at the Maimonides Medical Center in Brooklyn, New York, experiments that attempted to discern if the content of art prints could influence dream content. Several laboratories had studied the impact of pre-sleep experiences on dream content, but in our case the art prints were randomly selected once the research participant had gone to bed, so any influence would occur remotely, at a distance. In 1973, my colleagues and I published a paper on this experiment entitled "An Experiment in Dream Telepathy with the Grateful Dead." The six Grateful Dead concerts involved in this study were held in February 1971 at the Capitol Theater in Port Chester, New York, approximately 45 miles from Maimonides Medical Center. When judges tried to match the art print used each night with the research participant's reported dreams, they were successful more often than would have been expected by chance.

At the same time, I was conducting interviews with artists and musicians who had used LSD and other psychedelic drugs, ostensibly for creative purposes. Several members of the Grateful Dead consented to be interviewed and were represented in my published articles (e.g., Krippner, 1970). I did not know it at the time, but this collection of academic articles was the first in what was to become known as "Grateful Dead Studies." I had observed that members of the band were not only fine musicians but also intelligent, articulate, thoughtful commentators on many topics, including what became known as "The Grateful Dead Phenomenon," that mosaic of preparation, performance, and participation that marked each of the dozens of Dead shows I attended over the years.

For more than a decade, the Grateful Dead Caucus has met annually as part of the Southwest/Texas Popular American Culture Association in Albuquerque, New Mexico. Members of the Caucus represent a wide variety of disciplines: anthropology, business theory, communications theory, critical philosophy, ethnomusicology, history, literary studies, musicology, religious studies, and sociology, among others. Because members of this group have a common focus and a shared repository of data (much of it experiential), I have taken the position that their work is not multidisciplinary, not cross-disciplinary, nor interdisciplinary, but *transdisciplinary*—representing a discipline of its own (Minati & Collen, 1997). It is also postmodern (Anderson, 1990) since it questions academic authority, in this case what the "proper" areas of disciplined investigation "should" be.

The Grateful Dead in Concert: Essays on Live Improvisation comprises a collection of papers representing Grateful Dead Studies. Its editors have done a remarkable job in charting a transdisciplinary path for this exciting field. The quality of the essays they have included here demonstrates that Dead Studies is a legitimate and worthy enterprise. Finally, this collection provides models and methods for new scholars who might want to enter the field. Popular histories of the Grateful Dead (e.g., Harrison, 1980; McNally, 2002) have evoked poetic descriptions of the Grateful Dead Phenomenon, its "long, strange trip" and the many-faceted "luminous suspended moments" experienced at Grateful Dead concerts. Grateful Dead Studies has become a vibrant part of this strange luminous Phenomenon, and this book ensures its continuation and growth.

Bibliography

Anderson, W. (1990). *Reality Isn't What It Used to Be*. San Francisco: Harper and Row.
Harrison, H. (1980). *The Dead*. Millbrae, CA: Celestial Arts.
Krippner, S. (1970). "The Influence of 'Psychedelic' Experience on Contemporary Art and Music." In *Hallucinogenic Drug Research: Impact on Science and Society*, J. R. Gamage and E. I. Zerkin, eds., 83–114. Beloit, WI: Stash Press.
_____. (1999). "A Pilot Study in Dream Telepathy with the Grateful Dead." In *Perspectives on the Grateful Dead: Critical Writings*, R.G. Weiner, ed., pp. 11–17. Westport, CT: Greenwood Press.
_____, J. Hickman, N. Auerhahn, and R. Harris. (1972). "Clairvoyant Perception of

Target Material in Three States of Consciousness." *Perceptual and Motor Skills*, 35, 439–446.

———, C. Honorton, and M. Ullman. (1973). "An Experiment in Dream Telepathy with the Grateful Dead." *Journal of the American Society of Psychosomatic Dentistry and Medicine*, 20, 3–17.

McNally, D. (2002). *A Long Strange Trip: The Inside History of The Grateful Dead.* New York: Broadway.

Minati, G., and A. Collen. (1997). *Introduction to Systemics.* Walnut Creek, CA: Eagleye Books International.

Preface: Kaleidoscopic Entry to the Show

Through this collection of original essays, we hope to draw attention to some revealing facets of the Grateful Dead concert phenomenon, including aspects we find embedded within the surrounding experiential milieu and range of effects catalyzed by this phenomenon. The interlacing perspectives reflected in the variety of angles taken by this collection of essays produce a kaleidoscopic orientation to the study of Grateful Dead improvisation. The "First Set" and "Second Set" essays collected here emphasize careful analysis of the production, performance and reception of Grateful Dead music in the live concert setting. The "Third Set" essays explore the influence of this phenomenon on subcultural discourses, practices, rituals and values infusing and reaching beyond Deadhead experience. Our principal aim is to suggest points of entry for conducting a transdisciplinary reading of these phenomena, with emphasis on applying constructive threads of postmodern thought to articulate central facets of the music, experiences and community ideals spawned by Grateful Dead improvisation.

"First Set" studies influenced by musicology and ethnomusicology will explore the structural components of Grateful Dead improvisation by examining songs that have served nicely as vehicles for the collective exploration of musical and cultural ideas. "Second Set" reflections framed under the influence of recent Continental philosophies will address the production and reception of Grateful Dead music, with special attention to the operational influences of the affectional immediacy, performative attunement and lived-engagement conjured in the experiential setting of a Grateful Dead concert. These papers will also investigate transvaluations generated from exposure to these Dionysian festivals, and to their residual influence (for instance, through the non-commercial dissemination of audience and soundboard recordings of Grateful Dead concerts). "Third Set" observations drawing on postmodern research methods in sociology, cultural anthropology and communication theory will provide context for situating the "community" and cultural phenomena so essential to the interplay of Deadheads, band members, and Grateful Dead fans in general.

The purpose of this collection is to work out a kaleidoscopic frame of reference for exploring the "montage" structure and visceral significance of Grateful Dead improvisation. The papers collected here comprise multiple levels of analysis and numerous points of entry to suggest a basis for the claim that there really was something special about a Grateful Dead concert, and that there is something in this phenomenon to learn from and apply to the future development of music, mind and cultural forms of life.

This book follows a "show" format familiar to most *affectionados* of Grateful Dead music. We do not choose this structure haphazardly. The first tunings mark the opening to a series of inquiries about to unfold. They offer a few calibrating notes to fire up the circuits of attunement in preparation for liftoff. The "Encore" and closing refrain of "Greensleeves" mark the circuit of return, a last moment of reflection—in our case, on the magnitude of loss and the innocence of healing, as a reminder that life goes on in the face of the dead, and the dead return in the face of life. In between, the Grateful Dead invited fans to participate in the scene of their experiments with musical fusion and psychedelic improvisation. In the process, their concerts imparted experiences and impacted lives one set at a time, two or three sets to a show, each with its own special feel and nuances. Each set was a loosely structured collective voice, each song a focused *combinatorium*: multiple strands of thinking forming a multiplicity of musical ideas, much like an essay gives form to a multiplicity of insights and observations regarding its theme of attention.

We hope the essays in this book achieve similar liftoff. Each set opens with a tuning observation, followed by a loose "collective" of focused, reflective essays on Grateful Dead improvisation. The "First Set" essays investigate the emergence of several distinctive musical/lyrical forms of expression that soon became defining characteristics of Grateful Dead concerts. The "Second Set" essays investigate the experience of fusion improvisation packaged in simple lyrical structures dripping in profound ambiguity. The "Third Set" essays investigate the resulting community instantiations born from exposure to this musical complexity, which were themselves dripping in what Richard Rorty calls "the ungroundable but vital sense of human solidarity."[1] Make no mistake about this: these are scholarly writings, but their job "is to shed light ... not to master."[2] They open vistas on remarkable facets of the Grateful Dead experiment, viewed from scholarly angles immersed within the experience. The "Encore" and closing dose of "Greensleeves" bring our inquiry full circle. Not to be confused with throwaway tunes placating an audience's demand for "more," Grateful Dead encores were often a subtle reminder of the fragility of human existence, and the digestive strains of "Greensleeves" brought calm solace to the "re-entry" phase of the experience. But as Nietzsche and Robert Hunter continually remind us, death is not opposed to life: "What is living is just a sub-

Exploring the absent center. Oakland Stadium, October 9, 1976 (courtesy Michael Parrish, all rights reserved).

set of what is dead, and a very rare subset."[3] The Grateful Dead chose to live and perform in the stream of becoming. Their fans took this experiment to heart with an insatiable hunger. In the process, something happened the likes of which we may not see again, though fragments of its influence continue to infiltrate the dynamic of contemporary life. The essays in this book speak to these influences and their significance. In this meeting of refrains, a collective voice speaks to the life-affirming qualities of the "absent center" as a locus of improvisation. "Such a long, long time to be gone, and a short time to be there."[4]

Notes

1. Richard Rorty, "Method, Social Science, Social Hope," *Consequences of Pragmatism* (Minneapolis: University of Minnesota Press, 1982), 208.

2. Robert Hunter, "Terrapin (Lady with a Fan)," *A Box of Rain* (New York: Viking, 1990), 311.

3. Friedrich Nietzsche, *The Gay Science*, §109 in *Existentialism: Basic Writings*, R. Polt, trans. (Indianapolis: Hackett, 2001), 134.

4. Robert Hunter, "Box of Rain," *A Box of Rain*, 26.

INTRODUCTION: "SHALL WE GO?"

The Grateful Dead improvised in a style all their own, and people went to their concerts expecting to hear something unique in their experience. The band played improvisational music; but just as with everything else they did, they appropriated what was already shown to be possible, then transformed it, and made it their own. Grateful Dead improvisation surely exhibited salient qualities of traditional improvisation, but it also manifested some unique characteristics. The essays in this book address different facets of the "fusion" dynamic operating in Grateful Dead improvisation. These discussions serve as points of entry to a style of engagement reflecting a postmodern aesthetic sensibility with profound significance for how Deadheads engage their lives. Whether this style of engagement translates well to other walks of life is a question our authors take seriously. At times it seems as if the stakes of our unfolding lives might depend on how well we assimilate to the locus of power and precarious balance inherent in these transient encounters with collective improvisation. But where can we go with this? Is there something beyond the immediate enjoyment of these experiences worth exploring from all these angles?

The earliest English usage of "improvisation" dates from 1826, and its central characteristic is spontaneous, extemporaneous expression, whether composing, uttering or performing.[1] When discussing spontaneous performance in the context of modern music, theorists have generally narrowed their focus to two types of improvisation: hierarchical and associative.[2] Hierarchical improvisation operates whenever musicians play spontaneously and extemporaneously in front, or against the background, of an underlying structural framework. Imagine a musician playing a "jazz standard" solo in the context of a framework established by the rhythm section. In contrast, associative improvisation is more free-flowing, insofar as the underlying structure and framework are abandoned by musicians busy setting in motion suggestive new ideas leading to other new ideas. Even here, we will find evidence of a structural tension holding together the collective work of the ensemble. To pull this off, the musicians must listen to each other and use these musical ideas to contribute new ideas to expand the conversation in a manner tied to the other members of the group. In discussing this structural tension, Ingrid Monson draws attention to the relation between individual and group dynamic, describing "two levels on which the individual-versus-group tension operates: the relationship of the soloist (who may be a rhythm section member), and the relationship of each individual to the remainder of the rhythm section."[3]

Not only does the soloist improvise against the groove of the rhythm section, but members of the rhythm section also improvise collectively in establishing that groove. The essential thing is for each player to have something to weave into the musical unfolding conversation, so that the music is in fact an extemporaneous conversation between the players.

Bruce Ellis Benson accentuates this conversational dimension of improvisation when describing "composers, performers and listeners as partners in a dialogue," and the resulting music as "a conversation in which no one partner has exclusive control."[4] According to Benson, improvisation operates as a conversation within composition, listening and performance. To add credence to his view, Benson references an 1829 letter to Zelter, in which Goethe discusses the conversational nature of music. Goethe writes:

> Of all instrumental music, [a string quartet] is for me the most comprehensible: one has four rational persons conversing with each other, and believes that one gains something from their discourse and becomes acquainted with the peculiarities of their instruments.[5]

For Goethe, as for Benson, the conversation of improvisational music crosses functional lines, as the discourse creates space for listeners, performers and composers alike to speak with each other in a dialogue larger than one restricted to performers or composers or listeners alone.

Improvisation seems from the outset to require some underlying structure and framework to sustain the collective focus of the conversation. In the case of hierarchical improvisation, structural context is largely determined by the framework of the song. With associative improvisation, the particular song framework is largely abandoned, but a "collective" framework still operates to contain the free-form musical conversation.

Though the elements of spontaneity and conversation apply to improvisation in general, they fall short of describing the special dynamic operating in Grateful Dead improvisation. To be sure, the Grateful Dead improvised in both hierarchical and associative ways. They were improvising hierarchically any time a single soloist took off within the song framework established by other players in the band. Traditional blues tunes, cowboy songs, and numerous "cover" tunes allowed the various band members to improvise independently. At other times, their extended jams or segues between structured tunes brought out an associative dynamic, with each player suggesting and responding to musical ideas in conversation with the other members of the band. But in addition to these two modes of improvisation, the Grateful Dead also performed a third style of improvisation, possessing what David Malvinni terms a "transformational" quality that he traces to "the improvised experience of the in-between," which he identifies with "the space and tension between the hierarchical and associative [forms of improvisation]."[6]

All musical improvisation requires a certain level of musicianship and skill, not just in the individual but also within the ensemble. Players need to be proficient with their instruments, but they also need to be able to participate in a musical conversation with their band mates. They need to listen to the statements of the other players and then respond with a musical statement of their own. To improvise the way the Grateful Dead did presupposed both hierarchical and associative modes of improvising, but also an additional skill: each player had to learn to play so that in playing together, no one had to listen and respond to what the others were playing. They could focus on the song as a collective conversation manifesting "fusion" or "psychedelic" improvisation. The band recognized the tremendous effort it takes to play this way. As Jerry Garcia once remarked to David Gans, "You can't play the way the Grateful Dead plays without working at it. It's not something that just happened to us."[7] They had to practice: first to learn the structure of the songs; then to learn how each player could solo within that structure (hierarchical improvisation); then to learn how each instrument and player could participate in a free-flowing musical conversation no longer tethered to the structural framework of the song (associative improvisation); and finally, to play the song as a Grateful Dead song in which each player makes a musical statement not so much in response to another player's statement as in response to *the song itself*.

Phil Lesh has described this phase in the band's development as a lesson learned by going "back to the woodshed," the goal, in his words, being

> to learn, above all, how to play together, to entrain, to become, as we described it then, "fingers on a hand." [In the process,] each of us consciously personalized his playing: to fit with what others were playing and to fit with who each man was as an individual, allowing us to mold our consciousness together in the unity of a group mind.[8]

Garcia echoed this thought in another conversation with Gans: "When you're working in a band, you have to try to let everybody have his own voice the way he best sees it." In this same interview, Garcia emphasized the importance of practice in cultivating this art of listening beyond the specific voices of other players in order to have a meaningful conversation as a band. By the time the band performed on stage, it was as if each of the band members was soloing simultaneously. This emergent practice quickly defined the band's style of improvisational playing and generally marked the point where a song took flight as a Grateful Dead song. Whether playing a new cover tune or working out their own compositions, the band's performances of newer material began with each of the musicians playing the song within a contained structure, much like any other band. But after mastering this structure, each musician would begin experimenting hierarchically within the context of the song. Then, at some opportune moment, they would begin conversing associatively, listening to one another and responding through lateral dialogue with their own ideas. Finally, within the context of their respective roles in the band, each player would establish his own voice, conversing not so much with each other as with the song itself, which by then had become a Grateful Dead song.

Grateful Dead improvisation has always presumed an underlying structure, along with the ability to solo in the context of that structure, and the familiarity to carry on a collective musical conversation while abandoning that structure. In the process, while sometimes appearing chaotic and haphazard, the band managed to create something more compelling than a simple combination of musical parts. It produced a group synergy, one that expanded like a musical bubble to envelop the concert crowd in various combinations of rapture, ecstasy, and sublime attunement. As the essays in this volume aim to demonstrate, Grateful Dead improvisation represents a unique and significant form of interaction whose style of playing carried over into many other aspects of the Grateful Dead phenomenon, ranging from business practices and the formation of communities to a generalized world-view expressed in the lyrics of their songs. "Paradise waits / on the crest of a wave."[9]

Notes

1. *The Compact Edition of the Oxford English Dictionary* (Oxford: Oxford University Press, 1971), 1393.

2. Jeff Pressing, "Improvisation: Methods and Models," in *Generative Processes in Music: The Psychology of Performance, Improvisation, and Composition*, John A. Sloboda, ed. (Oxford: Clarendon Press, 1988).

3. Ingrid Monson, *Saying Something: Jazz Improvisation and Interaction* (Chicago: University of Chicago Press, 1996), 67.

4. Bruce Ellis Benson, *The Improvisation of Musical Dialogue: A Phenomenology of Music* (Cambridge: Cambridge University Press, 2003), x.

5. Johann Wolfgang von Goethe, in a letter to Karl Friedrich Zelter, November 1829. See *Goethe Briefe* (Hamburg: Christian Wagner, 1967), Vol. IV, 349.

6. David Malvinni, "Now Is the Time Past Believing: Concealment, Ritual and Death in the Grateful Dead's Approach to Improvisation," in *All Graceful Instruments: the Context of the Grateful Dead Phenomenon*, N. Meriwether, ed. (Newcastle: Cambridge Scholars Press, 2007), 5.

7. David Gans, *Conversations with the Dead: The Grateful Dead Interview Book* (Cambridge, MA: Da Capo Press, 2002), 68.

8. Phil Lesh, *Searching for the Sound: My Life with the Grateful Dead* (New York: Little, Brown, 2005), 56.

9. Robert Hunter, "Help on the Way," *A Box of Rain* (New York: Viking, 1990), 93.

First Set

Musical and Lyrical Elements of Grateful Dead Improvisation

Searching for the sound. Phil Lesh outside Club front (courtesy David Gans, all rights reserved).

NON-SYSTEMATIC THOUGHTS ABOUT IMPROVISATION

CRISTIAN AMIGO

The Grateful Dead: Non-Trip #1

In the late 1970s, I attended my first Grateful Dead concert at the Hollywood Sportatorium in Pembroke Pines, Florida. The Dead concert experience was already legendary, and even though I was not familiar with their music, I ached for that experience that I had read about and that many of my friends described in almost mystical terms. Besides, I was 15 years old and ready for it.

After traveling by car (in a caravan) along the two-lane road that led to this desolate tin-roof sports complex in the middle of nowhere (past a prison, no stores, no residences), we came upon the first contingent of Deadheads in the Sportatorium parking lot. Fifty to sixty people covered in mud, faces painted, and obviously "tripping out" (a term I learned that day), were climbing onto a makeshift percussion sculpture, playing and beating upon it in what seemed like some kind of strange ritual, so intent was their commitment and so seemingly random their sound and behavior. Definitely hippies, I thought, my parents having warned me about this type of people.

I grew up in a mostly Cuban neighborhood in Miami where playing percussion was not a random activity, even when informally practiced, so I was puzzled by this parking lot scene. These hippies seemed to be making disconnected incoherent sounds without a center that for me meant a structured sense of rhythm, although at the time I mistakenly expressed this as their having "no rhythm." No one seemed to listen to anyone else, and all were banging their instruments (they had drums, too) in what seemed to me an unsynchronized way. But, it was clear that despite the resulting sound they were having some kind of group experience, ecstatic, joyful, and kind of scary. It seemed, to my young ears and mind, like a din, a wall of noise, stoned hippies and their non-music. Crazy white people, *Americanos* for sure.

Full-throttle jamming. Winterland, December 31, 1978 (courtesy Pat and Dena Lee, all rights reserved).

I enjoyed the Dead show. They "jammed" and the songs were longish with lots of that noodle-y guitar playing so attractive to adolescent boys. Being an aspiring guitarist, I remember liking the mix of blues and country music elements that was new to my ears. However, what I found most compelling that night was the reaction of the crowd to the band and the music. Where I enjoyed the music, the audience was immersed in it; they were tuned in to the slightest nuances coming from the stage, to which they would react with movement, yelling, hands suddenly raised, fingers pointed toward the sky — active listening. They were into the Dead in a way that was beyond me. Unlike them, I was not able to turn my will and body over to the band and felt like an outsider. This was the alienating part of the experience — that I did not get it while everyone else did. I wanted to be transported too, but found myself alone in my head, bodiless.

Dirty, wasted, smelly people — what was there to like? Not partaking of hallucinogenics, not astounded by the music (I needed to be astounded by music back then for music to be great), and up past my usual bedtime, I went out to the car during the second encore and fell asleep in the back seat, not waking until my friends dropped me off at my apartment building later that evening. They had a tremendous time, and discussed the concert for a long time afterwards. It was as though we had been to two different events.

Not until many years later, during graduate school where I studied ethnomusicology, anthropology and philosophy, did I really begin to appreciate the Dead's music and their cultural phenomenon. Who were the Dead, anyway? A regular rock band, the original "jam band" from San Francisco? Or was the Dead a reflection of the band, their audience, the sound, the drugs, the culture, or some mix of all these things? The Dead were famous for their improvisations and had an audience who followed and participated in their lengthy improvisations (I had witnessed this) — a fact that is astounding in a world of downloaded three-minute pop songs. What was it about "improvisation" that was so central to this scene?

It is my thesis that, beginning in the mid–1960s, and primarily through musical and social forms of improvisation, the Dead were able to articulate and facilitate a cultural space wherein mostly white Americans, including themselves, were able to broach certain cultural limits or social mores that American society (at that time defined in exclusively white terms) had imposed upon them. What these mostly young people sought was a liberation of the body, and an expansion of their ultra-rational concept of mind to include unconscious, precognitive, and nonverbal elements, not just the pragmatic, utilitarian mind of their WASP culture.

Improvisation was central to this discourse — the ability to think on one's feet, to intuitively grasp what is essential in an artistic or social situation, to resolve a problem without the interference of logical propositions, to raise intuition to the status of a way of knowing. Of course, this discourse was a part of the cultural revolution of the 1960s writ large and not exclusive to the Dead phenomenon. But the Grateful Dead was one of the revolution's most public exponents, setting trends and inspiring the journey for countless persons.

By honoring bodily experience and knowledge beyond just propositional thinking, the Dead enabled their followers to participate in the world in ways that had previously been negatively ascribed to people of color, especially African Americans who were then (perhaps still?) seen by white America as sensuous and irrational, but whose cultural power as music makers was undeniable, even dominant in America. Through the Grateful Dead experience, the audience and the musicians themselves were liberated from some of the meaner restrictions imposed upon their bodies by the non-examined category of whiteness, without crossing the line into a completely segregated experience that was impossible at the time. They found themselves improvising (think sound sculpture) without restrictions, searching for expression, perhaps not yet grasping that collective improvisation in music (and ritual) can be a multilevel and complex experience with its own ideological structures and social imperatives, whether they inform a tea ceremony, a church service, a rite of initiation, a bebop tune, or a blues jam. Still, in the Civil Rights era of American history, and under the influence of jazz, the Beats, Zen Buddhism, drugs, and progressive values, the Dead opened a door for America's white youth to significantly expand their consciousness beyond the strictures of 1950s mainstream American society.

White Composition, Black Improvisation

In Western musical culture, "improvisation," and its practitioners, suffer in relation to improvisation's binary relationship to "composition." This relationship, and the cultural logic that affirms it, exposes deep cultural biases with respect to the associations that each term accrues to itself. At the most basic level, the binary of mind (composition) versus body (improvisation) leads to a string of metaphoric linkages that, linked to historical relationships of power, continue to produce real effects in the world.

Composition is seen as the apex of a universal musicality embodied in the single white, male subject at the top of a cultural and evolutionary hierarchy of all human beings. Composition represents rationality as opposed to improvisation/instinct, order vs. chaos, civilization vs. barbarism, knowledge vs. ignorance, science vs. superstition, health vs. disease, evolution vs. stasis, superiority vs. inferiority, and all of the other distinctions used by Western white men to distinguish themselves and their culture, to their benefit, from the *other* who threatens their dominance. The mind/body binary is perhaps most pernicious in its elevation of a white, male *mind* over the *body* of a person of color, or a woman, white or otherwise.

Although Western composers such as Bach, Mozart, and Beethoven (and their contemporaries) were all skilled improvisers, the practice of improvisation disappeared from classical music in the nineteenth century with the advent of the romantic hero. The "genius" became a symbol for the supremacy of the individual, his will, and the superiority and hegemony of the European over his colonial subject. The hierarchical order of a conductor leading the orchestra is another symbolic manifestation of this phenomenon.

Rationality being the highest value in Enlightenment European culture, it is "our" highest achievement, and indicative of the European rise from barbarism to civilization, of progress, an evolution that *others* have not attained. The rational white mind treads the ground of reality while the superstitious mind of color is caught in a self-spun web of illusions—two different kinds of minds in two different kinds of animals.

Improvisation denotes primitive bodies, led by facile instinct rather than systematic empirical analysis and application, by an innate sex drive (body) that threatens white women and white music. Improvisation is inherently lazy since it is not acquired through applied reflection, but rather by mindless (embodied), incoherent drives expressed as random — unimportant — musical impulses. Even though these old associations have long been discredited and do not stand up to critical analysis, their imprints remain in cultural attitudes and institutions, and in our limited case, in the composition/improvisation dyad that still informs American musical culture.

Musician and writer George Lewis, recognizing the cultural effects of this split, describes improvisation in America in terms of *Afrological* and *Eurological* perspectives, going so far as to suggest that the 1960s American art music avant-garde in the persons of John Cage, Earle Browne, Morton Feldman and others invented the term *aleatoric*, as a way of signifying "not-improvisation." These composers distanced themselves and their accomplishments from any African American (or Asian) precedents and reaped the institutional rewards of embracing the "mind" concept of Western art music culture. In this way the avant-garde could claim an unprecedented *invention* of aleatoric music, a music and practice that in many ways resembles aspects of improvisation, structure, and sound in African American and Asian art musics, which, in the case of African American art music, Cage had heard growing up in America, and in the case of Asian art music, had discovered as a student in Henry Cowell's music classes at Columbia in the 1940s.

Improvisation: African American Style

In the twentieth century, the preeminent international improvisational practice was in jazz, music of acknowledged African American origin. The great thematic improvisers such as Louis Armstrong and Bunk Johnson eventually morphed into the art music of bebop, where an extended and fast-developing theoretical and unprecedented musical virtuosity merged with a modernist ethos of progress in the likes of Charlie Parker, Thelonious Monk, Dizzy Gillespie, Miles Davis, et al. Despite the disdain of jazz by eminent critics such as Theodor Adorno, and the threat that jazz posed to the exclusive art credentials of classical music, and to white society, jazz conquered the world and became, as Miles put it, "black classical music." New musicians such as John Coltrane, Wayne Shorter, Sonny Rollins, Ornette Coleman, Cecil Taylor and countless others, including many whites, continued to push the technical and theoretical envelope-spawning movements, e.g., free jazz, and a union with world, especially African and Indian, music whose spiritual and religious values such as faith and transcendence existed alongside purely musical considerations, including a central commitment to structured improvisation.

The appropriation of the blues and rhythm & blues as central components of an emergent rock industry also did much to bring African ways of musicking to the American public and to the world, and blues-based improvisation in rock music entered a particularly fruitful phase with the emergence of artists like the Grateful Dead, Santana, and Jimi Hendrix, and many of the groups constituting the "British invasion" of America, including the Beatles, Yardbirds, Rolling Stones, Eric Clapton, Jeff Beck, and Led Zeppelin. White American and

British musicians were well aware of the African American precedents of their music and copied and recast the styles of Muddy Waters, Howlin' Wolf, B.B. King, Buddy Guy and many others. Progressive rock musicians were also aware of the accomplishments and techniques of the prominent American jazz musicians, and the fusion of jazz and rock was foreshadowed by Miles Davis' electric music in the mid to late 1960s and 1970s that additionally incorporated funk, R&B, and electric guitars into its sonic mix.

Musical Improvisation: Where Intuition Becomes the Modality Through Which Rationality Is Channeled

It is highly ethnocentric to imagine improvisation in American music only in the guise of African American music and musical practices originating in Africa. But clearly jazz was the first large-scale international musical movement to self-consciously consider "improvisation" a central part of its artistic ethos. Many classical music traditions such as Hindustani (North India), Karnatic (South India), and Javanese and Balinese gamelan music contain greater and lesser amounts of improvisation or elaboration. However, not many musicians in these traditions self-consciously refer to themselves as improvisers, although their elaboration of preexisting musical materials might look like "improvisation" from this American side of the world. Also, many European and North and South American folk music traditions (mostly admixtures of European, African, and indigenous elements) require minimal to significant elaboration by the musicians, dancers and singers. Is this improvisation? Or elaboration? It depends on whom you ask, and when, and in what context. In the contemporary globalized world, where musicians mix and match traditions with an ever-increasing naturalness and an international technological and cultural savvy, these types of questions become increasingly difficult to answer in any realistic manner, and difficult even to pose.

"Improvisation" is a flexible term that resonates differently in various musical, cultural, and social situations. In my own experience, the Spanish "improvisar" has an element of "inventar" (invent) attached to it, and in one guise, comes from being able to make do with less resources than those of the wealthy, resource-rich around you. *We* have to improvise because *they* have the economic power to name phenomena and to acquire and use tools that we do not have access to; we have to invent or improvise our own lower-tech, lower-cost versions and solutions. In this context, improvising well is a kind of flexible intelligence that requires astute attention and in-the-moment reaction.

In another guise, to improvise refers to moving beyond basic instructions in an oral musical tradition. For example, in order to advance beyond the basic melodic and harmonic frameworks of a standard song or composition, a student has to improvise, which in this case means accessing the musical sound and experience beyond the instructor's ability to name or discursively explain what "improvise" sonically means. It is a musical quality that language fails to account for but might be demonstrated by the instructor with a performance or a recording. Improvising becomes the means for achieving a culturally sanctioned level of musical achievement recognizable as such, as in competence playing the jazz standard *Autumn Leaves*, learning an Afro-Peruvian *lando*, or shredding a Metallica riff. Western conservatory-trained students also participate in this music-making beyond the notes, but generally identify the practice as interpretation rather than improvisation.

To some, improvisation will always be associated with the nonliterate oral tradition of others, and this is especially true for the Western art music tradition that requires composers to account for every musical gesture that constitutes a musical piece. But even this notion is fraying at the edges in the hands of realistic composers and performers who know that established systems of notation do not account for every musical parameter present in a realized piece of music or performance. Without the composer's indications, the players always automatically add elements that render a written score into actual music. This might include the amount of vibrato, decisions (or intimations) about tempo, timbral possibilities, amount of legato, etc. Is this improvisation even if the musicians do not recognize their contribution as such?

For me and other self-conscious improvisers, improvisation is a way, or an attempt, to bridge the mind/body dichotomy prevalent in our societies and in much music making. People play, walk, drive, and sometimes speak without thinking in logical propositions beforehand because they have previously acquired (through thinking and praxis) the tools that allow them automatically to participate in these experiences in the moment. In this sense, it is not a setting aside of mind but rather having mind automatically integrate various parameters into a gestalt, a performance whose myriad and simultaneous individual parameters would overwhelm the human subject if the brain had to account for them all in real time simultaneous, rational propositions. Try to walk this way to see if you can do it; try to play the head (melody) of Charlie Parker's "Donna Lee" to watch what happens—nothing, or a sonic disaster! Taken to the extreme, a person would narrate his/her life in the midst of experiencing it—a ridiculous situation. This would amount to explaining a life, rather than living or realizing life in the performance of a life. Aldous Huxley once wrote of the human brain as a limiting mechanism that filters reality, without which our biological being would be overwhelmed by the experience of an unmediated, simultaneous reality.

If a student has artistic talent and the discipline to develop its potential, she may be able to combine past lessons into new patterns and sounds in the moment of playing music, and this is the magic of improvisation: wide-awake presence and creation in the present tense. The participation of an audience in performance adds yet another element, whether just a few people in a club or a concert audience at Madison Square Garden. Improvisation does not always contain this now quality, but when it does, the cosmos opens and the musician and the astute audience member are in the stream of things beyond subject-object consciousness, or as the Buddhists say, "touching the ground of reality itself." Ponder that, but not too much. Better yet, listen to a live performance of "Dark Star."

Mandalas and the Dead
Graeme M. Boone

For Joe Donovan (1954–1998), psychedelic seer

In an early interview, Jerry Garcia invoked the concept of *mandala* to describe the Acid Tests, those mid–60s psychedelic festivals that provided a radical blueprint for what the Grateful Dead would aim to achieve in their music. He wove this word into an account that, in short order, invokes individual experience, drug use, metaphysics, experimentalism, existentialism, and communal identity, traits commonly associated with the Dead.[1]

> What the Kesey thing was depended on who you were when *you* were there. It was open, a tapestry, a mandala — it was whatever you made it. Okay, so you take LSD, and suddenly you are aware of another plane, or several other planes, and the quest is to extend that limit, to go as far as you can go. In the Acid Tests that meant to do away with old forms, with old ideas, try something *new*. Nobody was doing *something*, y'know, it was everybody doing bits and pieces of something, the result of which was something else. When it was moving right, you could dig that there was something that it was getting toward, something like ordered chaos, or some *region* of chaos.... It was magic, far out, beautiful magic.

By the time of this interview in mid–1969, the Dead had established their distinctive brand of open-ended, genre-blending rock 'n' roll, and the concept of *mandala* offers an evocative way to convey important things about it, balancing the centripetal identity of each song against the centrifugal force of their searching explorations and representing both in a cosmic wheel of time and motion that resonates with the Dead's philosophical and spiritual leanings. In that spirit, the present essay will attempt to situate the mandala concept in relation to the early Dead, defining it briefly in relation to Tibetan and Jungian traditions, considering the "Eastern" theme in American culture leading up to the psychedelic '60s, and plumbing the historical record regarding the Dead's own views.[2] In a later chapter ("Dark Star Mandala"), specific mandala constructions will be proposed for one song.

What Is a Mandala? The Tibetan Model

"Mandala" is a term with complex, divergent associations and, at the same time, a core identity whose appealing simplicity and directness have made it as enduring as it is adaptable. Originating in ancient India, the sanskrit word *mandala* conveys the idea of a circle, considered as defining a ring, a circumference, orbit, or globe; as demarcating a physical territory or multitude of some kind; or as representing a bodily or other totality.[3] All of these meanings find their place in its use as a focal concept in Hindu and Buddhist traditions, where the term designates not just a symbolic image, but a transformative field that may involve liturgy, sound, and metaphysical palaces, gods, demons, and other elements in relation to the sacred, transcendent self. These are projected not just onto the physical surface of a mandala image, but more importantly, in a metaphysical, sacred sense, into space and ultimately the body of the celebrant. The richness and cosmic multiplicity of mandala elements, varying also according to local and historical religious traditions, result in diverse and, especially when insufficiently understood, contradictory definitions that can obscure any clear and precise meaning for the noninitiate. That obscurity is redoubled by the secrecy in which much mandala teaching and practice are historically enshrouded.[4]

Most frequently cited in modern discussions are the Tibetan Tantric Buddhist mandala formulations, since these are the most meticulously detailed in their verbal prescriptions and visual imagery.[5] Two contrasting characterizations will serve to evoke the range of the Tibetan mandala concept; these focus respectively on what we might call its cosmological and liturgical identity (by the scholar Giuseppe Tucci) and on its revelatory, transformative identity (by the religious leader His Holiness the Fourteenth Dalai Lama).[6]

> It is the whole universe in its essential plan, in its process of emanation and of reabsorption. The universe not only in its inert spatial expanse, but as temporal revolution and both as a vital process which develops from an essential Principle and rotates around a central axis.... This, by the line of defense which circumscribes it, represents protection from the mysterious forces that menace the sacral purity of the spot or which threaten the psychical integrity of him who performs the ceremony; it also implies, by magical transposition, the world itself, so that when the magician or mystic stands in the center he identifies himself with the forces that govern the universe and collects their thaumaturgical power within himself [Tucci].
>
> *Mandala*, in general, means that which extracts the essence. There are many usages of the term *mandala* according to context. One type of mandala is the offering of the entire world system, with the major and minor continents mentally constructed, to high beings. Also, there are painted mandalas, mandalas of

concentration, those made out of colored sand, mandalas of the conventional mind of enlightenment, mandalas of the ultimate mind of enlightenment, and so forth. Because one can extract a meaning from each of these through practicing them, they are called mandalas. Although we might call these pictures and constructed depictions mandalas, the main meaning is for oneself to enter into the mandala and extract an essence in the sense of receiving blessing. It is a place of gaining magnificence. Because one is gaining a blessing and thereupon developing realizations it is called an extraction or assumption of something essential [Dalai Lama].

A third definition, by musicologist Ter Ellingson, illustrates how the concept of mandala can apply to sound itself.[7]

> The mandala of sound refers to a conceptual set of three mandalas, namely, the mandalas of the body, voice, and mind. These represent, in rough terms, transformations of the three doors of body, voice, and mind into perfected structural frameworks for the production in the self of the nature of a divine being. The bases for the transformations are, for the body, symbolic gestures, for the voice, mantras, or evocative vocalizations, and for the mind, meditation on deities, which simultaneously realizes their pride and clear appearance in one's own person. From the point of the media involved, we can characterize the three mandalas as mandalas of form, sound, and thought or meditation.... The bodily mandala may be extended into dance, and the vocal into vocal and instrumental music. Thus, instrumental music in its ritual mantra-generated context is also part of the mandala of sound.

Since the 1960s especially, Tibetan mandala paintings have become synonymous for many Westerners with the identity of the mandala concept. The best-known Tibetan mandala image in the West today is the Kalachakra sand mandala, promoted as part of the Kalachakra practice by the Dalai Lama.[8] The rich graphic geometry of this mandala includes an outer enclosure and a series of concentric circles; these enclose in turn a series of square figures, demarcating a multistory palace. In the middle of each palace wall, on three different stories, is pierced a gate area, in the form of a T surmounted by a multistoried arch. The full-fledged image can include numerous other lines, figures, and other elements, as well as colors, every one having its symbolic meaning and precise function. Figure 1 illustrates the ordered complexity of Kalachakra mandalic geometry.

The American East

Just as Asian populations have multiplied across the United States across the past two centuries and Asian art collections have grown in American museums, the spread of Eastern religion, as a practice and more generally a cultural influence, has proceeded with increasing speed and consequence.[9] Following on the development of trade relations between the United States, China, and other East Asian countries, the discovery of Hindu and Buddhist teachings by

Figure 1. Schematic diagram of the Kalachakra mandala.

the Transcendentalists, notably including Thoreau and Emerson, marked the beginning of a signal national involvement with Eastern spiritual traditions.[10] These and later writers, from Walt Whitman to T.S. Eliot and beyond, continued to show a fascination with the East as one aspect of what might be called (for the sake of efficiency, if not precision) a distinctively American spiritual engagement, involving intuitiveness, self-reliance, love of nature, belief in the transcendent and transformative possibilities of the individual, and social and religious nonconformity.[11] The development of Theosophy, like that of Christian Science, reflected a parallel tendency, though to more organized and less rebellious ends; Theosophists claimed an essential connection to the East and to Tibet, as reflected in the perennial best-seller, *The Tibetan Book of the Dead*, first edited in 1927 by W.Y. Evans-Wentz. Spiritualizing, Eastern-oriented trends such as these were integral to the rich and diverse American literary environment, forming a deep background to the cultural renewals of the 1960s.

The development of Buddhist teaching in twentieth-century America is most famously represented in the career of Zen Buddhist D.T. Suzuki. His lectures and writings, together with those of Alan Watts and other Western popularizers, were well known to post–World War II intellectuals, contributing to what has been called the "Zen Boom" of the later 1950s and '60s, most startlingly prevalent among Beat luminaries such as Jack Kerouac, Gary Snyder, Philip Whalen, and Allen Ginsberg.[12] The resonance between Zen and the Transcendentalist-inspired Beat sensibility is strikingly evidenced by Kerouac's sibling novels, *On the Road* (written before he discovered Buddhism) and *The Dharma Bums* (written after). With their emphasis on creative and social nonconformity, radical self-realization, spontaneous revelation, and the sacred dimensions of nature and everyday life, the Beats provided the immediate background as well as living presence and, as it were, cultural training for those young musicians who became the Grateful Dead. As Jerry Garcia once said[13]:

> I owe a lot of who I am and what I've been and what I've done to the beatniks from the fifties and to the poetry and art and music that I've come in contact with. I feel like I'm part of a continuous line of a certain thing in American culture, of a root.

In the 1960s, Zen Buddhism continued its rise in popularity with the establishment of schools, beginning with the San Francisco Zen Center in 1962. But the diaspora that followed the Dalai Lama's 1959 exile from Tibet also brought many Tibetan Buddhist monks to the United States, where they introduced a "new" tradition of Buddhism whose visual, liturgical, and philosophical richness made a striking cultural impact. As the use of psychedelic drugs proliferated, an encounter with Buddhism was inevitable, given its searching, self-questioning spirituality and countercultural resonances. Both Zen and Tibetan Buddhism played a major role in this encounter. The famous 1964 publication *The Psychedelic Experience*, a sustained, LSD-infused meditation on the *Tibetan Book of the Dead*, was one salient reflection; another was the popularity of Eastern or Eastern-sensitive philosophers and spiritual teachers, including Krishnamurti, Thomas Merton, and Alan Watts, whose recorded lectures were broadcast on radio and television in San Francisco during this period.[14] The pages of the *San Francisco Oracle*, the most famous Haight-Ashbury newspaper of the era, were studded with discussions, arguments, illuminations regarding Eastern thought. The environment of psychedelic San Francisco, then, we may safely say, was infused with it.

Allen Cohen, editor of the *Oracle*, recalls walking into the Thelin brothers' Psychedelic Shop on Haight Street — ground zero of the psychedelic Haight-Ashbury — "where the icons of the new emerging culture were gathered, displayed and sold. Books on Eastern religion and metaphysics and the Western occult were offered, along with Indian records, posters, madrases, incense, bead necklaces, small pipes, and other paraphernalia." Cohen found the atmosphere of the ordinary hippie pad to be "light, meditative, and creative with a mixture of rock and raga music, oriental aesthetics and vegetarian food," and noted a particular interest in Buddhism among Haight-Ashbury hippies.[15]

> One of the most generally preferred and admired spiritual paths was Mahayana Buddhism.... Hinduism, also, has a sensuous and sexual school of thought and practice called Tantra that influenced those who felt that the body and the soul, and the material and spiritual worlds could be yoked together in an ecstatic union. The word "LOVE" was a symbol or code for these ideas, mystical experiences, and practices. "LOVE" was the universal principle merging all and everything into an ecstatic unity. Thus the phrase often used by Hippies, "It's all love," had a more precise meaning than was generally understood.

Jung and the Pan-Cultural Mandala

Another aspect of twentieth-century mandala culture stems from the work of Swiss psychologist Carl Jung, who, pursuing a deep engagement with Eastern religious philosophies early in the century, developed his own particular enthusiasm for the mandala symbol as an archetypal art-form and organic, elemental representation of mental worlds. Jung's numerous writings on the subject freed the mandala from any necessary grounding in Buddhist tradition, while preserving the cosmological, incurving structure of the Buddhist concept. He associated mandalas with the dialectic of suffering and healing in the mind, but found that they permeate religious and mental expression generally, notably in their incorporation of a square.[16]

> As a rule a mandala occurs in conditions of psychic dissociation or disorientation.... In such cases it is easy to see how the severe pattern imposed by a circular image of this kind compensates the disorder and confusion of the psychic state—namely, through the construction of a central point to which everything is related, or by a concentric arrangement of the disordered multiplicity and of contradictory and irreconcilable elements. This is evidently an attempt at self-healing on the part of Nature, which does not spring from conscious reflection but from an instinctive impulse. Here, as comparative research has shown, a fundamental schema is made use of, an archetype which, so to speak, occurs everywhere and by no means owes its individual existence to tradition, any more than the instincts would need to be transmitted in that way.... Therefore, despite external differences, we find a fundamental conformity in mandalas regardless of their origin in time and space.
>
> The "squaring of the circle" is one of the many archetypal motifs which form the basic patterns of our dreams and fantasies.... Indeed, it could even be called the archetype of wholeness. Because of this significance, the "quaternity of the One" is the schema for all images of God.

Jung's vast concept of the mandala lay at the center of a teaching whose impact on later psychologists, artists, teachers, and healers proved to be as momentous as it was diverse.[17] As such, it invited Western or indeed pan-cultural applications, which intertwine with stricter Tibetan Buddhist ones in the iconic world of the psychedelic '60s. Mandalas were an integral part of the new landscape, conveying Buddhist, hermetic, holistic, or hallucinatory themes. The depiction of circles as motive forces, visual mazes, worlds, or cosmic environments was ubiquitous, as we see in the welter of peace symbols, moiré patterns, zodiac maps, planetary images, Taijitu yin and yang diagrams, light-show patterns, and other circular imagery common in concert posters and other artworks of the era. One can see, or project, mandalas in many of these images.[18]

As Allen Cohen wrote, in describing the psychedelic artwork of the *San Francisco Oracle*[19]:

> Most of the artists would conceive and manifest their designs in a state of expanded awareness. Thus, the *Oracle* pages correspond to the methodology of the Thanka art of Tibet and Byzantine art in which artists established a visionary state of mind, through meditation, chanting, abstinence and/or prayer, and tried to convey that vision in their painting. The perceivers of the art then could mount to that same elevation, and experience within their mind the same visionary state. So, looking at an *Oracle* could be a sort of occult trance experience communicated across the dimensions of space and time, through the tabloid medium, from one explorer of inner worlds to another. That was the magic, the fire, that spread from mind to mind with the *Oracle*. Motifs and techniques were universal — from ancient Chinese spirals to Sci-Fi. Wings, rays, auras, arabesques, swirls, unicorns, and centaurs, mandalas, collages, flying saucers and their inhabitants, op-art, flowers and paisley, nudes, feathers, and ghosted images were interwoven into a dazzling cross-cultural spectacle of multidimensional depth, pattern and flow.

The modern concept of mandala, then, follows many paths and has metaphorical as well as literal implications, depending as much on the cognitive functionality attributed to an image (or other thing) as on the image *per se*. For our purposes, it may be simplest to define mandala as a circular artwork with diagrammatic, meditative, and cosmic implications, but it is important to keep the other elements in mind, including reference to the East as an esoteric spiritual realm; "archetypal" and holistic suggestiveness; psychedelic pertinence; quadripartite structure; existence independent of any visual form; and above all, essential identity as a "transformative field."

The Dead vs. the East

Situated on the cutting edge — or perhaps more accurately, from the standpoint of this article, at a radiant center — of San Francisco's psychedelic world, the Dead would have been aware of the imagery and symbology discussed above; but one might think, judging by Dennis McNally's detailed biography or by numerous early interviews, that the spiritual East had relatively little prominence in their self-imagining.[20] That position is occupied rather by diverse Western themes, with music on the one hand — including folk, bluegrass, blues, rock 'n' roll, jazz, John Coltrane, Charles Ives, avant-garde, and (to a lesser extent) classical music — and folk/pop mythologies on the other, including rural Anglo-America, the Wild West, outer space, science fiction, and the Beats. To these themes was joined an intuitive, non-culture-specific cosmology or "quest" inspired by psychedelics and the Acid Tests, among other experiences. The many questions posed by earlier interviewers regarding musical and other influences were rarely met with references to the East; nor did discussions of transcendence, spirituality, "group mind," and other mystical matters elicit explicitly Eastern answers, or any others involving organized religion.

This state of affairs might be surprising if band members felt such influences to be close to the surface. But as the band's most frequent spokesman, Jerry Garcia, once said, in the very context of affirming the reality of his intense metaphysical experiences onstage, "I am so distrustful of anything that's invisible or occult or that can't be measured, tasted, or touched,"[21] and, more crisply, "I don't like the word *religion*. It's a bad word."[22] Garcia's lack of overt identification with Eastern religion evidently reflects a more general resistance to received doctrines (not to mention disciplines) and a distaste for ready-made explanations, as it were, for the extreme and intimate real-life experiences that had so strongly marked him: "I want it to surprise me, to continue to surprise me. I don't want to know anything about it."[23] Certainly this attitude must also be understood in light of his obsessive focus on the practice of music as a life mission.

Whatever band members did or did not happen to emphasize in early interviews, however, they were immersed in, and deeply affected by, Eastern art, music, and philosophy as it was popularized during this era. To mention just a few examples, Barbara Meier recalled that "Jerry got this little book of Buddhist sayings.... He steered me toward Buddhism and painting"; and in 1991 he told her that "if I were to think of myself in a spiritual context ... I'd think of myself as some sort of Buddhist."[24] Sara Ruppenthal Garcia recalls looking for a copy of the *Tibetan Book of the Dead* with Jerry during their first acid trip; David Nelson recalls that this trip was planned with regard to the related *Psychedelic Experience* book, and that during it they listened to Ravi Shankar recordings.[25] Phil Lesh's autobiography mentions early exposure to Western books that transmit Eastern or esoteric ideas; Tom Constanten mentions several more Eastern texts, calling them "guidebooks to the high country."[26] The band frequently consulted the *I Ching* in decision making.[27] They played for the "Zenefit" in November 1966 (on behalf of the S.F. Zen Center) and for the "Krishna Consciousness" show in January 1967 (on behalf of the S.F. Krishna Temple); performed at the Human Be-In, where Allen Ginsberg's Buddhist chanting opened and closed the event; and visited Maharishi Mahesh Yogi later in 1967.[28] It was Mickey Hart's momentous discovery, through Phil Lesh, of tabla player Alla Rakha that prompted the band to explore unusual time signatures in depth beginning in 1967, sparking a transformation in their approach to music.[29] Garcia discussed Indian classical music as fascinating; scattered references appear to Ravi Shankar, and to Indian music as part of eclectic listening habits.[30] The word "Zen" pops up frequently in writings by or about the Dead, as a kind of nonlinear descriptor.

A uniquely pertinent statement occurs in Lesh's later recollection of the final production stages for *Anthem of the Sun* in early 1968, during which he came up with a breakthrough mixing concept, audible on the album, of "the sound of a thousand-petal lotus, unfolding in constant renewal"—an unequivocal manifestation of Hindu and Buddhist symbology. One wonders if this idea could have been stimulated by Bill Walker's cover painting for that album, in process at that time, which, as Walker writes, was ultimately informed by this very concept.[31] As it happens, the most potent early Grateful Dead evocations of Eastern art, religion, and specifically mandalas are indeed found on their album covers, which include circular design elements with cosmic and Eastern-oriented imagery. The cover art for the first album, *The Grateful Dead* (1967), by Stanley Mouse and Alton Kelley, centers on a photograph of an Eastern religious bronze sculpture, backed by a photo of the sun's surface and surmounted with a rune-like inscription.[32] Rick Griffin's keenly hallucinatory cover art for the third album, *Aoxomoxoa* (1969), incorporates fertility and life-cycle elements into a cosmic, womb-like arc; its backside, like that of the preceding album, *Anthem of the Sun* (1968), includes a circular photograph of the Dead by Tom Weir, whose fisheye technique suggests cosmic-psychedelic resonances. But it is that second album, *Anthem of the Sun*, with a title itself already suggestive of nonwestern mysticism,[33] whose cover proves to be most striking from an Eastern point of view: it features a circular image painted by artist Bill Walker, made specifically for the album over a period of several months, that was directly grounded in Indian and Tibetan religious art. The painting could be called a mandala, being composed almost entirely of symbolic elements (serpents, flames, demonic or god-like figures) common in mandala designs. Walker, in his own later commentary on the painting, discusses this idea approvingly, finding that his painting "conforms to the basic structure" of a mandala as well as to its radiant cosmic spirituality. Further, he makes an essential connection between the themes of the painting and his personal experiences listening to the Grateful Dead in concert.[34] Basic elements of the painting are evoked in Figure 2.

Despite the imagery on these early album covers, the Dead did not plumb the sounds of the East for the music of the records themselves.[35] Rather, the album covers would seem to reflect a more general appreciation: opposed to the familiar West, free of its materialistic, pedestrian dualism, and encouraging of an intense, even hallucinatory meditative spirituality, the East represents an alluring "signpost to otherness."[36] When viewed through the broadest prism

Figure 2. Evocation of the painting "Anthem of the Sun" by Bill Walker (1968).

of native (U.S.) traditions, this otherness also seems ultimately to be as much about American maverick spiritualities as any movement "outward" toward the trans–Pacific world.[37]

Conclusion

The Dead's manager Rock Scully, recalling his acid-fueled impressions upon seeing the band perform for the second time in 1965, seems to put it all together, even at this early stage — not only Buddhism, but the Beats, the Transcendentalists, American folk and pop mythology — as he mulls on the Dead's radically intense, exploratory musical ambition[38]:

The individual, alienated tune does not exist, O my brothers! There is only this thing called *song*, an all-embracing Whitmanesque entity into which all songs empty themselves as if into the Mississippi. And like the Mississippi it's all one uninterrupted tune that includes—in Child ballad form—the folktale history of America. The entire story of our groaning continent contained in a twelve-bar song. Big American panorama, like Kerouac.

A moment of lucidity flashes by during which I try to remind myself that this is just a garage band on acid, but it's futile because in the core of my being I know I'm on to something big. Who says the bodhisattva has to come from Tibet? Why couldn't Soupy Sales be the Buddha? You have to leave an open mind about stuff like this. The idea is beginning to dawn on me, for instance, that the bodhisattva could easily be concealed in the person of, say, a ballad-singing country crooner. And from there it's only a small step to: Why couldn't the Grateful Dead become the greatest rock band in the world? Stranger things have happened.

Scully's vision of the band places Buddhism within an all-embracing psychedelic context. In so doing, it recalls the Acid Test characterization with which we began this study, in which Jerry implied that the mandala in particular can be a useful mode of understanding. Of course, Jerry did not stop there: "It was open, a tapestry, a mandala—it was whatever you made it." Why not a tapestry? Why not leave it open? The Dead's music, with its improvisatory, in-the-moment sensibility is, finally, whatever you make it; to insist on one path to understanding would be to deny other paths and understandings. In order to stay true to the Dead's identity, a "Dead mandala" would more appropriately serve as a possibility or opening than as an agent of control or finality.

Still, I contend that the concept of *mandala*, broadly understood, can be useful and, indeed, uniquely appropriate in relation to the Dead's early music, not least because of its very quality of "guided opening." It suggests a poetic holism, an incurving universe in motion; it conveys the meditative qualities of the music and the balance of forces within it, with their pull to order and to chaos, to center and to periphery; and it reflects the intensely spiritual, metaphysical world in which the Dead lived, with its distinctive tinge of psychedelic Easternness. In keeping with the nature of the mandala, visualization may be used as a point of entry, but the musical experience of "auditorization," including the state of being and becoming it generates, would constitute the essential key to a Dead mandala, which is, after all, a mandala of sound.

Notes

1. Lydon, 1969, rpt. in George-Warren, 1995, 61–64.
2. Regarding broader shared elements between Buddhist and Dead spirituality (including, among other things, emphasis on compassion and awareness; rejection of received belief systems in favor of direct experience; anti-materialism; dissolution of ego and the self; attainment of ecstasy through the transcendence of duality; and preparation for death), see Dodd, 1997 (entries listed under index heading "Spirituality");

Adams, 2000 (chapters by Hartley and Sutton); Weiner, 1999 (chapters by Gertner, Goodenough, Reist, Carr, and Noonan); and Gimbel, 2007 (chapters by Silberman, Fairlamb, Gass).

3. Macdonell, 1929, s.v. "Mandala."
4. Brauen, 1997, 7, 9 and 10.
5. For recent discussion of Asian mandala traditions outside of Tibet see ten Grotenhuis, 1999; Bühnemann, 2002.
6. Tucci, 1961, 23–24; Piburn 1993, p. 79; printed with the permission of the publisher. See also Trungpa 1991 and Leidy 1997. The Dalai Lama's definition involves the Tibetan parallel to the root Sanskrit word *manda: dkyil*, meaning "essence." See *Cologne Digital Sanskrit Lexicon*, viz. "manda;" and Kunsang, 2003, viz. "dkyil."
7. Ellingson, 1979, 29–30.
8. Cf. Brauen, 1997; Bryant, 1992; International Kalachakra Network Web site.
9. The terms "East" and "Eastern" are used for convenience here in referring to the cultures of East and South Asia, principally India, Tibet, China and Japan.
10. Cf. Tweed, 1992.
11. Cf. Gelpi, 1975; Sayre, 1992; Versluis, 1993; Moody, 1996; Oser, 1998; Taylor, 1999; Schmidt, 2005.
12. E.g. Suzuki, 1962; Goddard, 1938; Watts, 1958. Numerous good studies trace the broader history of Buddhism in the United States, including Fields, 1992; Seagher, 1999; Coleman, 2001.
13. Henke, 1991, repr. in George-Warren, 1995, 184. See also Scully, 1996, 23–24. Regarding the Dead and the Beats, see Ciocco, 2007; and Buddhism, Gass, 2007. Jerry was a wide-ranging reader. Kesey claimed him to be "as well read as anyone I'd ever met" (Greenfield, 1996, 76); Ron Rakow found him "reading all the time" (ibid., 96).
14. Leary, 1964; Krishnamurti, 1957–60; Merton, 1968; Watts, 1997. See also Badiner, 2002; and from a complementary perspective, Kripal, 2007.
15. Cohen, 1995. According to Mountain Girl, the Thelins "were good friends and came up to the [Grateful Dead] house often"; Troy, 1991, 83. Chet Helms recalls that Ravi Shankar was "already a cult influence" in 1966 Haight-Ashbury; Troy, 1991, 100. Charles Lloyd recalls that "you could hear my music and Ravi Shankar and the Dead and Hendrix on the radio"; Jackson, 1999, 127.
16. Jung, 1972, 3–4 (orig. publ. 1955). Elsewhere, he characterized the mandala archetype as "a pattern of order which, like a psychological 'view-finder' marked with a cross or a circle divided into four, is superimposed on the psychic chaos so that each content falls into place and the weltering confusion is held together by the protective circle," Jung, 1972, Vol. 1 (orig. publ. 1958).
17. Since Jung's time, use of the mandala concept as a means to understanding and meditation has become widespread, e.g. Argüelles, 1972; Hall, 1988; McLean, 1989; Cornell, 2006; Moss, 2007.
18. E.g. Atkinson, 2001, cat. nos. 13, 17, 30, 45, 50, 57, 68, 73, 85, 90, 100; also Grushkin, 1987, chap. 2; Cohen, 1991, 35, 362–363, and passim. As Mickey Hart once wrote, "The posters looked like what we were playing.... They resonated with the style of the times and described visually what the Grateful Dead, Big Brother, Quicksilver, and the Airplane were doing" (Hart, 1993).
19. Cohen, 1995.
20. Excluding major historical events (e.g. Ravi Shankar appearing at the Monterey Pops Festival, Ginsberg at the Human Be-In, Mickey Hart meeting Alla Rakha, the band meeting the Maharishi), the "Eastern element" is almost entirely absent from the account of McNally, 2002, chaps. 3–24, covering the history of the Dead, its members, and its environment between 1962 and early 1969. A different picture (as discussed presently) is drawn in Jackson, 1999; see also Troy, 1991 and 1994; Greenfield, 1996;

Gans, 2002; Lesh, 2005. Of course, not just different writers, but different band members too will have had different attitudes, variably represented in the written record. Kreutzmann, for example, "has a spiritual side that he hides from the band" (Scully, 1996, 163).

21. Gans, 2002, 73.

22. Gans, 2002, 214. Garcia was famously, with tongue in cheek, listed as (musical and) "spiritual" advisor on the cover of Jefferson Airplane's breakthrough LP, *Surrealistic Pillow* (1967); cf. Scully, 1996; Jackson 1999, 116. To the idea "during the Haight-Ashbury time and later, that you were the sort of spiritual advisor to the whole rock scene," Garcia once responded, "That's a crock of shit, quite frankly" (Wenner and Reich, 1972), repr. in George-Warren, 1995, 88. Garcia later characterized the band's spiritual power as a "seat-of-the-pants shamanism" (Henke, 1991), repr. in George-Warren, 1995, 182. Regarding the mid–60s, Owsley has said that "none of the people in Kesey's scene had any roots in the [ancient] shamanistic rituals at all" (Gans, 2002, 299). But references (by others) to Garcia as a "Buddha" figure are common, e.g. McClanahan, 1972, repr. in Dodd, 2000, 57; Meier, 1992, 56; Scully, 1996, 105; Greenfield, 1996, 21, 79; Gans, 2002, 73; and an early Ralph Gleason interview is entitled "Jerry Garcia, the Guru." See also the nuanced reactions in Hartley, 2000, 135ff; and the summative statement in Jackson, 1999, 475.

23. Gans, 2002, 214. Cf. the "ironic sacramentalism" discussed in Fairlamb, 2007. Garcia's sense of newly-minted spiritual existentialism, as it were, goes back at least in part to the Acid Tests. As Kesey recalls: "When the Dead's sound started to spark that acid consciousness, the way people moved to music absolutely changed. It was absolutely new and spontaneously creative. I don't think that kind of movement had ever happened before. It's not like Krishna. It's not like aborigines. It's not like Africans really. It's its own thing," Jackson, 1999b, 89.

24. Greenfield, 1996, 21; Meier, 1992, 56. The Dead's relation to Buddhism is evoked in Gass, 2007.

25. Greenfield, 1996, 57; Jackson, 1999, 71–72.

26. Lesh, 2005, 30, 35, 39, 83, 97, 128, 131; Constanten, 1992, 63.

27. Lydon, 1970; Gans, 1995, 118; Scully, 1996, 21.

28. Seagher, 1999, 99; Greenfield, 1996, 96; Grushkin, 1987, 103; Scully, 1996, 79–80; Lesh, 2005, 96–98; Cohen, 1991, 123 and 138; Contanten, 1992, 77; Scully, 1996, 124.

29. Hart, *Drumming*, 141–44 (mentioning that at the time he already owned a pair of tablas); Brandelius, 1989, 132–33; Jackson, 1999, 148; Gans, 2002, 68; McNally, 2002, 258; Lesh, 2005, 131–32. Hart recalls discovering Tibetan overtone chanting in the late '60s, which he describes as "a perfect universe, like a mandala of sound" (Hart, 2000). And the "Drummers' Chant," appearing in 1969 Dead shows, seems based on classical Indian drumming chants. More generally on the relationship of Hart and other band members to world music, see Vennum, 1997.

30. Gans, 2002, 69; Lesh, 2005, 39; Gans, 2002, 13.

31. Lesh, 2005, 128; also Jackson, 1999, 145; Walker, "Anthem." Regarding lotus symbology see Tucci, 1961, 27–37 and 114–15; Beer, 1999, 37–41; Fields, 2001, 146–49.

32. The inscription was originally a verse supposedly taken from the *Egyptian Book of the Dead*: "In the land of the dark, the ship of the sun is driven by the Grateful Dead." I have not yet found this line in various translations of the many constituent fragments of this "book," though it does relate to their themes and imagery. This verse had been used earlier, e.g. in an Egyptian-themed "advertisement" for the band drawn by Rick Griffin (*San Francisco Oracle*, 6, Feb. 1966, 28; repr. in Cohen, 1991, 142) and at the Human Be-In (cf. review by Steven Levine, ibid., 9; repr. in Cohen 1991, 123). But Garcia had the line obscured on the album cover before publication, finding it to be "a tad pretentious" (Troy, 1994, 105; Gleason, 1969, repr. in Dodd, 2000, 20). The Egyptian

theme would prove to be an enduring part of the Dead's world, recurring in later artwork (including that of *Aoxomoxoa*) and culminating with the Dead's famous trip to play at the Egyptian pyramids in 1978.

33. According to McNally, 2002, 273–74, the phrase is borrowed from James Churchward's geo-mytho-historical fabrication, *The Lost Continent of Mu* (New York: I. Washburn, 1931).

34. Walker, "Anthem." Walker also states that "although I was academically ignorant of the inner workings of a mandala in 1968, I 'saw' my world, both inside and out, in a mandala like way." Lesh has commented that Walker's painting "was so perfect for that album and so perfect for what we were doing then and who we were then" (Jackson, 1999b, re: 146).

35. The title of the first song on their first album, "The Golden Road (to Unlimited Devotion)"—also the name of their first fan club, forming in that era—would seem to be a pun on Hindu religious rhetoric, but "Eastern sounds" of the time (involving mainly sitars, tablas, or raga-like improvisatory runs) are scarce, one notable instance being the evocation of a tanbura drone on the released single of "Dark Star." Unequivocally Eastern themes are also exceedingly rare in Dead lyrics; one instance being the word "bodhi" used in Hunter's hallucinatory "China Cat Sunflower" of 1967; see Trist and Dodd, 2005, 55.

36. Walker, "Anthem."

36. Regarding Jerry's "signpost to otherness" formulation, see Wenner and Reich, 1972, repr. in George-Warren, 1995, 95.

37. Amid the vast literature on "outsider" impulses in American spirituality, see, for example (in addition to earlier citations), Moore, 1986, esp. p. 208, Jenkins 2000, and Partridge 2004.

38. Scully, 1996, 18.

Bibliography

Argüelles, José, and Miriam. *Mandala*. Berkeley: Shambhala, 1972.
Atkinson, D. Scott, Sally Tomlinson, and Walter Patrick Medeiros. *High Societies: Psychedelic Rock Posters of Haight-Ashbury*. San Diego: San Diego Museum of Art, 2001.
Badiner, Allan Hunt, and Alex Grey, eds. *Zig Zag Zen: Buddhism and Psychedelics*. San Francisco: Chronicle, 2002.
Beer, Robert. *The Encyclopedia of Tibetan Symbols and Motifs*. Boston: Shambhala, 1999.
Brandelius, Jerilyn Lee. *Grateful Dead Family Album*. New York: Warner Books, 1989.
Brauen, Martin. *The Mandala: Sacred Circle in Tibetan Buddhism*. Boston: Shambhala, 1997.
Bryant, Barry. *The Wheel of Time Sand Mandala: Visual Scripture of Tibetan Buddhism*. San Francisco: HarperSanFrancisco, 1992.
Bühnemann, Gudrun, ed. *Mandalas and Yantras in the Hindu Traditions*. Leiden, Netherlands; Boston: Brill, 2002.
Ciocco, Gary. "How Dead Beats Became Deadheads: From Emerson and James to Kerouac and Garcia." In *The Grateful Dead and Philosophy*, Steven Gimbel, ed. Chicago: Open Court, 2007, 63–74.
Cohen, Allen. "Additional Notes on the S.F. Oracle." *Haight-Ashbury in the Sixties* [CD-ROM]. Carlsbad, CA: Rockument, 1995. Posted online at: http://www.rockument.com/WEBORA.html.
_____, ed. *The San Francisco Oracle, Facsimile Edition: The Psychedelic Newspaper of the Haight-Ashbury, 1966–1968*. Berkeley: Regent, 1991.

Coleman, James William. *The New Buddhism: The Western Transformation of an Ancient Tradition*. Oxford; New York: Oxford University Press, 2001.
Cologne Digital Sanskrit Lexicon [Project hosted by the University of Cologne]. Posted online at: http://webapps.uni-koeln.de/tamil.
Constanten, Tom. *Between Rock and Hard Places: A Musical Autobiodyssey*. Eugene, OR: Hulogosi, 1992.
Cornell, Judith. *Mandala: Luminous Symbols for Meaning*. 2d ed. Wheaton, IL: Quest, 2006.
Dodd, David G., and Diana Spaulding, eds. *The Grateful Dead Reader*. New York: Oxford University Press, 2000.
Dodd, David G., and Alan Trist, eds. *The Complete Annotated Grateful Dead Lyrics: The Collected Lyrics of Robert Hunter and John Barlow, Lyrics to All Original Songs, with Selected Traditional and Cover Songs*. New York: Free Press, 2005.
Dodd, David G., and Robert G. Weiner. *The Grateful Dead and the Deadheads: An Annotated Bibliography*. Westport, CT: Greenwood, 1997.
Ellingson, Terry Jay. "The Mandala of Sound: Concepts and Sound Structures in Tibetan Ritual Music." Ph.D. diss., Univ. of Wisconsin–Madison, 1979.
Evans-Wentz, W. Y., ed. *The Tibetan Book of the Dead: Or The After-Death Experiences on the Bardo Plane, According to Lama Kazi Dawa-Samdup's English Rendering*. 3d ed. of 1957. With a new Foreword and Afterword by Donald S. Lopez Jr. Oxford: Oxford University Press, 2000. [1st ed. publ. 1927.]
Fairlamb, Horace L. "Community at the Edge of Chaos: The Dead's Cultural Revolution." In *The Grateful Dead and Philosophy*, Gimbel, ed. Chicago: Open Court, 2007, 13–25.
Fields, Gregory P. *Religious Therapeutics: Body and Health in Yoga, Ayurveda, and Tantra*. Albany: State University of New York, 2001.
Fields, Rick. *How The Swans Came to the Lake: A Narrative History of Buddhism in America*. 3d ed. Boston: Shambhala, 1992.
Gans, David, with the Grateful Dead. *Conversations with the Dead: The Grateful Dead Interview Book*. 2d ed. Cambridge, MA: Da Capo, 2002. [1st ed. publ. 1991.]
_____, ed. *Not Fade Away: The Online World Remembers Jerry Garcia*. New York: Thunder's Mouth, 1995.
Gass, Paul. "Buddhism Through the Eyes of the Dead." In *The Grateful Dead and Philosophy*, Gimbel, ed. Chicago: Open Court, 2007, 127–37.
Gelpi, Albert. *The Tenth Muse: The Psyche of the American Poet*. Cambridge, MA: Harvard University Press, 1975.
George-Warren, Holly, et al. *Garcia: By the Editors of Rolling Stone*. Boston: Little, Brown, 1995.
Gimbel, Steven, ed. *The Grateful Dead and Philosophy: Getting High Minded about Love and Haight*. Chicago: Open Court, 2007.
Gleason, Ralph. "Jerry Garcia, the Guru." In *The Jefferson Airplane and the San Francisco Sound*. New York: Ballantine, 1969. Rpt. in *The Grateful Dead Reader*, David G. Dodd and Diana Spaulding, eds., 20–38. [Interview dates from 1967.]
Goddard, Dwight, ed. *A Buddhist Bible*. 2d ed. New York: Dutton, 1938.
Grateful Dead. *Anthem of the Sun* [LP]. Warner Bros.–Seven Arts, 1968.
_____. *Aoxomoxoa* [LP]. Warner Bros.–Seven Arts, 1969.
_____. *The Grateful Dead* [LP]. Warner Bros., 1967.
Greenfield, Robert. *Dark Star: An Oral History of Jerry Garcia*. New York: William Morrow, 1996.
Grotenuis, Elizabeth ten. *Japanese Mandalas: Representations of Sacred Geography*. Honolulu: University of Hawai'i Press, 1999.
Grushkin, Paul. *The Art of Rock: Posters from Presley to Punk*. New York: Abbeville, 1987.

Hall, Manly P. *Meditation Symbols in Eastern & Western Mysticism: Mysteries of the Mandala*. Los Angeles: Philosophical Research Society, 1988.

Hart, Mickey. "Digital Interviews: Mickey Hart." Posted online at: http://www.digitalinterviews.com/digitalinterviews/views/hart.shtml, 2000.

———. "Foreword." In *Freehand: The Art of Stanley Mouse*, Stanley Mouse, Alton Kelley, and Walter Madeiros. Berkeley: SLG, 1993, 7.

———, Jay Stevens, and Fredric Lieberman. *Drumming at the Edge of Magic: A Journey into the Spirit of Percussion*. San Francisco: HarperSanFrancisco, 1990.

Hartley, Jennifer A. "'We Were Given This Dance': Music and Meaning in the Early Unlimited Devotion Family." In *Deadhead Social Science*, Rebecca G. Adams and Robert Sardiello, eds. Walnut Creek, CA: AltaMira, 2000, 129–154.

Henke, James. "Alive and Well: The Rolling Stone Interview with Jerry Garcia." *Rolling Stone*, October 31, 1991. Rpt. in *Garcia*, Holly George-Warren, ed. Boston: Little Brown, 1995, 180–189.

International Kalachakra Network. "The Kalachakra Mandala." Posted online at: http://kalachakranet.org/mandala_kalachakra.html.

Jackson, Blair. "The Cutting Room Floor." In *Garcia: An American Life*.

———. *Garcia: An American Life*. New York: Viking, 1999.

———. *Goin' Down the Road: A Grateful Dead Traveling Companion*. New York: Harmony, 1992.

Jenkins, Philip. *Mystics and Messiahs: Cults and New Religions in American History*. New York: Oxford University Press, 2000.

Jung, C. G. *Mandala Symbolism*, R.F.C. Hull, trans. Princeton: Princeton University Press, 1972. [Includes articles collected earlier in *The Collected Works of C.G. Jung*. Vol. 9, part 1: *The Archetypes and the Collective Unconscious*. 2d ed. Princeton: Princeton University Press: 1968.]

Kerouac, Jack. *The Dharma Bums*. New York: Viking, 1958.

———. *On the Road*. New York: Viking, 1957.

Kripal, Jeffrey. *Esalen: America and the Religion of No Religion*. Chicago: University of Chicago Press, 2007.

Krishnamurti, Jiddu. *Commentaries on Living*. D. Rajagopal, ed. 3 vols. New York: Harper, 1957–60.

Kunsang, Erik Pema, James Valby, Ives Waldo, and Jeffrey Hopkins. *The Rangjung Yeshe Tibetan-English Dictionary of Buddhist Culture*, version 3 [CD-ROM]. Kathmandu: Rangjung Yeshe, 2003. Posted online as *Online Tibetan English Dictionary* at: http://www.nitartha.org/dictionary_search04.html.

Leary, Timothy, Ralph Metzner, and Richard Alpert. *The Psychedelic Experience: A Manual Based on the Tibetan Book of the Dead*. New Hyde Park, NY: University Books, 1964.

Leidy, Denise Patry, and Robert A.F. Thurman. *Mandala: The Architecture of Enlightenment*. New York: Asia Society Galleries, 1997.

Lesh, Phil. *Searching for the Sound: My Life with the Grateful Dead*. New York: Little, Brown, 2005.

Lydon, Michael. "Dead Zone." *Rolling Stone*, August 23, 1969. Rpt. in *Garcia*, George-Warren, ed., 55–72.

———. "An Evening with the Grateful Dead." *Rolling Stone*, September 17, 1970. Posted online at: http://www.rollingstone.com/artists/thegratefuldead/articles/story/5935650/an_evening_with_the_grateful_dead.

Macdonell, Arthur Anthony. *A Practical Sanskrit Dictionary: With Transliteration, Accentuation, and Etymological Analysis Throughout*. London: Oxford University Press, 1929. Posted online at: http://dsal.uchicago.edu/dictionaries/macdonell.

McClanahan, Ed. "Grateful Dead I Have Known." *Playboy*, March 1972. Rpt. [with

additions and changes] in *The Grateful Dead Reader*, Dodd and Spaulding, ed., 53–85.
McLean, Adam. *The Alchemical Mandala: A Survey of the Mandala in the Western Esoteric Traditions*. Grand Rapids: Phanes, 1989.
McNally, Dennis. *A Long Strange Trip: The Inside History of the Grateful Dead*. New York: Broadway, 2002.
Meier, Barbara. "Jerry Garcia Speaks with Barbara Meier." *Tricycle: The Buddhist Review*, 1/3, spring 1992. New York: Buddhist Ray, 56–58.
Merton, Thomas. *Zen and the Birds of Appetite*. New York: New Directions, 1968.
Moody, A. David. *Tracing T. S. Eliot's Spirit: Essays on His Poetry and Thought*. Cambridge: Cambridge University Press, 1996.
Moore, R. Laurence. *Religious Outsiders and the Making of Americans*. New York: Oxford University Press, 1986.
Moss, Richard. *The Mandala of Being: Discovering the Power of Awareness*. Novato, CA: New World Library, 2007.
Oser, Lee. *T. S. Eliot and American Poetry*. Columbia: University of Missouri Press, 1998.
Partridge, Christopher, ed. *New Religions, a Guide: New Religious Movements, Sects, and Alternative Spiritualities*. New York: Oxford University Press, 2004.
Piburn, Sidney, ed. and comp. *The Dalai Lama, A Policy of Kindness: An Anthology of Writings by and about the Dalai Lama*. 2d ed. Ithaca, NY: Snow Lion, 1993.
Sayre, Robert F., ed. *New Essays on Walden*. Cambridge: Cambridge University Press, 1992.
Schmidt, Leigh Eric. *Restless Souls: The Making of American Spirituality*. New York: HarperSanFrancisco, 2005.
Scott, John W., Mike Dolgushkin, and Stu Nixon. *Deadbase X: The Complete Guide to Grateful Dead Song Lists*. Cornish, NH: Deadbase, 1997. [Updated website posted at: http://www.deadbase.com.]
Scully, Rock, with David Dalton. *Living with the Dead: Twenty Years on the Bus with Garcia and the Grateful Dead*. Boston: Little, Brown, 1996.
Seagher, Richard Hughes. *Buddhism in America*. New York: Columbia University Press, 1999.
Suzuki, Daisetz T, and Bernard Phillips, eds. *The Essentials of Zen Buddhism*. New York: Dutton, 1962.
Taylor, Eugene. *Shadow Culture: Psychology and Spirituality in America*. Washington, D.C.: Counterpoint, 1999.
Troy, Sandy. *Captain Trips: A Biography of Jerry Garcia*. New York: Thunder's Mouth, 1994.
_____. *One More Saturday Night: Reflections with the Grateful Dead, Dead Family, and Dead Heads*. New York: St. Martin's, 1991.
Trungpa, Chögyam, and Sherab Chödzin, eds. *Orderly Chaos: The Mandala Principle*. Boston: Shambhala, 1991.
Tucci, Giuseppe, and Alan Houghton Brodrick, trans. *The Theory and Practice of the Mandala: With Special Reference to the Modern Psychology of the Subconscious*. London: Rider, 1961. [Original Italian ed. 1949.]
Tweed, Thomas A. *The American Encounter with Buddhism, 1844–1912: Victorian Culture and the Limits of Dissent*. Bloomington: Indiana University Press, 1992.
Vennum, Thomas, Jr. "The Grateful Dead Onstage in 'World Music.'" In *Perspectives on the Grateful Dead: Critical Writings*, Robert G. Weiner, ed. Westport, CT: Greenwood, 1999, 41–54.
Versluis, Arthur. *American Transcendentalism and Asian Religions*. New York: Oxford University Press, 1993.
Walker, Bill. "Anthem: A Walkers Guide." Posted online at: http://www.billzart.net/files/AnthemGuide_2002-12-02_web.pdf.

Watts, Alan. "Beat Zen, Square Zen, and Zen." *Chicago Review*, XII/2, spring 1958. Posted online at: http://humanities.uchicago.edu/orgs/review/60th/15wattsindex.shtml.
———, and David Cellers, and Mark Watts, comp. *Zen and the Beat Way*. Boston: Tuttle, 1997.
Weiner, R. G., ed. *Perspectives on the Grateful Dead: Critical Writings*. Westport, CT: Greenwood, 1999.
Wenner, Jann S., and Charles Reich. "The First: The Rolling Stone Interview with Jerry Garcia and Mountain Girl." *Rolling Stone*, January 20, 1972. Rpt. in *Garcia*, George-Warren, ed., 78–95.

The Eccentric Revolutions of Phil Lesh

Brent Wood

From Modernism to Postmodernism

The Grateful Dead were born at the political and aesthetic crossroads of the modern and the postmodern in Western culture. The culture of "the Sixties," of which the Dead remain a primary emblem, is best understood as reflecting simultaneously the mature flowering of modernism and the emergence of postmodernism.[1] Contrary to the perceptions of many, the modernist utopianism characteristic of both capitalist ideologues and the counterculture did succeed in bringing about a brave new world in America — just not the one either side was expecting. Modernist-influenced perspectives of the time could not have grasped the implications of the postmodernity that would emerge from it. As cosmic irony would have it, the U.S. military played a significant role in the revolution, laying pipe for the future Internet, spurring on youth to widespread rebellion, discharging Jerome Garcia from the army, and introducing LSD to Robert Hunter and Ken Kesey. While Jacques Derrida and Gilles Deleuze worked at thinking their way out of the logo/phallo/ethnocentric orbits of Western rationalism, opening plurality through a keyhole and navigating with rhetoric turned inside out, in America groups of musicians soaked in acid began their own project of playing their way out of their own ethnocultural orbits. The Beatles brought African American music to Eurocentric ears, straight out of Liverpool, pivot of the slave trade.[2] Folk art and commercial art merged, then overthrew high art. Political multiculturalism may have been born kicking and screaming into the two-tone world of America, but its musical cousin was delivered already singing a brand new set of licks. In San Francisco, the musicultural mix was just right and the genie came swirling out of the bottle. Phil Lesh brought Modest Mussourgsky, Charles Ives and John Coltrane to play with his friend Jerry Garcia, who invited Scotty Stoneman,

Chuck Berry and a chorus of folk balladeers — including Robert Hunter. Naturally, they started a rock and roll band.

Acknowledged postmodernist aesthetics in the field of music don't seem to have much in common with the Dead's aesthetic at first glance. Hunter leans toward the Romantic, and most of the musical genres in which they work stem from the first half of the twentieth century. There's no "performance art" aspect to their music, no oblique subversion of technological alienation, and no identity politics. They do not do digital cut-and-paste (they are still into finger-painting), and they keep forgetting to remind people that they are artists. Nevertheless, they do indulge in a strange pastiche of styles; they use indeterminacy as a compositional principle; they blur the line between audience and performer; they break down barriers between genres and blend high art, folk art and commercial art. They are a process, not a product; they are a living demonstration of what Roland Barthes meant by "the Death of the Author"; they proliferate pluralities, creating a world in which incongruity ceases to imply irony. In the Grateful Dead's music, fragments of modernism and spirits of Romanticism dissolve into the dust of postmodernism and rise again, animated by liquid chaos courtesy of Owsley and the perpetual evolution machine of Phil Lesh.

In their general mode of performance as well as in their extended improvisatory passages the Grateful Dead are a musical manifestation of *becoming* in the way Deleuze and others use the word, always mutating beyond the stratifying impulse of the apprehending mind. The Dead's approach to "actualizing" possibilities on the fly in an ongoing multiplicity of dialogues prefigures by some 20 years Jean-François Lyotard's conception of the postmodern condition as defined by an ever-evolving web of "language games" that "refines our sensitivity to differences and reinforces our ability to tolerate the incommensurable" (Lyotard xxv). Lyotard's subsequent comment that postmodernity's central principle is "not the expert's homology but the inventor's paralogy" suggests that we think of the Dead as "inventors" engaged in paralogy — "speaking alongside one another" as well as "aside from" or marginal to the logocentric intellectual order. The ongoing struggle with consensus necessitated by the Grateful Dead's improvisational multiplicity is reflected in Lyotard's observation that in postmodernity "consensus is a horizon which is never reached" (61). The antiauthoritarian ethos of the Grateful Dead as actualized in their music may have created problems for record companies trying to package the Dead for mass consumption, but the audience naturally attracted to the band could easily imagine another unique concert just over that horizon.

In this sense Niklas Luhmann's characterization of what constitutes a "complex system" — one which has "more possibilities than can be realized" (Luhmann 25) — unquestionably applies to the Grateful Dead as both a musical and a social entity. Complex systems, postmodernism's characteristic organizational paradigm, are those comprised primarily of intricate sets of *relationships*, as opposed to sums of parts. They are open systems which interact with their environments, employing feedback loops which create a high degree of what Paul Cilliers calls "recurrency" and which operate "under conditions far from equilibrium" (Cilliers 12). The "complex system," according to these definitions, is nothing more or less than a living organism capable of self-organization or "autopoiesis"— a term especially suited to the kind of aesthetically-focused self-organizing system exemplified by the Grateful Dead.[3] The Grateful Dead are the agents of a kind of postmodernism that, like their renegade modernist counterparts James Joyce and Charles Ives, tirelessly cultivate plurality against the impositions of political and philosophical ideologies. If Joyce and Ives were paradigmatic modernists, artist-rebels working consciously against the expectations of the bourgeois and pushing the limits of perception and the coherent unfolding of the artwork, the Grateful Dead are quintessential postmodernists, helping to transform crumbling modernist social structures by providing a continuously morphing eccentricity for like-minded outsiders interested in anarchism, and offering a model of popular folk art as an alternative to the high-art sensibility of modernism. The Dead took the earlier synthesis of the cultural outsider and high art associated with the Beats to a hitherto unknown level of mass popularity, subverting the clutches of the commercial while making a living in and through its agency.

Not unlike that of the Merry Pranksters, the Dead's response to life amid a postmodern collage of representation and reality was to create their own "movie." The movie included plenty of traveling carnival footage, to be sure, but at its heart was an ongoing experiment in nonverbal human intimacy. As an alternative to the state of "hyperreality" in which human experience is subject to ubiquitous electronic mediation by postmodern technoculture,[4] the Grateful Dead (with the help of psychedelics) aimed at invoking a state of "superreality," an experience of reality in which our sense of mediation by our own habits of perception, mind and social customs is actively *minimized*. Electronic equipment, with the help of innovative sound engineers such as Owsley and Dan Healy, was focused on reducing the distance between listener and player.[5] The lyrics of the songs, especially Hunter's and to some extent John Barlow's, are capable in the concert setting of evoking a "superreal" mythworld which seems to encompass the contemporary possibilities of day-to-day experience in America, and ultimately to reinterpret America to itself.

Postmodernist Aesthetics and Psychedelia

Music's potential to manifest and reveal morphing cultural patterns is great, but few cultural theorists have seriously considered postmodernity as expressed in music. This is hardly surprising, as music has always baffled the theoretical mind raised on visual and textual culture. The foremost problem is music's minimal representational qualities; a second is its ephemeral existence; a third is music's natural role as a participatory art form, more suited to the group than to the individual. Finally, even the basic inner workings of most music remain a kind of "dark art" to most people, even many of those who are passionate about it, and its structures require a mind and ear trained by practice and performance to be understood.

Most discussion about popular music in terms of postmodernism has concentrated on the kinds of hyper-collage made possible by the electronic reproduction and distortion of sound, such as John Oswald's "cut-ups" or hip-hop's dense cut-and-paste compositional format. A focus on sounds-as-found-objects eases the first two difficulties somewhat, but not the third or fourth. The Grateful Dead's live music, moreover, is no less a hyper-collage than is hip-hop, or Oswald's electronic cut-up of "Dark Star," or the splicing together of various recordings of Grateful Dead live performances for *Anthem of the Sun*, for that matter — it just plays by different rules. Intertextuality in the Grateful Dead's music is not so easily grasped as that in hip-hop, for instance: there are few musical quotations, few deliberate juxtapositions of incommensurate styles, and only the audience tapers to turn the ephemeral momentary evolution of the music into a product. As "America's longest-running musical argument"[6] the Dead maintained itself as a forum for experimentation not with a variety of samples or "musical modules," as fellow Californian experimentalist Frank Zappa calls the standard combinations of motif and texture in Western music,[7] but with a variety of interpretations of interdependent musical ideas.

Postmodern art often acts as a challenge to what Fredric Jameson called "the cultural logic of late capitalism," even if already implicated within it. Jameson's famous essay (1984) and book (1991) of the same name discuss the intersection of political and artistic organization in the contemporary world, focusing largely on architecture and visual arts. Jameson's primary musical references, like those of most cultural critics, are John Cage and Philip Glass, composers who, while working in a high-art framework, create minimalist and/or chance-generated soundscapes which conceptually challenge both modernist and bourgeois aesthetics by deliberately working against their most basic assumptions. The enhanced tension between the fragment and the whole characteristic of modernist aesthetics breaks down in the work of these and other like-minded composers as continuity and discontinuity are relentlessly pushed to their limits.

In the Grateful Dead's improvisatory instrumental passages, one may hear a very different result emerge from a collectivist version of a similar process, as the band members simultaneously push the limits of identity of rhythms, harmonic progressions, and compositions. Even the compositions themselves often embody a multiplicity in which difference and repetition assume a characteristically postmodernist relationship with one another, although they may simultaneously embody Romantic and modernist sensibilities in lyric and structure. The Grateful Dead's art "product" embodies what Deleuze and Guattari call "becoming-other" as song is set into continuous variation which is also describable as "nomadic," "anarchic" and "schizophrenic." Moreover, the psychedelic listening and playing environment inevitably undoes the best-laid plans of mice and men, with chaos and tangent busily subverting intentionality of all kinds.

Dr. Lesh's Perpetual Motion Machine

It's easy enough to discuss the band's musical approach, organization, and environment in terms of basic postmodernist ideas such as those summarized above, but a more thorough analysis requires attention to the details of the music itself in its many incarnations over a long period. It also requires listening closely to the music from the perspective of bassist Phil Lesh. Why make Lesh the focus of the postmodern dimensions of the Grateful Dead, given that at heart it is an exercise in creative collectivism, and that its resulting irreducible multiplicity is an essential aspect of its postmodern quality? To begin with, Lesh's contribution to the music must be understood in the context of his relationship with Garcia, who found himself somewhat unwillingly the band's *de facto* leader in many respects due to the fact that most of the band members had stronger musical connections with him than with any other member. Garcia's attempts to back away from the musical center were more successful than his attempts to evade responsibility to the entire Grateful Dead organization and the Deadheads, which ultimately helped grind down his creativity and his health. As both *Harrington St.* and *Dark Star* reveal, Garcia was a product of the variety of cultural and genetic influences found in the port of San Francisco, and his constitutional multiplicity made him a perfect candidate to embrace both the transcendence of the self through psychedelics and the transcendence of musical genres and styles—the perfect foil for Lesh's orientation toward infinite musical multiplicity.

A dialogist at heart, Garcia couldn't play without a counterpart, and as the kind of dialogist who doesn't like taking breaks, he needed partners who could speak at the same time and harmonize. The bass is the minimal counterpart required for his upper, lyrical guitar voice, and of all the inspired choices Garcia made in his musical career, the unlikely decision to invite Lesh, a very white, intellectual ex-trumpeter and would-be avant-garde composer, to be the bassist for a band aiming to perform electrified dance music from the African American and European-American folk traditions would prove to be the one of greatest significance. The inclusion of Lesh in the band effectively launched the long strange musical trip for everyone, as the whirling dialectic of the unexpected between top and bottom began lift-off. The conversation began at the first bar of each concert, and they never liked to have the same conversation twice. Garcia's responsibilities as the "lead" guitar or highest instrumental voice were usually to interpret the melody of a song, to decorate a sung melody, or to create sustained melodic and rhythmic interest over a simple chord progression or series of scales for extended periods for the sake of the dancers in the audience. Unlike other guitarists who play these roles, however, Garcia's job wasn't primarily to tease new ideas from out of a solid ground. With Lesh on the bottom end, there was no solid ground. In fact, it was often Garcia who was put in the position of having to maintain order, to make some kind of sense of the swirling sea of improvisation beneath him for ears tuned to hear scalar melodies in the soprano as the primary voice of the music, and for bodies and minds in need of rhythmic regularity.

Both Garcia and Lesh have commented explicitly on the highly unusual nature of Lesh's playing style. In an early interview with Ralph J. Gleason, Garcia acknowledged that Lesh "doesn't play bass like anyone else; he doesn't listen to other bass players, he listens to his head" (Gleason 18). Later he remarked that Lesh "plays the bass as though he invented the instrument and nobody ever played it before him" (Jackson 261). It is of course true that none of the band members play in conventional "rock" styles, and the Grateful Dead can only be considered a "rock band" in a limited number of respects. Garcia's own sound is unique, as he brought rapid-fire, highly scalar, fiddle-like and percussive finger-picked, banjo-like licks to the electric guitar, transforming them with chromaticism and complex nontraditional rhythms, while eschewing the majority of rock 'n' roll stylings such as excessive distortion, repeated high-speed blues figures, minor pentatonic scales, long sustains and straight driving four-four rhythmic phrasing. While one of the keys to the band's unusual musical textures is that none of the members had come from a rock 'n' roll background, clearly Lesh had the farthest to travel to get to the Grateful Dead's electric dance party.

As documented in *Searching for the Sound*, European art music was Lesh's major influence, merging with experimental American approaches to orchestral composition such as that of Ives, and with the harmonic, melodic and timbral experimentation characteristic of improvised jazz such as Coltrane's. It was Lesh who best understood the essence of the experimental group improvisation approaches favored by groundbreaking artists such as Coltrane and aggressively brought that sensibility to the band. Tempering this jazz sensibility, however, was the fact that Lesh had never played the blues, the very root of jazz, to any substantial degree before turning on to the possibilities of musical texture offered by Coltrane, Miles Davis, Eric Dolphy and others. Instead, his basic repertoire as a child and young man had been European art pieces featuring trumpet and violin.

In *Searching for the Sound*, Lesh recalls being inspired to compose for bass guitar by the Rolling Stones' track "The Last Time," a rock standard which eventually became part of the Dead's repertoire. According to Lesh, Garcia pointed out that the "bass" riff inspiring him was actually being played on guitar (Lesh 43). This initial encounter would prove prophetic, as Lesh would often play a part more tenor than bass. In the mid–1970s, Garcia would comment on what it meant to hear Lesh's playing in a new light one night in the recording studio when Garcia listened to an isolated bass track for his solo record *Reflections,* sped up so the melody sounded an octave higher. Garcia compared Lesh's playing to that of a cellist, noting that his bass work made sense when heard as a single melody stretched over the entire length of the song played at a higher pitch.[8]

The root simplicity expected of a bass, in European art music no less than in folk and blues, occurs at only rare moments in Lesh's playing. Due to their oblique relationship to the perceived main melody or harmonic progression and to the delicacy with which the melodic and harmonic variations are approached, Lesh's counter-melodies sometimes sound like voices meant to be *internal* to a polyphony, such as that which might be played by a cello or other tenor instrument.[9] Lesh's melodies are often highly syncopated and generally busy and bubbly, using few articulations sustained for longer than an eighth note. Moreover, it is virtually impossible not to notice how often Lesh comes into the higher registers of his instrument. He frequently jumps from a low root to its higher octave as a starting point for melodic figures, sometimes intruding right into the guitarist's spheres for sustained periods or at moments one would least expect, creating tight harmonic and rhythmic interplay with the other instruments in the middle register, often dissonant in character. In the well-regarded "China Cat Sunflower — Know You Rider" from *Europe 72,* for example, Lesh runs busy licks right up under Garcia's vocal line as he sings, "I wish I was a headlight." The instrumental coda to "Here Comes Sunshine" from *Wake of the Flood* provides another example of this unusual effect. Not satisfied with that brief moment, on the coda to the subsequent track, "Eyes of the World," Lesh breaks out of the lower registers completely, taking what is essentially a guitar solo into the fade-out. In the studio recording of "Friend of the Devil" from *American Beauty,* Lesh often sounds as if he's parodying the conventional bluegrass elements of the song, coming in after the opening guitar phrase with a high-register, rhythmically complicated, "flat-picking" pattern light years from the bass's expected role in that genre, a sense furthered when the swinging drum part enters. Nevertheless, due to the complexity of the Dead's musical aesthetics, the song as a whole does not come across as parodic.

The majority of Lesh's playing consists of long phrases composed of series of brief melodic figures that swing in and around the main harmonic downbeats, forming a counter melody to the implied central melody — which often no one in the band is actually playing. At times the bass melody seems to specifically counter the guitars' own interpretations of the underlying musical structure in an ongoing conversation. Often both seem to be the case, as the bass part gives the impression that it "knows" in advance all the harmonic changes to come and is playing through them irreverently while offering comment on the guitarists' often more conventional approaches to the same progression. As Weir commented, "After thirty years of playing with him, you learn not to intuit what he's going to do because it's not possible. He can hear you thinking and make sure he's not supplying what you're expecting" (Jackson 260). As Garcia commented, "There's the required stuff and the elective stuff. For Phil, the required stuff is about one percent of what he plays" (Jackson 261). Very rarely, for example, does Lesh actually articulate a chord change with a root-note punch on time. Lesh's treatment of the R&B-style "shots" on B minor and A major, for instance, which occur between lines of "Eyes of the World," typify his approach. In the studio version, he plays the first two articulations as expected, leading the listener to anticipate the rest, then plays alternate pitches off the beat for the rest of the phrase. And the next time around, a few bars later, the phrase is different again. The same observations hold true for his live performances of the song.

In an early interview, Garcia acknowledged that Lesh's approach was proving to be a challenge for the rest of the band:

> [B]ecause of the way Phil plays, he makes it impossible for Bill [Kreutzmann] to rely on an old pattern, on a standard-type pattern. The problems we're having with all this is because all of us still think so musically straight, really, that it's difficult to get away from, that it's difficult to get used to not hearing the heavy two and four [Gleason 27].

Lesh comments explicitly on the early development of his approach:

> After playing a wrong note, for instance, I would quickly resolve it to a proper note — but then I took to repeating my mistakes (a simple matter, since the music was built out of repeating modules, or strophes) in order to resolve them differently each time. I soon began to see the dissonances caused by wrong notes, or right notes in the wrong place, as opportunities rather than liabilities — new ways to create tension and release, the lifeblood of music. This approach was to bear strange and wonderful fruit over the next five years of the band's development [Lesh 53].

Later, gigging regularly and having grasped the basics, Lesh began to think consciously about how he could mutate the music:

> I wanted to play in a way that heightened the beats by omission, as it were, by playing around them, in a way that added harmonic motion to the somewhat static chord progressions of the songs we were playing then. I wanted to play in a way that moved melodically but much more slowly than the lead melodies being sung by the vocalists or played on guitar or keyboard. Contrast and complement: Each of us approached the music from a different direction, at angles to one another, like the spokes of a wheel [57].

The wheel is supported by its many spokes, and there's no question that it turns energetically — but around what hub does it turn? Without a predictable bass line, melody line or drum part, the Grateful Dead's instrumental polyphony is truly a system without a fixed center. None of these typical frames of reference allows us as listeners to focus on it and make of it a kind of center for very long. Lesh's continuous variation continually propels us on, keeping dancers and listeners alike always "on their toes." His initiative pushed all the band members to "dance around" their expected parts, creating a kind of absence at the center of their songs, like a fire around which a circle of dancers move, or a pulsing spirit invoked by the music — a fire and spirit intimately connected with the audience's own individual spirits as they danced to the Dead.

Lesh's reference to the Grateful Dead's music as "strophic" characterizes almost every kind of popular music, and in folk, blues and dance music of all kinds, including the genres the Grateful Dead began originally to work with, the bass generally plays repeated simple rhythmic patterns at a steady pace, reflecting and motivating the cyclical rhythmic patterns of dancing. The interest that a bass is expected to generate is usually primarily rhythmic. The subtle rhythmic variations of the bass against a steady drumbeat, or vice versa, become very powerful in the context of extended and expected repetition as the tension of cycles against one another creates a rhythmic harmony between implied rhythmic patterns. Clearly this is the antithesis of Lesh's playing, which includes repetition only in relation to the underlying harmonic-rhythmic core of the music, almost never generating it himself. By his own admission Lesh finds it next to impossible to play exact repetitions of a given bass line. In this sense he can be understood like Coltrane and the free jazz pioneers as exemplars of the modernist impulse to "make it new" pushed to its practical limit in the context of popular music and dance music. He never repeats a passage exactly, and thus the sense of "homecoming" the listener feels at the return of a given familiar musical passage is always tempered. We are returning, but we are also moving ahead into new and alternate versions of the familiar.

Although the orbits Lesh implies in his approach to expected cyclical regularity are eccentric, they remain harmonious in an unusual way. And although unable to generate the same kinds of rhythmic dynamics as conventional bassists, Lesh nonetheless manages to create a great deal of rhythmic interest by producing continuous variation in the music's rhythmic cycles from the smallest to the largest. The implied minimal divisions of the music's pulse seem to shift continuously, and thus do the optimal dancing subdivisions. As he is constantly improvising and experimenting with new melodies and implied harmonies which in conjunction with the rest of the band's parts may not result in a desired effect, it is important to keep moving and not to create a sense of rest on any regular pulse or pitch beyond the absolute minimum required. In other words, Lesh's sense of harmonic freedom in turn motivates a rhythmic freedom. Though he naturally fell into "ruts" of sorts, Lesh always strove to find new ways to arrange his ideas by altering their relationship to the implied downbeats. His playing is uncommonly busy, with few silences or sustains, and although it includes hardly any extended repeated articulations of the same pitch in a rhythmic figure, it does maintain over longer passages a self-consistency which ebbs and flows in proportion to the demand to act as a unifying factor for the music as a whole. The sheer amount of movement in the bass produces an effect that is unique among bands performing material similar to the Dead's, and much of it is rhythmic in character.[10]

It is thus fair to describe the Dead as a band whose music operates largely without a dedicated conventional bass part. Indeed, the music's magical texture results precisely from its emphasis on true polyphony, a texture rarely heard today in any kind of popular music, with the exception of recreations of Renaissance vocal textures and J.S. Bach's instrumental and vocal compositions. It is decidedly difficult for the average listener today to discern and appreciate more than one melodic line at a time. Most popular music is mainly homophonic, comprised of a main melody and a harmonic accompaniment meant to provide a ground for it. Much rock music simplifies the recipe still further into the monophonic, featuring key passages in which guitar, bass and drums are all punctuating the same melodic-rhythmic figures. More elaborate popular music, like the Grateful Dead's, features a number of interdependent melodies, sometimes including bass parts which, like Paul McCartney's, for example, create a great deal of melodic interest. Seldom, however, do the rhythm guitar, keyboard or drum parts vary at the same time as the bass and lead guitar. Even more infrequently are there two kit drummers interacting while all this is going on. Still less frequently are all six parts being improvised at once, as they are in the Grateful Dead's music.

The listener with a highly developed ear will be able to hear three parts at once, but only the very few are able truly to appreciate four-part polyphony in an arranged piece of music, let alone a six-part piece being improvised on the fly. It is doubtful that very many Deadheads have developed the ear to understand and appreciate all six parts simultaneously. We compensate by listening to one part and then another in quick succession, taking advantage of our ability to predict the direction of the music and the Dead's characteristically slow tempos, and, in later years, sparser playing. We also let our bodies feel and understand the totality of the rhythm as it presents itself to us, even if we can't hear every individual articulation by the drummers. We compensate by using psychedelics and cannabis to temporarily turn up our brains to the awareness levels needed, and it is likely through the influence of psychedelics that the ambitious polyphonic improvisational goals of the Grateful Dead first evolved and made their own kind of sense. The Dead's music, no matter how many pratfalls the band took, was always evolving into new combinations beyond the ability of most listeners to hear all the constituent parts which together created the ever-changing snowflake of sound. The popularity and durability of these improvised performances as recorded and replayed countless times by Deadheads is partially explained by the impossibility of ever hearing the totality of musical relationships going on, or hearing exactly the same things in the same tape twice.

Despite this seemingly egalitarian plurality of musical texture, it is nevertheless necessary to privilege the absence of the conventional bass part as a key feature of the Grateful Dead's postmodernist dance music. It must not be forgotten that in spite of their free-flowing improvisation, frequent use of ballad tempos, and absence of a conventional bass part, the Grateful Dead were one of the most successful dance bands of their era. The unique character of this phenomenon can hardly be overstated. In spite of the fact that not a single member of the band played in a conventional dance music style, their live performances were entirely focused around dancing and never failed to stimulate the vast majority of the crowd in this respect, often to ecstatic heights and over marathon durations. The Grateful Dead were prime movers in the San Francisco dance renaissance of the late 1960s—unprecedented, as Ralph J. Gleason observed, "since the heyday of Glenn Miller, Benny Goodman and Tommy Dorsey" (Gleason 18).[11] Like these earlier big bands, the Grateful Dead's primary rhythmic mode is "swing" rather than "rock." In terms of assistance from elsewhere, there is no question that cannabis use encourages dancing, and the Dead have certainly had an abundant contribution on that front in their efforts to enliven large crowds. However, the same is not true for psychedelics, under whose influence the band evolved and many thousands of audience members enjoyed their concerts. In fact, although psychedelics tend to provide a surplus of creative energy, there is not generally a predisposition to dance in preference to other possible activities. Nevertheless, the Dead's rhythmic drive was powerful enough to attract and focus that psychedelic energy into bodily movement. Part of this effect may be the increased ability of the psychedelic-charged mind to appreciate the six-part polyphony that makes up the music. However, the adventuring psychedelic mind is just as likely to wander away from that task, and moreover the Dead's music inspired many to dance who weren't under the influence of any substances at all.

Paradoxically, it was Lesh's unwillingness and/or inability to play a basic rhythmic and harmonic foundation to their songs that allowed the Grateful Dead to evolve into one of American's finest dance bands. The bass' "erring" from this conventionally requisite role is much more significant than the wanderings of the other instruments, for several reasons. Our bodies are directly affected in a tangible way by the deep vibrations of the bass. The power of its motion is magnified compared with that of other instruments. Its sound occupies much of the acoustic "space" available as its overtones and undertones spread out into the upper registers and into subsonic physical vibrations. In highly amplified settings the bass' speakers move a greater portion of air than the rest of the band's speakers combined, provoking an inescapable physical response in the audience. Our bodies cannot help but rely on the bass to provide a minimal essence of a piece of dance music, a focusing of the rhythmic and harmonic motion of a piece into a single melody. Lesh's playing rarely fulfills that expectation. Like Hunter, Lesh never makes it easy for the listener or dancer to pin him down. Quite unlike Hunter's lyrics, however, symmetry is nowhere to be found at the Grateful Dead's bottom end.[12] Lacking this "bottom line," the listener's musical and physical awareness is forced "out" and "up" into the polyphonic interplay "above" where the bass is expected to be, where it sometimes encounters Lesh himself, playing the bass, but not the bass part we were unconsciously anticipating. Lesh's pragmatic response to the improvised polyphony of a jug band turned electric in the midst of psychedelic exploration, tempered by his desire for the ever-changing and his uncanny and highly developed ability to hear multiple voices in polyphony, became the key to creating a new kind of dance music.

In most African American dance music styles, such as funk, reggae, hip-hop, and rhythm and blues, whether played by African Americans or by others, there is an emphasis on sparse articulations which sculpt a silence implying rhythmic patterns which virtually force our bodies to manifest or realize them. The Grateful Dead, while certainly capable of great economy of phrasing and a wide dynamic range compared with most bands in a rock 'n' roll context, are nonetheless a great deal busier than most dance bands, largely due to the playing styles of Garcia and Lesh. Nevertheless, in spite of this polyphonic business, the space at the center of the songs, which Lesh ensures is there by refusing to occupy it for more than a measure or two at a time, provides a space analogous to that which funk provides in the tension between implied rhythmic parts. This is the anarchistic heart of the music as a totality, the heart that connects with the hearts of the dancers and transmits and receives anarchist energy to and from the concert crowd.

The Grateful Dead, as Mary Goodenough has commented, seem to have been summoned from the collective unconscious, which underlies the "already-here," but their commitment to improvisation made them always "yet-to-come." Their "group strategies," as part of the cultural revolution of the 1960s, might be characterized as a postmodern manifestation of the "mythopoeic *bricolage*" of oral societies discussed by Derrida in his seminal post-structuralist critique of the anthropological theory of Claude Lévi-Strauss back in the Summer of Love. *Bricoleurs par excellence*, the Grateful Dead are/were postmodernity's jug band. Regardless of how sophisticated their music or their equipment became, they continued to cobble together musical ideas the way a jug band cobbles together instruments from odds and ends and a mosaic of musical traditions. They incorporated found objects from their psyches, and from one another's, into a never-quite-coherent but highly functional system of poetry, music and myth around which a massive and disparate community could engage in freeing its selves through "otherness" while dancing its own "movie" of the end of modernity. In between Dr. Freud and Dr. Funkenstein, there was Dr. Lesh, the unexpected catalyst of the Grateful Dead's musicultural alchemy.

Phil's Court. Winterland, December 31, 1978 (courtesy Pat and Dena Lee, all rights reserved).

Notes

1. See DeKoven's *Utopia Unlimited* for a highly developed version of this perspective.
2. See Turner, *The Gospel According to the Beatles*.
3. Cilliers's assertion that autopoiesis "does not involve anything mystical" (12) and can be modeled mathematically, however, is well worth questioning, particularly the assumption that the two are mutually exclusive. As sociology student Jennifer Hartley discovered in writing a thesis on a core group of "Spinners" who whirled at Grateful Dead concerts, it is impossible for a description of a given phenomenon as observed from the outside to make sense of its spiritual dimensions (Hartley, 151–153). The two aspects may become the objects of mutually exclusive perspectives, but this does not imply that the aspects themselves are not coexistent. Without question, the Grateful Dead were a system capable of gelling spiritual energy, not just for Spinners but for most of their audience-participants.
4. See the work of Jean Baudrillard for an analysis of this condition.
5. Brad Lucas' comments on the connection between a distancing effect of the video screens in the 1990s and the unpleasant results of the transformation of Grateful Dead "movie" from carnival into mass spectacle demonstrate the importance of the principle of intimacy in the deployment of electronics (Lucas, 84–5).
6. Blair Jackson's phrase.
7. See *The Real Frank Zappa Book* for an elaboration of this concept.
8. Lesh later recalls a scene at the symphony in Belgium, where he sees but fails to meet a man who appears to be his double — the cellist. In an ironically rich episode, Lesh pursues the man backstage but cannot find him (Lesh, 206).

9. Blair Jackson aptly characterized Lesh's playing as "peals of fragile thunder," using one of Hunter's lines from "Crazy Fingers" (Jackson, 248).

10. Lesh's playing can also be criticized for many of these same reasons, not least because his avoidance of repetition precludes the development of certain kinds of rhythmic tension, which many musicians and listeners would maintain is integral to certain kinds of music, especially dance music, whether of European or African heritage. His quick melodic variations on a given basic chord can be perceived as interfering with the middle and upper voices as they shift the background overtone patterns in the sea in which the guitar and vocal parts are swimming. Moreover, his timing is often not as crisp as that of the guitarists, and his rhythmic variations, swinging sixteenth notes in and around downbeats and chord changes in sometimes unpredictable patterns, often lack the precision needed to really syncopate the underlying beat. This effect may be exaggerated by his use of a pick and the resulting micro-chronic delay it can insert between the fingers and the heavy strings of the bass. And when playing in vast, echoing arenas, Lesh's quick figures were often lost in the low-end sound-mush, exacerbating the impression of sloppiness. Lesh's approach to timing must also, however, be considered in the context of his unique position in relation to the rest of the band. Lesh joined the band after the drums, guitars, keyboards and vocals had been established, and without any previous experience on the bass. Whereas most bass players are expected to be ultimately responsible for maintaining rhythmic drive and strict tempo, Lesh was not initially in a position to seize that role. Before he had caught up with the rolling drive of drummer Bill Kreutzmann, a second drummer, Mickey Hart, joined the band and Lesh had to contend with two drum kits instead of one — a task demanded of very few other bassists then or now. Without a unified metrical framework being provided by a single drummer, Lesh's ability or inability to subtly move in and out of "the pocket" became largely irrelevant, as it became hard to know just exactly where the pocket was supposed to be. This sensibility is reflected in Hunter's line from "Mississippi Half-Step Uptown Toodeloo": "What's the point to calling shots—this cue ain't straight in line."

11. Lesh reports that Gleason told him he'd heard Dizzy Gillespie remark after hearing the Dead at the January 1967 "Human Be-In," "Who are these guys? They sure can swing" (Lesh, 98). Garcia told Gleason at the time that "our function is as a dance band. We feel that our greatest value is as a dance band and that's what we like to do" (Gleason, 27).

12. See Wood, "Robert Hunter's Oral Poetry," for a discussion of symmetry in his lyrics.

Bibliography

Adams, Rebecca, and Robert Sardiello. *Deadhead Social Science.* Walnut Creek, CA: AltaMira, 2000.
Cilliers, Paul. *Complexity and Postmodernism.* New York: Routledge, 1998.
DeKoven, Marianne. *Utopia Limited: The Sixties and the Emergence of the Postmodern.* Durham: Duke University Press, 2004.
Derrida, Jacques. "Structure, Sign and Play in the Discourse of the Human Sciences." *Writing and Difference.* Alan Bass, trans. Chicago: University of Chicago, 1978.
Dodd, David. *The Complete Annotated Grateful Dead Lyrics.* New York: Simon and Schuster, 2005.
Gans, David. *Conversations with the Dead.* New York: Citadel, 1991.
Garcia, Jerry. *Harrington Street.* New York: Bantam, 1995.
Gleason, Ralph J. "Dead Like Live Thunder." In *The Grateful Dead Reader,* David Dodd and Diana Spaulding, eds. New York: Oxford University Press, 2000. 17–19.

_____. "Jerry Garcia, the Guru." In *The Grateful Dead Reader*, Dodd and Spaulding, eds. New York: Oxford University Press, 2000. 20–38.

Goodenough, Mary. "Grateful Dead: Manifestations from the Collective Unconscious." In *Perspectives on the Grateful Dead*, R.G. Weiner, ed. Westport, CT: Greenwood, 1999. 175–182.

Greenfield, Robert. *Dark Star: An Oral Biography of Jerry Garcia*. New York: William Morrow, 1996.

Hartley, Jennifer A. "'We Were Given This Dance': Music and Meaning in the Early Unlimited Devotion Family." In *Deadhead Social Science*, Rebecca Adams and Robert Sardiello, eds. Walnut Creek, CA: AltaMira, 2000. 129–158.

Jackson, Blair. Introduction to "We Want Phil! An Interview" and "In Phil We Trust: A Conversation." In *The Grateful Dead Reader*, Dodd and Spaulding, eds. New York: Oxford University Press, 2000. 248–264.

Jameson, Frederic. *The Cultural Logic of Late Capitalism*. Durham: Duke University Press, 1991.

Lesh, Phil. *Searching for the Sound*. New York: Little, Brown, 2005.

Lucas, Brad. E. "Bakhtinian Carnival, Corporate Capital, and the Last Decade of the Dead." In *Pespectives on the Grateful Dead*, Weiner, ed. Westport, CT: Greenwood, 1999.

Luhmann, Niklas. *A Sociological Theory of Law*. London: Routledge, 1985.

Lyotard, Jean-Francois. *The Postmodern Condition*. Minnesota: University of Minnesota Press, 1985.

Perelman, Bob. *Writing/Talks*. Carbondale: Southern Illinois Press, 1985.

Tuner, Steve. *The Gospel According to the Beatles*. London: Westminster John Knox, 2006.

Weiner, R.G., ed. *Perspectives on the Grateful Dead*. Westport, CT: Greenwood, 1999.

Wood, Brent. "Robert Hunter's Oral Poetry." *Poetics Today*, 24:1, spring 2003.

Zappa, Frank. *The Real Frank Zappa Book*. New York: Simon and Schuster, 1990.

Discography

Garcia, Jerry. *Reflections*. Arista, 1976.
Grateful Dead. *Anthem of the Sun*. Warner, 1968.
_____. *American Beauty*. Warner, 1970.
_____. *Europe 72*. Warner, 1972.
_____. *Wake of the Flood*. Grateful Dead Records, 1973.

AMERICAN CHAOS: CHARLES IVES AND THE GRATEFUL DEAD

SHAUGN O'DONNELL

In the early 1990s, I participated in a graduate seminar exploring the music of the early modernist composer Charles Ives (1874–1954).[1] In the weekly readings I would come across critical reactions to his music, both negative and positive, that seemed vaguely familiar. Let me provide a few examples. One 1932 concert review labels Ives a "crude [naturalist], obsessed with the amateurish idea that loudness and harshness of sound testify sufficiently an artist's individuality," while another from 1939 describes his work as "the greatest music composed by an American, and the most deeply and essentially American in impulse and implication."[2] The reactions of musicologists exhibit the same range of sentiment as the critics. One dismissive author describes Ives's music as a "bizarre unintegrated mixture of daring sophistication and homespun crudity," while another states "there is an agreement between this music as expression and the bone-deep Americanism of the composer that commands attention."[3] Based on these comments, and hundreds more like them, it seems that we are discussing a quintessentially American music that inspires either absolute disdain or cult-like devotion in listeners. Given the context of this edited collection, my trajectory will already be obvious to readers, but at the time of the seminar, I had been "off the bus" and into the academy for several years, so the connection was not immediately apparent to me. However, as I studied his chaotic spatial American music more closely, the resonance between Charles Ives and the Grateful Dead became increasingly evident. Initially I believed these parallels were merely a strange subjective reaction to being a Deadhead working in post-tonal music theory, but research reveals that Ives is a real, tangible, direct influence on the band.

In his book *Searching for the Sound*, Phil Lesh identifies two American musicians who specifically exerted a "tremendous influence on the embryonic aesthetic of the Grateful Dead." One is the jazz saxophone legend John Coltrane and the other is the composer Charles Ives.[4] Coltrane may seem to be the more obvious influence because of his improvisational work in a popular style, as well as the plethora of supporting evidence, such as Lesh's glib comment summarizing the Grateful Dead's musical innovation: "All we did was steal what jazz musicians did and apply it to rock 'n' roll."[5] However, I find the alternative path of exploring some of the ways in which the band's music recalls the spirit of the latter figure, Ives, more intriguing. From nostalgic Americana to visionary transcendentalism, these iconoclasts have a great deal in common, but their most significant shared musical qualities are a postmodern eclecticism and a willingness to engage formal chaos in composition and improvisation. In this essay I emphasize one component of this resonance, the Grateful Dead's incorporation of Ives's signature pre-postmodern techniques of stylistic borrowing and juxtaposition.

To provide some historical context, I begin with a brief timeline of the Grateful Dead's initial interaction with Ives's music. Predating the founding of the band, as well as his studies with avant-garde composer Luciano Berio, Lesh first discovered Ives as an 18-year-old college music student via the book *Charles Ives and His Music*.[6] The authors, Henry and Sydney Cowell, were among the earliest advocates of Ives' music, presenting him as "one of the four great creative figures in music of the first half of the twentieth century."[7] Lesh, a trumpeter at the time, describes his encounter with the book:

> [T]he examples introduced me to truly original compositions: the song "The Majority," with its notated tone-clusters and unmetered barring, and the *Concord* Sonata, with its free polyphony for two hands written on three staves. It almost didn't matter what the music sounded like—it looked so cool on the page.[8]

The musical illustrations are radical enough to inspire a young musician to rethink performance practice entirely, as pianists can only perform the dense sonorities in the "Majority" example with a forearm or block of wood, and they need a very flexible sense of notated musical time to execute the "Emerson" example from the "Concord" Sonata.[9]

While Ives information and recordings were relatively scarce in the late 1950s when Lesh read the Cowells' book, it is certainly not the case today. Throughout this essay I recommend musical tracks that will enhance, clarify, and support my discussion. I urge readers to listen to the complete works mentioned in these **Listening** boxes, using whatever recordings are available to them. However, for those looking for a more concise experience, I reference approximate track times of specific commonly available commercial or online performances. **Listening #1** (below) includes the two Ives works already cited by Lesh. The opening passage of the song "Majority" illustrates the tones clusters and free meter in his description, and the opening passage of "Emerson" contains Ivesian polyphony, flexible meter, as well as a familiar Beethoven quotation.

Listening #1: Two Ives Works Cited by Lesh

Charles Ives, "Majority" [to 0:30] http://www.dramonline.org/tracks/majority[10]
Charles Ives, "Emerson," Piano Sonata No. 2, "Concord, Mass., 1840–1860" [to 0:25] http://www.dramonline.org/tracks/piano-sonata-no-2-concord-mass-1840-1860-i-emerson[11]

Lesh's reaction to the composer portrayed in the Cowells' book implies that he gravitated as much to Ives' ideas as to his sounding music. He continues:

> The power and freshness of his music, together with the story of his life (neglect, misunderstanding, unwillingness to compromise in order to earn a living as a musician, going into insurance and making a fortune, composing at night, using his wealth to promote new music other than his own), made him, in my eyes an artistic hero. All this before I ever heard a note of the music, as there were no recordings available to me until years later.[12]

Given these statements, it seems that the initial influence on Lesh was Ives the legendary American musical hero, and only later was it the sounding music.

This separation of idealized abstraction and literal sounding music parallels the conceptual duality of *substance* versus *manner* that Ives explains in his *Essays Before a Sonata*. Ives writes, "The higher and more important value of this dualism is composed of what may be called reality, quality, spirit, or substance against the lower value of form, quantity, or manner." He continues, suggesting that substance "has its birth in the spiritual consciousness" and is "appreciated by the intuition, and somehow translated into expression by 'manner'—a process always less important than it seems...."[13] Of course, we must keep in mind that manner, being the external reality of a work, that is, the sounds we actually hear, is necessary to communicate substance. This duality is particularly important in the context of my essay because the half-century that separates the music of Ives and the Grateful Dead generates substantial differences in manner: symphony orchestra versus rock band, classically trained versus vernacular singers, notated versus aural traditions, etc. In other words, the musical examples I am discussing sound rather different on the surface. The relations I am suggesting are deeper than these superficial parameters; instead they are at the level of substance. Still, once again, we can only examine this deeper similarity through the surface manner of the sounding music.

By April 1967, a live radio broadcast illustrates that the Grateful Dead had heard, rather than just read about, Ives' sounding music. Jerry Garcia and Lesh were guest disc jockeys on Tom Donahue's show on KMPX-FM in San Francisco. This was very early in their career, shortly after the release of their debut album, *The Grateful Dead*, and prior to their first New York performances planned for June of that year. During the show, they discussed and played 20 recordings that were major influences on them, as well as a couple of tracks from their album. As shown in **Table 1** below, nestled among less surprising recordings by artists such as Charles Mingus and Bob Dylan, there was just one "classical" track: the second movement of Charles Ives' Fourth Symphony!

Table 1: Playlist, Garcia and Lesh as Guest Disc Jockeys, April 1967

- Swan Silvertones—[song missing from circulation]
- Charles Mingus—"Wednesday Night Prayer Meeting"
- Blind Willie Johnson—"Lord I Can't Keep from Crying Sometimes"
- Ray Charles—"I Don't Need No Doctor"
- James Brown—"It's a Man's Man's Man's World"
- James Brown—"Ain't That a Groove"
- Bob Dylan—"Maggie's Farm"
- Ensemble of the Bulgarian Republic—"The Moon Shines"
- Charles Lloyd Quartet—"Dream Weaver"
- Junior Wells—"Ships on the Ocean"
- **Leopold Stokowski/American Symphony Orch.— Ives: Symphony No. 4, II**
- Ian & Sylvia—"Jealous Lover"
- Ian & Sylvia—"Four Rode By"
- Skip James—"Hard Time Killin' Floor Blues"
- Aretha Franklin—"I Never Loved a Man (The Way I Love You)"
- Righteous Brothers—"You've Lost That Lovin' Feelin'"
- Ike & Tina Turner—"River Deep, Mountain High"
- Lou Rawls—"Trouble Down Here Below"
- Rolling Stones—"Gotta Get Away"
- Otis Redding—"Day Tripper"
- Grateful Dead—"Cold Rain and Snow"
- Grateful Dead—"New, New Minglewood Blues"

It is interesting to note that despite Lesh's statement regarding two major aesthetic influences, John Coltrane is not included in this playlist. Lesh introduces the Ives movement, with an interjection by Garcia: "If you expect it to sound like a symphony—forget it [J.G.]— you'll be disappointed."[14] **Listening #2** directs readers to the archived radio show and suggests playing the introductory banter and first minute of the Ives movement.

Lesh comments on Ives' Fourth Symphony, stating, "This particular piece of music was welded into my DNA, ever since I'd heard the record mysteriously appear as background music for one of my finest trips," and he continues, describing it as "simultaneously sounding layers of different musics— hymn tunes, marches, popular songs of Ives's day — all woven together within a fantastical flux of sound."[16] **Table 2** lists the incredible number of popular tunes,

Listening #2: Garcia and Lesh Spin an Ives Movement

> Introduction by Donahue, Garcia, and Lesh [track 21, though identified as 22]
> http://www.archive.org/details/gd67-04-xx.prefm.vernon.9261.sbeok.shnf
>
> Charles Ives, Symphony No. 4, II [to 1:00] [track 22, though identified as 23]
> http://www.archive.org/details/gd67-04-xx.prefm.vernon.9261.sbeok.shnf[15]

religious and secular, Ives borrows in just the second movement of this symphony.[17]

Table 2: Borrowed Tunes in Ives, Symphony No. 4, II

- "The Beautiful River"
- "Beulah Land"
- "Camptown Races"
- "Columbia, the Gem of the Ocean"
- "Garryowen"
- "God Be with You"
- "Hail! Columbia"
- "Happy Land"
- "Home! Sweet Home!"
- "Irish Washerwoman"
- "Long, Long Ago"
- "Marching Through Georgia"
- "Martyn"
- "Massa's in de Cold Ground"
- "Nettleton"
- "Old Black Joe" "On the Banks of the Wabash"
- "Pig Town Fling"
- "Reveille"
- "St. Patrick's Day"
- "Street Beat"
- "Sweet By and By"
- "Throw Out the Life-Line"
- "Tramp, Tramp, Tramp"
- "Turkey in the Straw"
- "Westminster Chimes"
- "Yankee Doodle"
- Ives, *"Country Band" March*
- Sousa, *Washington Post March*

Possible additional borrowing:

- "Hello! Ma Baby"
- "Peter, Peter, Pumpkin-Eater"

Michael Tilson Thomas, the conductor of an excellent recording of this symphony, similarly describes it in this manner: "It's just a big stewpot of everything in musical society at that time ... and it makes reference to everything that's happening in America, particularly the onslaught of mechanization, the noisy aspect of modern civilization."[18] Though I recommend listening to the entire movement, **Listening #3** directs readers to an excerpt that captures the chaos of the "fantastical flux of sound."

Listening #3: A "Fantastical Flux of Sound"

> Charles Ives, Symphony No. 4, II [7:75–9:25] [track 22, though identified as 23]
> http://www.archive.org/details/gd67-04-xx.prefm.vernon.9261.sbeok.shnf[19]

Given the extreme complexity of Ives' music, it may seem like this is primarily an interest of Lesh's, but the whole band, including "Pigpen" McKernan, attended a performance of this symphony in December 1967 conducted by Leopold Stokowski in Carnegie Hall, and they were all "blown completely away." Mickey Hart even decided it was "life-transforming" and that they needed to do something similar with their music.[20] Along with the potpourri of tunes, what seems to have captured the band's imagination was how "the sense of space (height, width, depth) was palpable," as well as its transcendental qualities.[21] I might similarly point out these same three characteristics to describe my interest in the music of the Grateful Dead, although I only focus on the first component — the juxtaposition of source tunes — in this chapter.

One of Ives' core compositional techniques is musical borrowing, ranging from quotation through paraphrase to more general stylistic imitation. Musicologist Peter Burkholder identifies 14 different methods of borrowing in Ives' music, as shown in **Table 3**.[22] As readers may intuit, there is a great deal of overlap among these categories, and only a few are pertinent to my discussion, as shown in the bottom row of the table.

Table 3: Burkholder's List of Ives' 14 "Procedures for Using Existing Music"

1. modeling	8. stylistic allusion
2. variations	9. transcribing
3. paraphrasing	10. programatic quotation
4. setting	11. cumulative setting
5. cantus firmus	12. collage
6. medley	13. patchwork
7. quodlibet	14. extended paraphrase
My reduced list:	• quotation • medley • paraphrasing • stylistic allusion • collage

The first two items in my reduced list, quotation and medley, need less explanation than the others, but let me touch upon them briefly. Literal quotation plays a substantial role in Ives' music, and — in addition to the mayhem heard in the second movement discussed above — readers may recall the motive from Beethoven's Fifth Symphony at the end of the earlier "Concord" Sonata example.

Such literal borrowing plays a lesser role in the Grateful Dead's music, but it does exist, from the alleged Beethoven's Ninth Symphony reference in "Born Cross-Eyed" through "Ring around the rosie" in "Throwing Stones."[23] **Listening #4** offers one obvious example to illustrate my point, the instrumental "We Bid You Goodnight" at the end of "Goin' Down the Road."

Listening #4: Quotation (and Medley and Transcription and Paraphrase....)

> Grateful Dead, "Not Fade Away > Goin' Down the Road Feeling Bad" ["We Bid You Good Night" quote, track 24, from 4:35]
> http://www.archive.org/details/gd1971-04-05.sbd.cantor.gmb.96269.flac16[24]

As my caption suggests, this example also illustrates the overlap among Burkholder's categories. This is an instance of transcription, from vocal melody to guitar line. It is part of a medley, "Not Fade Away" into "Goin' Down the Road" into the instrumental "We Bid You Goodnight," all of which are borrowed. And, finally, Garcia's improvisatory quotation of the "We Bid You Goodnight" melody strays enough from the original to be understood as paraphrase. One might even consider the manner in which cover songs emerge and recede during the primordial flow of the second set the quintessential Grateful Dead enactment of both medley and quotation simultaneously.

As hinted at in the previous example, paraphrase plays a significant role in the Grateful Dead's music, and the technique is particularly noticeable in Garcia's solos. While this may stem from the jazz practice of keeping the head melody in mind while improvising, there is something simultaneously more literal and more stream-of-conscious in Garcia's approach. Throughout his solos we hear an impression of the song's vocal line, a stitching together of melodic fragments rather than totally free improvisation or a literal statement of the head. This technique is most common in the ballads, and **Listening #5** provides an example.

Listening #5: Paraphrase in a Garcia Solo

> Grateful Dead, "He's Gone" [solo, track 9, 3:54–4:32]
> http://www.archive.org/details/gd72-05-10.sbd.kaplan.1582.sbeok.shnf[25]

Many solos articulate the melodic fragments less directly than this example, and the rhythmic and pitch transformations frequently remind me of Ives' use of paraphrase specifically as illustrated by Burkholder in his research. A similar study could be made of the relation between Garcia's solos and his sung melodies.

More pervasive than any of those techniques is general stylistic allusion. Within the band's repertoire the broad range of style is self-evident and hardly needs explanation, but I am referring to closer stylistic juxtapositions that resonate with Ives. Within solo passages from "Sugaree," you might hear blues, banjo, and mandolin techniques, all representing individual American folk idioms, yet coalescing in Garcia's unique electric guitar style. **Listening #6** takes readers through three excerpts, first illustrating blues-influenced bending, then banjo-style arpeggiations, and, finally, mandolin-style tremolos.

Listening #6: Style Juxtaposition in Garcia's Solos

Grateful Dead, "Sugaree," Pembroke Pines, FL (May 22, 1997)[26]
- Blues-influenced bending [4:40–5:10]
- Banjo-style arpeggiations [8:10–8:40]
- Mandolin-style tremolos [9:54–10:22]

Even more interesting is the direct superimposition of independent musical styles. Lesh offers a clear blueprint of this kind of recomposition when he writes, "A good example of this technique is our version of the old Noah Lewis jug band tune 'Viola Lee Blues,' a traditional prison song. We electrified the song with a boogaloo beat and an intro lick borrowed from R&B artist Lee Dorsey's 'Get Out My Life Woman.'"[27] **Listening #7** takes readers through this process, from jug band version, through the rhythm-and-blues filter, to the Grateful Dead version. Furthermore, the incredible level of dissonance achieved in the Grateful Dead's extended "Viola Lee Blues" gives this derivation added meaning in the context of the Ives influence.[28]

Listening #7: Style Juxtaposition in the Arranging Process

Gus Cannon and his Jug Stompers, "Viola Lee Blues" [0:46–1:12][29]
Lee Dorsey, "Get Out My Life Woman" [0:05–0:38][30]
Grateful Dead, "Viola Lee Blues," Binghamton, NY (May 2, 1970) [1:00–1:30][31]

Borrowed music is not only incorporated sonically in Ives' compositions, many of his over 100 songs also include textual references to music or music making. This is perhaps my favorite resonance with the Grateful Dead, as they similarly spend much of their time making music about music, from "The Golden Road" to "Black Muddy River." And this brings me to a subtle example, the end of the song "Stagger Lee." I reproduce the closing verse and refrain below, and **Listening #8** refers readers to the corresponding musical passage.
Delia went a-walking down on Singapore Street

> A three-piece band on the corner played "Nearer My God to Thee"
> but Delia whistled a different tune ... what tune could it be?
>
> The song that woman sung was "Look out Staggerlee"
> The song that Delia sung was "Look out Staggerlee"
> The song that woman sung was "Look out Staggerlee"
> The song that Delia sung was "Look out Staggerlee"[32]

Listening #8: Grateful Dead Referencing "Nearer, My God, to Thee"

Grateful Dead, "Stagger Lee" [from 2:39][33]

In this excerpt, Delia walks past a three-piece band on the corner playing "Nearer, My God, to Thee"; this is a beautiful example of diegetic music in the Grateful Dead repertoire. This hymn plays a similar role in Charles Ives' song "Down East" in which the singer is reminiscing about tunes his mother used to play on her melodeon. I reproduce the final verse below, and **Listening #9** refers readers to the corresponding musical passage.

> Ev'ry Sunday morning, when the chores are almost done,
> From that little parlor sounds the old melodeon,
> "Nearer my God to Thee, nearer to Thee";
> With those strains a stronger hope comes nearer to me.[34]

Listening #9: Ives Referencing "Nearer, My God, to Thee"

Charles Ives, "Down East" [from 2:18]
http://www.dramonline.org/tracks/down-east[35]

This direct correspondence is interesting, but the technique is not unique, even if it may be decidedly American. Similar references, along with melodic quotations, are also common to Tin Pan Alley composers such as George M. Cohan and Irving Berlin. As Burkholder points out: "This format resembles any number of songs that mention a well-known piece and quote it near the end of the chorus."[36] However, the hymn tune *Bethany*, the one most commonly used for the text "Nearer My God to Thee," is one of Ives' most frequently quoted tunes. It makes instrumental cameos in dozens of works, where it is not always presented in such isolation, including two of the movements of the previously mentioned Fourth Symphony. What gives the Grateful Dead's usage a truly Ivesian twist is that Delia is whistling and singing *another* tune against the band on the corner, creating a diegetic Ivesian juxtaposition. In fact, for us outsiders, listening to Garcia's non-diegetic narration of the story, that is, hearing the song "Stagger Lee" itself, we have a collage of three musical streams. I cannot help but think of Ives in this context.

I conclude by identifying a few additional correspondences for future consideration, in no particular order of significance. First, they share a total immersion in literature, with Emerson and the Transcendentalists for Ives, and Kerouac and the Beats for the Grateful Dead. One might compare Ives' obsession with sports, particularly baseball, to Bob Weir, most notably his long forthcoming Satchel Paige musical.[37] They both share an environmentalist attitude. Ives' song "The New River" suggests the river gods were already dead from noise and pollution almost 100 years ago. In 1988, after decades of specifically not endorsing causes as a band, the Grateful Dead decided that the environment, particularly rainforest protection, was (and continues to be) in need of their political intervention.[38] Charles Ives and the Grateful Dead both demonstrate radical socioeconomic moderation. At the historic *Unbroken Chain* conference in 2007, band publicist Dennis McNally described Garcia's aversion to stockpiling money in his keynote address.[39] Ives similarly proposed a maximum property limit for all people in his essay "The Majority," and when he finally won the Pulitzer Prize in 1947, he gave the prize money away to a more needy composer.[40]

Finally, in the music of both Ives and the Grateful Dead there is simultaneously a nostalgic sense of the past, some works could almost be characterized as historical fiction, and a visionary sense of the future, nearly science fiction. The lyric "Moses came up riding up on a quasar, his spurs were a-jingling, the door was ajar" comes to mind as an apt example with its rapid succession of Moses, quasar, and spurs.[41] The result of this delicate balancing of nostalgia and modernism is an emphasis on the present, the now. Larry Starr eloquently describes this aspect of Ives' music:

> Ives is interested in the present. This is not the present of a particular time, place, person, or culture, rather it is an always extant and ever-changing artistic present: the current intellectual, emotional, and spiritual condition of creator, performer, and listener — in short, humanity. Ives's music seeks to engage the present as it is being lived and experienced, and to move with and through that present meaningfully into a new present enriched by the experience of the music. Aspects of the past, and potential for the future, are an inescapable part of the present, of course, and Ives's music directly acknowledges this. Yet the goal of his art almost always seems to be that of immersing us more deeply in the experience of the present, rather than in some past experience, real or imagined, or in some imagined future experience.[42]

One could easily replace the name Ives with the Grateful Dead throughout the above passage. In fact, I might argue that I have yet to read a better description of Grateful Dead music than this explanation of Ives by Starr.

> *Earlier versions of this essay were presented at Unbroken Chain: The Grateful Dead in Music, Culture and Memory (Amherst, MA, November 2007) and the Southwest/Texas Popular Culture/American Culture Association Annual Conference (Albuquerque, NM, February 2008). I wish to thank members of the Grateful Dead Caucus for their constructive feedback.*

Notes

1. The professor was H. Wiley Hitchcock (1923–2007), founder of the Institute for Studies in American Music.

2. Hugo Leichtentritt, "Musical Notes from Abroad," *The Musical Times*, 73.1071 (1932), 463. This is a review of the Slonimsky Pan American performances sponsored by Ives. Leichtentritt also writes: "These composers had hardly any aesthetic basis or any feeling for culture in sound, for life of form, for the essential elements of musical art." Alan Rich, quoting Lawrence Gilman's 1939 New York *Herald-Tribune* review of the "Concord" Sonata performed by John Kirkpatrick, *American Pioneers: Ives to Cage and Beyond* (London: Phaidon Press Limited, 1995), 32.

3. Gerald Abraham, *The Concise Oxford History of Music* (London: Oxford Uni-

versity Press, 1979), 824, as quoted by J. Peter Burkholder in *All Made of Tunes: Charles Ives and the Uses of Musical Borrowing* (New Haven: Yale University Press, 1995), 427, fn1. Henry Bellamann, "Charles Ives: The Man and His Music," *Musical Quarterly*, 19.1 (1933), 58.

4. Phil Lesh, *Searching for the Sound: My Life with the Grateful Dead* (New York: Little, Brown, 2005), 13–14.

5. Phil Lesh, "Dead's Lesh: 'We've got some unfinished music,'" interview by Denise Quan, CNN.com, online at: http://edition.cnn.com/2009/SHOWBIZ/Music/01/06/grateful.dead/index.html (accessed January 6, 2009).

6. Henry and Sydney Cowell, *Charles Ives and His Music* (New York: Oxford University Press, 1955). Lesh discovered this book as a student worker in the College of San Mateo library circa 1959; see Lesh, *Searching for the Sound*, 13. Lesh later audited courses with Berio at Mills College circa 1962, including at least one performance together according to the college's web site at: http://www.mills.edu/musicfestival/music_at_mills_history.php (accessed February 22, 2009).

7. Cowell, *Charles Ives*, 4. Lesh's encounter with this book may also be the genesis of the band's ongoing interest in Henry Cowell himself, as demonstrated by a 1996 improvisation with San Francisco Symphony conductor Michael Tilson Thomas. For more information and audio files of this performance, please see Michael Tilson Thomas conducts "An American Festival," San Francisco Symphony featuring Bob Weir, Phil Lesh, Mickey Hart, Vince Welnick (Bob Bralove) and Michael Tilson Thomas (on MIDI piano); "Space" for Henry Cowell, Davies Symphony Hall, San Francisco, June 16, 1996. Posted online at: http://www.archive.org/details/1996-06-16.sfo.aud-fm.vernon.19785.sbeok.flacf (last accessed on February 17, 2009). The event is also recounted in a Phil Lesh interview with David Gans, "Dead to the World," on KPFA 94.1 FM in Berkeley, CA, April 2, 1997.

8. Lesh, *Searching for the Sound*, 13–14.

9. Cowell, *Charles Ives*, Ex. 7, 160, and Ex. 1, 150.

10. *Charles Ives: Songs*, Vol. IV, Mary Ann Hart (mezzo-soprano) and Dennis Helmrich (piano), Albany Records TR080. Audio files are available at the given URL via institutional subscription to DRAM, formerly the Database of Recorded American Music.

11. *Charles Ives: "Concord" Sonata/Maurice Wright: Sonata*, Marc-André Hamelin, New World Records 80378.

12. Lesh, *Searching for the Sound*, 14.

13. Charles Ives, *Essays Before a Sonata* (New York: Norton, 1962), 75.

14. Additional information is available via the Internet Archive, http://www.archive.org/details/gd67-04-xx.prefm.vernon.9261.sbeok.shnf (last accessed February 17, 2009).

15. American Symphony Orchestra and Schola Cantorum of New York, conducted by Leopold Stokowski, assisted by David Katz and José Serebrier, Columbia MS-6775. This is the premier recording of the symphony.

16. Lesh, *Searching for the Sound*, 119.

17. Quotations list from the electronic version of James Sinclair's *A Descriptive Catalogue of The Music of Charles Ives* (New Haven: Yale University Press, 1999). Online at: http://webtext.library.yale.edu/xml2html/music/ci-d.htm (last accessed on February 17, 2009).

18. Michael Tilson Thomas, *Viva Voce: Conversations with Edward Seckerson* (Boston: Faber and Faber, 1994), 117–23. I highly recommend the recording *Charles Ives: Symphonies Nos. 1 & 4*, Chicago Symphony Orchestra & Chorus, conducted by Michael Tilson Thomas, Sony SK-44939.

19. American Symphony Orchestra and Schola Cantorum of New York, conducted by Leopold Stokowski, assisted by David Katz and José Serebrier, Columbia MS-6775.

20. Lesh, *Searching for the Sound*, 120.
21. Ibid., 119–20.
22. J. Peter Burkholder, *All Made of Tunes: Charles Ives and the Uses of Musical Borrowing* (New Haven: Yale University Press, 1995), 3–4.
23. Lesh, *Searching for the Sound*, 126, references Beethoven's Ninth Symphony.
24. This performance is commercially available on *Grateful Dead* ("Skull & Roses"), Warner Brothers 1935-2. ["We Bid You Good Night" quote, track 11, from 8:45.]
25. This performance is commercially available on *Europe '72*, Warner Brothers 2668-2. [Excerpted solo, disc 1, track 2, 3:37–4:15.]
26. This performance is commercially available on *Dick's Picks 3*, Grateful Dead Records GDCD-4021.
27. Lesh, *Searching for the Sound*, 59.
28. Like Ives, not only do the Grateful Dead directly juxtapose different sources, they also carve up the same source material for different songs. While "Viola Lee Blues" primarily borrows the groove of "Get Out My Life Woman," particularly the backbeat guitar punches, the song "Alligator" also literally quotes the drum introduction.
29. *Gus Cannon And His Jug Stompers: The Legendary 1928–1930 Recordings*, JSP Records.
30. *Lee Dorsey Selected Hits*, Charly Records.
31. This performance is commercially available on *Dick's Picks 8*, Grateful Dead Records GDCD-4028.
32. The lyric is also published as "Delia DeLyon and Staggerlee" in Robert Hunter, *A Box of Rain* (New York: Penguin Books, 1993), 56.
33. *Shakedown Street*, Arista Records ARCD-8228.
34. Charles Ives, *129 Songs*, H. Wiley Hitchcock, ed. (Middleton, WI: A-R Editions, 2004), 270–71.
35. *Charles Ives: Songs*, Vol. III, Paul Sperry (tenor) and Irma Vallecillo (piano), Albany Records TR079.
36. Burkholder, *All Made of Tunes*, 330–31. For example, Cohan's "The Story of the Wedding March" (1901, with Mendelssohn's wedding march) or Berlin's "Alexander's Ragtime Band" (1911, with "Old Folks at Home").
37. See Timothy A. Johnson's *Baseball and the Music of Charles Ives: A Proving Ground* (Lanham, MD: Scarecrow Press, 2004). Another shared trait with Weir might be Ives's song about a tragic cowboy death, "Charlie Rutledge."
38. For example, see the Grateful Dead Rainforest Press Conference at the United Nations, online at: http://forests.org/archive/general/gdrainf.htm (accessed February 20, 2009).
39. Symposium "Unbroken Chain: The Grateful Dead in Music, Culture and Memory" (Amherst, MA, November 16–17, 2007).
40. Ives, *Essays*, 172. Also mentioned in Cowell, *Charles Ives*, 115; and Rich, "Charles Ives," in *American Pioneers*, 32. The composer in question was John Becker.
41. Robert Hunter originally wrote this line from "The Greatest Story Ever Told" as "riding up on a guitar," but Weir sings "quasar" instead (Hunter, *A Box of Rain*, 90).
42. Larry Starr, *A Union of Diversities: Style in the Music of Charles Ives* (New York: Schirmer, 1992), 68–69.

Bibliography

Bellamann, Henry. "Charles Ives: The Man and His Music." *Musical Quarterly*, 19.1, 1933, 45–58.

Burkholder, J. Peter. *All Made of Tunes: Charles Ives and the Uses of Musical Borrowing.* New Haven: Yale University Press, 1995.

Cowell, Henry, and Sydney. *Charles Ives and His Music.* London: Oxford University Press, 1955.

Hunter, Robert. *A Box of Rain.* New York: Penguin Books, 1993.

Ives, Charles, and Howard Boatwright, ed. *Essays Before a Sonata, The Majority, and Other Writings.* New York: Norton, 1962.

Ives, Charles, and H. Wiley Hitchcock, ed. *129 Songs.* Middleton, WI: A-R Editions, 2004.

Johnson, Timothy A. *Baseball and the Music of Charles Ives: A Proving Ground.* Lanham, MD: Scarecrow Press, 2004.

Leichtentritt, Hugo. "Musical Notes from Abroad." *The Musical Times*, 73.1071, 1932, 461–64.

Lesh, Phil. "Dead's Lesh: 'We've got some unfinished music.'" Interview by Denise Quan for CNN.com. Online at: http://edition.cnn.com/2009/SHOWBIZ/Music/01/06/grateful.dead/index.html (accessed January 6, 2009).

———. *Searching for the Sound: My Life with the Grateful Dead.* New York: Little, Brown, 2005.

Rich, Alan. "Charles Ives." In *American Pioneers: Ives to Cage and Beyond.* London: Phaidon Press, 1995, 31–74.

Sinclair, James B. *A Descriptive Catalogue of The Music of Charles Ives.* New Haven: Yale University Press, 1999. Online at: http://webtext.library.yale.edu/xml2html/music/ci-d.htm (last accessed on February 21, 2008).

Starr, Larry. *A Union of Diversities: Style in the Music of Charles Ives.* New York: Schirmer, 1992.

Thomas, Michael Tilson. *Viva Voce: Conversations with Edward Seckerson.* Boston: Faber and Faber, 1994.

"Mr. Charlie Told Me So": Heidegger and the Dead's Early Assimilation to the Technology of the Blues

David Malvinni

"Rather, precisely the essence of technology must harbor in itself the growth of the saving power."[1] — Martin Heidegger

"And the ideas that I've pulled from blues musicians and from listening to the blues are from my affection for the blues which is like since I was a kid."[2] — Jerry Garcia

Today the Grateful Dead have become synonymous with the excesses of the 1960s rock scene. Yet for Deadheads, the band stands as an amalgam of improvisation with deep roots in American folk, blues, jazz, R&B, and country styles. Despite rejecting the status of "guru" throughout his career, it did not take long for Garcia's playing to attain legendary status in the San Francisco Bay area, and with the Acid Tests, for the band to do the same. It appears that from the start of their career, it was known that there was something different about the Dead's music, summed up by the Deadhead mantra, "There's nothing like a Grateful Dead show." Numerous explanations have been given to account for this for the last 43 years, in nearly every field of discourse imaginable. And yet as the memory of the band recedes into history, it is becoming difficult to explain to a noninitiate the authentic experience of Grateful Dead music.

In this paper, I will be juxtaposing Heideggerian philosophy with some musicological points drawn from the Dead's early blues repertory. Since the founding of the band, it seems that philosophizing about their music goes hand in hand with a musical appreciation of the Dead. Heidegger's later philosophy (post *Being and Time*), with its insights about the paradoxical destructive yet saving role of technology as a destining of Being, will serve as the framework for my reading of the Dead's early interpretations of blues music.

Experiencing the Refusal of Nearness

Heidegger's discourse on technology locates one of the disorienting/dizzying passages of the contemporary world, the shift from the machine as an autonomous tool to its (mis)appropriation in the "standing reserve" (*Bestand*), where everything awaits as the "ordering of the orderable."[3] He cites numerous examples of the standing reserve — the result of the demand for challenging (*Herausfordern*): the extraction and storing of nature's energy as in a hydroelectric plant, the mechanized food industry, man as a supply of patients in a clinic (human resource), and the airplane waiting on the runway for take-off (ensuring the possibility of transportation). The standing reserve indicates the axiomatics of the profit-making inherent in the industrialized and postindustrialized worlds, but also does more insofar as it reveals the essence of technology as "Enframing" (*Ge-stell*), as that which challenges man "to reveal the real, in the mode of ordering as standing-reserve."[4] For Heidegger, Enframing becomes a "destining" (noting the relationship of history to destiny), and he dwells on ways that the Enframing harbors within itself the supreme danger (the atom bomb) that paradoxically contains the "saving power" (quoting Hölderlin).[5]

Heidegger aligns his discourse with certain poets on whom he relies to help him think through the "unfolding" of Being. Indeed, Heidegger clearly privileges the voice of poetry in his discussion of the arts.[6] In his view, German poets like Hölderlin, Stefan Georg, Goethe, and Trakl offer an engagement with language that separates the experience of the poem from the inauthenticity of current modes of cultural activity unfolding under the sway of Enframing. He often speaks of the "nearness" of poetry and his thinking. Dwelling in "saying" can offer the double movement of the world: "To make appear, set free, that is, to offer what we call World, lighting and concealing."[7] The experience of saying is the double bind, where words paradoxically bring the world to us while at the same time concealing it. Today the danger is that language is caught up in calculation and challenging. For example, because of the calculation of fixed distances within set temporal parameters, the idea of the "nearness" of the world's region has been threatened:

> The all-out challenge to secure dominion over the earth can be met only by occupying an ultimate position beyond the earth from which to establish control over the earth. The battle for this position, however, is the thorough going calculative conversion of all connections among things into the calculable absence

of distance. This is making a desert of the encounter of the world's fourfold — it is the refusal of nearness.[8]

For Heidegger, the inability of mortals to listen, to hear language in the poem, has led at least in part to the withdrawal of nearness. In another text, Heidegger discusses the "fourfold" instantiation of dwelling as preserving: "saving the earth"; "receiving the sky as sky"; awaiting the "divinities as divinities"; and initiating mortals, or "being capable of death as death."[9]

While Heidegger does not address music in his writing, he often mentions how a poem "sings," and he does offer a short digression on the physical aspect of language — its spoken and written character. He questions whether we have experienced the "real nature of sounds and tones of speech."[10] His concern is that "physiology and physics" might determine the perspective of melody and rhythm, that is, that they might come to be understood in a "correct" and "calculating" way.[11] He does not spell out what melody and rhythm might mean for an experience of language, other than to say our experience is still "clumsy." But he does suggest in regard to styles of speaking that the "earth speaks in ["modes of mouth," *Mundarten*, or dialects], differently each time," and that the "body and mouth are part of the earth's flow and growth in which we mortals flourish, and from which we receive the *soundness* of our roots."[12] In an essay on Heidegger and Adorno, Andrew Bowie interprets the musicologist Heinrich Besseler, a student of Heidegger, as saying that man's being-in-the-world is melodic. Besseler's specific comment is that "music originally becomes accessible to us as a manner/melody of human being."[13] With respect to what Heidegger writes about the mouth and the sounding of our roots, I suspect Heidegger would concur with Besseler's statement.

The Blues as Mystical Event

Before turning to the Grateful Dead's music, we will quickly outline a historical context for the blues in the 20th century, the genre that was so important for the Grateful Dead and others in the 1960s San Francisco scene and beyond (especially London). This sketch is not meant to be comprehensive, but it will provide an orientation for how the Grateful Dead fit into the wider stream of American folk and blues music, and for understanding the folk/blues revival in the 1960s.

In Heideggerian terms, we propose that the folk blues of the African American in its rural, oral, and marginalized Southern origins names an *Ereignis*, a musical event (and moment) wherein mortals can dwell in the nearness of the earth, sky, and the divine, and intimidate death.[14] The *Ereignis* is a gift where there is an Opening "which brings all present and absent beings each into their own, from where they show themselves in what they are, and where they abide according to their kind."[15] The blues was authentic African American music which created an Opening or clearing for the community. In the moment of its sounding, the blues transported the listener to a world hitherto concealed, where for the first time African Americans could revel in the hidden power of their poetic expression.[16]

With African American music, the Enframing occurred in the recording industry's efforts to capitalize on Southern music in the 1920s, when the market for African American music opened up in a manner found to be lucrative. Like popular urban musics of the North, Southern music was added to the archive of the standing reserve, as record companies preserved the music of iconic blues guitarists like Charlie Patton, Blind Lemon Jefferson, Son House, and Robert Johnson (to name the most famous), among numerous other blues and jazz artists. The Library of Congress also recorded rural folk musicians on back porches, in prisons and schools across the South, in an attempt to save their music from oblivion.

These recording legacies represented efforts to "reveal the real," in Heideggerian terms. Though utterly modern in its subjective cry, blues was revealed on records as an old-fashioned music, a throwback to an earlier time in the South. And the music started to disappear even as it was still developing beyond Robert Johnson, in musicians like Bukka White and the early Muddy Waters. As African Americans from the South began their large-scale migration to Northern cities, and as mechanized farming grew rapidly during World War II, the rural life conditions which produced the folk music of the South receded. This concealment of the folk element of American music began a process that, following Heidegger, we will name the destitution of music.

However, because recorded and canned music were not highly valued in communal settings, live music continued to flourish in juke joints, bars, and taverns. With a powerful memory of folk music still alive, touring blues musicians from the Delta continued to play in the style of the previous generation, who in the 1930s included greats like Robert Johnson and Sonny Boy Williamson. But with transplanted Delta musicians like Muddy Waters and Willie Dixon, the style was changing with the advent of amplification.

In short, the technological advances in amplification did not destroy the blues, but transformed it for a modern audience. Amplification allowed the blues to survive in a tough new *national* marketplace for music. Blues still unfolded as *Ereignis*, as an event, which allowed mortals to connect to the world, and remained an exemplar of *poeisis*. To take a famous example, Willie Dixon's "Hoochie-Coochie Man," as sung by Muddy Waters and others, announces that "everybody knows I'm here," calling attention to the proud arrival of African Americans on the political scene, which would usher in the Civil Rights era in which the Grateful Dead took root.[17]

The Chicago blues was immediately appropriated by a new generation of brilliant white guitarists and bands in the 1960s, most prominently by Michael Bloomfield (who went on to play with Paul Butterfield) and Eric Clapton. The music produced in this blues revival was essential, authentic, and beautifully wrought. For the Dead, the white engagement with the blues created the context they would need to try to do something with the blues, to make it their own (*Ereignis* as Appropriation), and to turn it into a live Event (*Ereignis*) that altered lives.

The transition from a revivalist jug band to an electric blues band called the Warlocks is well known, and does not need to be rehearsed here.[18] What I find most significant is how the musical orientation of the Dead's members was clearly lodged in marginalized American vernacular forms rooted in *Ereignis*— jug, folk, hillbilly (Country & Western), and blues (country and urban), all folded together with influences from more contemporary jazz and avant-garde (experimental) music. Pigpen's own absorption in the blues through his father had a profound impact on the first sounding of the Dead, and Garcia noted in an early interview how the band was once mistaken for a Black R&B band.[19] As the band became a central addition to Kesey's Acid Tests, it was evident to those who had experienced them that they were not on the typical path of more commercial bands caught in the Enframing nets of the music industry. Like Kesey's Acid Tests, the Dead's music was imagined in the space of its transformative effects, in its capacity to facilitate new insights into "seeing" the world.

Before turning to some specific songs played by the Dead in their formative years, we will first show how, for Heidegger, technology contains destining paths (*Holzweg*) that might offer a "saving power" not unlike that experienced by Deadheads throughout the band's 30-year run of concerts.

Electrifying Music as the Saving Power in Amplification

For Heidegger, modern technology as revealed under Enframing is dependent on scientific advances as theorized by physics.[20] But this was not always the case. In earlier times, and most especially for the ancient Greeks, *techne*, the root practice of technological emergence, manifest a path of revealing and bore reference to the "arts of the mind and the fine arts." In fact, in these early manifestations of technology, Heidegger suggests, "*techne* belongs to bringing-forth, to *poiesis*; it is something poetic."[21] But as Enframing, modern technology leads to the standing reserve, and would seem to stand opposed to the granting of *Ereignis*. Yet in an unexpected reversal, Heidegger holds out the possibility that a destining of technology under Enframing might still be a granting (*ein Gewähres*), might bear within it an *Ereignis* as a coming-to-pass of truth (*Alètheia*, or unconcealment).[22]

Heidegger concludes "The Question Concerning Technology" by proposing that the "realm of art" might actually harbor the saving power within technology:

In Greece, at the onset of the destining of the West, the arts soared to the supreme height of the revealing granted them. They brought the presence of the gods, brought the dialogue of divine and human destinies to radiance. And art was simply called *techne*. It was a single, manifold revealing. It was pious, *promos*, i.e., yielding to the holding-sway and the safekeeping of truth.[23]

Again, for Heidegger, the revealing of art in the contemporary world is through the Word, the Saying, and the Showing of *poesis*, by which it can enter into dialogue with thinking.

But if art were to promise the "growth of the saving power" within technology, it can still be asked, why only poetry, and not the union of poetry and rhythm in music? And recalling how for Heidegger, man's essential being might be rhythmic-melodic, we propose to chart an artistic *Ereignis* in music, a new sense of the "Openness of the Open," as it were.[24]

Furthermore, given what Heidegger says about the relationship of technology to the saving power, it is more compelling that there be some technological event that gave birth to a new foundational art. In the twentieth century, the electrifying of musical energy radically altered the way music was created and heard. With this *Ereignis* of amplification, a new force entered the musical world. This amplification/electrification of music quickly ushered in a revolution, producing new styles of jazz, blues, country, and R&B, and culminating in the creation of rock 'n' roll in the mid–1950s.

If *Ereignis* did occur in electric music, we would propose that it happened in a myriad of ways with different groups, from Elvis to the Beatles to Pink Floyd. Judged from the vantage point of ecstatic audience reception among young people, a new beginning occurred with the onset of rock music. Heidegger writes of how a "new world" arises to accompany art, and of the "thrust" that enters history with new artistic endeavors.[25] This thrust would reach a pivotal climax with the coming-of-age of the first Baby Boomers during the late 1960s, a group for whom music was the main marker of group solidarity and identity, as witnessed by the territorializing gatherings of the Human Be-In, Woodstock and other large musical festivals (and counter-balanced to some extent by the deterritorializing impact of Altamont).

But something different marked the emergence of the Grateful Dead. The band's longevity, the lifelong commitment to a stunning array of styles, and the unmatched 30-year track record of improvisational concerts—each one more or less unique—made them a prime candidate for a Heideggerean "revival" capable of "bringing the gods to presence," that is, for being a "saving power" in dangerous times. The infinite task would be to show this in terms of the totality of their music, and especially their original music from the 1960s onward. From the beginning, each live show featured both subtle and intense forms of improvisation, espousing an Event/*Ereignis* that could not be missed. Following in the footsteps of Bob Dylan and The Band, who had both forged a musical dialogue with America's recent musical past, the Dead would write songs straddling the old and new that found their way onto classic albums like *American Beauty* and *Workingman's Dead*. By the early 1970s, they had turned to a jazz-flavored style that would lead to more extended improvisational flights of fancy in the tradition of "Dark Star," most prominently during the improvised heart of songs like "Playin' in the Band" and "Eyes of the World." But this is outside the scope of the present essay, which only addresses the influence of the blues on the early Dead.

To describe the "saving power" of the Dead, we will now focus on the sounding energy produced by the Dead's renditions of old and modern blues songs, which led to the band's first extended improvisatory music in original songs like "Dark Star" and "Alligator." If the Dead were caught in the net of Enframing insofar as they participated in the archive of the commercial music scene (something largely unavoidable for rock bands in this era), clearly, at the same time, they were drinking from the well of Heideggerian *Ereignis*, and right from the start.

Appropriating Blues as a Psychedelic Vehicle

Let us pause for a moment on the theme of *Ereignis: Er-eignis* has *eignen* at its root, meaning to appropriate; thus one way of understanding *Ereignis* would be as the gathering/granting process of making something one's own. It also conveys a sense for lingering in the moment, a mystical "oneness" with the moment before understanding and calculation set in.[26] Although there were some early originals, the Dead's first indications of what the future might hold were revealed in their versions of blues and R&B songs. Garcia said in an early interview that their music was about 40 percent original, and most of it was stolen bits and pieces. Of course, Garcia's statement does not do justice to the originality in how the band would incorporate other musicians' ideas.

Lesh mentions that after two months of rehearsals during the summer of 1965, they had melded the sound together as "the unity of a group mind."[27] He also tells us that as the house band at the In Room (in Belmont), they continually expanded their ability to improvise, playing Wilson Pickett's newly released smash R&B song "In the Midnight Hour" for 45 minutes (since the longest circulating version is just over 31 minutes—cf. *Fallout From the Phil Zone*—this is probably an exaggeration). Here, as with "Viola Lee Blues, the "background" musicians started to improvise in order to make the solo sound more interesting.[28] With respect to "Viola Lee Blues" (a Noah Lewis/jug band tune), Lesh writes:

> We electrified the song with a boogaloo beat and an intro lick borrowed from R&B artist Lee Dorsey's "Get Out of My Life Woman," and after each of the three verses, we tried to take the music *out* further—first expanding on the groove, then on the tonality, and then both, finally pulling out all the stops in a

giant accelerano, culminating in a whirlwind of dissonance that, out of nowhere, would slam back into the original groove for a repetition of the final verse. It was after a run-through of this song that I turned to Jerry and remarked ingenuously, "Man — this could be *art!*"[29]

What is striking is not that they borrow the intro lick, but that they appropriate the basic beat and the chord structure (I-IV-I-bVII-IV-I, with dominant-seventh inflections possible on each of the chords) from Dorsey's tune. In terms of the tempo, the Dead actually speed up the original, as they do on many of their covers (African American tunes are usually slower than their covers by white artists).

"Viola Lee Blues" is the first arranged song in which the band consciously sought to "stretch out." Performed in early 1966 (the earliest entry for this song in *Deadbase* is for a show on February 23, 1966), the Internet Archive includes interesting rehearsal tapes of the Dead working on their arrangement. Garcia discusses how they lopped off a half of a bar to make it an 11½ bar blues song, and he says, "Our way is quite a lot jazzier and it has newer rhythm."[30]

The Dead's "Smokestack Lightnin'" debuted soon after, at a bluesy show on November 19, 1966, at the Fillmore Auditorium in San Francisco.[31] The song was at least a decade old, having been recorded by Howlin' Wolf in Chicago for Chess Records in 1956. It was a popular song for other blues revival bands as well, including the Yardbirds and the Rationals (the Animals would release their own version in December of 1966 on MGM's American release of *Animalisms*).

From Weir's opening guitar riff, the Dead threw wide open the gates of the Chicago blues. Garcia's guitar solo reveals his uncanny ability to forge an original, personal style in an old genre. Pigpen's gruff voice, along with his unique ability to capture the *cri de coeur* of the blues, is mind blowing for a white singer. The blues coming from Pigpen's harmonica authentically recaptures the sound originated by the greatest harmonica player of the Chicago scene, Little Walter.[32] What did the Dead do differently in the instrumental parts from other white cover bands? Unlike the Yardbirds, the Dead kept the opening riff the same, as in the original. In the jam, however, Garcia masterfully quotes "Spoonful," a Dixon song (at about 3:48 on the tape), before bringing back the "Smokestack" theme. The solos reveal a stunning interplay between Pigpen's harmonica and Garcia's lines, producing a sound unlike any previously recorded versions.

The sound of the early Dead was ensconced and invested in a number of blues classics and ideas. Their first eponymous album is steeped in the blues, as Garcia acknowledges in the early Gleason interview:

> The material comes from blues, like some of the material is from blues, recent blues, like the last ten years' blues. Chicago style blues. Like "Good Morning Little School Girl" is a song that's in the public domain, by the way, and we didn't copyright any of this shit, the stuff that's traditional we left traditional. "Good

Morning Little School" is a traditional song but it's only as far as I know maybe 10, 15 year old.[33]

Furthermore, the Dead knew the blues was a powerful trip for audience participation—for example, at the famous afternoon free concert on Haight Street in March of 1968, they played an all blues and R&B show: "Viola Lee Blues," "Smokestack Lightnin'," "Lovelight," "Hurts Me Too," and "Dancin' in the Streets."[34]

One of their first great original psychedelic vehicles, Lesh's "Alligator," is built on blues-inspired motifs, as the jam outro illustrates well. Also from the blues tradition is their first original composition, written while they were the house band at the In Room (and also the reason they were asked to leave), "Caution (Do Not Stop on the Tracks)," about which Lesh writes of how at a show Pigpen's lyrics were delivered "with all the spooky, snaky, insinuating delivery he could summon."[35]

As is well known, most of the blues cover songs were led by Pigpen's powerful voice. Examples include "Big Boss Man," "It Hurts Me Too," "Big Railroad Blues," "The Same Thing," "Good Morning Little Schoolgirl," and "Katie Mae," which Garcia and the band complemented with their supportive playing.[36] Without Pigpen's voice, the Dead's blues renditions would not have come out as well—the weakest aspect of the blues revival for other white bands was always in the vocal parts, where the renditions would easily veer from the distinctness and earthiness of the African American voice. Great exceptions from this early era are Weir's version of "Minglewood Blues" and Garcia's "Deep Elem Blues."

Opening Doors to Improvisation

What did the blues allow the Dead to accomplish in their early years? First, if the Acid Tests and the early concerts are thought through the lens of *Ereignis*, blues was the vehicle that revealed the moment, allowing for the initial breakthrough.[37] The breakthrough was an ecstatic moment, where things were transformed—simple blues chords, rhythms, and patterns did not seem the same any longer. LSD, experimental lights show and a theater of the absurd with dancing would only heighten the swirling effect of the music. The blues was the genre and the musical language that first allowed the Dead to stretch out at these transformative events, which operated as a foundational moment in Heidegger's sense, signaling the grounding of a new relationship to Being.

The experience of the blues clearly informed the Dead's original compositions as well, even if they largely avoided the form of the 12-bar blues.[38] Pigpen's "Operator," while only performed at a few shows in 1970, offers a good example of the band's folkloric take on the blues. In the aftermath of Pigpen's departure from the band, the Dead would go on to refashion their blues repertoire, with songs like "U.S. Blues," and later on "Alabama Getaway" and "West L.A. Fadeaway." But the song I will focus on in the last part of this paper is a Pigpen/Hunter composition from 1971, "Mr. Charlie."

Like any great song, "Mr. Charlie" can be interpreted in a number of ways.[39] The interpretation I will venture here is that the song is part of the stream of African American blues music. Mr. Charlie is another name for "the Man," a white boss man who oppresses African American workers. The lyrics conjure up a magical landscape of voodoo and drums, as well as the sounds ("chuba chuba," etc.) of the Delta levee camps at the turn of the 20th century and before. The line "Mr. Charlie told me so" is typical of the multivalent lines so prominent in Hunter's and the Dead's songs—lines that can take on a multiplicity of meanings according to time and place. What is striking about the song is the simple and direct employment of African American musical tropes to create quite a traditional and direct blues song, including a drum intro, a guitar riff running throughout, the 12-bar blues form, and the call-and-response in the refrain. The performances of this song were tight, lacking the long expansions of musical space so prominent in songs like "Viola Lee Blues" and "Smokestack Lightnin'." Garcia's solo, conveyed over the two choruses, shows a masterful compression of ideas, in a unique, personal style.

It was as if, by deconstructing the electric blues style in their earlier appropriations of Chicago and Delta blues, the band was now able to reach an essential purity in their expression of the blues—a shoot 'em up, shotgun sound, as Garcia once phrased it. After Pigpen's death, the Dead never performed the song again, not even in the '90s when a number of neglected songs from the early period began filtering into the set lists.

The Saving Power of the Dead Archive

I will close with a consideration of the Enframing inherent in the Grateful Dead's archive and legacy. On the one hand, the existence of the Grateful Dead's massive tape and video content collected in the vault is an excellent example of the standing reserve, where things wait ready to be called up for use. Further, the use of the vault for commercial gain confirms that the musical energy has entered the Enframing of the music industry. The Dead offer a steady stream of musical products—CDs, downloads, and DVDs—from their vault, completely outside the band's commitment to noncommercial, authentic art and the *Ereignis* of their live concerts. For Heidegger, this is an inevitable process, given the nature of modern Enframing, where the purpose of technology is for things and energies to be stored up for later consumption and profit.

But Heidegger holds out hope within the Enframing that "precisely the essence of technology must harbor in itself the growth of the saving power." As we have tried to show, the early Dead's dedication to the African American blues offers a double resistance to the pop orientation of the music industry. On the one hand these songs were conceived by their creators as a resistance to a dominant white culture, and on the other hand the songs could not be repackaged by the Dead and simply released and sold as "hit singles," as it were, for a mass audience. And judged by the later Dead, the blues never lost any appeal for the band. Indeed, right up until Garcia's death, the Dead were still trying out new versions of old blues songs—for example, Garcia's take on Muddy Waters' "Rollin' and Tumblin'," from shows in June of 1995. Weir, of course, became the standard bearer for blues songs, singing Pigpen's former repertoire, including "Smokestack Lightnin'" and "The Same Thing," but also adding new songs like Robert Johnson's "Walkin' Blues," and Willie Dixon's "Wang Dang Doodle."

Ereignis beckons. Sandstone Amphitheatre, July 4, 1990 (courtesy Barry Barnes, all rights reserved).

Perhaps the "saving power" of the Dead is only now starting to come into full existence, and because of technology. Technology, of course, persists on many levels. In this essay, "technology" has so far referred to the electrification of the blues, but it can also mean the digitalization of the musical vault mentioned above. And this names the paradox of the Enframing: that the storing up of the Dead's primal energy as an archive in the standing reserve now offers us an entrance into a world that is past. Without the Enframing, we would not have recordings and other sources with which to discuss the *Ereignis* of the Dead. To appreciate the vastness of the band's archive is no longer difficult, for the music is available to anyone with access to the Internet. Much of the archive is now available digitally, and much of it for free: Web sites like Internet Archive have entire streaming concerts available; for video content, YouTube features rare and unreleased footage, as well as songs taken from their official releases. In addition to soundboard shows in the vault, there are thousands of audience tapes that were made by tapers at Dead shows, providing a different perspective on the music. At the very least, from these precious sources the uniqueness of the Dead, if not their greatness, emerges for the noninitiated. *Ereignis* beckons.

Notes

1. Heidegger, *The Question Concerning Technology*, 28.
2. Gleason, "Jerry Garcia the Guru," reprinted in *The Grateful Dead Reader*, Dodd and Spaulding, eds., 32.
3. Heidegger, *The Question Concerning Technology*, 17.
4. Ibid., 20.
5. Ibid., 24 and 28, respectively.
6. Heidegger, *The Origin of the Work of Art*, 73.
7. Heidegger, *The Nature of Language*, 93.
8. Ibid., 105.
9. Heidegger, *Building, Dwelling, Thinking*, 150–51.
10. Heidegger, *The Nature of Language*, 98.
11. Note that in Heidegger's usage, the "correct" understanding of a subject is usually superficial and, as such, denotes it is derived from the history of metaphysics, which for him must be deconstructed.
12. Heidegger, *The Nature of Language*, 98–99 (author's emphasis).
13. Bowie, "Adorno, Heidegger, and the Meaning of Music," 259.
14. Resisting translation, we will retain throughout this essay the German term "Ereignis," which can be translated as event, appropriation, or enowning. In the 1956 *Zusatz* (addendum) to *The Origin of the Work of Art* (written in the mid 1930s), Heidegger writes (against) Hegel that "art is considered neither an area of cultural achievement nor an appearance of spirit; it belongs to the *disclosure of appropriation [Ereignis]* by way of which the 'meaning of Being' can alone be defined" (p. 86). Note that the root of the word "eignen," which means to own, comes from "augen," the eyes.
15. Heidegger, *The Way to Language*, 127.
16. The spiritual and the work song had already done this, but under the premise of slavery—as a necessary counterpart to a harsh existence. By contrast the blues was a free, spontaneous reaction to the oppression still present in the South.
17. The Dead did in fact play "Hoochie Coochie Man," sung by Weir, at the sound check at Deer Creek, July 2, 1995. Had Garcia lived there probably would have been a Dead version of this song. Also note that a few months earlier (03/28/95, at a rehearsal for the Omni show in Atlanta), they were messing around with "Big Boy Pete," the classic R&B song sung by The Olympics (inspired by "Stagger Lee") that they had played at a few shows in 1966 and once at a rare acoustic show in 1978 (November 17, Loyola University), and lastly in 1985 as a show opener (November 21, Henry J. Kaiser Convention Center).
18. For a quick summary, see David Hadju, "How the Dead Came to Life," posted online at: http://www.rollingstone.com/news/story/7582743/how_the_dead_came_to_life/print, August 25, 2005 (retrieved October 19, 2008). Also Lesh reports that Garcia told him it was "Pigpen's idea to turn Mother McChree's into an electric blues band," in Lesh, *Searching for the Sound: My Life with the Grateful Dead*, 54.
19. Gleason, "Jerry Garcia the Guru," in *Reader*, 32: "We played in a spade show, in fact, like a rhythm and blues show. And we were received. I think we were a shock to them, because the music we were playing was heavy blues, certainly heavier than any of the spade were doing, they were doing all the lighter stuff."
20. Heidegger, *The Question Concerning Technology*, 14.

21. Ibid., 13.
22. Ibid., 32.
23. Ibid., 34.
24. Heidegger, Addendum to *The Origin of the Work of Art*, 86.
25. Heidegger, *The Origin of the Work of Art*, 77.
26. For more on this line of thinking, see "The influence of Schleiermacher's second speech On Religion on Heidegger's concept of Ereignis," by Alexander S. Jensen (June 2008), on the web at: http://findarticles.com/p/articles/mi_hb3545/is_4_61/ai_n28571768/pg_2?tag=artBody;col1 (retrieved October 17, 2008).
27. Lesh, *Searching for the Sound*, 56.
28. Ibid., 58–59.
29. Ibid., italicized words are Lesh's. The mention of a "boogaloo" is fascinating; Lesh most likely is referring to Tom and Jerrio's 1965 smash hit "Boo-Ga-Loo," which was released within the Latin dance craze in the 1960s with songs like Ray Barretto's 1963 "El Watusi."
30. Gleason, "Jerry Garcia the Guru," in *Reader*, 21. The half bar "deletion" occurs with the change to the IV chord (C), when instead of playing two bars, they play one-and-a-half.
31. It is striking to see the African American roots of an early Dead show. This particular night included: "Hi-Heel Sneakers" (Chicago blues song recorded by Tommy Tucker [Robert Higginbothom], covered by the Rolling Stones in 1964); "Pain in My Heart" (Otis Redding–Phil Walden, based on Allen Toussaint, also covered by the Stones); "Cold Rain and Snow" (traditional); "Beat It on Down the Line" (1961 country blues song by Jesse Fuller, who was living in Oakland and played throughout the Bay area); "Cream Puff War" (original); "The Same Thing" (Chicago blues style, by Willie Dixon); "He Was a Friend of Mine" (prison song, sung by Leadbelly, and later by folkies like Eric von Schmidt and Bob Dylan, and then by the Byrds); "Dancin' in the Streets" (Motown classic sung by Martha and the Vandellas, co-authored by Marvin Gaye); "Smokestack Lightnin'"; "King Bee" (Slim Harpo, 1957, again covered by the Stones on their debut album in 1964); "Midnight Hour."
32. Little Walter invented the sound of the electrified harmonica; frustrated at the volume of the electric guitars, he held the harmonica to the microphone and cupped his hand around it to produce the aching sound of the blues harmonica, one that can nearly approximate the range of a saxophone.
33. Gleason, "Jerry Garcia the Guru," *Reader*, 20–21. "Good Morning Little Schoolgirl" was actually first recorded in 1937 by Sonny Boy Williamson I, and marks a transition from the solo guitar art of the Delta blues to the ensemble style of the Chicago blues. Also, after the first verse, Pigpen changes the lyrics from Sonny Boy's original.
34. On Internet Archive there is an audience tape — perhaps the only one in existence — of this amazing concert; both "Viola Lee Blues" and "Smokestack Lightnin'" reveal the Dead in top form.
35. Lesh, *Searching for the Sound*, 91. Biographer Dennis McNally, in his *A Long Strange Trip: The Inside History of the Grateful Dead*, relates that "Caution" was based on a fragment from the Them song "Mystic Eyes," (p. 92). What they took most prominently from the song was the bass line. Them was conceived as the backup band for Van Morrison, and, curiously, descriptions of their live shows at the Maritime Hotel in Belfast bear a resemblance to a Dead show. Also note that one of the staples of Them from 1964 onward was "Turn on Your Lovelight." See the video of "Mystic Eyes" online at: http://www.dailymotion.com/video/x1v1yu_them-mystic-eyes-et-gloria_music (retrieved October 22, 2008).
36. Of these songs, "Katie Mae," by Lightnin' Hopkins, showed off the incredible ability of Pigpen to approximate the soul of the down-home blues; the song was accom-

panied by the sparse and tasteful playing of Garcia on acoustic guitar in shows from 1970.

37. I am thinking of "breakthrough" in Adorno's sense. In his analysis of Mahler's music, a breakthrough occurs when the composition seems to fall apart, when the formal element can no longer contain the substantive elements. For Adorno, the substantive element is always already a mediated moment. He writes that Mahler's tonal chords are "the explosive expressions of pain felt by the individual subject imprisoned in an alienated society." *Quasi una fantasia*, London; New York: Verso, 1992, 85.

38. Given the importance of the blues, this may seem surprising, yet other revival bands, like the Rolling Stones, also never employed the twelve-bar blues in their original compositions—the one exception being "19th Nervous Breakdown."

39. See "The Annotated 'Mr. Charlie,'" online at: http://arts.ucsc.edu/GDead/AGDL/charlie.html (accessed October 18, 2008).

Bibliography

Bowie, Andrew, and Tom Huhn, ed. "Adorno, Heidegger, and the Meaning of Music." In *The Cambridge Companion to Adorno*. Cambridge: Cambridge University Press, 2004.

Dodd, David. "The Annotated Grateful Dead Lyrics." Online at: http://arts.ucsc.edu/GDead/AGDL/.

_____, and Diana Spaulding, eds. *The Grateful Dead Reader*. Oxford: University Press, 2000.

Hadju, David. "How the Dead Came to Life." Posted online at: http://www.rollingstone.com/news/story/7582743/how_the_dead_came_to_life/print, August 25, 2005 (retrieved October 19, 2008).

Heidegger, Martin. "Building, Dwelling, Thinking." In *Poetry, Language, Thought*, Albert Hofstadter, trans. New York: Harper and Row, 1971.

_____. "The Nature of Language." In *On the Way to Language*, Peter D. Hertz, trans. San Francisco: Harper and Row, 1982.

_____. "The Origin of the Work of Art." In *Poetry, Language, Thought*, Albert Hofstadter, trans. New York: Harper and Row, 1971.

_____. "The Question Concerning Technology." In *The Question Concerning Technology and Other Essays*, William Lovitt, trans. New York: Harper and Row, 1977.

Jensen, Alexander S. "The Influence of Schleiermacher's Second Speech on Religion on Heidegger's concept of Ereignis." *The Review of Metaphysics*, June 2008. Online at: http://findarticles.com/p/articles/mi_hb3545/is_4_61/ai_n28571768/pg_2?tag=artBody;oll (accessed October 17, 2008).

Lesh, Phil. *Searching for the Sound: My Life with the Grateful Dead*. New York; Boston: Little, Brown, 2005.

McNally, Dennis. *A Long Strange Trip: The Inside History of the Grateful Dead*. New York: Broadway Books, 2002.

DARK STAR MANDALA
GRAEME M. BOONE

If it is true, as argued earlier in this book,[1] that the Grateful Dead's early music can profitably be framed in mandalic terms, the question remains of how one might go about doing that in a specific case. This task could be accomplished in diverse ways and to diverse ends. The present essay will construct one kind of mandala for the song "Dark Star," the most famous and mythologized song in the Dead canon, as performed during their early, psychedelic era (1967–69).[2] It will organize the most readily observable episodes in the music into a circle of structured meaning, visualized by a diagrammatic evocation of the mandala of musical sound.[3] This will also entail consideration of the song's musical and expressive world; the role played by the lyrics in that world; the evolution of the song across many performances; and the later, grander development of the song.

Spirituality and Identity in "Dark Star"

Comments about "Dark Star" made by band members and by their close associate, lyricist Robert Hunter, give us a sense of the overarching metaphysical qualities they attribute to it, prime candidates for incorporation into a mandala.[4]

> [LESH:] As we played around with it, it started expanding itself into a flood of endless melody, and from there into some scarifying, chaotic feedback, and back to the original theme, almost of its own accord—as if the music wanted to be expanded far beyond any concept of "song." [....] This theme, because of its infinite mutability, became our signature space-out tune, consciously designed to be opened up into alternate universes—a tone poem reflecting the possibility that the collapse of a star into singularity in our universe could be the birth of another complete universe.
>
> [HUNTER:] I think the images may have been the thing that recommended that you could go ahead and take this out into those dimensions.

[GARCIA:] No question. The reason the music is the way it is, is because those lyrics did suggest that to me. That's what happened. They are saying, "This universe is truly far out." That's about it. You could take whatever you will from that suggestion. For me, that suggestion always means, "Great, let's look around, let's see how weird it really gets."

These qualities are perceived with no less intensity by many Dead fans. As Jim Powell, long-time student of "Dark Star," has written[5]:

"Dark Star" is the kernel of wide open possibility at the core of the Dead's repertoire, the essential seed promising unlimited intergalactic space journeys at the speed of total mindwarp. [...] It is the most exploratory of Dead tunes and the trippiest, the one where the acidic whistle of the dark interstices is heard most starkly, where you might turn any corner and step off into the void. It is the Dead's spirit of musical adventure at its strangest, wildest, most vehement, weirdest, dreamiest, and the place where the leading wave of the Dead's music is most often audible being created in mid-air.

Lesh and Garcia perceive the song as not only highly flexible, but an outright call to cosmic exploration — a transformative field, as it were, whose purview would include "alternate universes." This characterization resonates with Garcia's description of the Acid Tests as provoking awareness of different "planes" of existence, and a quest "to extend that limit, as far as you can go"[6]; and in fact "Dark Star" can be viewed as one kind of purely musical transmutation, or distillation, of the essential Acid Test experience. Since the Dead viewed the Tests as a key formative experience behind their band — the "Big Bang," as Phil wrote[7] — it is logical that Test elements should have surfaced in their music, nowhere more so than in this "archetypal jamming" song.[8] Jerry's description of "Dark Star" in development, typifying the Dead's way of working on new music, recalls his characterization of the Tests[9]:

[ACID TESTS:] Nobody was doing *something*, y'know, it was everybody doing bits and pieces of something, the result of which was something else.
["DARK STAR":] As always with Grateful Dead stuff, my version just dies somewhere and the Grateful Dead's version takes over.... But as it opened up and we got really risky, when we started to drop the rhythm and just went all over the place, by then I realized that the Grateful Dead version, the x version, was way more interesting both to me as a player and also to me as an audience.

The fascination in "Dark Star" with "seeing how weird it gets" relates directly to the creative chaos Jerry so admired in the Tests: "When it was moving right, you could dig that there was something that it was getting toward, something like ordered chaos, or some region of chaos." Garcia said elsewhere[10]:

[ACID TESTS:] We were doing the Acid Test, which was our first exposure to formlessness. Formlessness and chaos lead to new forms. And new order. Closer to, probably, what the real order is. When you break down the old orders and the old forms and leave them broken and shattered, you suddenly find yourself a new space with new form and new order which are more like the way it is. More like the flow. And we just found ourselves in that place [1972].

[GRATEFUL DEAD:] As a musician I like form but there's a part of me that wants there to be underform, like the form after chaos, that kind of fractal form. I long to take ideas down those roads. Now it remains for me to figure out ways to suggest the use of those things where the stuff is satisfying intellectually so I feel like I'm playing and I'm being honest in a formal sense but I'm also allowed to be innovative in a way where I can get a chance to surprise myself [1990s].

A pronounced interest in extreme exploration, with its metaphysical resonances, is thus one essential aspect of "Dark Star," which is balanced against the song's fixed and centering elements. It seems no coincidence that the song came into being during the creation of the album *Anthem of the Sun*, whose mandalic cover painting evokes something of these qualities.

The Lyrics

Being integral to the song's mystique as well as its expressive power, Robert Hunter's lyrics have been much discussed over the years.[11] Simple but intensely evocative, they evoke disintegration and loss on different levels, from the cosmic to the psychological and emotive. The imagery is defiantly threatening and hallucinatory, but turns to a more intimate, even romantic denouement in the chorus, which, borrowing transparently from T.S. Eliot,[12] shares his gentility of language and sentiment, lending "Dark Star" an unexpected "twist" of sophistication, seriousness, and connection to literary tradition.

> Dark star crashes, pouring its light into ashes
> Reason tatters, the forces tear loose from the axis
> Searchlight casting for faults in the clouds of delusion
>
> Mirror shatters in formless reflections of matter
> Glass hand dissolving in ice petal flowers revolving
> Lady in velvet recedes in the nights of good-bye
>
> *Shall we go, you and I, while we can*
> *Through the transitive nightfall of diamonds?*

The cycle of movement from form to formlessness, being to nothingness, cosmos to chaos, is repeated in each line. But it is also belied by the constant renewal of images, which, like the simple, structured flow of lines and rhymes, anchor us in "being"; and by the chorus, which displaces (depending on one's interpretation) hallucinatory imagery with the tranquil beauty of a nighttime sky and the offer of companionship. The lyrics, then, suggest cosmic wheels of motion involving order and chaos, inner and outer worlds, immanence and ephemerality.

The musical setting of the lyrics reinforces (more subtly) their unsettling as well as (more obviously) their classical-meditative qualities. Performed quietly rather than loudly, with melancholic tenderness rather than violence or overt aggression, the "Dark Star" melody's unhurried, falling lines and vaguely baroque-sounding counterpoint produce an effect of pensive reflection and intimacy, countering the external, galactic aspect of the lyrics with the effect of an internal, emotive cosmos whose humanizing impact is cemented in the chorus ("Shall we go...?"). Analogous to the fateful name of the band itself,[13] the paradoxical title of its most famous song thus ended up a marker for twin identities, a psychedelic yin-yang adventure of life and death, alienation and companionship, appearance and reality.

Approaching a Mandala

The resonance between the lyrics and music of "Dark Star," the Acid Tests, and the Dead's ultimate sense of identity makes it seem particularly compelling to explore a mandalic way of experiencing, or modeling, this song. Discussions by Tucci and His Holiness the Dalai Lama would seem appropriate for the metaphysical dimensions of such a mandala, including the ideas of whole universe or world system; the universe as temporal revolution and vital process, developing from an essential principle and rotating around a central axis; the mystics standing at the center of the circle as collecting and radiating the thaumaturgical power; the external, circular threshold as holding forces at bay that threaten the psychic integrity of the song and its celebrants; and the extraction of essence, reception of blessing, and gaining of magnificence.[14] Also significant is the duality of nirvana and samsara, suggested by the opposition between everyday reality and the contrasting, life-transforming state of pure being, awareness, connection, and flow, involving, in certain respects, the dissolution of Self, which members evoke as the "peak experience" that makes all the rest worthwhile.[15]

> [GARCIA:] Truth is something you stumble into when you think you're going someplace else, like those moments when you're playing and the whole room becomes one being—precious moments, man. But you can't look for them and they can't be repeated. Being alive means to continue to change, never to be where I was before. Music is the timeless experience of constant change.
>
> [GARCIA:] To get really high is to forget yourself. And to forget yourself is to see everything else. And to see everything else is to become an understanding molecule in evolution, a conscious tool of the universe. And I think every human being should be a conscious tool of the universe. That's why I think it is important to get high.... I'm not talking about unconsciousness or zonked out, I'm talking about being fully conscious. Also I'm not talking about the Grateful Dead as being an end in itself.
>
> [LESH:] When we get onstage, what we really want to happen is, we want to be transformed from ordinary players into extraordinary ones, like forces of a larger consciousness.
>
> [LESH:] After this many years, man, there's nothing awesome about it at all, except those moments. Those moments, when you're not even human anymore—you're not a musician, you're not even a person—you're just there.... Those moments—they're a state of grace, in a sense.

[LESH:] I think every song we play, everything we do should be able to open up at any moment.... I'd just as soon get outside! That's what we're all about!

Many different mandalas could be projected to capture some element or vision of "Dark Star." My goal here, originating with the problem of effective music analysis, will be to take account of the most salient and basic structuring features in the music—riffs, harmonies, verses, choruses, and other major episodic elements—which, recurring in numerous performances up to early 1969, constitute the basic, *de facto* working structure of the song, and to place these in a visual environment that evokes, at the same time, its freewheeling and "world-making" identity. That identity includes the overarching forces of order (Greek "cosmos") as well as chaos, informing the road map, as it were, of both the song's basic formal organization and its improvisatory explorations. While informed by the imagery and expression of the lyrics, this visualization does not attempt to incorporate them in any direct manner.

"Dark Star" was, of course, anything but static. As Jerry put it[16]:

All of our music ... is really a process. "Dark Star" is a good example. It's not a work, it's not like an opus—now it's done, here's the tune, play it this way always, everybody play this tempo always, here are the expression marks. It isn't like that. What we do is an ongoing procedure. The procedure sometimes coughs up a magical relationship with the music and other people can dig it too. We're definitely a process band.

Thanks to the assiduous taping of concerts and, across the years, preservation and dissemination of those tapes, we have an extraordinary record of the "process" of "Dark Star" across its musical life—hardly exhaustive, given the concerts and innumerable rehearsals that are not known to have been recorded, but remarkably "complete" nonetheless. With these recordings in hand, it becomes possible to trace the monthly and sometimes daily "process" of the song as it evolves. For present purposes, which require close analysis of each performance, we shall restrict our attention to the early evolution of the song, book-ended by its two early publications; this period ranges from its first recording as a two-minute studio single (recorded c. November 1967) through the Fillmore West run that produced the classic performance released on *Live/Dead* (recorded on February 27, 1969). At the end of this chapter, we will further extend our consideration to performances up through April 1969.

The list of extant early recorded performances of "Dark Star," given in Table 1 at the end of this essay, illustrates the song's growing length during this time; and a tabulation of its most prominent and distinctive episodes illustrates its progressive growth in complexity. To propose, as I am doing, one synchronic mandala for the diachrony of these widely varying renderings might appear to marginalize the song's progressive variability, or to reflect a teleological bias according to which later performances, longer and far more exploratory, represent the realization, rather than alteration, of the song's earlier identity. The latter stance would reflect the conviction, conveyed by band members and

Table 1:
Appearance of Basic Episodes Across Early Performances of "Dark Star"

Key to Table 1: • Presence of a specific musical episode or idea (absence of • indicates absence of the episode); [•] Instrumental performance of the normally sung verses and choruses (found in recording no. 1 only); ▬ Evocation of a musical idea, falling short of a full-fledged statement; — Gap in the recording, possibly causing the loss of an episode; **t1** First instrumental tag; **jt** Jerry's theme; **V1** First sung verse; **C1** First sung chorus; **t2** Second instrumental tag; **sr** Jerry's "starting riff"; **ve** Verse episode; **m** Modal shift, usually to the minor; **r** Arpeggio-riff episode; **vd** Volume-dial episode; **gr** Growling episode; **fb** Feedback; **sp** Space; **np** New chord progression; **ns** New song; **cl** Climax episode; **pc** Post-climax episode; **V2** Second sung verse; **C2** Second sung chorus; **t3** Third instrumental tag

no.	date	place	timing	t1	jt	V1	C1	t2	sr	ve	m	r	vd	gr	fb	sp	np	ns	cl	pc	jt	V2	C2	t3
1.	67.11.14	American Studios, Hollywood	2:35	•		[•]	[•]																	•
2.	67.11.14	American Studios, Hollywood	2:39	•		[•]	[•]																	•
3.	67.11–12	[studio-produced single]	2:42	•		•	•																	•
4.	68.01.17	Carousel Ballroom, San Francisco	4:48	—		•	•	•	•	•														•
5.	68.01.20	Municipal Auditorium, Eureka	[1:55]	•		—	—	—	—	—	—	—	—	—	—	—	—	—	—	—	—	—	—	—
6.	68.01.22	Eagle's Auditorium, Seattle	5:43	•	▬	•	•	•	•	•														•
7.	68.02.03	Crystal Ballroom, Portland	5:37	•		•	•	•	•	•														•
8.	68.02.14	Carousel Ballroom, San Francisco	5:57	•		•	•	•	•	•											▬			•
9.	68.02.22	King's Beach Bowl, Lake Tahoe	6:21	—		•	•	•	•	•														•
10.	68.02.24	King's Beach Bowl, Lake Tahoe	6:49	•		•	•	•	•	•														•
11.	68.03.16	Carousel Ballroom, San Francisco	7:24	•		•	•	•	•	•														•
12.	68.03.26	Melodyland Theater, Anaheim	7:16	—		•	•	•	•	•														•
13.	68.03.30	Carousel Ballroom, San Francisco	8:54	•		•	•	•	•	•	•													•
14.	[68.08.20]	Fillmore West, San Francisco	15:38	—		•	•	•	▬	•	•	•	•	•										•
15.	68.08.21	Fillmore West, San Francisco	13:45	•		•	•	•	•	•	•	▬	•											•
16.	68.08.22	Fillmore West, San Francisco	11:58	•		•	•	•	•	•	•													•
17.	68.08.23	Shrine Auditorium, Los Angeles	15:27	•		•	•	•	•	•	•													•
18.	68.08.24	Shrine Auditorium, Los Angeles	11:19	•		•	•	•	•	•	•													•
19.	68.08.28	Avalon Ballroom, San Francisco	10:42	•		•	•	•	•	•	•													•
20.	68.09.02	Nelson's Farm, Sultan, Washington	14:05	•		•	•	•	•	•	•													•
21.	68.10.12	Avalon Ballroom, San Francisco	14:51	•		•	•	•	•	•	•							▬						•
22.	68.10.13	Avalon Ballroom, San Francisco	13:31	—		•	•	•	•	•	•								▬					•
23.	68.10.20	Greek Theater, Berkeley	10:19	—		•	•	•	•	•	•													•
24.	68.11.01	Silver Dollar Fair, Chico, Cal.	12:07	—		•	•	•	•	•	•									▬				•
25.	68.11.06	Pacific High Studios, San Mateo	12:22	—		•	•	•	•	•	•													•

no.	date	place	timing	t1	jt	V1	C1	t2	sr	ve	m	r	vd	gr	fb	sp	np	ns	cl	pc	jt	V2	C2	t3
26.	68.11.22	Veterans' Hall, Columbus, Oh.	11:51	—	•	•	•	•	•	•	•	•	•	•	•	•	•	•	•	•	•	•	•	•
27.	68.12.07	Bellarmine College, Louisville	13:25	—	•	•	•	•	•	•	•	•	•	•	•	•	•	•	•	•	•	•	•	•
28.	68.12.29	Gulfstream Park, Hallandale, Fl.	10:25	•	•	•	•	•	•	•	•	•	•	•	•	•	•	•	•	•	•	•	•	•
29.	69.01.17	Civic Auditorium, Santa Barbara	13:18	•	•	•	•	•	•	•	•	•	•	•	•	•	•	•	•	•	•	•	•	•
30.	69.01.24	Avalon Ballroom, San Francisco	18:57	—	•	•	•	•	•	•	•	♮	•	•	•	•	•	•	•	•	•	•	•	•
31.	69.01.25	Avalon Ballroom, San Francisco	14:04	•	•	•	•	•	•	•	•	•	•	•	•	•	•	•	•	•	•	•	•	•
32.	69.01.26	Avalon Ballroom, San Francisco	[9:41]	•	—	•	•	•	•	•	—			—	—	—	—	—	—	—	•	•	•	•
33.	69.02.02	Labor Temple, Minneapolis	15:19	•	•	•	•	•	•	•	•	•	•	•	•	•	•	•	•	•	•	•	•	•
34.	69.02.04	Music Box, Omaha	[13:11]	—	•	•	•	•	•	•	—			—	—	—	—	—	—	—	•	•	•	•
35.	69.02.05	Memorial Aud., Kansas City, Mo.	11:39	•	•	•	•	•	•	•	•	•	•	•	•	•	•	•	•	•	•	•	•	•
36.	69.02.06	Kiel Auditorium, St. Louis	[14:02]	•	•	•	•	•	•	•	—			—	—	—	♮	—	—	—	•	•	•	•
37.	69.02.07	Stanley Theater, Pittsburgh	14:03	•	•	•	•	•	•	•	•	•	•	•	•	•	•	•	•	•	•	•	•	•
38.	69.02.11	Fillmore East, New York	12:29	•	•	•	•	•	•	•	•	•	•	•	•	•	•	•	•	•	•	•	•	•
39.	69.02.12	Fillmore East, New York	[4:58]	—	—	•	•	•	•	•	—			—	—	—	—	—	—	—	•	•	•	•
40.	69.02.14	Electric Factory, Philadelphia	18:34	—	•	•	•	•	•	•	•	•	•	•	•	•	•	•	•	•	•	•	•	•
41.	69.02.15	Electric Factory, Philadelphia	22:29	•	•	•	•	•	♮	•	•	•	•	•	•	•	•	•	•	•	•	•	•	•
42.	69.02.21	Dream Bowl, Vallejo	20:48	•	•	•	•	•	•	•	•	•	•	•	•	•	•	•	•	•	•	•	•	•
43.	69.02.22	Dream Bowl, Vallejo	[21:10]	•	•	•	•	•	•	•	—			—	—	—	—	—	—	—	•	•	•	•
44.	69.02.27	Fillmore West, San Francisco	21:48	•	•	•	•	•	•	•	•	♮	•	•	•	•	•	•	•	•	•	•	•	•
45.	69.02.28	Fillmore West, San Francisco	19:37	•	•	•	•	•	•	•	•	•	•	•	•	•	•	•	•	•	•	•	•	•
46.	69.03.01	Fillmore West, San Francisco	23:00	•	•	•	•	•	•	•	•	•	•	•	•	•	•	•	•	•	•	•	•	•
47.	69.03.02	Fillmore West, San Francisco	20:01	•	•	•	•	•	•	•	•	•	•	•	•	•	•	•	•	•	•	•	•	•
48.	69.03.15	Hilton Hotel, San Francisco	20:28	•	•	•	•	•	•	•	•	•	•	•	•	•	•	•	•	•	•	•	•	•
49.	69.03.22	Rose Palace, Pasadena	14:46	•	•	•	•	•	•	•	•	•	•	•	•	•	•	•	•	•	•	•	•	•
50.	69.03.28	Student Center, Modesto	23:11	•	•	•	•	•	•	•	•	•	•	♮	•	•	•	•	•	•	•	•	•	•
51.	69.03.29	Ice Palace, Las Vegas	[15:34]	•	•	•	•	•	•	•	—			—	♮	♮	•	♮	—	—	•	•	•	•
52.	69.04.04	Avalon Ballroom, San Francisco	20:02	•	•	•	•	•	•	•	•	•	•	♮	•	•	•	•	•	•	•	•	•	•
53.	69.04.05	Avalon Ballroom, San Francisco	17:23	•	•	•	•	•	•	•	•	•	•	•	•	•	•	•	•	•	•	•	•	•
54.	69.04.11	University Auditorium, Tucson	19:58	•	•	•	•	•	•	•	•	•	•	♮	•	•	•	•	•	•	•	•	•	•
55.	69.04.12	Student Union, Salt Lake City	21:37	•	•	•	•	•	•	•	•	•	•	•	•	•	•	•	•	•	•	•	•	•
56.	69.04.13	Ballroom, U. of Colo., Boulder	[23:56]	—	•	•	•	•	•	•	•	•	•	•	•	•	—	—	—	•	•	•	•	•
57.	69.04.15	Music Box, Omaha	20:21	•	•	•	•	•	•	•	•	•	•	•	•	•	•	•	•	•	•	•	•	•
58.	69.04.17	Washington Univ., St. Louis	21:35	•	•	•	•	•	•	•	•	•	•	•	•	•	•	•	•	•	•	•	•	•
59.	69.04.20	Clark University, Worcester, Mass.	21:13	•	•	•	•	•	•	•	•	•	•	•	•	•	•	•	•	•	•	•	•	•

no.	date	place	timing	t1	jt	V1	C1	t2	sr	ve	m	r	vd	gr	fb	sp	np	ns	cl	pc	jt	V2	C2	t3
60.	69.04.21	The Ark, Boston	[20:57]	•	•	•	•	•		•	•				•		–	–			•	•	•	•
61.	69.04.22	The Ark, Boston	[27:21]	•	•	•	•	•		•	•	–		≈			–	–			•	•	•	•
62.	69.04.23	The Ark, Boston	20:56	•	•	•	•	•		•	•	–	–						≈		•	•	•	•
63.	69.04.27	Labor Temple, Minneapolis	26:30	•	•	•	•	•		•	•				•		•		≈		•	•	•	•

Table 1 lists the 63 extant recorded "Dark Star" performances by the Grateful Dead from the origins of the song in 1967 up to the end of April 1969. (Other recordings for other dates in this period may exist, but are not widely known at present.) From this list are excluded the late-1968 performances by the spinoff band "Mickey and the Hartbeats," which lack the participation of Weir and Pigpen. For each recording, the table lists the date, venue, and time length. The association between specific dates and recordings seems generally reliable, but there are exceptions. Thus, no. 14 had been provisorily dated by others to earlier 1968 for musical reasons (or, lacking firm evidence, to the placeholder of "68-12-31?"), but the performing style suggests that this is the missing performance of 68-08-20. There has been disagreement over the dating of no. 25, but the musical style suggests participation by Tom Constanten on organ, and a date in November. And another, fragmentary recording that has been disseminated without a date, 4:04 in length, turns out to be the end of no. 37, from 69-04-17. The timing given for each song corresponds to the length of the song itself, which may be shorter than the length of source audio files (since these may include additional time before or after the song). Many files have a small amount of music missing from the beginning or end of the song. Brackets are placed around song timings in instances of what appear to be extensive gaps in the recording. Each column in the table, to the right of the song timings, indicates the presence or absence of a specific episode on each recording; dashes (–) indicate a tape gap as the possible cause for absence of certain episodes. The order of episodes, moving left to right, follows the order of unfolding of the song, to the extent that it is consistent (most of the improvisatory episodes in the second jam having no fixed sequential order). Distinct, recurrent episodes such as occur in the second jam occur far more rarely in the first, where it would seem that they are more or less avoided. Such episodes as do appear in the first jam are not noted in the present table, for reasons of space. Examples would include SR (frequently evoked, though not stated outright, in earlier first jams); VD, played on 69-03-29; R, played on 69-04-13; and NS, evoked on 68-10-12.

fans alike, that "Dark Star" did, across the years, have a growing but also persistent identity and meaning; that it did exist as *something*. And I do want to capture something of that something. More importantly, though, the mandala, properly understood, does allow for differing interpretations that are germane to every extant recorded performance of this period.

The list of Table 1 is complete only insofar as commonly available recordings would suggest; it will almost certainly be rendered obsolete by the future dissemination of obscure tapes.[17] Among the securely documented performances between November 1967 and March 2, 1969, this list indicates the recorded survival of 47 different dates, including four studio recordings; up through April 1969, it indicates 63.[18]

Close analysis of the recordings listed in Table 1 allows us to project the mandala image shown in Figure 1, based on episodes occurring in the music. The relative consistency of these episodes across many performances (as reflected in the columns of Table 1) allows for clarity and consistency in the image, but it should not be exaggerated. The band members' predilection for "worrying," layering, and tinkering with improvisatory ideas within and among performances ensures that these ideas shift, transform, re-combine, appear, and disappear, producing a variability that hinders any attempt at a simple and definitive categorization. The firm distinction between one idea and another, or even "idea" and "non-idea," can prove elusive. As a result, the sorting of musical ideas must be provisory and interpretive, and works best when limited to the clearest episodic constructions. Providing auditory illustration of those I have found to be clearest and most distinctive, Table 2 gives their timing of placement in the song as performed on August 23, 1968, February 27, 1969, and April 15, 1969.[19]

Since the present essay concentrates on matters of tonal organization (extending to consideration of melody, harmony, and counterpoint) and on elements that can be represented in distinctive episodic constructions, its analyses do not incorporate numerous other subtle or ongoing textural elements. Any listener to these recordings would be likely to notice, for example, the increasing presence of trap drumming over time, which becomes a major element of second jams in the course of early 1969. This shift is not indicated in Table 1 nor Figure 1; nor are the shifts between relatively straight and swing rhythm, nor the change of keyboardist from Pigpen to Tom Constanten in late November 1968, nor Jerry's and Phil's changes of guitar, nor their distinctive use of different melodic registers, nor Jerry's frequent changes of guitar tone during solos, nor Bob's evolving approach to backup guitar, nor Phil's use of different bass styles, nor the many crescendos and decrescendos that unfold during jams. Thus it is evident that a great deal more musical data is excluded than included; but this is for reasons of simplicity, elegance, and efficacy as well as sheer information management. To the extent that the image of Figure 1 is successful in its own right, I see these exclusions as one of its nicer aspects.

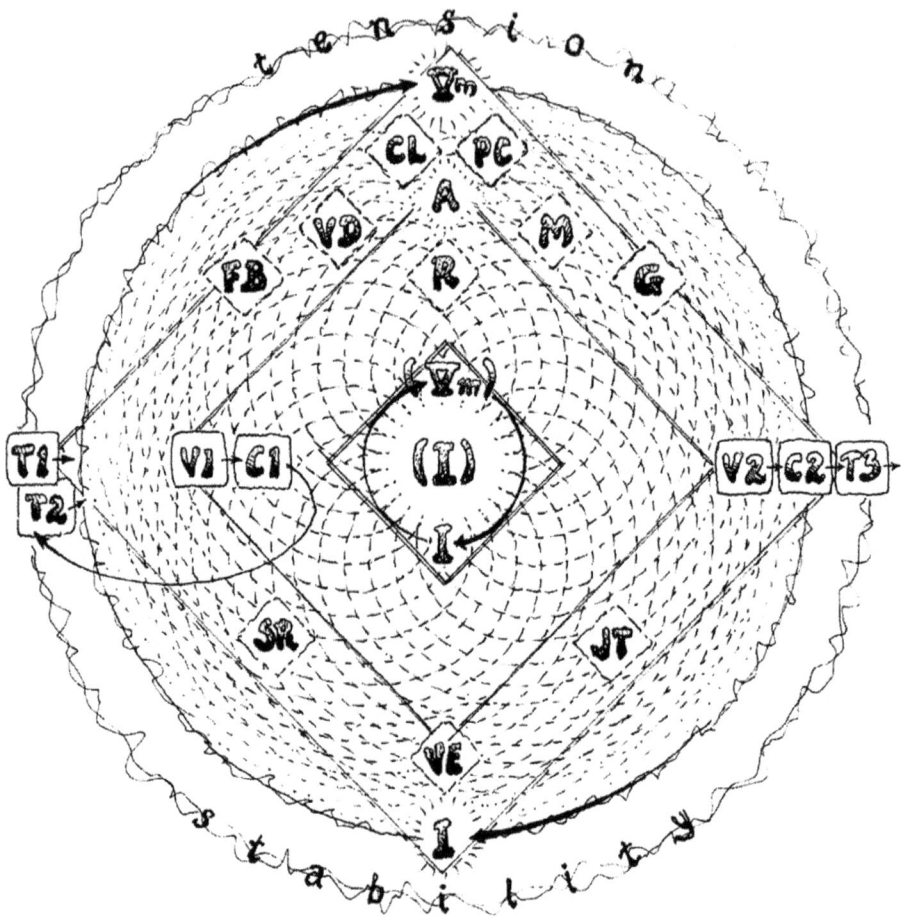

Figure 1. A mandala image for early "Dark Star."

Components of the Mandala

At the center of Figure 1 is the primal point of tonal reference, namely, the tonic A-major chord in the key of A, which (following traditional music-analytical symbology) is labeled as I ("one" in Roman numeral form). This essential home chord is placed in parentheses, however, because its status as tonal ground is challenged by the song's very structure, both in the sung verses, which lead not to I but to Vm ("five minor," meaning the chord of E minor, located on the fifth degree in the key of A), and in the improvisations, which frequently leave the I chord in abeyance; even the elaborately composed ending of the song leads definitively away from I.[20] The tonal ground of the song thus incorporates an inherently ambiguous and ephemeral element, suggestive of both identity and nonidentity. Borrowing Buddhist terminology, one could say that this ephemerality, more than a straightforward tonic anchor, is key to the "absolute power" or "consciousness" that the musicians seek in their explorations. "Dark star," indeed, "crashes; ... shall we go, while we can?"

Immediately surrounding that center point and forming the core harmonic identity of the song is the chord cycle of I–Vm (A major–E minor), labeled as DSP (*Dark Star progression*). This progression, like other chord progressions in other rock songs, provides the basic, insistently repeated harmonic movement that, as rendered by the band, is instantly recognizable to fans as defining the musical ground upon which the song is built. DSP appears at crucial stability- and identity-defining moments in the song, including the beginning and ending of both jams and the beginning of both sung verses; and it is associated in these places with a calm, quiet stability of texture, atmosphere, and dynamics. DSP also outlines the melodic and tonal frame of the song, namely the mixolydian mode on A.[21] But alongside these grounding functionalities, DSP incorporates instability, partly for the same reasons the I chord does. It cedes to Vm during the sung verses; it is challenged by other chords and inflections during improvisatory explorations and even static, calm passages; and above all, it is itself ambiguous, thanks to the changeable contrapuntal and rhythmic voicings of its Vm chord, which can evoke bVII (G major) as well as Vm (E minor). For that reason, Vm, like I at the core of the image, is placed in parentheses.[22] DSP is represented in Figure 1 as a radiant, dualistic cycle, with "(Vm)" situated above (moving upward, evoking relative uncertainty or instability) and I below (moving downward, evoking certainty and stability).

Along the horizontal axis or diameter of the image, the most basic, fixed episodes of the song are inscribed in their temporally unfolding order from left to right. We begin with T1 (*first instrumental tag*), an introductory bit of melody that signals the beginning of the song. Sometimes this tag begins in silence (at the beginning of a set, for example); sometimes it evolves out of the flow of preceding improvisation. In either instance, it represents a liminal opening, or "doorway," to the "Dark Star" universe. After an initial jam that may last for up to several minutes, there ensues V1 and C1 (*first sung verse, first chorus*); these will vary from performance to performance in subtle ways, but their basic musical structure and arrangement does not change. At the close of C1, a distinct pause on Vm leads to a modified reprise of T1, here labeled as T2 (*second instrumental tag*), signaling a re-beginning of the song[23]; an elliptical arrow marks this return to the liminal left. Just as T1 was followed by an initial jam, T2 leads to a second jam, which is always longer than the first, but also ultimately cedes to sung verses (V2 and C2).[24] These in turn lead directly and inevitably to T3 (*third instrumental tag*), which takes us decisively out of the song, slowing and quieting it down to near silence, evaporating its textures, and erasing its mixolydian-A tonality like a composed fadeout, usually followed without pause by another song's beginning. C2 and T3, bound together, are musically distinct from C1 and T1/T2, but share their tinge of quiet classical calculation and increase dramatically their suggestion of baroque-sounding harmony and counterpoint.

Composed, fixed episodes, in addition to providing core elements (lyrics, sung melody and accompaniment), thus demarcate and anchor the horizontal boundaries of "Dark Star": its inception (T1), its "rebirth" after the thudding stop of C1 (T2); and its "demise" (the passage of C2 through T3). These boundaries mark the threshold around which the DSP, with its anchor of I, either does (inside) or does not (outside) apply to the musical sound; where the song either *is* (inside) or *is not* (outside). Given the importance of limit-exploration for the Dead, and in this song in particular, that threshold is itself a radiant and intensely signifying place, and these tags have a special meaning for Dead fans. Significantly, both ends of the song are quiet, especially the ending, which is sometimes near inaudible. Also significant, though in a more mysterious way, is the fact that the band often fluffs T3 during this era. Some performances (such as the one included on *Live/Dead*) seem to exemplify what the ending was supposed to sound like in terms of specific notes clearly played; many do not. It is as if the idea and mood of the ending were more meaningful than its detailed actualization, which (exquisitely?) tiptoes, wheezes, or stumbles in near-silence following the exertions and crescendos of an increasingly extended and unpredictable jam.

The open spaces of the image falling between, above, and below the episodes of the horizontal axis are not empty; on the contrary, they represent the arena of the two instrumental jams. Being essentially inchoate, defining the changeable circle of the song's musical and expressive limits (above and below T1 and T3) as well as the stable harmonic core of its DSP — providing the grand "air" and environment, as it were, within which the relatively brief, directed sung verses breathe — these jams follow no rigorous sequential unfolding and are given no labels or fixed trajectory within the mandala. Rather, they explore among a number of recognizable, recurring ideas and episodes, each having its own musical and expressive meaning, and each represented symbolically around the vertical axis of the image. The mandala sorts these events according to two opposable hemispheres: those falling beneath the central core represent agents of tonal stability or anchoring, while those rising above represent agents of tonal tension or questioning. It should be noted that in order to account for the large amount of musical material shared by the two jams; to conceive them as constituting, in combination, the unified projection of a larger musical space; and to preserve the overarching, incurving circularity of the mandalic song as a whole, no attempt is made in it to distinguish between the two jams, even though they do represent two distinct stages in the unfolding of the song. The first jam is always shorter, and preparatory in some sense, for the grander, more extended meditations of the second; and it mostly avoids the full statement of episodic constructs that lends dramatic structure and meaning to the second jam. In Figure 1, as in Table 1, it is the second jams that provide most of the distinctive, recurring episodes.

Within the lower hemisphere are placed the stabilizing episodes of SR (*starting riff*), VE (*verse episode*), and JT (*Jerry's theme*), all of which are present on the earliest currently circulating concert recording of January 17, 1968. SR is the bit of melody Jerry uses to launch most second-jam solos; it occurs at a point of maximal solidity and calm in the DSP, and goes all the way back to the very first known, studio recordings of the song in 1967 (nos. 1–3), in which no jamming occurs. Unlike the second-jam solos, Jerry's first-jam solos tend not to begin with SR although, in earlier performances, they do evoke it fleetingly. JT is a distinctive, memorable riff that Jerry almost always plays toward the end of both the first and second instrumental jams; its tonal, rhythmic, and melodic centeredness and clarity help to re-center and stabilize DSP, preparing the singing of the verses. VE is an instrumental evocation of the sung verse that occurs almost always "in the middle" of the second jam, and never in the first jam. This episode incorporates the song's first melodic line (e.g., "Dark star crashes, pouring its light into ashes"), played by Jerry on lead guitar. It then continues into a free improvisation over the harmonic phrasing of the sung verse, which shifts from DSP to Vm. This passage is suggestive of tension and exploration; but, contrary to the sung verses, it concludes with a return in energizing or even triumphant fashion directly to DSP, thereby surmounting (if temporarily) any instability. Being based on the melody and harmonies of the sung verse, VE represents a major point of arrival and anchoredness within the jam; but for the same reason, its length (in beats and measures) is also strictly defined. As the jams get progressively longer, VE takes up progressively less of their time and creative energy, eventually beginning to drop out entirely, as seen in performances of April 1969.

By contrast with the "stabilizing" SR, VE, and JT ideas of the lower hemisphere, which are ultimately governed by the tonal anchors of I and DSP, other ideas explore tension or instability, and are accordingly placed in the upper hemisphere, ultimately governed by the "challenge" of Vm as an exploratory tonal space. These ideas develop and multiply over time, as the jams get longer and more involved. In the early phase of "Dark Star" that is presently under discussion, they include—in order of chronological appearance in the jams—A (*high-A arrivals*), PC (*post-climax*) and CL (*climax*), all first appearing in early 1968; M (*modal shift*), R (*arpeggio riff*), and VD (*volume dial*), first appearing in August 1968; and G (*growling*) and FB (*feedback*), first appearing as distinct sound-objectives in early 1969. With the exception of the relatively frequent A, these "tension" episodes are most frequently confined to the longer and more exploratory second jam; they may coexist or overlap in various ways.

R (*arpeggio riff*) provides a major way station in second jams as a point of arrival but, at the same time, functions as a goad to unsettling exploration;

it is the opposite, in this sense, of VE, which it most often follows. In R, Jerry insistently repeats a specific broken-chord pattern based on the chord of Vm; like his other, more variable insistent riffs, this arpeggio invites and even demands intensification, and therefore exploratory "questioning," from the other players. This episode can go on for two minutes, has no defined ending, and frequently includes a heightened sub-episode in which Jerry plays the same arpeggio transposed one octave above. Another episode that often pops up nearby is M (*modal shift*), in which one or more players (most frequently Bob, but sometimes Jerry or Phil; often they do not "agree" on a strategy) make a modal shift, from the mixolydian (i.e., a kind of major scale) usually to the aeolian or dorian (i.e., types of minor scale).[25] Such changing of modes provides a stark and trenchant, but clearly "tonal," means of signifying departure from I (major) and from DSP; since this episode is never developed in a structured way, it also signifies entry onto uncharted and unpredictable musical terrain.

In VD (*volume dial*) episodes, Jerry turns his guitar's volume dial up and down while playing, to create a swelling effect without crisp attacks, sounding like a bowed violin or cello; though not introducing any harmonic tension *per se*, this technique introduces a kind of timbral tension and functions as another exploratory signpost, eliciting textural experimentation from the band. In G (*growling*) episodes, Jerry creates a sandpapery, curdling sound like a growl through simple electronic and picking effects—the opposite effect of the smooth volume-dial episode, but similar in goading the band to "get strange" by means of a timbral shift. FB (*feedback*) may characterize a jamming episode, but is properly an electronic effect that emerges in certain timbrally exploratory situations; originally a byproduct of high amplification, it was eventually recognized by Jerry as a virtual "instrument" in its own right, and exploited for that purpose.[26]

These five episodes, R, M, VD, and (ultimately) G and FB, often occur in proximity to one another during second jams, but their nature and placement is somewhat unpredictable. By contrast, two other "tense" moments follow a more predictable sense of progression through peaks and resolutions; these are both based on A (*high A notes*, located an octave and a sixth above middle C, that Jerry frequently reaches in his improvisations), namely, CL (*climax riff*) and PC (*post-climax riff*). "A" is not an episode *per se*, but rather a point of articulation, a crux of tension or affirmation that occurs in many places during Jerry's solos; for that reason, it is not represented among the episode columns of Table 1. Flexibility of use notwithstanding, high A is important as demarcating both minor and major climax points, and orienting the highest plateaus or peak areas of Jerry's improvisations. Two proper episodes, CL and PC, are based on this climactic A, extrapolated into a full-fledged area for limit exploration. Normally occurring near the end of the longer, second jam, these episodes mark an ultimate confrontation and resolution of expressive tensions in early performances of the song, posing the drama of *Vm vs. I* in its most epic, *fortissimo* terms, and ultimately resolving that drama in favor of DSP and I after what usually amounts to an insistent, questioning crescendo on Vm.[27] Both CL and PC are based on distinct, insistent riffs played by Jerry.

Taking account of all the elements described above, we incorporate into our mandala the most commonly recurring and distinctively salient episodes found in performances of "Dark Star" up through February 1969. Progression through the song triggers the play of forces, ranging between stability and instability, questioning and affirmation, that defines its improvisations. Figure 1 places the various elements on a ground of interlocking spirals, radiating from the core of the image, which evoke the open-ended and integrative nature of the jams in relation to these episodes, as well as their ultimate origin in I and in DSP. Quadrilateral lines evoke broader connections and a sense of meaningful symmetry among the structural elements. Near the top and bottom of the image are placed Vm and I, respectively, symbolizing DSP writ large, that is to say, the overarching, dialectic power of its constituent harmonies as agents, and limits, of stability (I) and tension or instability (Vm) in the song as a whole.[28] The hovering fringes of the border evoke the threshold of questing tensions that define the musical limits of the early "Dark Star." The resulting image is in effect the opposite of Bill Walker's "Anthem" painting, incorporating abstract, alphanumerical, Western symbols rather than evocative, figurative, Eastern ones and emphasizing the literal musical field of the song over its transcendent, spirit-world expressive resonances.

The Greater Mandala

Having projected one essential mandala for the earliest years of "Dark Star," I shall not resist the temptation of a second one in recognition of the remarkable, and even more iconic, development of the song after that time. Although the *Live/Dead* recording of February 27, 1969, is the most famous and widely known of all "Dark Star" performances, it is conservative by comparison with many later ones, which are especially beloved of Dead fans for that very reason and which, retrospectively, color appreciation of the earlier ones as well.

Later "Dark Star" performances would suggest their own mandalas, in keeping with the evolving musical and expressive identity of the song. With that in mind, the image shown in Figure 2 aims to reflect a different, newly emergent identity as heard in performances through April 1969. This mandala could be labeled as "greater," inasmuch as it enfolds and exceeds the "lesser" mandala represented in Figure 1.[29] In it, the previous limits of the song, defined by the ultimate centripetal force of I and DSP, are extended through the incorporation of centrifugal episodes that seem tonally or thematically free of that force. The cosmic circle-limit of the song is no longer defined by tension and stability within one tonality, but has extended to include a more extreme exploration of cosmos and chaos, embracing *in potentia* all musical possibilities. Although it is not intended to reflect the still more radical "Dark Star" performances of later years, this image more closely reflects the comments of band members cited earlier in this essay, regarding the "far out," "alternative-universe" scope of the jamming.

Within the "tension" hemisphere of the lesser mandala, we noted that A, CL, and PC had been defined by their relationship to DSP and would always ultimately direct the music back to it. By contrast, R, M, VD, FB, and G, often occurring in tandem, had represented the development of a timbral and textural, and not just properly tonal, exploration. This second path is the one that historically led more decisively away from DSP, as shown in Figure 2 by the reappearance of these episodes outside of the "tension-stability" circle. The limit of that movement toward "instability" would prove to be SP (*space*), finally reached on April 4, 1969, as an actual sonic dwelling place within "Dark Star."[30] Providing an ultimate answer to the "call of the weird," SP leaves behind tonality, rhythmic meter, and familiar texture entirely, exploring the outer fringes of a musical "chaos" that is no longer immediately identifiable with the initial, core elements of "Dark Star" or indeed any other popular music, save the most experimental (even if it was the elemental, hovering ambiguity of DSP, together with the song's lyrics, that ultimately prompted the band to explore SP within this song).

Within the "stability" hemisphere, SR, VE, and JT had always been defined by their relationship to DSP and always led (back) to it. But other episodes, especially after February 1969, suggest a more radical form of tonal "anchoring" which, like SP, simply turns its back on DSP. Thus, NP (*new progression*) denotes any passage where one or more players (usually Bob or Phil) settle on a new and different chord progression, evoking a tonal centeredness and a musical grounding or identity, but one that just doesn't happen to belong to what one would have thought of as "Dark Star." A more radical version of this idea is NS (*new song*), where the strength, decisiveness, and familiarity of a new and different chord progression suggest the incursion of a new song, creating an even more potent threat to (or opening up of) what one would have thought was the integrity of "Dark Star." In the early years pertaining to the "lesser mandala," these regions were rarely entered with decisiveness, although the inherent blurriness of DSP and the restless flair of Bob and Phil, in particular, resulted in the occasional momentary adumbration of another chord progression. It was not until April 1969 that the distinctive and highly recognizable instrumental jam known as "Main Ten" imposed itself, complete with coordinated multiinstrument riffs and 3+3+4 rhythmic meter, as a bona fide episodic "song" digression contained within "Dark Star" jams. Later on, other songs, complete with singing and lyrics, would come to be interpolated into (or tacked

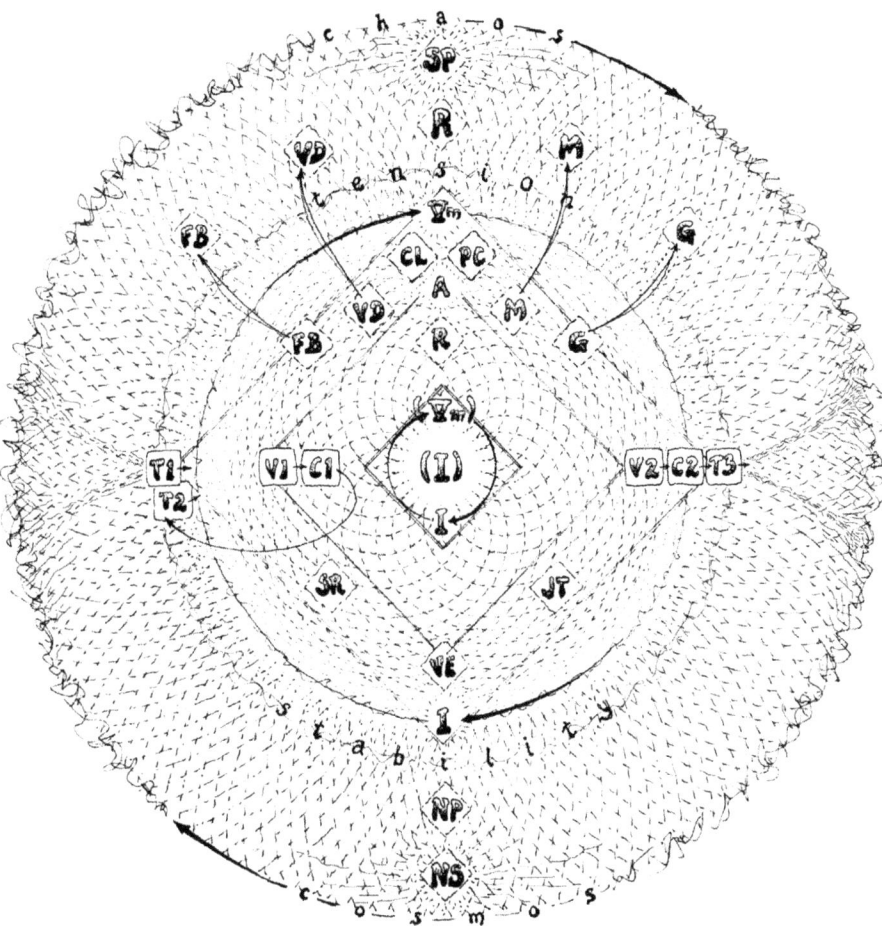

Figure 2. Greater "Dark Star" mandala image.

onto) increasingly open-ended performances of "Dark Star," to the point of provoking fan controversies over what should properly constitute its identity-limit.

These, then, are the extremes of the "Dark Star" ontology by April 1969, namely, the rhetorical chaos of SP and counter-cosmos of NS, both balanced by increasingly sustained, jazz-inspired improvisations on DSP and Vm. To the identity-delimiting, horizontal "palace gates" of T1 and T3, then, are added two new, vertical gates of an identity-transgressive kind. It is from this perspective that Lesh could visualize "Dark Star" as "expanding beyond any concept of 'song,'" or that Tom Constanten, who performed with the Dead during the key year of 1969, could speak of it as a continuum, reaching beyond any simple concept of identity or even time: "'Dark Star' is going on all the time.

It is going on right now. You don't begin it so much as enter it. You don't end it so much as leave it."[31]

Conclusion

The images of Figures 1 and 2 are primarily music-analytical, aiming, as it were, at a "prosaics" of episodic schematization.[32] But they attempt something of a poetics too, evoking ways in which those musical events orient themselves within the song's universe of sounding meaning to create the transformative field that has so strongly affected band members and listeners alike. These images are doubly metaphorical; not only do they abstract and symbolize musical events, but they present those events in a format that arises from my own intuitive, empirical, and intimate experiences as a music analyst and fan of the Dead's music since 1969. Those experiences have unfolded independently of the immediate creative work and community that brought the music into being, and independently also of any profound engagement with Eastern religion. Most importantly, the images were created many years after the performances in question, on the basis of recordings, whereas it is the original performances themselves, as lived, evanescent experiences, which surely constitute the true mandala of the song — a sound-mandala existing in and through the act of its creation, analogous to the *It* Jerry was referring to when he said of the Acid Tests that *it was a mandala*. Any image or other artifact crafted to evoke that experience will by nature be derivative and, to a greater or lesser degree, alienated from it; those qualities must ultimately be understood to pertain to the recordings, too.[33] Figures 1 and 2 suggest mandalic agency, therefore, only in the most generous (or generic) sense, inasmuch as they do convey something of the transformative field in performances of "Dark Star," touched as they were by the psychedelic geography of the spiritual East.

A comment by David Gans, long-time performing musician, writer on the Dead, and host of the Grateful Dead Hour, brings home the limitations of such images in relation to "Dark Star." Like the Dead's music, a mandala is finally what you make of it.[34]

> I found the mandala presentation interesting but ultimately unsatisfying. I don't know if it's possible to map the universe of Dark Star, and although I wanted your chart to be a shining beacon, I think it was of necessity the barest of outline maps where what we need is a 4- (or more-) dimensional relief map.

Table 2: Locating Events in Specific Recordings

Musical Event	August 23, 1968	February 27, 1969	April 15, 1969
t1 opening tag	0:04	1:20	0:00
DSP* Dark Star progression	0:09	1:24	0:04

Musical Event		August 23, 1968	February 27, 1969	April 15, 1969
sr	starting riff	(0:27)	—	—
a*	high A	2:18	2:15	2:26
jt	Jerry's theme	2:28, 3:43	5:01	0:47, 6:16
V1	first sung verse	5:40	6:04	6:53
C1	first sung chorus	6:13	6:39	7:28
t2	modified opening tag	6:36	7:05	7:51
DSP*	Dark Star progression	6:40	7:10	7:57
sr	starting riff	—	—	—
a*	the high note A	9:44	8:08	9:08
r	arpeggio riff	(7:32)	11:19	12:45
g	growling episode	—	13:10	15:06
m	modal shift	—	13:28	—
ve	verse episode	8:09	18:18	—
vd	volume dial	11:15	—	14:31
sp	space	—	—	(c. 8:55), c. 16:00
ns	new song	—	—	17:18
cl	climax riff	12:32	19:29	12:21
pc	post-climax riff	12:53	20:39	—
jt	Jerry's theme	13:29	20:48	18:26
V2	second sung verse	14:02	21:26	18:52
C2	second sung chorus	14:35	22:02	19:25
t3	closing tag	15:01	22:31	19:53

Note: The first and third dates above (August 23, 1968, April 15, 1969) can, at the present time, be streamed from the Grateful Dead collection at http://www.archive.org; the second (February 27, 1969) was published on the Dead's 1969 album, *Live/Dead*. For ease of use, the timings given above take the beginning of the audio track as 0:00 (though that beginning may occur during the jam, or silence, that precedes the beginning of the song). Only the beginning, or early salient moment, of the appearance of any event is indicated. For those marked with asterisks, the timings indicated are merely illustrative, since these episodes appear many times during a performance. None of these performances includes every episode; SR happens to be missing from all three.

Notes

1. Cf. Boone, "Mandalas and the Dead," in the present volume.
2. The song has been frequently discussed in print, e.g., in addition to the citations mentioned below, Shenk and Silberman, 1994, 50–52; Wybenga, 1997, 61–65.
3. For closer analysis of "Dark Star," see Boone, 1997 (one recorded performance) and 2007 (all early recorded performances); also Skaggs, and the timelines in Scott, 1997, 588.
4. Lesh, 2005, 101–2. Hunter and Garcia in Bowman, 1995, 4.
5. Shenk and Silberman, 1994, 51. See also the many accounts related in Scott, 1997, and Getz and Dwork, 1998–2000.

6. "Mandalas and the Dead," xx.

7. Lesh, 2005, 141.

8. Lesh, quoted in Bowman, 1995, 4. As Hunter put it, "What the Dead do on 'Dark Star' is what the Dead are, that's what they do best. What defines the Dead is 'Dark Star,'" Bowman, 1995, 2.

9. Lydon, 1969, repr. in George-Warren, 1995, 61; Bowman, 1995, 4.

10. Wenner and Reich, 1972, repr. in George-Warren 1995, 95; Bowman, 1995, 6.

11. E.g., Trist and Dodd, 2005, 49–51; Dodd, 2003; Boone, 1997, 83–85. The lyrics were written simultaneously and in concert with the elaboration of the music. As Hunter recalls it: "I actually heard the Grateful Dead playing it and those were the words it seemed to be saying. I'm going to take a big stretch here and say the music seemed to be saying that and I transcribed it." See Bowman, 1995, 3; Jackson, 1999, 135.

12. T. S. Eliot, from "The Love Song of J. Alfred Prufrock," which strikes, of course, a less romantic pose: "Let us go then, you and I, / When the evening is spread out against the sky / Like a patient etherized upon a table." Hunter comments: "If there had been no 'The Love Song of J. Alfred Prufrock,' then I don't think 'Dark Star' would have fallen the way it did. Beyond that, it's just my kind of imagery, the sorts of things I see, the sort of things that occur to me to say. I can't find any other source imagery for the song," Bowman, 1995, 3. Eliot's verses in turn recall Verlaine's classic "La Bonne chanson": "N'est-ce pas? Nous irons, gais et lents, dans la voie / Modeste que nous montre en souriant l'Espoir." (Is it not so? You and I shall go, gay and slow, down the path / So modest, that is shown to us, smiling, by Hope.)

13. As Hunter wrote regarding the band name "Grateful Dead": "I know that my own input into the scene, my words, were heavily conditioned by that powerful name. It called sheaves of spirits down on us all. It expressed a deep and mystic hope about the nature of eternity," Trist and Dodd, 2005, xiv.

14. Cf. "Mandalas and the Dead" in this volume.

15. Garcia, quoted in Lydon, 1969, Wenner and Reich, 1972, and Henke, 1991, repr. in George-Warren, 1995, 64, 95, and 182, resp. Lesh, quoted in Gans, 2002, 110 and 166.

16. Bowman, 1995, 7.

17. Recordings of different "Dark Star" performances are currently available from various online sources, of which the most conveniently comprehensive include http://www.archive.org and http://www.dead.net.

18. For lists of performances of "Dark Star," see Scott, 1997, and Powell, 2003.

19. These recordings are currently available either in streaming format online at: http://www.archive.org (08/23/68; 04/15/69), or commercially (02/27/69) released on the Grateful Dead album *Live/Dead*).

20. For close analysis of this and other elements of the song structure see Boone, 1997, which differs in some details from the present analysis.

21. "Mixolydian," meaning in effect a major scale or key, but with a lowered seventh degree (i.e., in the key of A, the note G natural instead of G sharp).

22. In Boone, 1997, "(Vm)" was sometimes labeled as "not-I," and Arabic rather than Roman numerals were used for chord names, in order to give a differently open-ended cast to the analysis.

23. T2 differs musically from T1 in having a line of higher guitar counterpoint added to T1's simple melody.

24. The central core of the mandala (involving "(I)" and the DSP), signifying the radiant center of the music, is not intended to represent one point along this temporal axis, but rather the core that informs the whole interior of the mandala space, vertically and horizontally, in variable ways.

25. Modal shifts (while remaining in the home key of A) must be distinguished from the movement, far more common, toward insistence on the Vm chord (E minor)

during improvisations, which entails no change of mode since the minor-V chord occurs naturally in the mixolydian mode. A shift from the home mode of mixolydian to a minor mode, with lowered third degree, represents a different kind of "threat" to the home key and its attendant DSP. Other modes, including the ionian and phrygian, are also alluded to in the course of improvisations, but with greater rarity and brevity than the minor.

26. Jerry describes the musical value of feedback, as well as "volume dial" and other sound effects, in Gleason, 1969, 29–30. Before January 1969, feedback occurs sporadically in "Dark Star," but not so clearly as a distinct episodic sound objective. Of course, feedback had already been long established in Dead jams by 1969, but as Mountain Girl has said of "Dark Star," "It was an excuse for the band to get really weird with a lot of feedback and harmonics and stuff. They'd usually only play 'Dark Star' if they were pretty high. It was frequently the peak of the concert when they played 'Dark Star.' It could be a wonderfully harmonious experience or it could sound like a subway collision at high speed," Troy, 1991, 91.

27. This observation supersedes the observation made in Boone, 1997, 198, on the basis of fewer recordings, that the grand return to DSP during CL appeared unusual or even unique to the *Live/Dead* performance. It remains true, however, that different performances treat this episode in widely varying ways; some rely strongly on DSP while others avoid it completely, allowing it to re-emerge only afterward.

28. The Vm symbol at the top of the image is not parenthesized because, unlike the ambiguous voicing of "(Vm)" within the DSP (evoking bVII as well as Vm), the most common voicing of exploratory harmonies during the jams unambiguously suggests Vm as the focal "non-I" goal, having the unequivocal note E as a persistent element. By contrast, bVII, emphasizing the root note G and pointedly lacking E, is not a significant harmonic destination or vehicle during jams.

29. For closer analysis, see Boone, 2007, and, more broadly, Powell, 2003, where the two approaches mentioned here are labeled as the "First" (up to 1969) and "Second" (1969–72) of four evolutionary stages in the history of "Dark Star."

30. As shown in Figure 1, SP is adumbrated, though not quite achieved, in the performance of Nov. 22, 1968, during a concert that was considered exceptionally good, at least by some; Lesh, 2005, 138. The definition of "space" will depend on one's criteria, and the band's approach to it is variable. In this context, I take it to involve the unequivocal abandonment of tonal anchoring in melody and harmony, as well as marked textural exploration. Of course, SP had arisen earlier in other Dead songs and jams, and came to represent a major episode in its own right within Dead shows, independent of any particular song; but it also had a special relationship to "Dark Star."

31. Lesh, 2005, 101; Greenfield, 1996, 126.

32. Regarding the term "prosaics," see Morson and Emerson, 1990, 15.

33. As Weir has famously stated, "The tapes always lie," Gans, 2002, 182. That is not to deny or diminish the attainment of mandalic experiences by listeners purely on the basis of recordings, but the distinction remains essential.

34. Personal e-mail communication, March 12, 2009, referring to Boone, 2007, in which more primitive versions of Figures 2 and 4 were presented. It seems likely that Gans has the full history of "Dark Star" in mind, not simply the early years.

Bibliography

Boone, Graeme M. "'Dark Star' Revisited." Paper presented at "Unbroken Chain: The Grateful Dead in Music, Culture, and Memory, A Public Symposium, November 16–18, 2007." Amherst, MA, November 16, 2007.

———. "Tonal and Expressive Ambiguity in 'Dark Star.'" In *Understanding Rock: Essays in Musical Analysis*, John Covach and Graeme M. Boone, eds. New York: Oxford University Press, 1997, 171–210.

Bowman, Rob. Liner notes to John Oswald and the Grateful Dead. *Grayfolded* [CD]. Toronto: Swell/Artifact, 1995.

Dodd, David. "The Annotated 'Dark Star.'" Posted online at: http://arts.ucsc.edu/gdead/AGDL/darkstar.html (rev. 2003).

———, and Alan Trist, eds. *The Complete Annotated Grateful Dead Lyrics: The Collected Lyrics of Robert Hunter and John Barlow, Lyrics to All Original Songs, with Selected Traditional and Cover Songs*. New York: Free Press, 2005.

Eliot, T. S. "The Love Song of J. Alfred Prufrock." In *Prufrock and Other Observations*. London: The Egoist, 1917.

Gans, David, with the Grateful Dead. *Conversations with the Dead: The Grateful Dead Interview Book*. 2d ed. New York: Da Capo, 2002. [1st ed. publ. 1991.]

George-Warren, Holly, et al., eds. *Garcia: By the Editors of Rolling Stone*. Boston: Little, Brown, 1995.

Getz, Michael M., and John R. Dwork. *The Deadhead's Taping Compendium: An In-Depth Guide to the Music of the Grateful Dead on Tape*. 3 vols. New York: Holt, 1998–2000.

Gleason, Ralph. "Jerry Garcia, the Guru." In *The Jefferson Airplane and the San Francisco Sound*. New York: Ballantine, 1969. Rpt. in *The Grateful Dead Reader*, Dodd and Spaulding, eds. (New York: Oxford University Press, 2000), 20–38. [Interview dates from 1967.]

Grateful Dead. "Dark Star" b/w "Born Cross Eyed." Warner Bros., 1967.

———. *Live/Dead* [LP]. Burbank: Warner Bros.–Seven Arts, 1970.

Greenfield, Robert. *Dark Star: An Oral History of Jerry Garcia*. New York: Morrow, 1996.

Henke, James. "Alive and Well: The Rolling Stone Interview with Jerry Garcia." In *Rolling Stone*, October 31, 1991. Rpt. in *Garcia*, George-Warren, ed., 180–189.

Lesh, Phil. *Searching for the Sound: My Life with the Grateful Dead*. New York: Little, Brown, 2005.

Lydon, Michael. "Dead Zone." *Rolling Stone*, August 23, 1969. Rpt. in *Garcia*, George-Warren, ed., 55–72.

Morson, Gary Saul, and Caryl Emerson. *Mikhail Bakhtin: Creation of a Prosaics*. Palo Alto: Stanford University Press, 1990.

Powell, Jim, et al. "Dark Star." In *The Deadlists Project*. Posted online at: http://www.deadlists.com/dlsite/dark_star.txt (dated 2003).

Scott, John W., Mike Dolgushkin, and Stu Nixon. *Deadbase X: The Complete Guide to Grateful Dead Song Lists*. Cornish, NH: Deadbase, 1997. [Updated website posted at: http://www.deadbase.com.]

Shenk, David, and Steve Silberman. *Skeleton Key: A Dictionary for Deadheads*. New York: Main Street Books, 1994.

Skaggs, Steven. "'Dark Star' as an Example of Transcendental Aesthetics." [n.d.] Posted online at: http://arts.ucsc.edu/GDead/AGDL/ds.html.

Verlaine, Paul. *La Bonne Chanson*. Paris: Lemerre, 1870.

Wenner, Jann S., and Charles Reich. "The First: The Rolling Stone Interview with Jerry Garcia and Mountain Girl." *Rolling Stone*, January 20, 1972. Rpt. in *Garcia*, George-Warren, ed., 78–95.

Wybenga, Eric. *Dead to the Core: An Almanack of the Grateful Dead*. New York: Delta Trade, 1997.

"Where All the Pages Are My Days": Metacantric Moments in Deadhead Lyrical Experience

Revell Carr

The lyrics of Robert Hunter, John Perry Barlow and Bobby Peterson constitute a fertile field, loaded with meaningful metaphor and allusion. Drawing from deep wells of American folklore and mythology, as well as from the writings of a wide range of philosophers, prophets and poets, the content of the Dead's lyrics deserve as much critical analysis as any facet of the Grateful Dead culture complex. There have been a number of significant books and essays that deal with the literary content of the Grateful Dead's songs, most notably David Dodd's comprehensive tome, *The Complete Annotated Grateful Dead Lyrics* (2005). The analysis of lyrics in the context of Deadhead culture, however, requires something other than a straight literary analysis of poetics or prosody. From the perspective of a folklorist, a linguist or an ethnomusicologist, the lyrics of the Grateful Dead need to be analyzed not just for their antecedents in American and British traditional music and poetry, but specifically for their meaning and function in the individual and collective lives of Deadheads.

The Grateful Dead's lyrics were actively appropriated by Deadheads, who imbued fragments of lyrics with significance that built, to adapt the terminology of Arjun Appadurai, a unique *mediascape*, an extensive complex of images, narratives, sounds, and meanings, which Deadheads inhabited as it was created (1996, 35). The popular image of the Grateful Dead is often one of a stereotypical hippie community, rejecting the mainstream media in favor of a do-it-yourself ethos. Anyone who looks carefully at the Grateful Dead, however, will see that they have been pioneers in the use of electronic media since their earliest experiments at the Acid Tests, and that they built for themselves an independent media empire unrivalled in American vernacular music. Not only have the Dead mastered the art of songwriting and recording, both live and in the studio, they have also developed substantial video, print, and digital media sold through a merchandising arm that was, until very recently, entirely in-house.

Appadurai says that "Mediascapes, whether produced by private or state interests, tend to be image-centered, narrative-based accounts of strips of reality, and what they offer to those who experience and transform them is a series of elements (such as characters, plots, and textual forms) out of which scripts can be formed of imagined lives, their own as well as those of others living in other places" (1996, 35). The success of the Grateful Dead as an enterprise was largely due to their audience's power to transform the band's mediated elements and to take the "strips of reality," in the form of song lyrics, iconography, band mythology, etc., and extrapolate them into a world of "imagined lives." In ways more literal than literary the lyrics of Grateful Dead songs came to life in the reality that was shared by participants in the Deadheads' society. This chapter will examine several ways that Dead lyrics took on significance beyond the boundaries of the songs themselves.

I begin by discussing the use of lyric allusions in Deadhead argot or slang — cases in which the surreal landscape of the song intersected with the constructed reality of the Deadhead world. Then I examine the aphoristic qualities of the Dead's lyrics, considering how fragments of songs, separated from their original context, became the building blocks of the Deadhead world view, communicated through such Deadhead generated art as posters, bumper stickers and T-shirts. Next, I look at Deadhead responses to certain lyrics, during the course of a musical performance, when specific phrases became predictable moments of audience/band interaction. And, finally, I will illustrate ways that the Dead's lyricists used lyrics to create what I term "metacantric moments," which drew the audience closer to the band, encouraging Deadheads to feel connected with what was happening on stage, and in the personal, emotional lives of the band members.

The River Keeps a Talking — Lyrics in Deadhead Argot

Probably the most obvious way that the Grateful Dead's lyrics shaped the world of Deadheads is their use in Deadhead argot or slang. Several Dead scholars, particularly Natalie Dollar (1999, 2007) and Jeremy Ritzer (2000), have looked at ways that Deadheads use language gleaned from the songs of the Grateful Dead and related musicians to create and reinforce their sense of community identity. Dollar's work examines the cultural speech codes of Deadheads, which are built upon fragments of lyrics and references to band mythology or imagery, and how fluency in those codes was an important part of membership in the Deadhead community (2007, 183). She cites as an example the Deadhead expression that one who "gets it" is said to be "on the bus," the most definitive statement of membership in Deadhead argot (Shenk and Silberman, 1994, 210). This expression refers to the band's involvement with Ken Kesey's Merry Pranksters and their famous bus, as well as to the Dead's musical tribute to that bus, "The Other One," with its oft quoted line, "The bus came by and I got on/ that's when it all began" (Hunter, 1990). This is just one example of a Deadhead speech situation that brings together the history, the mythology, the narrative of the band and the meaningful reality of Deadhead communities (Dollar, 2007, 178).

Another example is the term, "Shakedown Street," which was used to describe the Deadheads' parking lot marketplace (Shenk and Silberman, 1994, 215). The song "Shakedown Street" was released in 1978, and this usage of the term seems to have emerged in Deadhead argot sometime in the early '80s, at the time when the customs and lifeways that would define Deadhead culture as it is known today were being codified. Just as the Shakedown Street of the song takes on a different image in the mind of each listener, the real Shakedown Street took on a different appearance and character in every different city or venue. As Deadheads strolled down Shakedown Street, the lyrics of the song might inform their experience, reassuring them that all it takes is a little "poking around" to find the "heart of town" (Hunter, 1990).

Shakedown Street was a street of dreams that became real, where the cultural economy of Deadhead society was centered, with musicians, food stands, clothiers, jewelers, drug dealers, and ticket scalpers making a very real living. Deadheads needed a town center, a gathering place for the community, and so they created it and named it for a song in the Dead's oeuvre. This example is particularly potent because it has now extended beyond the specific domain of Deadheads and into the larger culture of jam bands in general. Today, over 13 years after the official disbanding of the Grateful Dead, Shakedown Streets can be found at festivals and concerts featuring any band from the jam band scene, or from the Dead's extended family. The majority of people at these concerts would not identify themselves as Deadheads, and yet they know the term and its implications.

In my own essay on Deadheads' supernatural narratives, published in *Perspectives on the Grateful Dead* (1999), I discussed a number of cases in which lyrics were employed to describe or categorize the "magic" that Deadheads experienced in the context of the show. The most common was the "miracle," a term derived from the classic Bob Weir number "I Need a Miracle." Whether it was a "miracle ticket," a miracle ride to the next show, or a miracle bag of weed, the Deadhead beliefs in the power of optimism and positive thinking made it possible to literally manifest the miracles they needed "every day" in the real world (Carr, 1999, 206–7).

Lyrics also played an important role in a common magical belief among

Deadheads that the Grateful Dead had the ability to influence the weather. As the song "Black Peter" asks, "Who can the weather command?" many Deadheads have said that a song with rain in the title or in the lyrics ("Looks Like Rain," "Cold Rain and Snow," "Mission in the Rain," "Samba in the Rain," etc.) could actually presage the coming of rain, while a song like "Here Comes Sunshine" could have the opposite effect, banishing rain and conjuring sun (Carr, 1999, 209). The most striking of these weather control narratives involved a 1980 concert in Portland, Oregon, where it was said that during a particularly hot version of "Fire on the Mountain," Mount Saint Helens spewed one of its huge plumes of ash, which was still falling on Portland when the audience came out of the show. Deadheads who tell this story rarely explicitly say that the Dead "caused" the mountain to erupt, but most agree that the intensity of the song and the eruption were somehow connected (Carr, 1999, 209–10). In all of these weather control narratives, it is specifically the lyrics or titles of songs, not the music, that serve as the perceived trigger for this effect.

Other uses of lyrics in Deadhead argot, many of which are documented in Shenk and Silberman's *Skeleton Key* (1994), include the use of "Hey Now!" from the song "Iko Iko" as a greeting (143), the term "Sugar Magnolia" from the song of the same name used to describe a particularly attractive Deadhead woman (274), and the term "Steal your face" from "He's Gone," which soon came to reference the Dead's most recognizable icon, also known as the "skull-with-lightning-bolt" (273). Coded speech is clearly central to membership and participation in Deadhead culture and it is significant that most, if not all, of these codes emerge from the bands' lyrics. The creation of these shared meanings has been a collaboration between a collective of artists and a community with shared affinity for that art. But this is just the beginning of the ways that lyrics informed and literally manifested in the reality of the Deadheads' world.

Speak with Wisdom Like a Child — Aphorisms

Much has been made about the ambiguities that Robert Hunter, Bobby Petersen and John Perry Barlow built into the lyrics they wrote for the Grateful Dead. Deadheads often cite the Dead's lyrics the way some people cite bible verses, or the works of Shakespeare, using their knowledge of the literature to find a quote appropriate to almost any situation or circumstance. This fact did not escape the attention of the Dead's lyricists themselves, who were acutely aware, particularly in the wake of the Manson murders and the Dead's own bad trip with the Hell's Angels at Altamont, that the band's mediascape could be received as a quasi-religion or cult, which could be taken to a dark place if they let it. Hunter knew that if there were to be a Deadhead "belief system" that the lyrics would be the source texts. But in the mid–1970s, lyricists Barlow and Hunter agreed that they would "never write anything that could be easily taken to form dogma" (Barlow, 2007). The result was a collection of lyrics that are both obscure and illuminating, that seem to provide guidance while never committing to a particular direction.

Hunter referred to this in an interview with Blair Jackson as his "notion of evocativeness rather than pat statements" to which Garcia added, "The lack of specificness. It was the power of the almost expressed, the resonant..." (1992, 209). This approach, they claimed, was inspired by the ambiguous metaphors and cryptic imagery of traditional British ballads, such as those found in the collection of Francis James Child. As Hunter remarked to Blair Jackson:

> Jerry favors a certain type of folk song. He loves the mournful death-connected ballad, the Child ballad stuff. This is a venerable source which has always spoken to him, and to me as well, which is one reason we got together writing songs—because of that haunting feel that certain traditional songs have [1992, 117–8].

In the anthology of his lyrics, *Box of Rain*, Hunter explained in more detail his intentions with regards to creating lyrics that could take on a life of their own in the mind of the listener.

> My inclination has been to forgo printing lyrics on the jackets of recordings and let the songs live out their lives in the listener's ear.... My versions of these songs are no more "the real ones" than those that may have spoken to some of you through the music darkly twenty years ago. I hope that seeing the intended words will provide you with an interesting, if not always convincing variant on the words some of you *actually* heard [Hunter, 1990, 2].

Writing this way is far more difficult than it might seem. All of the Dead's lyricists possessed the rare ability to articulate thoughts and images that could be ambiguous enough to allow for multiple interpretations, while remaining true to a fundamental consistency of tone and overall world view. The structure of these lyrics was rarely coherently narrative, but consisted largely of fragments of imagery and brief, thought-provoking aphorisms that echo the aphoristic writings of philosophers from Socrates to Confucius, Friedrich Nietzsche to Walter Benjamin, and Benjamin Franklin to Ralph Waldo Emerson. The Dead's lyricists used the form of the aphorism to sidestep the problems of linear narrative, choosing to embrace the fragmentary nature of human experience by focusing on the smallest configurations of knowledge, the dialectical images that Walter Benjamin termed "monads." These monads represented to Benjamin "a revolutionary chance in the fight for the oppressed past" (Benjamin, 1968, 262–263). While Hunter and Barlow may have been reluctant to lead the Dead's followers into revolution, their lyrics nevertheless served an emancipatory function for Deadheads, helping them to liberate themselves from the oppressive effects of modernity.

The aphorisms that emerged from the lyrics of Dead songs, based in folklore, philosophy and religion, are central to Deadheads' mediascape. They appear on T-shirts, posters and bumper stickers, inspire Deadhead art, and provide Deadheads with ambiguous truths, which can illuminate moments of darkness. Many times, when caught in a no-win situation, have Deadheads thought of the line from "The Wheel,"—"If the thunder don't get you then the lightning will!" Many times have Deadheads thought of an unkind person, "If you plant ice you're gonna harvest wind" ("Franklin's Tower"). The list goes on and on: "Once in a while you get shown the light in the strangest of places if you look at it right" ("Scarlet Begonias"); "One man gathers what another man spills" ("St. Stephen"); "Without love in the dream it will never come true" ("Help on the Way"); "Never give your love unto a foolish heart" ("Foolish Heart"); "Goes to show you don't ever know" ("Deal"). These fragments of songs did indeed take on a life of their own, acting as signposts, directing Deadheads along the road to becoming better Deadheads, better people, yet never supplying easy answers to a complex world.

The Music Plays the Band — Metacantrics and Audience Interaction

The spiritual aspects of the Dead show cannot be denied, and I would argue the Dead's canon has provided a *poesetic* holy text offering Deadheads guidance while never becoming dogmatic. Lyrics quickly became a means through which Deadheads could feel a communicative link with the band and one another. Just as a congregation in a Baptist church calls back to the preacher, during a Grateful Dead show there were moments when the entire audience would either join in on a specific lyric, or would respond with wild ovations to a specific line. In some cases this response differed depending on the venue. For example, a line from "Truckin'"—"New York's got the ways and means"—generally received a big response in the Northeast, but did not cause much of a stir in California. On the other hand, the ecstatic "California!" in the chorus of "Estimated Prophet" was greeted with the most enthusiasm when sung in the band's home state of California. But this kind of audience reaction was not limited to "shout-outs" to a favorite state or town, it was one of the ways that band and audience transcended the fourth wall of performance. Whether it was the audience telling the band, "Thank you for a real good time," during "Loose Lucy," or taking over the end of the show with a neverending "love won't fade" chant, these moments provided a direct form of verbal feedback from the audience to the band.

These moments of connection were not random or accidental. The Dead's lyricists, Hunter in particular, infused their songs with moments that were not merely communicative, but which had the uncanny quality of seeming to comment on the experiences that all were sharing. This is not unheard of in music; for example, in my own research on sea chanteys, I have found numerous examples where the lyrics of a work song described the action of singing a song while working, e.g., "Heave and bust her is the cry/as we raise this yard into the sky" (Hugill, 1961). Until recently, however, there was no standardized term to describe this phenomenon. In 2006, ethnomusicologist Katherine Meizel coined the term *metacantric*, based on the latin "canto"— to sing — and the greek "meta" used in its modern epistemological sense to mean "about its own category." In its purest sense, metacantric describes the act of singing about singing, but I have extended it to include the case of work songs, where the singers are simultaneously in the midst of another act, and they are singing about their own actions. So, more than simply "singing about singing," metacantrics can mean "singing about the actions of the singer and the listener in the moment of singing."

The term has another level of meaning, because it is also a play on the term "cantometrics," a term promoted by folklorist Alan Lomax (1968). Cantometrics is a system of musical analysis developed by Lomax that is supposed to relate statistical data on the sound production of traditional song styles to statistical data on sociological traits, attempting to show direct correlations between singing style and social norms in various cultures. So while "cantometrics" designates a method for quantitatively measuring the salient features of singing styles and their relationship to cultural features, "metacantrics" designates a quality of music that is dependent upon the circumstances of performance within a cultural milieu.

Metacantric moments occurred frequently in a Deadhead's experience of the Grateful Dead concert. When Bob Weir sang, "You know it's gonna get stranger, so let's get on with the show," or, "It's gonna be a long, long, crazy, crazy night," during "Feel Like a Stranger," Deadheads knew that he was not talking about some fictional show on some undetermined night, he was referring to the show occurring in the present, the night happening at that very moment, and Deadheads received those lyrics as a promise of what to expect. So, while Hunter wrote lyrics that were intentionally ambiguous, designed to be potentially metacantric, those lyrics only became metacantric when heard by an audience engaged in the act being sung about. So when Weir sings, "Everybody's dancing," it is not metacantric if the listener is lying in bed listening to it. If, however, he or she is up and dancing with a bunch of friends, whether to a live performance or a recording, the lyric becomes metacantric. In other words, no song or lyric is inherently metacantric, it only becomes so when the performance of the lyric intersects in space and time with a listener who is acting out the narrative, or who perceives that the lyric refers to their actions or state of being in real time. Thus, metacantrics can be related to the old saying, "If a tree falls in the forest and no one is there to hear it, does it make a sound?" The metacantrics of a song are completely dependent on the performances' context and the coincident actions of the listener.

Metacantric lyrics such as this can be found in some of the Dead's earliest songs, such as "Mindbender," in which the singer and the listener both

Metacantric moment in the making, July 1989 (© Lloyd Wolf/www.lloydwolf.com).

experienced the lyric "it's bending my mind" as a commentary on what was happening at that moment. Likewise, when early audiences heard the lyric "I can't come down," from the song of the same name, the band's first original composition, many of them probably identified closely with the sentiment. Metacantric lyrics in early Dead songs also geared themselves toward communicating directly to the audience that they were welcomed to "come and join the party every day" ("The Golden Road") and that everyone would be accepted because "who you are and what you do don't make no difference to me" ("I Can't Come Down"). As the Deadhead scene developed, this sort of metacantric communication reflected unique aspects of the Deadhead world. Especially in the late '80s and early '90s as new Heads were entering the scene, lyrics seemed to follow their every move. When Garcia sang, "I see you've got your list out" ("Touch of Grey"), chances were that a good portion of the audience did indeed have their set list out, and when he sang, "When it seems like the night will last forever" ("Black Muddy River"), Deadheads cheered because it did seem that the night would last forever, or at least they hoped it would.

But of course it did not, and it seems that even the eventual end of the band, and the end of Jerry Garcia's life, were foreshadowed in the Dead's mediascape for many years. Particularly after his diabetic coma in 1986, songs like "Black Peter," with its lyrics like "One more day, I find myself alive," took on even more poignancy than they had before. It was during songs like this that

Deadheads felt that Jerry was talking directly to each member of the audience, that he was letting the audience in on his private thoughts. Of course this was at least partially illusory, the words came from Hunter, but he fashioned those words specifically for Garcia, knowing full well the singer's extraordinary ability to convey the meaning of a song. Hunter was also deeply aware of the feelings of intimacy that Deadheads believed they shared with Garcia. So when Garcia said, "I love you more than words can tell" ("Brokedown Palace"), Deadheads believed him because it was part of a conversation between singer and audience that had been going on for years. Likewise, when Garcia sang, "It looks like the old man's getting on" ("Brown-Eyed Women"), Deadheads could feel the weight of time on his shoulders and in his voice.

"Unbroken Chain," a song on the album *From the Mars Hotel*, was, until 1995, never performed live. Deadhead lore that circulated since at least the mid–1980s said that if the Dead ever played that song in concert it would be at the last show. As it happened, during the Dead's last tour in the summer of 1995, the band did break out "Unbroken Chain," and it was indeed played at the last Grateful Dead concert on July 9, 1995. This fulfillment of a prophecy that emerged from Deadhead lore is perhaps one of the most striking examples of the way that song, mythology and reality intersected in the Grateful Dead's milieu, but the last year of the Dead seemed to be especially rich with intertextual metacantric moments. That final tour was plagued by violent incidents. Deadheads were struck and killed by lightning at the June 25 show at RFK Stadium in Washington, D.C., recalling at once a plethora of references to lightning in the band's lyrics and iconography. One of the worst incidents on that final tour was after the July 5 show near St. Louis, MO, when a platform/balcony at a campground collapsed on a large group of Deadheads, seriously injuring over 100 people. The following night the band dedicated their show to these fans, and many Deadheads commented that one of the most poignant moments of that show was the song "Brown Eyed Women" with its lyric,

> Tumble down shack in Bigfoot County.
> Snowed so hard that the roof caved in.
> Delilah Jones went to meet her God
> and the old man never was the same again[1]

Indeed, the old man never was the same again. The ambiguity of Hunter's lyrics once again appeared to be metacantrically narrating the unfortunate reality of the situation — a little over a month after this tragic concert Jerry Garcia, the "old man," died of heart failure.

"My Words Fill the Sky with Flame"— Conclusions

Many of the authors found in this book are dedicated to exploring and potentially explaining the numinous nature of the Deadhead experience, and each comes at the question from a different theoretical or disciplinary perspective. The phenomena described in this chapter represent just a few of the ways that Deadheads received the mediascape of the Grateful Dead and transformed it from representation to reality, from expression to experience. The capacity to make manifest that which is spoken is traditionally associated with either gods or illusionists. The Grateful Dead and the Deadheads were neither of these. Because they understood the frightening potential for their audience to ascribe to them godlike powers, the members of the Grateful Dead consciously sought to undermine or negate these tendencies, and purposefully avoided making dogmatic pronouncements. Yet the band could not control how their output was received and in the process of developing an ambiguously benign mediascape, they created an even more fertile field for the imaginations of their audience to take root. The results of this interaction between musicians and audience were no illusion — Deadheads and the Dead literally built a world out of their collective imaginations that was as real as any imagined community, whether cult or nation-state.

What is perhaps most significant about this form of band/audience interaction is that the penetration of Dead lyrics into reality is both personal and collective. As the individuals who comprise the collective Grateful Dead culture disperse and diffuse into other communities and other cultures, the lyrics and their interpretations are transmitted to new listeners and new audiences, who will make their own realities out of them. The Grateful Dead's mediascape will only continue to grow and change as the world changes with it, and the meanings ascribed to lyrics may change with time, but this is as it should be. What will not change is the power of the Grateful Dead's music and lyrics to transform listeners, and, in turn, for those listeners to transform reality.

Note

1. Robert Hunter, "Brown Eyed Women," *A Box of Rain* (New York: Viking, 1990), 29.

Bibliography

Appadurai, Arjun. (1996). *Modernity at Large: Cultural Dimensions of Globalism.* Minneapolis: University of Minnesota Press.
Barlow, John Perry. (2007). Keynote Address. Southwest/Texas Popular Culture Association Annual Conference. Albuquerque, New Mexico.
Benjamin, Walter, and Hannah Arendt, ed. (1968). *Illuminations.* New York: Schocken Books.
Carr, James Revell. (1999). "Deadhead Narratives of the Supernatural: a Folkloristic Approach." In *Perspectives on the Grateful Dead: Critical Writings*, R.G. Weiner, ed. Westport, CT: Greenwood Press.
_____. (2007). "Black Muddy River: The Grateful Dead in the Continuum of American

Folk Music." In *All Graceful Instruments: The Contexts of the Grateful Dead Phenomenon*, Nicholas G. Meriwether, ed. Cambridge: Cambridge Scholars Press.
Dodd, David. (2005). *The Complete Annotated Grateful Dead Lyrics*. New York: Free Press.
Dollar, Natalie. (1999). "Understanding 'Show' as a Deadhead Speech Situation." In *Perspectives on the Grateful Dead: Critical Writings*, R.G. Wiener, ed. Westport, CT: Greenwood Press.
_____. (2007). "'Songs of Our Own': The Deadhead Cultural Communication Code." In *All Graceful Instruments: The Contexts of the Grateful Dead Phenomenon*, Nicholas G. Meriwether, ed. Cambridge: Cambridge Scholars Press.
Hugill, Stan. (1961). *Shanties from the Seven Seas*. London: Routledge & Keegan Paul.
Hunter, Robert. (1990). *A Box of Rain*. New York: Viking.
Jackson, Blair. (1992). *Going Down the Road: A Grateful Dead Traveling Companion*. New York: Harmony Books.
Lomax, Alan. (1968). *Folk Song Style and Culture*. Washington, D.C.: American Association for the Advancement of Science.
Ritzer, Jeremy. (2000). "Deadheads and Dichotomies: Mediated and Negotiated Readings." In *Deadhead Social Science: You Ain't Gonna Learn What You Don't Want to Know*, Rebecca G. Adams and Robert Sardiello, eds. Walnut Creek: AltaMira Press.
Shenk, David, and Steve Silberman. (1994). *Skeleton Key: A Dictionary for Deadheads*. New York: Doubleday.

"Not Just a Change of Style": Reading *Workingman's Dead* as an American Commentary with Americana Roots

Erin McCoy

An album that begins with "the first days are the hardest days" is an album aware of its place, born from the roots of experience.[1] The Grateful Dead's *Workingman's Dead* was simultaneously a seminal project and a prophetic commentary. Fresh off the highs and lows of the 1960s, *Workingman's Dead* offered a weary, bluesy deviation from the Grateful Dead's acid-rock sound. But in true Grateful Dead fashion, it also conjured a species of hope within its framework of lyrical disappointment.

Released in 1970, amid a hangover from the high times, turbulence and deaths marking the country's passage out of the '60s, the album was not only a departure from the band's previous four releases[2] in terms of production efforts, but also marked the first Dead album to feature original songs showcasing the band's blues, folk and country roots. With their fifth release, the Dead exhibited a conscious shift toward a studio sound, as distinct from the "live" experience reflected on their prior records, which largely chronicle the psychedelic beginnings of arguably one of the most influential bands of the last 40 years. The earlier records do not feature the blue-collar, Americana ethos of the band, which, on *Workingman's Dead*, surfaces in Robert Hunter's lyrics and the band's "new" rootsy sound.

After coming together midway through the turbulent 1960s to mine the rich musical energies of the new electric sound, the Grateful Dead's first release for the 1970s is a wise and conciliatory album. The record progresses into a sonic journey detailing the plight of the universal Everyman as he explores the dawn of a new decade where only fragments of the hope and revolution from the previous decade seem possible. *Workingman's Dead*, where speakers lament the droll routine of everyday life, underscores both the plight of the quintessential American proletariat and the politically tumultuous nature of American life in the wake of the 1960s. Librarian and Dead historian Richard Pipes noted,

> In their personal lives, the band no longer lived together in the same Haight-Ashbury neighborhood, but had moved to the "country" suburbs of Marin County, a very different environment. Acid was left behind, cocaine began to creep in, and they began to have families, houses, [and] "workingman's" responsibilities and sensitivities.

The record demonstrated the national appeal of the Dead (it yielded the group's first Top 100 hit) and also developed the band's new working-class message. Equal parts social commentary and social warning, the music and lyrics of the album are a seminal contribution to the American experience.

Utilizing the roots of American sound, the album takes on the tone of an oral adage where both the lyrics of Robert Hunter and its Appalachia-inspired finger-picking and call-and-response song arrangements take the listener simultaneously backwards and forwards in time. The bluegrass infusions on songs like "Cumberland Blues" are deftly coupled with the Crosby, Stills, and Nash–like harmonies on "Uncle John's Band." The roots of this new sound were actually present at the beginning of the band's career, as reflected in Garcia's recollections of the burgeoning music scene preceding the formation of the Grateful Dead: "Bluegrass bands are hard to put together because you have to have good bluegrass musicians to play…. So we put together a jug band…. It was Pigpen's idea…. He wanted me to start up an electric blues band" (Wenner & Reich). According to traveling rock historian and Grateful Dead companion Barry Drake, these Americana roots played a key role in the transition from psychedelic compositions to the cultural translations reflected in the "new" sound epitomizing *Workingman's Dead*:

> Taking an acoustic stance in 1970 was exactly what that moment was calling for. It was a retreat and a sanctuary from a lot of craziness and a re-appreciating of our musical roots. That's what 1970 was all about. When The Dead returned to their roots (certainly Jerry Garcia's and Robert Hunter's), they were very comfortable with that musical form. It's actually what they did best. It took awhile for the general audience to align themselves with this "new" Grateful Dead sound, which was simply the popular music sound of the time.

Significantly, the mood of the band was changing as well:

> By 1970, the idealism surrounding the Bay Area music scene … had largely evaporated…. [*Workingman's Dead*] was the Dead's response to that period. The record was a statement about the changing and badly frayed sense of community

in America ... it was a work by and about a group of men being tested and pressured at a time when they could have easily pulled apart from the madness and stress and disappointment [Gilmore, 50].

The album cover itself is indicative of the band's new attitude, as the band is depicted as a bunch of vaguely-sketched outlaws hanging out in a dust-bowl-type town in some forgotten enclave of the anonymous American dream. The visual representation of this disenchanted attitude furthers itself as soon as we hear the beginning "mariachi/calypso" acoustic strums of "Uncle John's Band" (Peters, 61). The song is set "by the riverside," which, according to lyricist Robert Hunter, is "...figurative. Uncle John was a Kansas City drifter who had a flea circus, little critters in band uniforms you could only see under a magnifying glass..." (Peters, 62). Fresh on the heals of being pegged the flagship band of the Haight-Ashbury scene, the Dead were under a cultural microscope, for their reflections and statements about the '60s were important to believers of the trampled moral sensitivities of the New Left.

The Dead decided to surprise and soothe their audience. They made themselves over in a new image framed by a new sound, and most fans were leery when they first heard the album (Zwerling). But long-time fans and new listeners quickly warmed to the music, and "almost immediately," as Peters observes,

> fans adopted the concept of Uncle John's Band as the Grateful Dead's alter-ego in the tradition of the Beatle's *Sgt. Pepper's Lonely Hearts Club Band*, a notion that was clearly supported by the fact that the song didn't sound anything like the band they'd always known [Peters, 62].

This new "alter-ego" offers Dead freaks an immediately soothing caress of wisdom in its opening lines: "Well, the first days are the hardest days / don't you worry anymore." This is further welcomed into the soothing entreaty from Garcia's "think this through with me / whoa-o what I want to know is / are you kind? ... will you come with me / won't you come with me?" In one broad stroke, kindness is instilled as a paramount virtue for America, and the tribulations of the past are discarded by this friendly escape from the disillusionment of the tumultuous '60s.

The Dead just want this new America, emerging from a decade of fits and starts in the emergence of radical change and thought, to "come with [them]." The band is aware that their listener's choice is the "buck dancer's choice," but couples this with the sentiment that the emerging America "know[s] all the rules by now." The lost ones can "come with [the band] or go alone," which reflects the band's attunement to the circumspect new attitude of its listeners. They are Americans cast in a sea of disillusionment, but there "ain't no time to hate / barely time to wait." The pied-piper imagery of "Uncle John" portrays a man whose wisdom is informed by a storytelling crow who has "come to take his children home" (Dodd). The Dead's comforting new perspective features a workaday speaker who "live[s] in a silver mine" called "Beggar's tomb." When the band "beg[s] [the listeners] to call the tune," the music instills a trust in the audience. The jilted thoughts and hopes for a better America were not foolish ones that should cause listeners to mistrust their own judgment. After all, "Uncle John's Band" recognizes the new attitude, where the opposition's "wall[s] are built of cannonballs/ [and] their motto is *Don't Tread on Me*," yet they encourage the listener to "call the tune." It's as if the listeners, the people, are still in control, and the poignant ambivalence of the band ("how does the song go?") further underscores the underlying sense of trust in their fellow '60s survivors. After all, there are still "things to talk about / here beside the rising tide" of the new decade.

Where this Uncle John is taking his children, however, is first represented by a balladeer-type reflection on the bad side of peace, love, and understanding. "High Time" simultaneously lauds the ethos of the Grateful Dead's heyday, as well as the sad aftermath of that excitement. In this new decade, "the wheels are muddy/ got a ton of hay" and the speaker's message is urgent: he's *having*, he could *show* you, and you and he *could still have* a high time. Similar to a dramatic monologue, the speaker seems to reply to the unnamed listener's newfound hesitation. He considers the aftermath of the golden era and wearily replies, "Well, I know," as if anticipating the listener's doubt, and, "Don't be that way," as if responding to it. The song is also a nod to a cultural movement in America, where those disenchanted with the '60s were shifting their attention to nature and the simple life.

The ground is shaky in "High Time": the "leader" of this new era "won't draw," "tomorrow come trouble/ tomorrow come pain," and "nothing's for certain/ it could always go wrong." Yet all the audience has to do to survive is to "come in when it's raining" and "go out when it's gone." The listener can figure this out; we can sense an ability to discern the good and bad, and despite the false promises of the earlier period, the new age will still experience high times, as will America.

Like "Uncle John's Band," "High Time" focuses on tomorrow. With the events of the early seventies looming in the cultural consciousness—Nixon's election, the Vietnam War—the band, despite its option for "high times," warns prophetically that rough roads lie ahead. The worries of America are legitimate, according to the Grateful Dead, but at the heart of that understanding, the band still believes in a silver lining for the future.

The silver lining, of course, may first be addressed by a silver bullet. The earlier warnings from "High Time" are personified by the Dire Wolf, a giant beast to whom the speaker repeatedly begs "please don't murder me." The Grateful Dead, however, take a calm and rational approach to this creature of iniquity, despite the foreboding imagery of a swampy "Fennario" where "wolves are running round" and the winter cold "froze ten feet underground." It's a hedonistic, predatory setting for a song; it could be likened to the aftermath of the summer of love, where the media has now entered and made the pleasant, New Age scene a pop culture commodity ("We Were Just Happy Freaks, Man," 56). The speaker in "Dire Wolf" sits to eat and says his prayers, and then is never seen again. He wakes up to the Dire Wolf grinning at him through his bedroom window. He sits down for a game of cards with the monster and is greeted to a deck cards "all the same," cutting always to the Queen of Spades. The Queen of Spades is the cousin of the Tarot's Queen of Swords, who "suffered great loss" and is "possibly the bearer of evil and slanderous words ... mourning. Privation. Loneliness. Separation ... a card of death" (Dodd). While perhaps an oblique reference to the death of the band's friends, like Janis Joplin, the significance of this lyric pertains also to the death of a dream — the dream to which the Dead and their fans and fellow New Age thinkers had directed their aspirations. By placing the song in a cold and foreboding climate, the addition of the "boys [singing] 'round the fire" reminds the listener that the Dead are aware of the bad that has preceded this era, and they feel that the average American of the early '70s needs to be mindful of the bad experiences while remembering the good, produced through a sing-a-long reassurance of good times past. The warm and sharp styling of Jerry Garcia's steel pedal accents the warmth of the central melody and counterbalances the song's harsh setting.

While the speaker begs not to be murdered, the band continues playing as if they are going down with the ship no matter what. The group, throughout *Workingman's Dead*, is able to find a balance between the darkness of America's past and an optimism for the future. The balance of shadows and light, however, is never more emphasized and garishly addressed than in the semi-vitriolic "New Speedway Boogie." An obvious reference to the distressing and ominous violence at Altamont, the song sticks out from the rest of *Workingman's Dead* by its tightness; the song is musically taut, and its anxious sound underscores its tense lyrics, so there's little room for the band to wander musically. "New Speedway Boogie" is, essentially, a missive to America on how *not* to conduct itself in the future. The speaker's anger after the breakage of his old ideals is transparent, and he immediately establishes himself as a wary authority: "Spent a little time on the mountain/ spent a little time on the hill." The speaker's seen it all at this point, and he has pointed advice that is delivered with cunning ambiguity. Lyrics like "Please don't dominate the rap, Jack" warn listeners that new ideas are best now; the previous plan didn't work. Also, "I don't know/ But I been told/ It's hard to run with the weight of gold/ Other hand I've heard it said/ It's just as hard with the weight of lead" is simultaneously a pointed memorandum to Altamont and to America's reaction as well. Jerry Garcia elaborated to *Rolling Stone* in 1972, "Altamont showed us that we don't want to lead people up *that* road anymore, taught us to be more cautious ... it was the music that generated Altamont" ("We Were Just Happy Freaks, Man," 58). The speaker backpedals a little in order to maintain the mentality of the peace and love movement, admitting that "I saw things getting out of hand / I guess they always will / I don't know whose back's that strong / Maybe find out before too long / One way or another / this darkness got to give." The band, the people, and the fractured communities of America have all grown tired and mistrustful of the scary results of something that started with such good intentions.

But the average American experience, the blue-collar morality of those left in the aftermath of the peace and love movement, is still one that the Dead understands. "Cumberland Blues" is a veritable hoedown of banjos, spiky guitar jangling, and Appalachia bluegrass harmony vocal styles (Zwerling). The song is gentler and more prone to musical tangents than the angst-ridden "New Speedway Boogie." It features the empathetic lyric "Lotta Poor Man got the Cumberland blues/ he can't win for losing/ lotta poor man gotta walk the line/ just to pay his union dues" that exhibits compassion for the common disillusionment in America. Also, the song's knee-slapping beat is instantly a familiar workingman's folk sound, comforting in its admission of the exhausting transformation of the audience's adjustment in becoming an ex-member of the New Age and a new member of the working class. After all, "some other fella's makin' nothin' at all / and you can hear him cryin ... can I take your shift in the mine?" We have to go back, we sense them telling us; we "gotta get down" to the mines, into the deeper and undiscovered territories of America, sung with an urgency that reflects both a call to arms and a cornerstone of the American folk experience. Barry Drake casts this movement exhibited by the Grateful Dead as a core facet of the American folk experience:

> That's what American Folk Music has always been about. Psychedelic Hippies were looking inward through "The Canyons of Their Mind." Folk musicians were always floating down the Columbia River to the Grand Coulee Dam, up the Mississippi to Memphis, from California to the New York Island and from the Smokey Mountains to the Pacific Ocean.

In this way, the line "[we] just don't know/ if [we're] going back again," simultaneously conjures ideas of *leaving* the past behind as well as *going back* to the past for the good of America's future.

In "Black Peter," the Dead offer a glimpse into the bleak expectations that their prevailing optimism aims to conceal elsewhere on the album. The song is a tragic *chanson* that mimics the attitude of a smug America, one that is pleased to be "right" about the silly optimism of the '60s. The era is "layin' [in its] bed and dyin'," and an "angel" alludes to the "weather down here/so fine" as if the era and speaker are destined for Hell. The plaintive "one more day/ I find myself alive/ tomorrow maybe go/ beneath the ground" warns against the bad side of the counterculture drug experience, rising to a crescendo of "see here how everything/ lead up to this day/ and it's just like/ every other day that's ever been." That era is over, and this is its elegy. Enhanced by folksy harmonies and hobo-style harmonica accents, the speaker entreats its audience to "run and see" the new era, as the old one is "lyin' in pain."

The crudest, and perhaps most authentic exemplar of America's new workingman ethic is "Easy Wind." Sung in the deep machismo voice of Ron "Pigpen" McKernan, the song adds a new character to the Grateful Dead's folklore. Unlike the forlorn Poor Peter, the mysterious Black Peter, and the speed-demon Casey Jones, the narrator of "Easy Wind," is an "unsavory denizen ... who smashes boulders with a jack-hammer by day and chases women across the bayou by night" (Peters, 69). Oddly, the song was heavily influenced by both Delta Blues and a Robert Frost poem, which inadvertently compliments the past-and-present dichotomies of the album; one can hold a job in manual labor while remembering the idealistic past (Peters, 70). The sound is a "...contrast between ... straight bugaloo rhythm and a slow-cruise triplet groove," yet retains the authentic and plain voice of a workingman (Peters, 70). The singer is unabashedly masculine, which maintains the true essence of the working class; his ideal woman would be one who "doesn't hide [his] liquor/try to serve [him] tea." Also, the inescapable sexual imagery of "ballin' jack hammers" and "my rider" as a reference to the speaker's "woman," accentuates the testosterone-driven image, while the strong bass-line reaffirms this aural interpretation. The song's message is simple: America is instructed to go back to nature, as "the river keep a-talkin'/ and ya never heard a word it say" alludes to the increased distance from nature that modern America will be fostering in the future. The band is also unwilling to forget its past; the "easy wind/across the bayou today" was not what they encountered when they were busted in New Orleans (Pipes). This is not the first time the band references the ills of drug use on the album; "High Time" refers explicitly to drugs, as does "Casey Jones."

The latter, "Casey Jones," is not just the most obviously drug-infused song on the album, it is also the most cautionary — offering the most foreboding warning of what is to come for America. There is definitely a "double entendre of [the lyric] 'watch your speed'" (Peters, 70). It begins with an unabashed recorded "snort" like that of someone doing a pinch of cocaine, and moves on with a distorted version of the popular American tale of John Luther "Casey" Jones, a train engineer who was known for his train's distinctive whistle (Dodd). It is a modern fairy tale for the new America, culled from years of folk legend and music (Dodd), where the motto "trouble ahead/trouble behind" is repeated as if to emphasize the newest thread in our cultural fabric. Lyrics like "trouble with you/ trouble with me/ got two good eyes/ but we still don't see" admit that the speaker and the audience need to "watch [their] speed." That "this notion / just crossed" the speaker's mind is telling — he and America are not quite prepared for the new policies and politics of the '70s, but they're all speeding straight into it, while "the fireman screams and the engine just gleams." Someone, in this case a fireman, sees the culture train "come round the bend" and "know[s] it's the end," but the engine, like the people of America who were setting up for a revolution and received only embitterment, still surges ahead at full speed.

This might be the most important Americana message *Workingman's Dead* wants to impress upon its listeners: you know you are headed for some bad times, but give it a shot anyway, because we still believe progress can be made. The beauty of *Workingman's Dead* is that it does not apologize for the chaos, havoc or enlightenment of the 1960s—it insists on remembering the past while blazing trails to meet the future. It admits to its flaws—drug use, ambivalence, being unprepared—and it embraces the hopes for the future while maintaining honesty. The album is dignified because it doesn't attempt to hang on to the psychedelic illusions of the '60s, lyrically or musically. The concerns of the popular culture are crossed with laments of the past and predictions of the future while establishing the band as a new doppelganger of its old psychedelic self. While exploring its roots, the Grateful Dead are able to affirm hope in the future, all the while seemingly wise enough to know that "it's not just a change of style."

Notes

1. All lyrical references in this paper are taken from Robert Hunter's *Box of Rain*. Songs referenced include "Uncle John's Band," "High Time," "Direwolf," "New Speedway Boogie," "Cumberland Blues," "Black Peter," Easy Wind," and "Casey Jones."
2. *The Grateful Dead* (1967), *Anthem of the Sun* (1968), *Aoxomoxoa* (1969), and the double live album *Live/Dead* (1969).

Bibliography

Brandelius, Jerilyn Lee. *Grateful Dead Family Album*. New York: Warner Books, 1989.
Dodd, David, comp. "The Annotated Grateful Dead Lyrics." Online at: http://arts.ucsc.edu/gdead/AGDL/gdhome.html.
Drake, Barry. "Re: USC-Upstate Conversation." Personal correspondence. Jan. 8, 2008.
Gans, David, ed. *Not Fade Away: The On-Line World Remembers Jerry Garcia*. New York: Thunder's Mouth Press, 1995.
Garcia, Jerry. "'We Were Just Happy Freaks, Man': Garcia in His Own Words." *Rolling Stone* issue 717, September 21, 2005.
_____, Charles Reich, and Jann Wenner. *Garcia: A Signpost to New Space*. San Francisco: Straight Arrow, 1972.
Gilmore, Mikal. "Jerry Garcia." *Rolling Stone*, 717, September 21, 2005.
Grateful Dead, et al. *Workingman's Dead* [CD]. Burbank, CA: Rhino, 1970.
"Grateful Dead Discography." Online at: http://www.deaddisc.com/GDFD_Grateful_Dead.htm.
Hunter, Robert. *A Box of Rain*. New York: Viking, 1990.
Kurlansky, Mark. *1968: The Year That Rocked the World*. New York: Random House Trade Paperbacks, 2005.
Meriwether, Nicholas G. *All Graceful Instruments: The Contexts of the Grateful Dead Phenomenon*. Cambridge: Cambridge Scholars Press, 2007.
Peters, Stephen. *Grateful Dead: What a Long, Strange Trip: The Stories Behind Every Song 1965–1995*. New York: Thunder's Mouth Press, 1999.

Pipes, Richard. "Re: Grateful Dead Goes Academic." Personal correspondence. Jan. 11, 2008.
Zwerling, Andy. "Workingman's Dead: Grateful Dead." Online at Super Seventies Rock-Site!, http://www.superseventies.com/spgratefuldead1.html, Nov. 8, 2007.

SECOND SET

Some Philosophical Contours of Grateful Dead Improvisation

Rosemont Horizon, March 1993 (courtesy Barry Barnes, all rights reserved).

IMPROVISED PHILOSOPHY
ALAN TRIST

A commentary on the hexagram *Ch'ien* (the Creative) says, "The Creative is easy." Like much of the *I Ching*, this encourages us to take a different viewpoint because in the ordinary sense creativity is not easy — there is hard work, struggle; success is elusive. What does the *I Ching* mean? My intention here is to weave together an understanding from many voices.

Phil Lesh once remarked about the experience of a "good night," perhaps a very good night: "We couldn't play a wrong note."[1] This suggests that the Grateful Dead, at such a time or timeless moment, were in the grip and understanding of a condition of creation greater than themselves. The Force was with them, metaphysically. Was the Creative then easy? If we suspect so, then there is another question: What is the nature of the condition that makes it so?

In the Native American tradition, novelist Forrest Carter says in a description of the worldview among the Apache:

> Considering themselves a part of, not the master of, all things around them, and feeling no arrogance towards these things, they attributed the same Will and Spirit to them. They had observed that all things have Life, and therefore Purpose.... They had seen the wind bring rain, scattering it across the Life parts for their needs. If not a creator of Life, then Wind was a conductor of Life ... as was man. Therefore, Wind had Purpose, and so, Spirit. To the Apache the moods of Wind were real, not poetic; sullen, tempestuous, tender, soothing, violent, fresh, stale, loving — expressions of their own Spirit temper.[2]

The moods of Wind. Of a good night, I suspect Phil referred to notes played flawlessly not only in the melody of a well practiced song (the "head" in jazz terminology), but also, and perhaps more so, in the improvisational music then taking off from the harmonic and rhythmic foundation of the head. The moods of Wind were in play and the musicians profoundly in synch with them. The audience flowed with them too, for now another often noted ingredient of the Grateful Dead concert experience is in evidence — the "X-Factor" or "Seventh Member" — described variously as the presence of the audience's collective

Rosemont Horizon, March 1993 (courtesy Barry Barnes, all rights reserved).

energy consciousness in the mix, or the Wind itself, or both. Without distinction, on a good night all elements were present in arriving at the transcendent.

I once witnessed an occasion when something more occurred. Within an improvisational space, a new composition emerged in the moment, all parts complete, coming together into an instantly distinguishable and balanced work poised and sustained at a higher level of composition, apparently without effort.[3] The creative was easy. The Greeks would have called this *homonoia*, the spirit of concord, unanimity, and oneness of group mind.[4] In political philosophy it might be called *hamarchy* (Greek *ama*, together, *-archy*, rule, "together rule"), a rare and useful word, enabling us to avoid plunging further into metaphysics. Francis Lieber, who worked in the Lincoln administration, coined the term to fill a gap he found in the forms devised for the rule of order in society: anarchy, monarchy, plutocracy, oligarchy, synarchy, democracy, and convoluted admixtures, masquerades, and transitionary forms.[5]

In contrast to the absolutism of *autarchy*, a category into which he puts all other forms, Lieber defines hamarchy as "...that polity, which has an organism, an organic life ... in which a thousand distinct parts have their independent action, yet are by the general organism united into one whole, into one living system."[6] He is here affirming freedom and anticipating general systems theory formulated a century later.[7] He is also anticipating and advocating an ideal form, an *-archy* not yet seen but one experienced in the musical conversation on a good night when improvisation is flowing.

The "I Ching" says, "The beginning of all things lies still in the beyond in the form of ideas that have yet to become real. But the Creative ... has power to lend form to these archetypes of ideas.... The clouds pass and the rain does its work, and all individual beings flow into their forms."⁸ Catching *the moods of Wind.*

As expressed by the band, "Improvisation is built on trust, love, and time in the groove ... and intuition ... and playing together, and listening really closely ... and really listening closely ... and conversation. You have to have something to say, and someone has to be able to come back and encounter that, and then go with it, and take off. You have to give people space to do what they're supposed to do. Freedom is what we really all live for. Musical freedom is one of the most beautiful things in the world. Listen really deep ... listen more than you play, really ... it's about listening. And if you're hung-up or something, you sit back and sandbag it for awhile and listen to everybody else because something's coming your way ... coming your way ... and that's where the trust comes in."⁹

Notes

1. A "good night" is Deadhead code for those luminous occasions when the music reached a level of non-ordinary excellence. The mostly unmentioned subtext of much Taper discussion and trading concerns whether the tape in question records such a night or not, the subjective nature and pharmacological underpinning of its identification notwithstanding. Nevertheless, certain agreements as to good nights are said to exist.

2. Forrest Carter, *Watch for Me on the Mountain*, 1978. A novel of Geronimo's resistance to oppression. Pressed from the south by Mexico, and from the north and east by America's "Manifest Destiny" in the final phase of that continental action, the Apache nation were concentrated in the Sierra Madre, their ancestral homeland, where their own destiny played out.

3. This was a gratifying experience for my primary job as the Grateful Dead's music publisher for, in contrast to the normal vagaries of dating a composition, the date and time to the second of the actual moment of creation was on the tape, upon which knowledge the claim to copyright is fixed. However, this particular jam-song did not develop further.

4. Greek concepts and their personifications as gods and goddesses are quite confusing. The sophists saw Homonoia as the political equivalent of "Philia," friendship, a bond that could work wonders amongst warring states. She was also closely identified with Theban "Harmonia" who, as the daughter of Ares and Aphrodite, was the product of the union of the antithetical forces of war and love. She is most well known as the personification of musical harmony.

5. Francis Lieber, *Manual of Political Ethics*, 1864. I discovered this odd word and the provenance of its coinage while looking up the meaning of another word in the Oxford English Dictionary. Turned out that the possibly sinister "Synarchy," capitalized, is not mentioned in my 1971 OED edition, though the lower case form is defined as "to rule jointly; participation in government." This does not inspire much confidence, but the illustrative quotation from Lieber's *Manual of Political Ethics* did, not least because it defined synarchy in contrast to an even more obscure word: "Hamarchy,"

then, signifies something entirely different from the ancient synarchy, which merely denoted a government in which the people had a share together with the ruler proper. "The ancient synarchy" is a phrase irresistible to an anthropological sensibility, connoting visions of council in the long house where community rules and, hopefully, mitigates power. But what is hamarchy? Turning to this, the OED was brief and self-referencing, giving only the definition and usage I've mentioned from Lieber: "...a living system." Such are the epiphanies of poking around in the dictionary. I did not find it in Webster. Perhaps only Lieber used the word, a failed coinage, but not a failed idea (see note 6).

6. Hamarchy, of course, is the natural order of things. In their new book, *The Superorganism: The Beauty, Elegance, and Strangeness of Insect Societies*, Bert Hölldobler and Edward O. Wilson describe ant colonies in which, and I quote Lieber again, "...a thousand distinct parts..." are indeed "...by the general organism united into one whole, into one living system." Superorganisms exist also in the plant world. From time to time such are reported in the news. No sooner had a mushroom mycelium complex been identified in eastern Oregon, which covered half that region, than one was reported from Africa that may cover half the continent. (The authors of *Superorganism* report that various species of Leafcutter Ants, consummate agriculturalists if only of one crop, cultivate a fungus deep in their colonies whose fruit, a tiny mushroom, is the sole food for their young.) Tim Flannery, who discusses *Superorganisms* at length for *The New York Review* (Vol. LVI-3, February 2009), admits that anthropomorphism is dangerous ground but usefully distinguishes between human and insect societies in pointing to the necessary condition for globalization to evolve hamarchically, through the application of intelligence: "When conferring an honorary degree upon the man who invented the term 'superorganism,' President Lowell of Harvard University said [in 1928] of William Morton Wheeler that he had demonstrated how ants 'like human beings can create civilization without the use of reason.' Create perhaps, but there is no question of maintaining this first global civilization without resort to humanity's defining faculty. As the twenty-first century progresses we'll doubtless find ourselves trying to shape our planet-sized nest as carefully as an ant colony does, but the great difference is this: in the case of the human superorganism it will be our *intelligence* that will guide us. We have to hope that we shall find ourselves living sustainably in a global superorganism whose own self-created intelligence has been bent to the management and the maintenance of its life systems for the greater good of life as a whole."

7. Ludwig von Bertalanffy, *General System Theory*, 1968. The development of systems theory in the early part of the twentieth century was crucial to the emergence of modern science, being an interdisciplinary and holistic perspective in contrast to the reductionism and specialization of the nineteenth century. This change of perspective is still underway.

8. Richard Wilhelm, trans., *The I Ching; or Book of Changes*. I have carried the commentary which tripped off this essay, "The Creative Is Easy," around in my head for more than 30 years. It nagged. However, I cannot now find the citation, much as I have searched Wilhelm and my old notes. Perhaps it was from a different translation. If it is a phantom memory, so much the better for the intent of this essay!

9. Transcribed from an interview on Iclips.com with Mickey Hart, Bill Kreutzmann, Phil Lesh and Bob Weir on the occasion of The Dead's *Change Rocks* Obama Benefit concert, Philadelphia, October 2008.

"POURING ITS LIGHT INTO ASHES": EXPLORING THE MULTIPLICITY OF BECOMING IN GRATEFUL DEAD IMPROVISATION

JIM TUEDIO

> Okay, so you take LSD, and suddenly you are aware of another plane, or several other planes, and the quest is to extend that limit, to go as far as you can go. In the Acid Tests that meant to do away with old forms, with old ideas, try something *new*. Nobody was doing *something*, y'know, it was everybody doing bits and pieces of something, the result of which was something else. When it was moving right, you could dig that there was something that it was getting toward, something like ordered chaos, or some *region* of chaos.
> — Jerry Garcia (1969).[1]

"We're just trying to be right behind our noses," comments Garcia in describing the "moment by moment" manifestation of musical ideas as the driving force of Grateful Dead improvisation. The precision of this comment should not be underestimated. "He finds a way," writes Michael Lydon; "a few high twanging notes that are in themselves a song, and then the others are there, too, and suddenly the music is not notes or a tune, but what those seven people are *exactly*. The music is an aural holograph of the Grateful Dead." The emerging musical multiplicity manifests shifting balances, some of which "last longer than others, moments of realization that seem to sum up many moments, and then a solid groove of 'yes, that is the way it is' flows out, and the crowd begins to move. Each time it is Jerry who leads them out, his guitar singing and dancing joy," conveying both the band and the audience to a place "where the struggle to understand ends and knowledge is as evident as light."[2]

At the same time, we find out later, Lesh was learning to play his bass "in a way that heightened the beats by omission, as it were, by playing around them," in a manner that "cogenerates not only rhythm, but [also] the nature and rate of harmonic motion, so that the archetypal character of the music is clearly defined."[3] The Dark Star → Spanish Jam → U.S. Blues medley from June 23, 1974 offers a signature example, in comparison to which there are literally hundreds more. And those are just the really great examples, from shows where the magic was firing on all cylinders. Factor in several thousand additional examples of musical symbiosis sprinkled throughout the concert performances so diligently, lovingly, compulsively recorded to tape by archivists and circulated over the years, and it becomes clear that something distinctive was clearly happening at Grateful Dead shows, something reflecting a special convergence of "bits and pieces of something," as Garcia so aptly points out.

Grateful Dead concerts were punctuated with intensities of affectional immediacy traversing musical space like Deleuzean lines of flight, nomadic assemblages, creative articulations shaping the production and reception of musical multiplicities. Musical notes were no longer measured in relation to a musical scale "but in terms of differential relations and coefficients such as selective pressure, catalytic action, speed of propogation, rate of growth, evolution, mutation, etc."[4] The musical forces were transposed into "flows of intensities," musical "lines of flight" no longer subordinated to the point, no longer travelling point to point, but traversing instead a space of affective immediacy in which "experimentation has replaced all interpretation, for which it no longer has any use."[5]

As Deleuze and Guattari point out, the practice of freeing our musical line of flight from bondage to a fixed point of reference entails liberating our performative attunement from "points of subjectification that secure us, [or] nail us down to a dominant reality." To accomplish this, they suggest "tearing the conscious away from the subject in order to make it a means of exploration," and "tearing the unconscious away from significance and interpretation in order to make it a veritable production."[6] The audiences embracing Grateful Dead music comprised people who were especially receptive to this experiment, people who found a "home" in the seam of attunement co-generating the performative and receptive contours of the musical experience. At the heart of the experiment was the band's special relationship to "the one," which was less a fixed point of reference than an orienting feel for what was in play; in other words, something of an "ongoing subconscious kind of thing that's there when you need it."[7] As Garcia remarks:

> Rhythmically, you always know our policy is that the one is where you think it is. It's kind of a Zen concept, but it works well for us. It makes it possible to get

into a phrase where I can change into little phrase spurts ... and then turn that into a new pulse.... Then I'm inside of a whole irregularly rotating tempo in relation to what the rest of the band is playing, when they're playing, say, the original common time. It produces this ambiguity, but all I have to do is make a statement that says, "End of paragraph, AND, one," and they all know where it is. We all have that kind of privilege — it's partly something we've allowed each other, and partly something we've gained the confidence to be able to do just by spending *a lot* of time playing together.[8]

When Deleuze and Guattari introduce their discussion of rhythm and musical improvisation in *A Thousand Plateaus,* they do so with reference to chaos. "Sometimes chaos is an immense black hole in which one endeavors to fix a fragile point as a center." They reference the child who "takes shelter" from the dark by humming her way into the "calming and stabilizing" insulation of a familiar song, by which she can conjure a "calm and stable center in the heart of chaos."[9] The song works like a "wall of sound," effecting a transition "from chaos to the beginnings of order in chaos," but this centering frame of reference is not yet stable: it remains "in danger of breaking apart at any moment." Soon it starts to feel like home, though, but only because the child has managed to "draw a circle around that uncertain and fragile center, to organize a limited space" to help maintain a fragile balance and keep the "forces of chaos" at bay. "Now we're at home," in a familiar abode of "periodic repetition," sustained by the sonorous power of the familiar refrain. With this "jump" from chaos to sheltering milieu, the child gains confidence and "opens the circle a crack, opens it all the way, lets someone in, calls someone, or else goes out oneself, launches forth ... in order to join forces with the future." In this act of launching forth, the child "hazards an improvisation," by which it is able to "join with the World, or meld with it" once again. "One ventures from home on the thread of a tune." These are all moments of the Refrain:

> Sometimes chaos is an immense black hole in which one endeavors to fix a fragile point as a center. Sometimes one organizes around that point a calm and stable "pace" (rather than a form): the black hole has become a home. Sometimes one grafts onto that pace a breakaway from the black hole.[10]

So initially, we find ourselves menaced by "nonlocalizable, nondimensional chaos, the force of chaos, a tangled bundle of aberrant lines." This is the black hole that threatens to absorb us into the nothingness of pure disorientation. Struggling to find a seam of trust, we turn to familiar landmarks to constitute a stabilizing "milieu," an assemblage of territorial forces organized in terms of a periodic repetition of elemental components. We hope these territorial forces will provide a "bedrock or ground" to insulate us from exposure to the ever-present chaos, which continually threatens our stabilizing milieus "with exhaustion or intrusion." The solace of rhythm "is the milieu's answer to chaos."[11] The components of the milieu are directional, reflecting a flight from chaos. When these components cease to be directional and become "dimensional" instead, the milieu becomes a "territory," achieving the "signature" of a "temporal constancy" and "spatial range" that serves to express a meaningful code comprising an "interior zone of a residence or shelter, the exterior zone of its domain, more or less retractable limits or membranes, intermediary or even neutralized zones, and energy reserves and annexes."[12]

> There is a territory precisely when milieu components cease to be directional, becoming dimensional instead, when they cease to be functional to become expressive. There is a territory when the rhythm has expressiveness [or the mark of a signature].... The expressive is primary in relation to the possessive; expressive qualities, or matters of expression, are necessarily appropriative and constitute a having more profound than being. Not in the sense that these qualities belong to a subject, but in the sense that they delineate a territory that will belong to the subject that carries or produces them. These qualities are signatures, but the signature, the proper name, is not the constituted mark of a subject, but the constituting mark of a domain, an abode. The signature is not the indication of a person; it is the chancy formation of a domain.[13]

While it is not my intention to bury us in the unfamiliar cadence of a specialized discourse, the points I am importing from Deleuze and Guattari speak to the heart and challenge of the human experiment in living. The manner in which we overcode our bodily and social existence with territorializing motifs and counterpoints accounts for how we can take possession of a "critical distance" to help hold at bay "the forces of chaos knocking at the door."[14] And of course, this is all familiar to us in the midst of our experiences, but not always apparent. "There is a whole art of poses, postures, silhouettes, steps and voices." In their more refined forms, these expressive qualities "entertain variable or constant relations with one another (that is what matters of expression *do*): they no longer constitute placards that mark a territory, but [serve now as] motifs and counterpoints that express the relation of the territory to internal impulses or external circumstances."[15] These expressive styles serve as our abode against the menacing threat of destabilizing chaos. But they can also threaten to capture us in their wake, congealing the forces of innovation, closing us off, romanticizing our refrain and superimposing on our bodies the territorializing values and expectations of other people and systems on whom we grow increasingly dependent for validation and affirmation.

Deleuze and Guatteri speak here of "stratifications" that slowly draw us into compromising assemblages, "consolidations" that capture us within circuits of forces operating as "linear causalities," "hierarchies" and "framings" to shape and define the unfolding of our lives. But while these stratifications serve to congeal our lives within determinative relations, all the while cajoling us to follow along on paths that are no longer "for our steps alone," they cannot eradicate the interruptive forces of "play" that would serve the destratifying impulse within us. Yes, the chaos menaces us from within, too. Only now the issue is our own, and the challenge is to find ears for the solicitations that

At the cutting edge of deterritorialization. Rosemont Horizon, March 1993 (courtesy Barry Barnes, all rights reserved).

would liberate these destratifying forces and work for the production of a more open, fluid form of existence.[16]

For Deleuze and Guattari, music plays a crucial role in all of this, not only in forms that reinforce territorializing rhythms and practices, but also as a cutting edge of deterritorialization. In its capacity to decode and destratify the compromising assemblages holding our bodies hostage to the rhythms and compressions of our territorialized existence, music "invades us, impels us, drags us, transpierces us; it takes leave of the earth, as much in order to drop us into a black hole as to open us up to a cosmos," thereby "effecting the most massive of reterritorializations," for instance, through conjugations of ecstasy or hypnosis.[17]

Of course, Deleuze and Guattari are not referring here to those "assembled" refrains of "territorial, popular or romantic" forms of music, which serve primarily to reinforce the imposing of territorializing formulas of existence on us from beyond the inner-circuit of intensities in which our own-most creative potential circulates. They refer instead to "the great cosmic machined refrain," to a form of music that "turns loose" an "untempered, widened chromaticism." Drawing on the work of Gisèle Brelet, they formulate the challenge to musicians in the following way:

What needs to be shown is that a musician requires a *first type* of refrain, a territorial or assemblage refrain, in order to transform it from within, deterritorialize it, producing a refrain of the *second type* as the final end of music: the cosmic refrain of the sound machine.... [B]eginning from popular and territorial *melodies* that are autonomous, self-sufficient, and closed in upon themselves, how can one construct a new chromaticism that places them in communication, thereby creating *"themes"* bringing about a development of Form, or rather a becoming of Forces? The problem is a general one because in many directions refrains will be planted by a new seed that brings back modes, makes those modes communicate, undoes temperament, melds major and minor, and cuts the tonal system loose, slipping through its net instead of breaking with it.[18]

What Deleuze and Guattari suggest in regard to Schumann's concertos applies as well to the deterritorializing powers of Grateful Dead improvisation:

In Schumann, a whole learned labor, at once rhythmic, harmonic, and melodic, has this sober and simple result: *deterritorialize the refrain*. Produce a deterritorialized refrain as the final end of music, release it in the Cosmos—that is more important than building a new system. Opening the assemblage onto a cosmic force. In the passage from one to the other, from the assemblage of sounds to the machine that renders it sonorous, from the becoming-child of the musician to the becoming-cosmic of the child, many dangers crop up: black holes, closures, paralysis of the finger and auditory hallucinations ... a note that pursues you, a sound that transfixes you. Yet one was already present in the other; the cosmic force was already present in the material, the great refrain in the little refrains, the great maneuver in the little maneuver. Except we can never be sure we will be strong enough, for we have no system, only lines and movements.[19]

Weirdness with trust. Formless routes to new forms, pressing to extend the limits. Ambiguity overflowing with rich connotations, a musical assemblage taking us out into an ethereal space of hallucinatory imagery enriched with interlacing passages of tranquil beauty and twisting, wrenching, spiraling tonalities of chaos, all rotating about a single axis, and serving to open a phase space, a matrix full of unbridled possibilities, an event of transfixed rapture, and then safe passage back again, to a center of reference that bears the mark of a formative dynamic. When this works, there is a "non-signifying communication of energies, a complex dissemination of forces between the performers in an ensemble," and the "sociality of improvising musicians" is conjured by "transversal relations" of "undecidable complexity."

To accomplish music that "opens onto a cosmic space" by means of a "non-hierarchical process of lateral connections between sounds, genres and musicians," there must be "a moment of becoming-music at which the boundaries between performer and performed, between audience and compositions, between musician and instrument, between musicians and each other are all blurred: this is the moment of the opening onto 'the Cosmic,' which is also an experience of sociality ... [viewed as an] inherent capacity to break down the distinctions between inside and outside which [otherwise] guarantee the stability of individual subjectivity."[20] In trade, the listener/dancer is offered over to "an experience of 'all-body eroticism'" liberated from the formulaic constraints of the "regulated ... rock sound-dance apparatus." While this comment from Jeremy Gilbert is made with respect to the "rhythmic drive, chromatic range and multi-timbral soundscapes of the best Disco music," he proposes:

> The same argument might be made about the ecstasy of complexity engendered by those intense "peak" moments which characterize improvisatory musics, from traditional American banjo music to the guitar-playing of the Grateful Dead's Jerry Garcia, moments which may not be characterized by great speed or volume or extremes of pitch, but almost always by a momentary affect of notes colliding in a space too small to contain them, bursting out onto some new, smoother space with photons bouncing in unimagined directions in and out of existence altogether. In these moments ... a becoming-music is enacted which draws a line of flight away from the physical-ideological constraints of the gendered body or fixed musical genres: a body without organs; a smooth, cosmic space.[21]

As Patti Sotirin writes, in a fascinating discussion of "Becoming-woman," Deleuze is primarily concerned with "unfettering possibility to experiment with what a life can do and where a life might go."

In other words, Deleuze affirms the possibilities of becoming something else, beyond the avenues, relations, values and meanings that seem to be laid out for us by our biological make-up, our evolutionary heritages, our historical/political/familial allegiances, and the social and cultural structures of civilized living. There is in this a radical affirmation of the sort of possibilities for becoming that we cannot think of in logical or moralistic terms: becomings that can only be felt or sensed or conjured, that require us to take risks and experiment in ways that affirm the vitality, the energies and the creative animations of existence.[22]

My interest in this paper is to set up some ideas for the purpose of conceptualizing the improvisational dynamic of Grateful Dead music and to track some of the experiential influences on Deadheads and counter-cultural movements spawned by the immense popularity of this musical innovation. My larger objective is to contextualize performative and experiential dimensions associated with the production and reception of Grateful Dead music as a dynamic, ground-breaking form of musical improvisation — effecting a style and intensity of musical engagement exhibiting the capacity to serve as a catalyst for compelling transformative experiences, and often affecting personal and community engagements beyond the scope of the live concert setting. There is little doubt in my mind that the musicians performing this music dedicated their efforts to promoting "the great health" celebrated so unabashedly in the writings of Friedrich Nietzsche, "a health such as one does not simply have, but also constantly acquires and must acquire, because one is giving it up again and again, and must do so!"[23] And in the name of this health we dedicate our efforts to engage "a world so over-rich in what is beautiful, strange, questionable, terrible and divine, that our curiosity as well as our thirst for possession is beside itself—alas, nothing will satisfy us anymore!" How can we contain our enthusiasm, once we pass through "the transitive nightfall of diamonds?"

> A different ideal runs ahead of us, an odd, seductive, perilous ideal which we would not like to persuade anyone to follow, because we do not so easily grant anyone *the right to do so:* the ideal of a spirit that plays naively, that is, not deliberately but from overflowing fullness and power, with all that up to now was called holy, good, untouchable, divine.[24]

"Words Half Spoken and Thoughts Unclear": Synchronicity, Ambiguity, and Exposure to Excess in the Transvaluative Dynamic of Grateful Dead Music

The layered meaning of a word is not unlike the performative disposition of a Grateful Dead song. Layered fragments of sense catalyze a dynamic interplay between component elements of understanding, much the way layered fragments of instrumentation instantiate each singular expression of Grateful Dead music. Affinities between iterations of a particular song harbor the unique, singular flavor of each performance, just as a series of words and their definitive sense harbor the singular performative expression instantiating any specific use of these words in discourse.

The *Live/Dead* performance of "Death Don't Have No Mercy" from March 2, 1969, is a singularly compelling example of the performative disposition of a Grateful Dead song. So, too, is the *Live/Dead* performance of "Dark Star," recorded just three nights previous to this. These are not hybrid compositions signaling excessive interventions of a studio mentality. These performances have come to signify singular performative expressions of "aleatory" *communitas*. Their very possibility as performances grew from the root of Jerry Garcia's fascination with aleatory phenomena.[25] Aleatory music is born from exposure to risk and chance. The performance of this music manifests a synchronic transversal logic of productive intentionality. The productive intentionality instantiates the aleatory order inherent in the music, and the performance itself comprises a living instantiation of aleatory *communitas*. The resulting openness to serendipity flowers from the uncertainty and contingency inherent in this multiplicity of singular musical dispositions. As exemplars of "primal Dead" music, these specific Fillmore West versions of "Death Don't Have No Mercy" and "Dark Star" were a key accelerant in the cultivation of philosophical attunements in the music, community and subcultural attraction of the Grateful Dead. A group commitment to aleatory music in live concert settings fueled the band's 30-year reign as iconic symbols of the radical, apolitical "spirit" of counter-culture community that emerged from the late '60s San Francisco music scene. These specific performances are by no means the only gems to emerge from the archives. They simply typify rare moments when interweaving threads of musical resonance, layered fragments of interlocking temporality, and synchronic instrumentation coalesced for one special suspended moment into a space of rapture unlike anything we have ever heard, before or since. The synchronicity of these performative elements produces music in a moment of instrumentation when the ear of the listener is in command of a higher authority. And if we want to test this hypothesis, we can go straight to the evidence. It is right there, waiting for us, every time we revisit the recordings.

My first encounter with this phenomenon came in 1969, when I stumbled onto "Viola Lee Blues" in a used record bin. Most of the records in this bin were 25 cents, but this Grateful Dead record was 35 cents, ended with a 10-minute song and featured front and back covers that resisted my efforts to make sense of them. I had no clue about this band, but I figured I knew what a 10-minute song would feel like. Now, if I had taken my cue from the ambiguity inherent in the cover art, from the promisingly undecipherable logographs and recursive imagery on the front cover to the double-negative mirror imagery dominating the back, I might have been more attuned to the possibility of something totally unexpected. As it was, five or six minutes into "Viola Lee Blues," I simply disappeared in the temporal suspension of a musically altered state of mind, as if drawn to a state of pure attunement. At 10 minutes in, I was back in my body, saturated in wonder, and positively hooked on my newfound access to lived-immediacy.

But my greatest surprise was yet to come. Until I heard the band live, three years later, by which time I had stumbled onto a used copy of *American Beauty* and invested in a brand-spanking-new copy of *Europe 72*, I had no idea a song could manifest a life of its own, or that an entire crowd of transfixed auditory surveillance instruments could modulate to identical frequencies of dancing attunement without the slightest absence of personal engagement. The soundscape was so clean as to be nearly invisible, and seemed to permeate the attunement of my musical awareness, while a strangely recurring excess of visual imagery poured its light into ashes in the midst of a pulsing light show. Even the familiar songs were fresh and new. Years later, the tapes from this show would validate my sense that more was happening here than could ever be explained in the space between my ears.

As Calvino's Marco Polo remarks to Kublai Khan in *Invisible Cities*, the virtues of the implicit can be lost to the clarity of words: "Memories images, once they are fixed in words, are erased," Polo said. "Perhaps I am afraid of losing Venice all at once, if I speak of it. Or perhaps, speaking of other cities, I have already lost it, little by little."[26] Attunement to the dynamic interplay of Grateful Dead music is initially experienced as an implicit phenomenon. If we pursue a more explicit articulation of the implicit sense traversing this attunement, we could risk losing the very substance of the implicit. For if implicit content is the sustaining ground of experiential attunement, can we be sure this attunement will survive translation into explicit terms? Whatever has been incorporated into our life as an implicit orientation to complexity and the free-flowing dynamic of elemental ingredients of an improvisational musical experience loses depth in the translation to conscious discourse. We balance this risk by resisting the imposition of traditional categories of thought and seeking to break open a space for new possibilities.

A Grateful Dead phenomenology exposes the bodymind character of improvisational rapture, registers a Deadhead's disengagement from socially constructed temporalities, recognizes the free-play structure of collective group dynamics driving the music, and grapples with evocative, ambiguous shades of meaning inherent in the delivery of lyrical passages. But already we face an additional complexity that carries us beyond phenomenology to a hermeneutical/genealogical accounting of the engaged role of perception in the dynamic of performance: For, as Marco Polo says, "I speak and speak, but the listener retains only the words he is expecting…. It is not the voice that commands the story; it is the ear."[27] The performative attunement implicit in the production of Grateful Dead music undergoes immanent translation through the receptive attunement of the listener, connecting one implicit domain of experience with another. In the process, a residual excess of sense outstrips the boundaries of normality, giving space to new possibilities, lateral moves in the untamed regions of operant thought, where the event of music displaces the mind into a performative realm where it "rains" originality, invention and novelty.

In the event of giving speech to that which has no language, sense is trapped in a certain frame that closes off myriad experiences in which other possibilities live and breathe, just as a memory trapped in a certain frame of explicit articulation closes off myriad experiences in which the past lives and breathes. We might explore how Grateful Dead music plays a role in developing "an ear for rain." The experiential sense inherent in the music resists domestication in its implicit form, but the frontal significance and lateral implications of the lyrical text and the untamed regions of performative structure inherent in the musical dynamic also sustain an overflowing experience in which "words half spoken and thoughts unclear" bear the weight of experience by means of a subtle, agile leap above the weight of things, a leap to embrace the fragility of the ephemeral, where the sparseness of words supplies openings to an expansive new play of possibilities. Grateful Dead music is often as much about the silence in the words as it is about the evocative affectivity of their deep resonance with human experience. There is, for instance, a move in Grateful Dead music drawing us to a reconfigured sense of home, seen now as a meeting place of wild and domestic, a liminal intersection of self and other, where translation, as the ultimate vehicle of connection, moves us from our own partiality in the direction of a bonding abstraction. In the process, through glimpses of fragments, we are delivered over to a new sense of inter-relatedness and relation to place.

Garcia captured the liminal attraction of this sense of home in a comment to Alice Kahn in 1984: "I like things wide open," he remarked, "with question marks hanging over it, everything changing — nothing settled."[28] In the Reich interview from 1972, Garcia likens this to serving as a medium of translation in which signification is exchanged for implicit indicators of open possibilities concretely inscribed in the dynamic of the present:

> I think of the Grateful Dead as being a crossroads or a pointer sign, and what we're pointing to is that there's a lot more universe available, that there's a whole lot of experience available over here. We're kinda like a signpost and we're also pointing to danger, to difficulty, we're pointing to bummers. We're pointing to whatever there is, when we're on — when it's really happening.[29]

Tracing back to a 1969 conversation with Michael Lydon, Garcia adds a crucial note of caution in response to a comment where Lesh suggests the Grateful Dead might be "trying to save the world." It's true, he says, "we are trying to make things groovier for everybody," and the point is to help make it "so more people can feel better more often, to advance the trip, to get higher, however you want to say it."

> But we're musicians, and there's just no way to put that idea, "save the world," into music; you can only *be* that idea, or at least make manifest that idea as it appears to you and hope that maybe others follow. And that idea comes to you only moment by moment, so what we're going after is no farther away than the end of our noses. We're just trying to be right behind our noses.[30]

Hinting in his next breath that everything hinges on the power of the implicit, Garcia likens the performance of music to a "yoga":

> ... something you really do when you're doing it. Thinking about what it means comes after the fact and isn't very interesting. Truth is something you stumble into when you're playing and the whole room becomes one being — precious moments, man. But you can't *look* for them and they can't be repeated. Being alive means to continue to change, never to be where I was before. Music is the timeless experience of constant change.[31]

These comments provide context for Garcia's fascination with aleatory music and, more generally, with the power of uncertain events and the chance firing of contingencies bearing the weight of profit and loss. Playing off the affectional immediacy implicit in the space of a group musical improvisation, Garcia had the uncanny ability to play musical notes dripping with contingencies and conveying the radical singularity of a moment's singular performative disposition. In doing so, his musical expression embraced "the whole 'odyssey' idea" inherent in journeys, voyages, trips and scales,[32] and traversed an atmospheric attunement of shared intuitions. "The Grateful Dead has some kind of intuitive thing," and everyone involved "experiences it on their own terms."

> I don't know what it is or how it works, but we recognize it phenomenologically. I know it because it's reported to me hugely from the audience, and it's some-

thing that we know because we've compared notes among ourselves in the band. We talk about it, but all those things are by way of agreeing that we'll continue to keep trying to do this thing, whatever it is, and that our best attitude is to consider it a stewardship, in which we are the custodians of this thing [p. 154].

"Wings to Fly": Love's Refrain in the Ideational Space of a Grateful Dead Soundscape

Grateful Dead concerts were renowned for the power of the music to draw their fans into a coalescent phase space of affectional immediacy. The phase space might suddenly open to the hymnal chords of an emerging cascade of melodious tonality signaling the arrival of a rapturous "Wheel"—or we might find ourselves absorbed in the crystalline rapture of a touching "China Doll" flowing to the surface on the cresting notes of a jam so delicate we can hardly breathe without soaring out of our skin from the joyful sorrow lodged within this musical space depicting an overwhelming and incomprehensible loss. "If you can abide it..." the song will take you in: what happens next is at the mercy of "forces torn loose from the axis."

The possibilities brought to life in these experiential attunements were at the heart of the crowd dynamic at Grateful Dead shows, and help to explain how live Grateful Dead performances could resonate with chords of desire, recognition and affinity in proportion to the dynamic of a person's psychic life. The marvel is how this connotative musical resonance could catalyze and calibrate a person's experiential attunement to new possibilities without sacrificing the precious melody of the implicit or violating the sovereign domain of love's refrain (and how it continues to do so in the performative space of the recorded music). In these rarefied moments of musical engagement, the ear of the listener comes under command of an affectional immediacy where vision is clearest and obstructions are denied. Grateful Dead soundscapes could embrace the rarefied possibility inherent in these possibilities—*give them wings to fly*—and in the affectional immediacy of love's refrain we might discover our boundaries are really just thresholds drawn in sand. Later, this might be retracted in a cunning victory for the forces implanted in us by others. But the soft awakening is sure to continue deep in the refuge of a lingering hollow and in time we begin to feel ourselves waiting patiently, close by, in the shadows of another life.

For those who knew what to expect, Grateful Dead soundscapes were highly sought after experiences. Deadheads discovered a form of existential transportation harbored in the improvisational nuances of these musical soundscapes: they found intimate proximity to a life calling them forth to themselves, and passage across mood-lit waters of affective immediacy to shores of possibilities brimming with actualizable energies. Word of these experiences soon gave considerable impetus and urgency to the quest for concert tickets and residual fragments of the recorded shows. The goal was simple enough: *be there* when disarticulating chords coalesce with melodic tones to signal a passage to existential rapture. Or get the tape.

Exposed to these transgressing adventures of the human spirit, the more fortunate Deadheads discovered "wings to fly," wings for conscious passage unbridled by normalizing schemas, dependent modes of articulation or other sedimented forms of stratification. Soon enough, some of these Deadheads learned to work the magic of recording tape, which proved proficient at translating these magical affective transformations into soundscapes capable of emanating from home stereos. Distribution networks spawned a hunger for steadily degrading copies of singular concert performances, and the magic was on. As the Grateful Dead sound crew steadily increased its mastery of acoustical science, cutting-edge sound systems helped to translate interlacing performative dispositions into compelling experiential soundscapes. With such a stellar vehicle for transmitting the music, the innovative textures of the ensemble sound made every show its own space of possibilities. Spaces became places, and it soon got to feeling like home no matter where your airplane happened to land. Tourheads carried the vibe onto the highways and byways of the great American frontier, with bumper stickers announcing the interplay of absurdity and transversal thought in stealth-like counterculture voices certain to connect with members of the tribe: "No left turn unstoned." "Question assumptions." "Dare to think for yourself." "Wherever we go the people all complain." "Who are the Grateful Dead and why are they always following me?" Demand for tickets and concert recordings grew in proportion to a Deadhead's attraction to this newfound access to the plane of immanence. Word got out: there's nothing like a Grateful Dead concert. If you could track the sound, you were on the bus. But to accomplish this, you had to trust the implicit structure of the music, and this meant exposing yourself to the transvaluative dynamic of Grateful Dead music.

This exposure took place within a dynamic interface of experiential attunements constituting the live (or recorded) soundscape of the concert setting. In particular, the musical dynamic of a Grateful Dead soundscape seemed to foster an ideational space for conscious travel unfettered by traditional patterns of meaning and signification. This ideational space manifested a coalescent tonality of liberating emotional and philosophical attunements, often trading on experimentation to dismantle *a priori* sediments of interpretation. The possibilities brought to life in these experiential attunements were at the heart of the crowd dynamic at Grateful Dead shows. Of special interest to me is how one's orientation to this soundscape opened up possibilities for *letting be in the face of the still to come*, and how the face of these possibilities resonated with chords of desire, recognition and affinity in proportion to the affectional immediacy of one's engagement with the music. Nothing could be more emblematic of the Grateful Dead synergy than the countless deterritorializing lines of flight embodying the overarching complexity of love's refrain as a calling forth to a plane of immanence on which a life "unfurls and opens to experimentation."[33]

There's no point to generalizing here. The circumstance of engagement in these instances is always singular. The moodscape is always in transit. The ambiguity cashes in every investment. The underlying depth and overarching promise coalesce around the bass and lead guitar motifs, implicitly anchored in the incessant interplay of performative dispositions: searching, probing, pacing, circling, cutting through, congealing sounds in various nuanced arrays of measured tone and counter-tone. Add to this the special orientation of Deadheads to the music and lyrical measure of the band, interweaving a resonance of shared experience with the singular intensity of their own personal rapture, and we have the rudimentary components of an "ideational" space. The ideational space of a Grateful Dead soundscape is actually a place of conscious exploration. It instantiates a situated life-experience which, though familiar in its tonal quality still becomes partially unfettered from the stratifications of everyday life. In this way Deadheads might experience a liberation from expectations of conscious assimilation to the stratifications of meaning and significance already operating on us in virtue of our relationship to the organism of our social composition. This ideational space became the context for their reception of the music as, for instance, in those "peak" ecstatic moments spanning the episode of a suspended jam within the main body of any number of tunes performed by the band in concert. Far from locating themselves as appreciative listeners operating *in regard* of the music, Deadheads generally "lost" themselves in the "affective immediacy" of a lyrical soundscape, lodged in a rich interplay of ideas and possibilities brimming with territorializing intensities and destratifying lines of force.

The Deadhead's reception of the performative measure of a Grateful Dead love song — their trust in both the emotional and lyrical measure, in particular — reflects a resolute anticipation of the unfathomed "still to come" received as something accessible to discovery through experimental passages of open possibility. Drawing on Deleuze and Guattari, we might say specific songs serve to sustain our movement between "the surfaces that stratify [us] and the plane that sets [us] free."[34] The song itself becomes a provisional stratum on which we can lodge ourselves long enough to "experiment with the opportunities it offers." Our dancing embodiment, in turn, provides support for our attunement to these passages of open possibility. And because dancing helps calibrate our own personal measure of the song, the "singularity-in-the-moment" feel of the experience coalesces with a "flowing suspension" of temporal orientation to plant us in a rapture of affective immediacy. Yet even in the midst of this wonderful synchronous flow we can face our greatest challenge, *letting be in the face of the still to come*. We look to the soundscape for our inspiration, for in the music resides the voice of a muse who speaks to the question brewing within us: to hold or release, grow or withdraw, reach for the gold ring or let her pass by ... until at some point threads of attunement coalesce from a cacophony of lines of flight and a suggestive, compelling intuition strikes like lightning:

> remain poised
> in pursuit of perfection
> otherwise life is too honest
> and harsh to digest
>
> or fall
> in bad habits,
> fade into woodwork
> grain by grain
> and disappear without a trace.

Already the searchlight is "casting for faults in the clouds of delusion," looking to open a space for discovery, for growth, for engagement with the promise of an intuition. "Shall we go, / you and I / while we can?"[35]

> yes, poised on the cliff
> with groundswells of silence
> and wings for feet
> something else beckons you
>
> *not this, not now*
>
> like some dark alley
> on a moonlit night
> passing silently
> as if barking fences
> and rustling leaves
> were the soundtrack
> of hope
> and deliverance.

In a crevasse of the darkest hollow, life shakes free of the stratifications binding us to the organism of our social constitution and harnesses the wings of the muse:

> don't be fooled
> by the storied remainders
> the moment is *everything*.

But of course this is just the beginning, for "the wheel is turning," and as the possibilities grow bolder and more perceptive they also become increasingly entangled within shifting contexts of consideration. Pressures build and love blooms or quakes amid uncertainties torn loose from the axis.

When the question comes we have two chances: one to get it right, and one to get it wrong. Only then do we discover if our answer is made of blood, wine, or *pharmakon*, or what it means for the ear to judge the opening gesture and meaning of the sudden exposure.

Sometimes we get it wrong, if only for the dream of getting it right, and we wonder why we had to stand forward at that moment and speak from the heart when no one was sure of anything more than to trust the implicit ambiguous register of experience where joyful possibilities linger dangerously close to the point of expression and feed on the hunger released in their name.

We can float only so long before the compression from waiting cancels the gift of patience and sends us pressing, probing in retreat for a connection so implicit we wonder how it could ever subsist without the structure and support of words.

Vulnerable, exposed, concerned or curious, the question recedes in silence to await the fate of the answer. Life is like this: what matters most is the love in the heart, not the words that express it.

The muse instills this experiment in trust as an affirmation of life. The music, in turn, delivers a place to dwell in the message. We do not affirm life by establishing or affirming propositional constraints on the possibilities of this life. We affirm life only by trusting beyond what is cast in the logic of our own compelling instantiations of meaning and significance — that is, by engaging in a collective performance, not unlike that of the band members themselves.

The collective performance of Grateful Dead music manifests a multiplicity of singularities swarming to an "indeterminate 'plan of composition'" or flowing under the influence of an indefinite "plan of consistency." These "plans" operate implicitly, embracing the "still to come" and its attendant possibilities for displacement and transvaluation. Through exposure to innovation, resistance to normativity undergoes a transvaluation, taking its leave of domination, hierarchical power, and every "transcendental illusion" that might constrain it to the scope of obedience prescribed by representational limits of exclusion and measure.[36]

Garcia suggests something similar while reminiscing on the formlessness inherent in the early Acid Tests, where the Grateful Dead's performative gesture to a new space of freedom was especially well suited to engaging possibilities on the plane of immanence:

> Formlessness and chaos lead to new forms. And new order. Closer to, probably, what the real order is. When you break down the old orders and the old forms and leave them broken and shattered, you suddenly find yourself a new space with a new form and new order which are more like the way it is. More like the flow. And we just *found* ourselves in that place. We never decided on it, we never thought it out. None of it....
>
> What we're really dedicated to is not so much *telling* people, but to *doing* that thing and getting high. That's the thing; that's the payoff, and that's the whole reason for doing it, right there.[37]

In the process, Deleuze would note, what is hereby affirmed "is precisely the Being of becoming, the one of multiplicity, the necessity of chance." That is, we learn to trust the affirming intuition in its wholly implicit form of deliverance. The whole spectacle is born to fly on wings of fragile confidence. "Dionysus is a player," Deleuze continues.[38] "The real player makes of chance an object of affirmation; he affirms the fragments, the elements of chance," and so embraces the affirmation of joy even as the test of despair and suspension of love's refrain return him to the fragile dominion of his soft awakening. The personal yield is a transvaluation of the human life force, something the Grateful Dead were renowned for instigating; and though in the final analysis the members of this band were not *responsible* for these accomplishments of transvaluation, they were surely the catalysts and consummate tricksters; kindred spirits to all who wandered into this festival of excess with a hunger for the point of contact as a point of *exposure*, for the form of being that is equally well a *letting-be* "delivered [over] and abandoned to its finitude." That is, they delivered us to the "finite here and now" in the face of the immeasurable sense of all that is still to come.[39]

Through Grateful Dead music, one can access this spirit of *letting be in the face of the still to come*. Immersion in the uncharted immediacy of the rolling timbre of Grateful Dead jams and poignant spatial interludes delivers us to a space of *affectional immediacy* in which our life can recuperate from the practices of normalization and exclusion that otherwise serve to constrain our attunement to possibilities for living *beyond* our contingently prescribed boundaries of self-containment.[40] This, in turn, provides direct experience of philosophical dispositions invested with the qualities of a transversal logic, effectively exchanging hierarchical modes of valuation for lateral displacements of meaning and sense. Such dispositions can alter the fundamental dynamic of interpersonal relations by embracing the counter-tonal measure of love's refrain. Trusting implicit love yields more than calm solace in the face of uncontainable measures of alterity: it also opens us to the immeasurable domain of the still to come, like the song the morning brings when you wake beside the dream of love that cast you out for sleep. "Life may be sweeter for this, I don't know / see how it feels in the end."[41]

As this attunement influences our affective relation to love's refrain, the impact can be profound. As we temper our impulse to control outcomes (through an open receptivity to the uncharted possibilities of the still to come), life acquires newfound urgency in the face of unyielding openness. Suspending the urge to master, our new attunement harbors the full range and density of the human experience and draws us closer to the spectacle of life's unfolding: "Beneath the sweet calm face of the sea / swift undertow."[42]

Notes

1. Jerry Garcia, quoted in Lydon, "Dead Zone" (August 1969), reprinted in George-Warren, ed., *Garcia*, 61 and 64.
2. Ibid., 72.

3. Phil Lesh, *Searching for the Sound*, 57 and 50.
4. Gilles Deleuze and Felix Guattari, *A Thousand Plateaus*, 48.
5. Ibid., 162.
6. Ibid., 160.
7. Blair Jackson with David Gans, "Talking with Garcia," *The Record*, June 1982, reprinted in *Garcia* (1995), 154.
8. Ibid., 155.
9. Deleuze and Guattari, *A Thousand Plateaus*, 311.
10. Ibid., 312.
11. Ibid., 313.
12. Ibid., 314–15.
13. Ibid., 316.
14. Ibid., 320.
15. Ibid., 318.
16. cf. ibid., 335–36.
17. cf. ibid., 348.
18. Ibid., 349–50.
19. Ibid., 350.
20. Jeremy Gilbert, "Becoming Music: The Rhizomatic Moment of Improvisation," in *Deleuze and Music*, Buchanan and Swiboda, eds., 124–25.
21. Ibid., 126. Cf. Deleuze with Guattari, *A Thousand Plateaus*, 474–500.
22. Patty Sotirin, "Becoming-woman," in *Deleuze and Music*, 99.
23. Friedrich Nietzsche, *The Gay Science*, §382, in *Existentialism: Basic Writings*, Guignon and Pereboom, eds. (Indianapolis: Hackett, 1995), 162.
24. Ibid.
25. "Aleatory" derives from the French "alea" (chance), and means "depending on uncertain events or contingency as to both profit and loss" or "pertaining to luck," where one might speak of "the aleatory element in life" *(Webster's 2nd Edition, unabridged*, 1940). In a point of reference to the influence of aleatory music on the emergence and evolution of Grateful Dead music, Garcia references the term with a certain mischievous glee in one of his early *Rolling Stone* interviews in speaking about his formative attraction to jazz improvisation.
26. Italo Calvino, *Invisible Cities*, 87.
27. Ibid., 135.
28. Alice Kahn, "Jerry Garcia and the Call of the Weird" (1984), reprinted in *The Grateful Dead Reader*, Dodd and Spaulding, eds., 203.
29. Jann S. Wenner and Charles Reich, "The First Rolling Stone Interview with Jerry Garcia and Mountain Girl" (1972), in *Garcia*, George-Warren, ed., 95.
30. Michael Lydon, "Dead Zone" (1969), reprinted in *Garcia*, George-Warren, ed., 64.
31. Ibid.
32. Jackson and Gans, "Talking with Garcia" (1982), reprinted in *Garcia*, George-Warren, ed., 155.
33. The underlying philosophical orientation of this discussion is drawn from Deleuze and Guattari, *A Thousand Plateaus*, with special attention to the chapter "How Do You Make Yourself a Body Without Organs?" (pp. 149–66). The quote is from p. 159.
34. Deleuze and Guattari, *A Thousand Plateaus*, 161.
35. Robert Hunter, "Dark Star," in *A Box of Rain* (New York: Viking, 1990), 54.
36. See Antonio Negri, *Time for Revolution* (New York: Continuum, 2003), 198–203 and 258–61.
37. Wenner and Reich, "The First Rolling Stone Interview with Jerry Garcia and Mountain Girl" (1972), in *Garcia*, George-Warren, ed., 95.

38. Deleuze, *Pure Immanence*, 86–87. Cf. Deleuze, *The Logic of Sense*, 60.
39. See Jean-Luc Nancy, *A Finite Thinking*, 3–47.
40. This notion of "affective immediacy" traces to an unpublished paper by Charles E. Scott on "Affectional Immediacy in the Space of Painting." While Scott's focus is on "sensibilities" and "affective dispositions" present in paintings and the people attuned to them, his intuitions about the experience of these paintings carry over to the experience of improvisational forms of music.
41. Robert Hunter, "Crazy Fingers," in *A Box of Rain*, 45.
42. Ibid.

Bibliography

Buchanan, Ian, and Marcel Swiboda, eds. *Deleuze and Music*. Edinburgh: Edinburgh University Press, 2004.
Calvino, Italo. *Invisible Cities*. New York: Harcourt Brace Jovanovich, 1974.
Deleuze, Gilles. *The Logic of Sense*. New York: Columbia, 1990.
_____. *Pure Immanence*. New York: Zone Books, 2005.
_____, and Felix Guattari. *A Thousand Plateaus: Capitalism and Schizophrenia*. B. Massumi, trans. Minneapolis: University of Minnesota Press, 1987.
Dodd, David G., and Diana Spaulding. *The Grateful Dead Reader*. New York: Oxford University Press, 2000.
Gans, David. *Conversations with the Dead*. New York: Citadel Press, 1991.
George-Warren, Holly, ed. *Garcia: By the Editors of Rolling Stone*. Boston: Little, Brown, 1995.
Hinter, Robert. *A Box of Rain*. New York: Viking, 1990.
Lesh, Phil. *Searching for the Sound*. Boston: Little, Brown, 2005.
McNally, Dennis. *A Long Strange Trip*. New York: Broadway Books, 2002.
Meriwether, Nicholas. *All Graceful Instruments: The Contexts of the Grateful Dead Phenomenon*. Newcastle: Cambridge Scholars Publishing, 2007.
Nancy, Jean-Luc. *A Finite Thinking*. Stanford: Stanford University Press, 2003.
Natoli, Joseph, and Linda Hutcheon. *A Postmodern Reader*. Albany, NY: SUNY Press, 1993.
Negri, Antonio. *Time for Revolution*. New York; London: Continuum, 2003.
Nietzsche, Friedrich. "The Gay Science." Richard Polt, trans. In *Existentialism: Basic Writings*, Charles Guignon and Derk Pereboom, eds. Indianapolis: Hackett, 1995.
Scott, Charles E. "Affectional Immediacy in the Space of Painting." In *Internationales Jahrbuch für Hermeneutik*, Günter Figal, ed. Tübingen: Mohr Siebeck, 2008.
Tuedio, Jim. "Community Through Excess: Bataille's Festival of Rapture and the Deadhead Concert Experience." In *Dead Letters, Vol. III*, edited by N. Meriwether. Columbia, SC: Dead Letters Press, 2006.
_____. "The Grateful Dead Parallax." In *Dead Letters, Vol. II*, N. Meriwether, ed. Columbia, SC: Dead Letters Press, 2003.
_____. "Nothing to Hold (You Can't Let Go): Embracing the Uncanny in Grateful Dead Songs of Home." In *Dead Letters, Vol. IV*, N. Meriwether, ed. Columbia, SC: Dead Letters Press, 2009.

"Searching for the Sound": Grateful Dead Music and Interpretive Transformation

Jason Kemp Winfree

> I have spent my life
> Seeking all that's still unsung
> Bent my ear to hear the tune
> And closed my eyes to see
> — Robert Hunter

> The hermeneutical experience also has its own rigor:
> that of uninterrupted listening — Gadamer [TM, 465].

Pause for a minute. Linger over the breadth of the run, the sheer duration, the extensive and wide-ranging catalogue of songs, say from 1968, when the Grateful Dead acquired a sound all their own, through June 1995. Already it is a phenomenon with its own history, distinct periods, monumental events, year- or decade-long moods. Like a family with multiple roots and complex histories, lineages manifest and fade: lost characteristics resurface like a long-gone sister's countenance in new life with its own future; definitive voices and voicings pass and ghost the edges of everything that follows, which is nourished but no less disconnected from them; transient interests, infatuations, flirtations, hit like spring fashions and summer romance, shallow, enjoyable distractions. Listening to the music today, almost 15 years after Soldier Field in Chicago, the experimentation and verve of that 30-year run still surprises and delights. But the continuity of the phenomenon — no doubt elusive, and yet, there it is! (you know it when you hear it, you know it when it's missing) — is no less impressive. The Dead's sound, the moods, songs, punctuations, fumbles, and heat have left their mark. It is familiar. We know the format; we sing the songs; we remember that moment of silence in Stella Blue under the blue light, the vibrations of earthquake bass, the dissemination of dissonance and the gentle release and return to sweet form. The Grateful Dead have made history, are history, have a history. Today, 40 years separate the '68 sound and the present. We know the development, we can trace it. Blues and folk to psychedelic blues and improvisation, country, Americana, jazz, rock and roll, in countless combinations and doses.

Pause again. An entirely different 40 years separated the full-throttle Grateful Dead of 1968 and the sounds of 1928, or if you prefer, the Acid Test of '65 and barn dances and juke joints and churches of the first quarter of the twentieth century. The continuity we experience in listening to the history of the Dead today cannot begin to approach the relation of the band to the music of its past, the music of what Greil Marcus has called "the old, weird America."[1] Listening today to Charlie Monroe's "Rosa Lee McFall," the Rev. Gary Davis' "Samson and Delilah," or Woody Guthrie's "Going Down the Road Feeling Bad," we undoubtedly get some sense of the strangeness of that music, have a sense of what philosopher Hans-Georg Gadamer calls aesthetic alienation[2]: ours is not the world of depression-era dustbowl migrants or African Americans with immediate family who suffered the brutality and inhumanity of slavery. But our alienation from the music that expressed those lives is nevertheless mediated by a history of development, interpretation, and appropriation heavily determined by the Grateful Dead. Our listening is tuned by the ears they showed in the early-to-mid sixties and which they cultivated for the next 30 years after that. How many more people today appreciate Mississippi John Hurt or Merle Haggard or Jesse Fuller because of the Dead? How many, because of the Dead, know something of Lightnin' Hopkins or the Stanley Brothers or the Mississippi Sheiks, even if they are not really aware of it? How many, like one interviewer, think *Old and in the Way* to be the best bluegrass album of all time (certainly it has enjoyed a long run as the best-selling bluegrass record ever)?[3] In any case, listening to the old, mostly rural music that so influenced and interested Mother McCree's Uptown Jug Champions, the Warlocks, and then the Dead, our expectations regarding melodic line and lyrical order are more or less met. The "old, weird America" is still old and weird, but in a different light, more accessible, and because of that access, at the same time, more cut off, more determined. What exactly is the relation of the Dead to that past, though? How does their creativity feed and fuel it, savor and consume it? How does the past well up in their exploratory musical articulations, reshaped, refined, transformed?

These questions concern the relation of history and interpretation. That is also to say, however, they immediately bear on fundamental ontological problems, issues concerning being and time, the temporality of historical being in its receptive and productive capacities. Within the history of Western conceptuality, though, both the notion of history itself and the ontology corresponding to it are ambiguous, at least doubly and tensely determined. Clarifying this ambiguity will help situate the philosophical significance of Grateful Dead music and its striking coincidence with hermeneutic phenomenology, which is characterized in large part by an insistence on the ontologically generative and constitutive role of interpretation in historical experience.

On the one hand, then, history is construed as a set of past events, a sequence of causal relations that have the capacity to be narrated, isolated, excavated, recovered, retrieved. This is the history of historiography, which appears in academic libraries no less than boutique gift shops, serving understanding no less than manipulative ideology. The events recounted by historiography have their ontological parallel in the idea of the substantial subject, the "doer behind the deeds," as Nietzsche critically observed, a discrete being clearly demarcated, set apart from others, self-determining, self-directing, and willful.[4] This is what it means to be a substantial subject: quite literally to stand under (sub) the flux of change as the being supportive of becoming. Reflecting on this, it is easy to see how these determinations of history and ontology reinforce one another. As a substantial, self-identical being, I have a history, a past, a set of causal relations into which I am placed, but across which I nevertheless endure. And history itself is just the history of the substantial subject writ large. Behind every event, historiography seeks the causal agents, the doers behind the deeds. At the same time, the event itself is treated more or less as a discrete, identifiable being with a life all its own. Such is the history of the Civil War, jazz, or the Grateful Dead. What is more, the historian herself is taken to be a more or less neutral, autonomous agent bracketing herself from her work, just another doer behind the deed of historical research. The practice of historiography everywhere implies the metaphysics of the substantial subject, and this subject measures its substantiality in large part against the changes the historian records.

There is also, however, the more profound question of what it means to *be* historical. The being of historical existence and the history of a being are not the same. There is a world of difference, in other words, between the happening or event-character of that which is narrated by historiography, and the historiographical narration itself. To the extent that such narration takes its object as belonging to the flux of change, it is no doubt correct. But the linear representation of that belonging, which posits a doer behind the deed, is adumbrated at best, reifying at worst, and in any case inadequate to the complexity of the dynamic of historical being. The past of historical existence is excessive to the neutrality of an artifact, excessive to the logic of sequential causal order, excessive to the representation of linear temporality. With respect to historiography, the colloquial way of putting things is instructive here: we say not only that something has been discovered, but that a discovery has been *made*. Historiography not only records, it produces, it forms and shapes. Its truth, like that of art, is interpretive. And whatever form its specific interpretive development takes, it is rooted in the ontological structure of historical existence itself, expressive of its fundamental openness.

In contrast to the classic metaphysics of substance, which takes the finitude of the subject to be a limit that defines a space of self-enclosure and self-presence, hermeneutic phenomenology understands existential finitude as an opening onto the world, the capacity for experience, the condition of play. To be finite and historical is to be exposed, that is, open to what is other than oneself, set outside or ahead of oneself in being-possible. Martin Heidegger expresses this succinctly when he says of existence that possibility is higher than actuality.[5] (This is why the possibilities are dizzying.) By that he means that at any given point, our situatedness, how we find ourselves, our attunement (*Befindlichkeit*), is determined by our being fundamentally unfinished, by being thrown into our potentiality. Our situatedness always opens onto a horizon of possibilities, which is in turn always determined in its possibility by that situatedness. In being-possible we are fundamentally open, determined as undetermined, but always from the here and now, and never in a free-floating way. Possibility is concretized in our being-here, literally in German, our *Dasein*, our existence. What is more, at every point, the openness of existence is developed, articulated, expressed, without for all that being closed down, completed, or consummated in grand achievement. At every point, existence is, by virtue of its very structure, interpreted, laid out. For this reason, "Interpretation does not, so to speak, throw a 'significance' over what is nakedly objectively present and does not stick a value on it" (BT, 150). Rather, as indicated by its Latin root (*interpreter*, from *interpres*), interpretation concerns negotiation, a working out that takes place at and as a site of intersection and communication, the negotiation between our situatedness and its possibility, which constitutes our existence. Interpretation is the articulation of openness, first and foremost an ontological structure.

If we follow these aspects of Heidegger's ontology, as developed in the existential analytic of *Being and Time*, it is clear they take their force from their explanatory power, their rigor and comprehensive vision. To say that existence is fundamentally open does not mean, of course, that we are psychologically, emotionally, ethically, intellectually, culturally, or spiritually open. It means rather that these factical ways of being-in-the-world develop out of a more fundamental ontological condition. We can refuse as well as accept; contest as well as celebrate; challenge as well as affirm. But we do so only because we are vulnerable or enthused, always already touched by what is other, open to the outside, as it were. We shut down because we are threatened, but we can be threatened only because we are already exposed. We flourish and play and enjoy, but we do so also only because we are already exposed. In this respect, the fundamental conditions of the Grateful Dead phenomenon are no different than those of trauma or banal everydayness. What is striking about the Grateful Dead, though, is that at times it seems remarkably aware of this condition, highly attuned to it, affirming its generative and productive capacities along with their fundamental uncertainty and unpredictability.

In contrast to the metaphysics of the substantial subject, hermeneutic ontology shifts the locus of understanding from the visual to the auditory, from sight to hearing. The substantial, neutral subject who can choose to close his eyes, look away, or look elsewhere, proves poor compared to the richness of the situated being who cannot help but hear, and whose hearing is the locus of exposure and communication with the world, which incessantly gives itself to be heard. "Listening to ... is the existential being-open of Da-sein [i.e., existence]," writes Heidegger. "Hearing even constitutes the primary and authentic openness of Da-sein for its ownmost possibility of being" (BT, 163). In other words, hearing is a constitutive mode of the openness of existence, its being-possible, and without it that existence could not be developed or articulated. Existence is most itself, given over to its possibilities and its being-in-the-world, insofar as it hears. And listening names something like the alertness of that fundamental openness, its intensification and affirmation, its directedness toward the interpretive development and articulation that will carry it through.

Listening to the Dead talk about their music, it is remarkable how much their own discourse reflects this emphasis within hermeneutic ontology. "The Grateful Dead listens to the Grateful Dead," Mickey Hart tells David Gans in 1984. "Jerry's listening to me; I'm listening to me; Bobby's listening ... we're all listening to each other, and we're making this grand agreement as to where it should be."[6] When there is no agreement, when the Dead aren't happening, it is because they are not listening to each other, because they do not hear and resonate with the whole of the sound in that moment, because they are unable to sustain the sensitivity to their very conditions, which more than anything else defines or shapes their most powerful musical expression. Hence Phil Lesh's frustration when the band plays ahead, locking into something that becomes static, be it rhythm, scale, or mode. "I find it really difficult. Not so much because I can't think of what to play—there's so much going on ... when I say that everyone is playing ahead, I mean that they're not listening" (CD, 162). In such a situation, there is sonic space, notes can be played that fit, but they fail to speak, fall flat without any real resonance. What's missing in these instances is what Lesh calls the psychic or psychoacoustic space necessary for agreement, space that is carved out, staked out, awaited and sometimes inhabited by attuned listening. In this respect, listening has everything to do with attending to the conditions of possibility that might allow something special and arresting to occur, caring for and cultivating those conditions such that the music can transcend its mechanical and technical correctness. Bob Weir's remarks concerning the band's openness make the point succinctly and plainly: "We're always going to play real loose; we're always going to play kind of open, and we're going to try to create an opportunity for something new to happen every night" (CD, 179). I suspect Garcia liked Bruce Cockburn's song "Waiting for a Miracle" so much because, at least in part, it expressed this idea so clearly, its lyrics a sort of meta-reflection in the song of how Garcia understands the conditions of music-making. In this vein, echoing Weir, Garcia says, "It has to do with creating a situation in which miracles can happen, amazing coincidences that all of a sudden put you in a new musical space."[7]

In his development of Heidegger's insights, Hans-Georg Gadamer emphasizes the conversational, or dialogical, dimension of hermeneutics. That he does so helps clarify the parameters and stakes in maintaining the space required by creative musical expression. Gadamer stresses that genuine conversation cannot be forced, indeed, no more so than the miracle to which Garcia gestures above, the event the Grateful Dead aim to cultivate. Conversation is more like something we fall into, something that happens to us, than something we do or direct. In this respect, Garcia's remarks regarding the relation of the band and the audience are just as apropos of what happens within the band itself: "It isn't something that I'm doing, and that's what makes it special" (CD, 215). Accordingly, Gadamer identifies in the dynamics of conversation two co-determining features: on the one hand, there is the necessity of relinquishing control, and on the other, the requirement of being guided by the subject matter, the issue at hand. Otherwise put, what counts in conversation is the issue, not the subjectivity of the interlocutors, which subjectivity must in fact be set aside in its claim to authority and position of dominance if genuine dialogue is to transpire. When that subjectivity insists too much, the conversation breaks down, just as the music breaks down under the same conditions, the assertion of egos. That is why Gadamer underscores that "it belongs to every true conversation that each person opens himself to the other, truly accepts his point of view as valid and transposes himself into the other to such an extent that he understands not the particular individual but what he says."[8] When the issue at hand in the conversation prevails, when it takes shape through the attunement of interlocutors who listen and give it the space required for its manifestation, the world itself comes into being, meaning is disclosed, truth happens.

Again, the coincidence with the Dead's description of their own musical practice is remarkable. Hart, Weir, and Garcia echo the co-constitutive requirements of successful dialogue: the displacement of subjectivity and the yielding to the issue itself, effected in part through genuine openness to the other. Hart: "You bring the best parts of yourself to it and you see how it goes with everybody else. You have to compromise, surrender—give yourself up to it" (PB, 18). Weir: "You've got to listen to the whole sound and *play what the music needs*" (PB, 51, my emphasis). Garcia: "When you're working in a band, you have to try to let everybody have his own voice the way he sees it" (PB, 52). All of which is to say, the mutual agreement which Hart and Garcia both explicitly invoke is less a matter of harmonious *judgment*, which would still reflect the stance of any number of substantial subjects, than it is an accord or *attunement* that finds a frequency of resonance that takes on a life of its own.[9] I emphasize this because it so clearly marks the very core of the Grateful Dead phenomenon: the ontological structure of openness is lifted up, doubled, affirmed, redeployed, intensified in collective improvisation, conversation rather than monologue, ensemble interaction rather than solos. The band understands this about itself, acutely aware of the conditions of its occurrence.

> KREUTZMAN: Traditionally, drum solos had to be full-bore blowouts—
> HART: Ours are conversations, not solos. We're trying to sculpt air.
> KREUTZMAN: Both of us are catalysts when we're on stage. We just kick each others' tails around.
> HART: We take the drum solo as a walk through a particular landscape, what feels like us each time [PB, 67].[10]

The same point is emphasized in another register by Garcia when he says, "Weir and I have a long, serious conversation going on musically, and we've designed our playing to work against and with each other. In a way his playing puts my playing in the only meaningful context it can enjoy" (PB, 54). Insofar as these conversations take place freely, that is, within limits that do not determine the outcome but rather make possible a kind of to-and-fro, they are the medium of play, and the music plays the band.[11]

I began with a question about the Dead's relation to the music of the past, and in the course of development have emphasized the ontological dimension of interpretation and the privileged role of conversation in their music-making. In doing so, I have shifted the focus of the question away from basic historiography to the ontological character of historical-finite being. That is, I have treated the happening of historical being as exemplified in Grateful Dead musical interaction, rather than directly addressed the history of a given subject. The dynamism characteristic of live music performance is also telling regarding the Dead's relation to the past, though. Indeed, as Gadamer emphasizes, every interpretive event, every historical happening, involves a fusion of horizons. While we have seen this above in terms of the requirement of taking the other's position as valid and transposing oneself into it, it is no less true of the relation of present and past than it is of co-present interlocutors, even if this point seems counterintuitive at first glance. It is worth dwelling on this by way of conclusion.

Hermeneutically speaking, the relation of the present to the past differs from that of two presents more in degree than in kind. To be sure, the aesthetic alienation I emphasized at the outset of the essay does pose a barrier to understanding and enjoyment. Cut off from its original context, the artwork has no one to answer for it, no one to defend it, explain it, or place it.[12] But the contemporaneity of interlocutors never guarantees agreement—imagine a musical conversation between Merle Haggard and Culture Club—and agreement is just as likely between past and present. To see this, it is necessary to

A conversation plays the band. Winterland, October 20, 1974 (courtesy Pat Lee and David Thomson, all rights reserved).

emphasize once again that agreement is not a matter of judgment, but resonance. Because of this, the past can even be received by the present in ways that reverberate more powerfully or sensitively than in its original historical context.[13] In such a case, there is then yet another fusion of horizons yielding to the issue itself, an interplay that is just as mutually augmenting and transforming as that between players in a happening band. Indeed, any given tradition lives only by way of such fusion, persists only in appropriative transformation, survives only at the cost of alteration. In a sense, this means there is little point in speaking about the tradition's "original" form, since any meaningful encounter with it changes it. Precisely and only through such changes it persists, lives on, is given an entirely new life rather than merely a new lease on life. To receive a tradition is, then, to take it up as one's own, in a word, to own it. Musically, this happens when the performer inhabits the song, when a song is found suitable for the singer, fitting for the player, when it is worn comfortably as it is carried into a new context that gives it new meaning. But doing so also changes the recipient. The contours of the appropriated past shape the future, just as the future reshapes its past. And in this way, we see how the radical experimentation of the Dead, exemplified in open collective improvisation, is so compatible with the traditional songs of their repertoire. "Rosa Lee McFall" is antithetical to "Dark Star," as "Friend of the Devil" is to "Playing in the Band," only from the vantage point of criticism, judgment, formality. Undoubtedly, they resonate differently, but that they resonate is what keeps them in circulation, and that resonance is the mark of fused horizons— those of the band members with each other, and those of the band with its past—which echo and reverberate across the entire historical-ontological space of their musical conversation. Like the fusion of horizons that shapes the event of truth in conversation, the fusion of horizons between past and present, their agreement in resonance, is a kind of intensification and carrying through of the ontological openness that makes it possible.[14]

Asked whether he spends much time mining the tradition for new material, Garcia says no, rather he listens just to listen, "and every once in a while something jumps out and grabs me" (CD, 32). But that is how the tradition works, rather than through efforts of pure and painstaking preservation. Gadamer's understanding of hermeneutical experience is again illuminating: "The nature of hermeneutical experience is not that something is outside and desires admission. Rather, we are possessed by something and precisely by means of it we are opened up for the new, the different, the true" (PH, 9). Moreover, it does so entirely because "our sensitive-spiritual existence is an aesthetic resonance chamber that resonates with the voices that are constantly reaching us, preceding all explicit aesthetic judgment" (PH, 8). Extending this metaphor, we can say that in any given instance, resonance requires the proper balance, the proper weight and space, in order for reverberation to sound. For the Dead the resonance chamber quickens best the more evocative and the less declarative the song. This is why Garcia says he is drawn to the folk tradition, and above all the fragmentary character of so many of the songs. Speaking with Mary Eisenhart in 1987, he says, "I prefer the open — you don't know what happened, we don't know what happened, it's not... It's like the storyteller makes no choice — and neither do we. And neither do you, and neither does anybody else. I prefer that. I prefer to be hanging."[15] And regarding "Two Soldiers" in particular: "There's so little to it that you just barely understand what happened. Undoubtedly it was originally 20 verses. But it's got a beautiful melody and it's just real evocative. It's the kind of thing I'm a real sucker for."[16] The same can be said of "Cold Rain and Snow," the only tune that graced the Dead's repertoire through their entire history, or even "Jack-a-Roe," which Garcia taught to Dylan (and which appears on 1992's *Good as I've Been to You*, the first in a series of albums explicitly returning to the American folk song). And it is perfectly consistent with this, although certainly more astonishing, that "Greatest Story Every Told" is based on a rhythmic coincidence with the melody from "Froggy Went 'A-Courtin'" (which also, incidentally, appears on *Good as I've Been to You*).[17] As it turns out, Garcia's remarks in 1966 are prescient of the years to come, all the way up to "Days Between" and "Lazy River Road": "Our ideas about writing songs are not particularly affected by rock and roll," and this because in all its energy rock lacks the openness of fragmentary form (PB, 79).

The depth of connection between the American folk tradition and the Grateful Dead's original songs is wonderfully attested in Robert Hunter's anecdote about "Cumberland Blues." Evidently, someone who had worked in the Cumberland mines mused to him, "I wonder what the guy who wrote this song would've thought if he'd ever known something like the Grateful Dead was gonna do it."[18] In light of that kind of resonance, it is not surprising that Garcia speaks of his collaboration with Hunter much in the same way as he speaks of his attraction to the fragmentary form of much traditional American folk music. In a 1976 interview, he says, "I edit his work an awful lot and, for example, a tune like 'U.S. Blues' really will start off with three hundred possible verses. Then it's a matter of carving them down to ones that are singable. Other songs are like stories. A lot of times I edit out the *sense* of Hunter's songs" (G, 123). "Friend of the Devil" and "Terrapin" in particular stand as examples where Garcia removes entire verses, drawn by a less determinate, more evocative register than he is by the strength of narrative continuity. Hunter, too, though, is also aware of this, attuned to the open structure and sense of the songs. As he tells David Gans in 1978, "I'd really prefer not to get into tearing apart the symbology of my songs, and I'll tell you why: symbols are evocative [not explanatory], and if there were a more definite way to say things, you'd say them that way" (CD, 23). Yet another fusion of horizons, let's say between Hunter, the musical tradition, Ginsberg, Rilke, et. al. And, again, it is as though "Terrapin" says as much, a meta-reflection on what is happening in the songs themselves, in the fusion of horizons that gives birth to them and passes them on: "The story teller makes no choice/soon you will not hear his voice/his job is to shed light/and not to master."[19] "You know, people hear their own songs," says Hunter. "If you can cue them into their own thought processes, then later — when they can find out what the words really are — they might realize that it was their own interpretation they were listening to. I *like* that" (PB, 86). So, the Grateful Dead carry a tradition of music, "espouse American traditional music" (CD, 187), create the context for yet another fusion of horizons. I think Garcia has something like this in mind, at least in part, when he speaks of the Grateful Dead as "custodians of this thing" (CD, 53).

Notes

1. Greil Marcus, *Invisible Republic: Bob Dylan's Basement Tapes* (New York: Henry Holt and Company, 1977), 87 ff.
2. Hans-Georg Gadamer and David E. Linge, trans. and eds., *Philosophical Hermeneutics* (Berkeley: University of California Press, 1976), 4. Hereafter cited as *PH*.
3. Steve Weizman, "Chat with Jerry Garcia," in *Garcia: By the Editors of Rolling Stone* (Boston: Little, Brown, 1995), 121. Hereafter cited as *G*.
4. Friedrich Nietzsche and Walter Kaufmann, trans., *On the Genealogy of Morals* (New York: Vintage Books, 1989), I: 13.

5. Martin Heidegger and Joan Stambaugh, trans., *Being and Time* (Albany: State University of New York Press, 1999), 38. Hereafter cited as *BT*.

6. David Gans, *Conversations with the Dead: The Grateful Dead Interview Book* (New York: Citadel Press, 1991), 251. Hereafter cited as *CD*.

7. David Gans and Peter Simon, *An Oral and Visual Portrait of the Grateful Dead: Playing in the Band* (New York: St. Martin's Press, 1985), 50. Hereafter cited as *PB*.

8. Hans-Georg Gadamer, Joel Weinsheimer and Donald G. Marshall, trans., *Truth and Method*, 2d rev. ed. (New York: Continuum, 1998), 383.

9. "The whole thing is this mutual agreement that allows the whole thing to happen. I'm conscious of that. It's definitely that for me" (*PB*, 52).

10. Cf. Garcia's remark: "I don't know why those guys [Weather Report, Chick Corea, Return to Forever, Al DiMeola], with all their ability, don't have a concept that is sort of like ensemble improvisation. They're certainly capable of doing it but they don't for some reason.... That whole generation of players ... they all have that thing of real rigid solo structures. I don't know why they have chosen to tie themselves down like that. I think it really limits the dynamism that's available to them in the music" (*CD*, 32–33).

11. Garcia: "The ones I love are the ones where it's slippery. The best of everything is all around.... I don't know how to explain it, but it's easy. That's just the coolest feeling in the world. Lesh: "When 'it' plays instead of me ... well, as Karl Wallenda put it, 'The wire is life. All the rest is just waiting around'" (*PB*, 61).

12. Significantly, this constituted the weakness of writing over the oral tradition for Plato, making possible all forms of sophistry and abuse. Plato, *Phaedrus*, in *Collected Dialogues*, edited by Edith Hamilton and Huntington Cairns (Princeton, NJ: Princeton University Press, 1961).

13. Cf. Heidegger, we can understand the Greeks better than they understood themselves. At a performance in Berlin in 2000, Herbie Hancock reminded a crabby audience of how, when he first played the city in 1977 with the Headhunters, he was booed, but how a few years later everyone was dancing in their seats.

14. Hart's conversation with Kreutzmann, Garcia's conversation with Weir, Hunter's conversation with the band, the band's conversation with its own history, its conversation with the traditional musical forms upon which it draws—all this piles up as a complex fusion of horizons that has a life of its own.

15. Mary Eisenhart, "Transcript: Jerry Garcia Interview" (November 12, 1987, Part 1 of 4), 7. Online at: http://www.yoyow.com/marye/garcia.html.

16. "Well, this tune starts off with a Boston boy and a friend sitting around a campfire, and the Boston boy is saying, 'I'll do what you want me to provided you write to my mother, if I ... if something happens to me.' So we don't know what the other guy wanted him to do.... Then he talks about his mother a little, and then they go off to the battle. And then there's a great verse of battle stuff that has incredible lines in it. And the battle is over, and at the end of the battle the people who are dead, left on the hill after the battle, are the boy with the curly hair, the Boston boy, and the person he was talking to. So there's nobody to write to mother, and it ends" (ibid.).

17. "It ['Greatest Story Ever Told'] actually started out with a pump that Mickey had—he recorded the pump and told me to write a song [laughs]. I ran the pump tape and built a chord structure around it. Mickey suggested that I pattern the song after 'Froggy Went A-Courtin' and He did Ride.' So I sort of patterned the melody after that" (*CD*, 138–39).

18. Stephen Peters, *The Stories Behind Every Grateful Dead Song: What a Long Strange Trip* (New York: Thunder's Mouth Press, 1999), 68.

19. Robert Hunter, *A Box of Rain* (New York: Viking Press, 1990), 311.

Bibliography

Eisenhart, Mary. "Transcript: Jerry Garcia Interview, November 12, 1987, Part 1 of 4." Online at: http://www.yoyow.com/marye/garcia.html.

Gadamer, Hans-Georg, and David E. Linge, trans. and ed. *Philosophical Hermeneutics*. Berkeley: University of California Press, 1976.

Gadamer, Hans-Georg, Joel Weinsheimer, and Donald G. Marshall, trans. *Truth and Method*. 2d rev. ed. New York: Continuum, 1998.

Gans, David. *Conversations with the Dead: The Grateful Dead Interview Book*. New York: Citadel Press, 1991.

_____, and Peter Simon. *An Oral and Visual Portrait of the Grateful Dead: Playing in the Band*. New York: St. Martin's Press, 1985.

Heidegger, Martin, and Joan Stambaugh, trans. *Being and Time*. Albany: State University of New York Press, 1999.

Hunter, Robert. *A Box of Rain*. New York: Viking Press, 1990.

Marcus, Greil. *Invisible Republic: Bob Dylan's Basement Tapes*. New York: Henry Holt, 1977.

Nietzsche, Friedrich, and Walter Kaufmann, trans. *On the Genealogy of Morals*. New York: Vintage Books, 1989.

Peters, Stephen. *The Stories Behind Every Grateful Dead Song: What a Long Strange Trip*. New York: Thunder's Mouth Press, 1999.

Plato. *Collected Dialogues*. Edith Hamilton and Huntington Cairns, eds. Princeton, NJ: Princeton University Press, 1961.

Weizman, Steve. "Chat with Jerry Garcia." In *Garcia: By the Editors of Rolling Stone*. Boston: Little, Brown, 1995.

Plato's *Pharmakon*: Grateful Dead Concerts and the Politics of Getting High

Elizabeth Carroll

According to Grateful Dead historian Dennis McNally, "The parking lot and interior of every Dead concert" were spaces of "a no-holds-barred orgy of pot, LSD, nitrous oxide and other substances."[1] Without a doubt, drugs were a central feature of the Dead concert experience; however, their presence held multiple and often contradictory meanings. Some considered their use as sacramental, as in a spiritual ritual; some felt their use was purely recreational; for others, taking drugs meant something else; and a few avoided them entirely. Over the years, some drugs maintained a consistently positive reputation among Deadheads, such as LSD, mushrooms, and marijuana, while the popularity of other drugs rose and fell as trends, values, and availability changed in the community. Moreover, for almost all Deadheads, some important distinctions had to be made among the various substances: "drugs" simply couldn't be lumped together in one category without glossing over important differences in the substances that term was meant to cover. Although drugs occupied a central role in the Grateful Dead scene, no consensus among Deadheads was ever reached on the values, meanings, or impacts of their presence.

As a Deadhead myself, I traveled to many Grateful Dead shows over a nine-year period, and during that time, I witnessed a wide range of behaviors, attitudes, and perspectives associated with drug use. At the extreme, drugs functioned in oppositional terms: as agents of liberation, sacraments of ritual, and technologies of ecstatic experience; but also as substances of addiction, overdose, and criminal sanctions. What are we to make of the competing narratives of drug use: celebration and liberation, on the one hand, and destruction, death, and imprisonment on the other? Without generalizing or oversimplifying, what meaning can we make of the presence of drugs at Grateful Dead shows, and how can we account for the contradictory effects they produced on a subculture practically defined by their presence?

To answer these questions, it is necessary to situate discourses in a historical context. In the late twentieth century United States, dominant discourses, on the one hand, were cast in combative ("war on drugs") and absolute ("just say 'no'") frameworks. The Deadhead subculture, on the other hand, created an alternative rhetoric of drugs, one that challenged and reframed dominant legal, social, and medical discourses on the value and meaning of drugs. The community defined its own norms and prohibitions concerning certain drugs and rituals of drug use (a contentious and unsettled set of norms and prohibitions, but present nonetheless), and these norms and prohibitions differed dramatically from those found in mainstream American culture. My research reveals that band members and Deadheads' narratives of drug use form an alternative rhetoric of drugs in at least two ways: first, by introducing alternative definitions, metaphors, and images relating to drugs that move us beyond the limited, binary thinking commonly associated with dominant discourses on drugs (legal/illegal, recreational/abusive, drug-induced/drug-free, etc.); second, by calling into question dominant assumptions about issues not commonly considered in public debates about drug use, for example, matters that relate to cognitive liberties, responsible citizenship, and body politics more generally.

This alternative rhetoric emerged from multiple sites, including Deadheads' experiential narratives and behavior at shows, printed interviews with band members, and lyrics to the Grateful Dead's music. Using ethnographic methods of data collection, including interviews with Deadheads and personal observations at Dead concerts, I have begun to piece together this alternative rhetoric of drugs, which is the subject of this essay. To interpret the data I collected, I rely on Jacques Derrida's analysis of the *pharmakon,* which I define and describe in the next section, to attempt to capture the multilayered and contradictory meanings that emerged in the narratives. As Grateful Dead scholar Jeremy Ritzer points out, Deadhead culture was polysemic, capable of producing multiple meanings.[2] Derrida's writing on the *pharmakon* offers a lens through which we might consider this polysemic, alternative rhetoric of drugs in a Grateful Dead context.

The Pharmakon

The concept of the *pharmakon* captures the multiplicity of meaning, including the contradictions and wide-ranging uses of drugs at Grateful Dead shows. *Pharmakon*—the Greek term from which we derive pharmacy, pharmacist, and pharmaceutical — is defined as both medicine and poison. As a contranym (a word that means a thing and its opposite), it reveals the competing definitions and functions of drugs in the Grateful Dead scene, disrupting the dualistic thinking that accompanies dominant discourses on drugs (e.g., glorifying/condemning, allowing/prohibiting). Moreover, the *pharmakon* refuses monolithic categories (such as addiction) and effectively calls into question the binary (and artificial) separation of drug and drug-free experiences.

In his extended essay "Plato's Pharmacy," Derrida deconstructs the *pharmakon* in Plato's writings, arguing that the entire western metaphysical tradition is based on a binary conception of inside/outside that is unstable in its opposition, most notably in the opposition of speech/writing. In Plato's *Phaedrus*, the god Theuth presents the king with gifts for the people. The most important gift he presents, according to Socrates, is writing, a *pharmakon* which Theuth describes as a "remedy" (*pharmakon*) for the problems associated with memory; the king, however, disagrees with him, claiming that writing is a "poison" (*pharmakon*) to memory because it can allow people to forget. In translations of Plato's writings, *pharmakon* has been translated variously as remedy, poison, (either the cure or the illness or its cause), philter, drug, recipe, charm, medicine, substance, spell.[3] No single word in English captures the play, the range of meaning involved in the *pharmakon*'s signification; therefore, Derrida points out, every time *pharmakon* is translated, the translator must decide something ultimately indeterminable — whether to translate the term as "medicine" or "poison" — and thereby reduce the meaning of *pharmakon*. The *pharmakon* in Plato's writings, Derrida explains, introduces a play of oppositions: remedy/poison, good/evil, inside/outside, true/false, and, far from being limited by them, the *pharmakon* enables the coming into play of oppositions without allowing its meaning to be restricted to the concepts whose boundaries it creates.[4] In other words, the *pharmakon* usefully captures the multiple meanings involved in a rhetoric of drugs without forcing a translation to a term that will ultimately reduce its meaning to either medicine or poison. Like the *pharmakon* in "Plato's Pharmacy," the Grateful Dead *pharmakon* cannot be clearly defined as either "medicine" or "poison": it must mean both at once for it to account for the range, complexity, and competition of the meaning of drugs in the Grateful Dead scene.

If we attempt to isolate the extremes of the medicine/poison binary, we can identify some markers at either extreme (e.g., marijuana more clearly in the "medicine" category, heroin located closer to "poison"), but, as we see upon closer examination, even at the extreme, the *pharmakon* refuses to be fixed as either medicine or poison. This refusal forms one aspect of the Deadhead socialization process that is rhetorically induced, meaning that part of how one becomes a Deadhead is through a restructured, revised relationship to drugs and drug use. As one bumper sticker on a Dead tour commanded, "D.A.R.E. to think for yourself!" Playing with the drug war propaganda, this imperative on a Deadhead bumper sticker called on readers to question dominant assumptions about drugs and to form new opinions about how and in what contexts drugs could operate as either poison or medicine or both.

This alternative rhetoric of drugs, structured by the logic of the *pharmakon*, acted on Deadheads, through a process of identification with other Deadheads and the music of the Dead, to alter values, assumptions, beliefs, and judgments from the dominant culture: initiation into Deadhead subculture carried alternative ways of thinking and talking about drugs, and these alternatives formed cultural attitudes toward drugs that ultimately affected matters that, on the surface, would seem unrelated or only indirectly related to drugs— these matters we might refer to as the ideological dimension of this alternative rhetoric. Matters related to Deadhead identity, community, and aesthetics cannot be separated from the *pharmakon*.

The Pharmakon *as Medicine*

Narratives of the Grateful Dead's origins place the band's emergence in the context of the Acid Tests, events that Hal Espen describes as "wild, euphoric, Dadaist affairs that celebrated noise, nonsense, and open-ended improvisation."[5] Although the Acid Tests lasted only a short while in the late '60s, they established the framework for the entire Grateful Dead experience: "Those acid-fuelled evenings became the inspiration and the model for the next three decades of Grateful Dead concerts, each of which sought to invoke, in some measure, the crazed, beatific spirit of the Acid Tests."[6] As band member Jerry Garcia put it, "The Acid Test was the prototype for our whole basic trip."[7] A foundational aspect of the Grateful Dead's origins, LSD's good reputation in the scene held up throughout the entire 30-year trip of the Grateful Dead and continues, along with most other drugs, to be available today at shows played by the band's remaining members. Band members and fans reported mostly positive results of LSD use, oftentimes describing life-changing, spiritual experiences with the drug. As Dead lyricist John Perry Barlow has said, "I'm convinced that the best thing I ever did was to take LSD."[8] Among the Grateful Dead, Barlow was not alone in his excitement about the life-transforming potential of acid. As Garcia explains, "LSD just changed everything. For me, personally, the effect was that it freed me because I suddenly realized that my little attempt at having a straight life ... was really a fiction and just wasn't going to work out. The realization made me feel immensely relieved."[9] Throughout the Grateful Dead's history, LSD use functioned for many fans as a transformative (medicinal) aspect of the Dead show experience.

Life-changing and mystical experiences populate Deadhead narratives of psychedelic drug use (LSD, mushrooms, mescaline) at shows, and much of the language Deadheads used in these narratives redefined terms from popular use or created new terms altogether for describing experiences that couldn't be described using language from dominant discourses. The rhetorical power of new and alternative definitions for drugs and drug-related experiences opened the possibility of new meaning, and new drug-related terms and definitions proliferated in the Deadhead community. As a significant rhetorical strategy, definitions set the parameters within which subsequent discussion on an issue can occur (Chesbro). In *Skeleton Key: A Dictionary for Deadheads*, 57 out of 466 definitions directly relate to drugs (and many more indirectly refer to drugs). To explore one example, many Deadheads defined psychedelic drugs as "sacraments," a term which, in *Skeleton Key*, is defined this way: "Like members of the Native American Church, some Heads prefer not to call marijuana and psychedelics 'drugs,' with that term's connotations of illness, abuse, and law enforcement. They prefer the word 'sacraments,' appropriate to the respect and gravity with which they use these substances."[10] This redefining of marijuana and psychedelics refers to the mystical, ritualistic aspect of a show that many experienced through a combination of psychedelics and the Dead's music. This alternative definition, as mentioned in the dictionary, is also a distancing from dominant definitions of psychedelics that connote disease and criminality.

Kirsten T., telling the story of her first mushroom trip at her first show, spoke of the Deadhead who sold her the mushrooms and accompanied her and her friends on their journey not as a "drug dealer" but as a "trip tour guide," which is not a synonym for "drug dealer." She understood his role as introducing them to the community and teaching them about some of its fundamental aspects. She explained how she was "taught by a wonderful person who recognized his role as a high responsibility to be [their] tour guide." She was "so moved by his trip about organic drugs" that she resolved for years that "[organic drugs] were all [she'd] ever take." Clearly, this "trip tour guide" provided more than the mushrooms: he provided a perspective on the community and the role (and type) of drugs within in it. Her worldview changed completely after that night: "I knew that there was so much more out there that I'd never known before. I'd never seen or felt so much beauty, so much to live for. Hope. Excitement. A huge community of people who live like this! Screw the high school world. This is where it's at! Most real experience I'd ever had." Her description of the experience was not uncommon among the newly initiated in the Deadhead social world, and it shows the power of psychedelics and a new language to describe them in the formation of Deadhead identity. In her case, a "trip tour guide" (as an alternative to the definition of "drug dealer") conditioned the possibility that life-changing, positive experiences with drugs could occur and that, through her experience with mushrooms and her trip tour guide, she and her friends were initiated into the Deadhead community.

In addition to the redefining of old terms and proliferation of new words to account for Deadheads' experiences with (especially psychedelic) drugs, positive associations with psychedelics were also reflected in much of the imagery and iconography associated with the Grateful Dead. Psychedelic art — tie dyes, posters, stickers, etc. — sold inside the show and in the parking lot mimicked the visual distortion and brightness of color one experiences while taking hallucinogens. Psychedelic lettering and tie-dyed backgrounds on these images communicated symbolically a powerful message about the interrelated experiences of psychedelic drug use and seeing a Dead show. Many images associated with psychedelic experience were integrated into Grateful Dead iconography, and these representations (as with all images) carried rhetorical impact.

In "The Rhetoric of the Image," theorist Roland Barthes describes the multiple levels of meaning and message carried through an image. According to Barthes, many linguistic messages accompanying images carry both a denotational and connotational meaning.[11] Barthes' argument helps explain the rhetorical power of a T-shirt I bought at a run of shows in 1987 that blended a psychedelic linguistic and imagistic message with representations of the Grateful Dead. It was a tie-dyed T-shirt with a skeleton with roses on the front and the list of spring tour stops on the back. On the front, above the skeleton, was written "Grateful Dead Spring Tour 1987"; below the skeleton, in swirling, psychedelic letters, was the invitational message: "It's worth the trip." The denotational linguistic message was clear to any Deadhead: the Dead's spring shows were definitely worth whatever effort it would take to make the long, involved road trip to follow this tour. Cleverly ambiguous, this message draws on the enriched connotational message embedded in the notion of "trip," referring both to the journey to get to the show and the psychedelic "trip" on hallucinogenic drugs that many experienced at any given show. As one of the Grateful Dead's more familiar icons, the skeleton with roses signifies the Grateful Dead itself and adds another layer of meaning to the implicit, underlying message: the notion of "trip" bears subliminal reference to the "life" trip, which always ends in death but is nevertheless worthy of the effort. The imagery and linguistic message both support the idea that tripping and seeing the Dead go together, and the implication is that trips of this kind are worth whatever costs one must pay to experience them.

The Pharmakon *as Poison*

Along with the extremely positive reports and images of the psychedelic experience, however, there were also problems even with the most accepted drugs at shows. There were freak-outs and bummers along the way even with the most celebrated of the drugs in the Grateful Dead *pharmakon*. If we look closely, we find a bit of the *pharmakon*'s poison even in the use of psychedelics. Not everyone passed the Acid Test, or at least not every time. As Deadicated

The gathering storm. Summer tour, 1989 (© Lloyd Wolf/www.lloydwolf.com).

Mamma, a frequent poster on a Deadhead Web site, puts it, sometimes "psychedelics turned on us," meaning that some Deadheads could not rely on them consistently to function as medicine. Jim S., a serious acidhead for years, used to think nothing of "a ten-strip on the tongue that brightened everything [and] put a smile on [his] face." But one night in 1990 at a Dead concert at the Capitol Center in Maryland, he took some liquid LSD and missed the show, remembering nothing as he came out of his bad trip. He spent the rest of his tour days free from psychedelics. The *pharmakon* accounts for LSD's function as medicine while accounting for its poisonous effects, even in the most ideal of circumstances. In general, though, LSD and other psychedelic drugs, such as mushrooms and mescaline, were described in favorable, celebratory language and images.

In contrast to the general acceptance of psychedelics, though, ambivalence (and sometimes outright disapproval) characterized attitudes toward other drugs, such as heroin, cocaine, and nitrous—controversial substances that carried community prohibitions and caused heated debates. Alongside narratives of consciousness-expanding, life-changing euphoria that describe some drug-related experiences, another set of narratives describe the less desirable effects caused by drugs. The most serious are the stories of early deaths of band members and Deadheads who overdosed or died gradually as the result of hard drug use.

Unquestionably the most prohibited drug in the subculture, heroin was nevertheless readily available for those seeking it out. Garcia's heroin addiction factored into the discourses (and silences) surrounding heroin use. When band member Bob Weir started singing "Victim or the Crime" on stage with the Dead in the '80s, a storm of controversy followed from objections to the use of the word "junkie" in the song's first line, "patience runs out on the junkie." In the essay "The Crime, and Its Victims," Gerrit Graham, author of the lyrics to the controversial tune, recalls the outrage expressed by many: "The j-word! Good God, the hue and cry. Desperate wails of scandalized sensibility! Indignant bellows of outraged morality!"[12] He remembers Barlow saying, "'Weir must not — cannot — be allowed to stand up there next to Jerry and sing that line.'" As Graham explains:

> [P]eople were suddenly so high-minded that they wouldn't even say the word (whence j-word), much less why Weir couldn't sing the line, because we were all supposed to understand automatically what the problem was and why Jerry must be protected from this unthinkable offense. Words like "inappropriate" and "unsuitable" were getting heavy workouts.... [Weir] did finally broach the subject with Garcia, and Jerry said, "I don't give a fuck, sing what you want"[13] [Graham, "The Crime," par. 6].

Revealing a demand for silence on the subject of "junkies," this story shows the deep discomfort Deadheads felt about naming and describing Garcia's relationship with heroin. Objections to the word "junkie," I believe, grew out of its connotations of pathology, addiction, and deviance — terms from which many in the community wanted to distance themselves and their drug use. Most people think it is impossible to use heroin and not be a junkie, and the truth of the matter is less important than keeping open the possibility that one's relationship with heroin — or any drug, for that matter — might be thought of in terms that fall outside of the binary logic of addict/non-addict. Lyrically, "Victim or the Crime" also complicates the binary logic associated with heroin through its paring of opposites in the lines of each verse: "Am I living truth or rank deceiver / Am I the victim or the crime; Is destruction loving's twin / Must I choose to lose or win," etc. (Graham, "Victim").[14] The narrator of the song can only raise but not answer these questions. Within the logic of the *pharmakon*, either/or answers are impossible to come by: resisting the binary logic associated with addiction, the song reflects the ambiguity of the Grateful Dead *pharmakon*.

According to Graham's account, the value judgment from some in the community lies not in the questions the song asks but in the language of "junkie" that frames it. The "Victim" controversy reveals the extent to which the language of drugs functioned rhetorically in Grateful Dead discourses as an expression of cognitive liberty (D.A.R.E. to think for yourself) and not as an identity marker (a "junkie," for example). Even after he quit using heroin, Garcia was unwilling to condemn it: "It's tough for me to adopt a totally anti-drug stance.... For me, it was like taking a vacation while I was still working, in a way. I was on for eight years. It was long enough to find out everything I needed to know about it, and that was it."[15] Unfortunately, he was unable to maintain that distance and detachment, but the sentiment nonetheless expresses the desire to use an alternative rhetoric to describe the power of drugs. Taking a vacation as an analogy for heroin use carries no prohibitive or moral implications.

As a metaphor, the "trip" offers a rhetorical framework for considering drug use that simply frames it as another kind of journey, a metaphor that departs radically from the metaphors of war and illness found in dominant discourses. As rhetorical theorist I.A. Richards has argued, metaphor structures cognition, meaning that, far more than a linguistic strategy, metaphor conditions thought in ways that determine the contours of meaning. The metaphor of the trip offers an alternative way of thinking about drugs that refuses the logic of disease and war circulating in dominant discourses. Additionally, the metaphor of taking a vacation implies that one can maintain agency and control in the act of using heroin, thereby refuting the notion that heroin is always a substance of addiction, a condition in which agency is given to the drug rather than the user.

In the Grateful Dead *pharmakon*, we often find a refusal to make a clear distinction between the medicine and the poison, even in relation to the most controversial of drugs. This refusal might be best understood as a larger refusal to take a stand on the life/death opposition, the ultimate of binaries (and implied in any conversation about heroin). The band's name, imagery, and attitude toward death and mortality represented by the Grateful Dead resists the life/death binary and opens up the meaning of the *pharmakon* beyond a definition for drugs. Molly Lewis considers the possibility that some band members died from their drug use because they "sacrificed themselves for the music," a perspective that assumes a relationship between the making of their art and the drugs they were consuming: a medicine for the music and a poison for the artist.

In addition to the crises and complications individuals experienced with addiction or dependency, drug use in the Grateful Dead scene was also targeted by strict federal and state laws. Many Deadheads were criminalized by these laws and penalized with exceptionally harsh sentences, especially for the use and sale of schedule I drugs (LSD, mushrooms, ecstasy) and mandatory minimum sentencing — the result of an escalation of the War on (some) Drugs in the '80s and '90s. This war succeeded in making criminals out of thousands of Deadheads busted by federal agents and sentenced to long periods of jail time. This issue was big enough to concern the band, even as they were trying to distance themselves from their drug culture image in the early '90s. As Phil Lesh said in 1994 during the Dead's induction into the Rock & Roll Hall of Fame, "I'd like to say to the thousands of Heads who are currently serving maximum sentences that there's still hope for a miracle in America, so keep the faith."[16] The Grateful Dead scene could never completely separate itself from the dominant culture, though it felt worlds away. Drug laws drew users and sellers of drugs at shows into the criminal justice system as a result of George H.W. Bush's declaration of "war not only on drugs but also on groups of American people."[17] Deadheads were victimized specifically by the "carrier weight law," which included the "carrier" substance in the weight of the substance someone was busted for carrying; for example, the weight of the paper or sugar cubes was included in measuring the amount of the drug one was carrying.[18] Some of the most accepted of drugs within the Grateful Dead scene resulted in some of the harshest sentences in the U.S. criminal justice system. Medicine for the community was often considered poison from the perspective of the law, a contradiction that victimized both band members and Deadheads throughout the Grateful Dead's history.

While many of the *pharmakon*'s victims were caught in the legal system, others were victimized through their various addictions. Some Deadheads abstained from drugs completely at shows because they were recovering from drug problems. These Deadheads formed a group called the Wharf Rats, and although they were drug-free, the Wharf Rats, like other Deadheads, also derived their group identity in relation to drugs. Modeled after 12-step programs, the Wharf Rats blended aspects of Grateful Dead culture with language from Narcotics Anonymous and Alcoholics Anonymous, using slogans such as "One show at a time," and "Let go, Let Jerry."[19] In other words, regardless of whether or not individuals took this or that drug at a particular show, the meaning of the Grateful Dead could not be extracted from drugs, particularly its psychedelic drug-related emergence in the context of the Acid Tests. Drug and drug-free operate here not as opposites, but in other kinds of relations, such as cause and effect.

The Grateful Dead as Pharmakon

Not everyone at a Dead show took drugs, or at least not at every show, but the psychedelic experience was never more than a metaphor away, the "long, strange trip" evoking meaning for all Deadheads, whether or not they happened to be high on psychedelic drugs. Operating at the level of metaphor, the *pharmakon* refuses to commit to the binary logic of drug and drug-free experiences. As mentioned earlier, the metaphor of the trip posed a powerful alternative to the dominant culture's metaphors of war and disease for drug use. For Dee Flanagan "psychedelic means not a drug but a force, a strength — being able to peer through and beyond and behind What Is Going On, to extract something essential from it, and fuel my life trip with that essence."[20] Psychedelic drugs were both essential for this perspective and nonessential in terms of achieving this state of mind once that perspective had been established as a metaphorical framework for the Grateful Dead experience. After one has taken psychedelic drugs, a psychedelic experience without drugs is possible. As Kirsten T. explains, "Once you've had an ecstatic experience with the music and drugs, the tracks have been laid in your brain, and there's the contact high. Not exactly the same [as taking drugs] but so similar. You get to the same place — high as a kite on the music." The only difference between taking or not taking psychedelics at shows is that without them, as Jim S. puts it, "Everything was basically the same, except I had no problem driving my car when [the show] was over!"

The blurring of drug/drug-free experiences expands the *pharmakon*'s meaning beyond "drugs" and calls into question the logic of binary thinking on a number of conceptual terrains. In "The Rhetoric of Drugs," Derrida explains that the *pharmakon* calls into question "the very genealogy of a vast number of conceptual oppositions: nature/culture, nature/convention, nature/artifice, emancipation/alienation, public/private, etc." (11).[21] *Pharmakon* as movement across these binary oppositions places our discussion both within and outside experiences with drugs. The *pharmakon* positions us between two places (a thing and its opposite), in a movement between oppositions, an experience, like the "trip," often associated with drugs. In the concept of the *pharmakon*, as Derrida describes it:

> We have at stake here no less than the self, consciousness, reason, liberty, the responsible subject, alienation, one's own body or the foreign body, sexual difference, the unconscious, repression or suppression, the different "parts" of the body, injection, introjection, incorporation (oral or not), the relationship to death (mourning and interiorization), idealization, sublimation, the real and the law, and I could go on.[22]

In other words, although the *pharmakon* is defined as medicine and poison, conceptually it implies much more than drug use. It is, I believe, at the center of what the Grateful Dead meant in the historical context of late twentieth century U.S. culture: the Grateful Dead itself functioned as a *pharmakon*—as a cure for the individual and a poison for the state, and vice versa. The *pharmakon* is available as meaning and metaphor for the Grateful Dead itself, which was, as Garcia claimed, "an addictive factor that's useful in some people's lives."[23] In response to alienation, repression, and boredom that characterized life in the United States under late twentieth century capitalism, the Grateful Dead offered a cure to the individual. Taking psychedelics and seeing the Dead, from the user's perspective, were antidotes to the poison of social, economic, and political repression. In other words, those "products"—drugs and the Dead—considered as dangerous were, from the user's perspective, often considered "fit for the liberation of the 'ideal' or 'perfect body' from social oppression, suppression and repression, or from the reactive violence which constricts originary forces or desire, and indeed constricts the 'primary processes.'"[24] In this sense, taking LSD and seeing the Dead were technologies for gaining access to an idealized state of mind, calling into question the limits imposed by laws and social mores. In claiming one's cognitive liberties, Deadheads refused to abide by prohibitions and norms that denied the right to explore one's consciousness. Moreover, the use of drugs at Grateful Dead shows complicates the naturalization of addiction and deviance associated with drugs in the modern period.

To provide historical context, it is important to note that the addict and the alcoholic emerged as categories of identity only in the eighteenth and nineteenth centuries, alongside the rise of the eugenics movement and capitalist development. Those considered "feeble-minded" (the catch-all term for those with cognitive disabilities, physical impairments, addiction, etc.) came under institutional and state control. The attempt was to eliminate disease and deviance from the body politic and institutionalize those with bodies and minds unfit for labor. Many of the most basic assumptions about drug use and addiction formed only 200 years ago. Far from describing anything "natural" or "commonsense," the dominant discourses on drug use are a product of history and social construction.[25]

It just so happens that LSD can powerfully intervene in one's thinking in ways that reveal the very constructedness of categories of difference and language. As such, the opening of the human mind through hallucinogens can operate as a poison to state control. As Barlow argues, "LSD is dangerous because it promotes the idea that reality is something to be manipulated rather than accepted.... LSD is illegal because it endangers Control. Worse, it makes authority seem funny.... LSD is illegal because it threatens the dominant American culture."[26] From the prohibitionist (representatives of the state) we have the following reasons for drug prohibitions: "The need to protect society from everything we associate with drug use: irresponsibility, non-work, irrationality, unproductivity, delinquency, promiscuity, illness, and the social costs it implies, and, more generally, the destruction of the social bond" presented as "the protection of a 'natural' normality of the body, of the body politic and the body of the individual-member."[27] LSD use at Grateful Dead shows endangered the very idea of the law because it caused one to question submission to the state and its rules, and, within the logic of capitalism, anything that promotes non-work has negative value that must be challenged. According to Terence McKenna, "The psychedelics are a red-hot social/ethical issue precisely because they are deconditioning agents. They will raise doubts in you ... because their business is to dissolve belief cycles."[28] Like LSD, the Grateful Dead was a deconditioning agent, a vehicle for personal, social, and political transformations. This aspect of the Grateful Dead *pharmakon* was perhaps its most revolutionary because it pointed to new ways of thinking, new ways of living together and solving problems. The implications were far more transformative than a simple reform of drug laws: the Grateful Dead *pharmakon* acted as a remedy for government's failure to act in the interest of the people and its suppression of basic human rights, including rights to explore one's consciousness.

Garcia imagined a new kind of government as a result of the Grateful Dead *pharmakon*. As he told Charles Reich in a 1972 interview:

> I think basically the Grateful Dead is not for cranking out rock and roll, it's not for going out and doing concerts or any of that stuff. I think it's to get high.... To get really high is to forget yourself. And to forget yourself is to see everything else. And to see everything else is to become an understanding molecule in evolution, a conscious tool of the universe ... [not] unconscious or zonked out, I'm talking about being fully conscious ... the Grateful Dead should be sponsored by the government.... It should be a public service ... and they should set us up to play at places that need to get high."[29]

Here the Grateful Dead, like LSD, is represented as the vehicle for getting high, a remedy for unconsciousness or limited, narrow thought, as medicine for the people and for the state. Garcia assumes that democracies should encourage consciousness exploration and that cognitive liberty is a basic human right and therefore something that free societies should encourage and support.

In what Barbara Johnson terms "lateral association," by following all senses of the word *pharmakon*, Derrida brings into play many other contexts in which the word is used by Plato, thus folding onto the problematics of writing such "other" domains as medicine, painting, politics, farming, law, sexuality, festivity, and family relations.[30] Two related terms in this "lateral association" well worth exploring in a Grateful Dead context are *pharmakeus* and *pharmakos*. These terms are etymologically linked to *pharmakon*: *pharmakeus*, or "sorcerer, magician, or poisoner," and *pharmakos*, or "scapegoat." These terms connect with the *pharmakon* in a textual, signifying chain, meaning that the use of one term invokes the presence of the others and so are involved in a discursive relationship: the magician and the scapegoat are implied in any discussion of "drugs." The Grateful Dead as *pharmakeus*, as sorcerers, is a common enough reference in discourses on the magical and synchronous events that occurred at Dead shows. As Blair Jackson writes, "Few words are as integral a part of the Dead Head lexicon as 'magic.' It is the one term — with all its implications of Merlin, brujos, shamen, and psychic legerdemain — that almost every Dead Head will arrive at eventually to explain what it is that separates the Grateful Dead from other bands."[31] We might also consider that the Grateful Dead as *pharmakeus* (magicians) could act as catalysts for a revolutionary process involved in transforming consciousness.

The Grateful Dead as *pharmakos*— the scapegoat for social ills—conjures up familiar narratives as well. For example, in the '80s, the Dead were banned from more than a few venues because the people in the area blamed them for saturating their communities with drugs and corrupting their young. As Brent Paterline explains:

Many members of communities where the Grateful Dead played disliked the arrival of Deadheads because of their blatant drug use. They believed that when Deadheads arrived there would be an influx of drugs into the community, which would find their way into local neighborhoods and schools. This fear of drugs was often combated by the communities' agents of social control. Local police departments often stepped up their operations, using undercover agents and other means to try to catch the sellers and users of drugs at Grateful Dead concerts.[32]

Far from the illness itself, though, "what many community members feared or disliked most about Deadheads was simply the lifestyle itself.... To them, Deadheads were freaks who ignored America's values of monetary success and status. They were seen as a threat to the American middle-class way of life and to the general norms of a community."[33] The Grateful Dead offered alternatives to the limited ways of thinking and behaving in late twentieth century America and changed thousands of lives, mostly for the better, in a movement of consciousness expansion as well as the opportunity for life-changing experiences.

Much more could be written in the story of what drugs meant in the Grateful Dead scene. What I have attempted to show in this essay is that the competing meanings and uses of drugs in a Grateful Dead context may be accounted for in the rhetorical framework of the *pharmakon*. As the sets of competing narratives that frame drugs as either medicine or poison refuse to be reconciled, the Grateful Dead *pharmakon* opens the space for an alternative rhetoric of drugs, one that offers new conceptual frameworks— definitions, metaphors, and images— as well as the space to explore one's own consciousness in drug or drug-free experiences.

Notes

1. McNally, *A Long Strange Trip*, 579.
2. Ritzer, "Deadheads and Dichotomies," 248.
3. Derrida, *Dissemination*, 71.
4. Ibid., 103.
5. Espen, "American Beauty," 284.
6. Ibid.
7. Shenk and Silberman, *Skeleton Key*, 5.
8. Ibid., 18.
9. Ibid., 102.
10. Ibid., 252.
11. Barthes, *Image Music Text*, 33.
12. Graham, "The Crime, and Its Victims," par. 5.
13. Ibid., par.6.
14. Graham, "Victim or the Crime."
15. Espen, 284.
16. Shenk and Silberman, 33.
17. Elwood, *Rhetoric in the War on Drugs*, 27.

18. Shenk and Silberman, 32.
19. Ibid., 316.
20. Ibid., 232.
21. Derrida, "The Rhetoric of Drugs, 11.
22. Ibid., 13.
23. Haas, "Still Grateful After All These Years," 130.
24. Derrida, "Rhetoric," 14.
25. Trent, *Inventing the Feeble Mind*.
26. Shenk and Silberman, 186.
27. Derrida, "Rhetoric."
28. McKenna, "Psychedelic Society," 43.
29. McNally, 578.
30. Derrida, *Dissemination*, xxv.
31. Jackson, "Deadheads," 154.
32. Paterline, "Community Reaction to Deadhead Subculture," 185.
33. Ibid.

Bibliography

Adams, Rebecca, and Robert Sardiello. *Deadhead Social Science: You Ain't Gonna Learn What You Don't Want to Know*. Walnut Creek, CA: AltaMira, 2000.

Barthes, Roland, and Stephen Heath, trans. *Image Music Text*. New York: Hill and Wang, 1977.

Chesbro, James. "Definition as Rhetorical Strategy." *The Pennsylvania Speech Communication Annual*, 41 (1985), 5–15.

Derrida, Jacques. "The Rhetoric of Drugs." *Differences*, 5.1 (1993), 1–25.

_____, and Barbara Johnson, trans. *Dissemination*. Chicago: University of Chicago Press, 1981.

Dodd, David G., and Diana Spaulding, eds. *The Grateful Dead Reader*. New York: Oxford University Press, 2000.

Elwood, William N. *Rhetoric in the War on Drugs: The Triumphs and Tragedies of Public Relations*. Westport, CT: Praeger, 1994.

Espen, Hal. "American Beauty: The Grateful Dead's Burly, Beatific Alchemist." In *The Grateful Dead Reader*, Dodd and Spaulding, eds. New York: Oxford University Press, 2000.

Graham, Gerrit. "The Crime, and Its Victims." In *The Annotated Grateful Dead Lyrics*, David Dodd, ed. 2004. Available online at: http://arts.ucsc.edu/gdead/agdl/votc.html.

_____. "Victim or the Crime." Available online at: http://arts.ucsc.edu/gdead/agdl/vict.html.

Haas, Charlie. "Still Grateful After All These Years: In Which the Grateful Dead, Pinup Uglies of the Haight-Ashbury, Become the House Band of the Age of Certain Doom." In *The Grateful Dead Reader*, Dodd and Spaulding, eds. New York: Oxford University Press, 2000.

Jackson, Blair. "Dead Heads: A Strange Tale of Love, Devotion, and Surrender." In *The Grateful Dead Reader*, Dodd and Spaulding, eds. New York: Oxford University Press, 2000.

McKenna, Terence. "Psychedelic Society." In *Hallucinogens: A Reader*, Charles S. Grob, ed. New York: Putnam, 2002.

McNally, Dennis. *A Long Strange Trip: The Inside History of the Grateful Dead*. New York: Broadway, 2002.

Paterline, Brent. "Community Reaction to Deadhead Subculture." In *Deadhead Social Science: You Ain't Gonna Learn What You Don't Want to Know*, Adams and Sardiello, eds. Walnut Creek, CA: AltaMira, 2000.
Richards, Ivor Armstrong. *The Philosophy of Rhetoric*. New York: Oxford University Press, 1965.
Ritzer, Jeremy. "Deadheads and Dichotomies: Mediated and Negotiated Readings." In *Deadhead Social Science: You Ain't Gonna Learn What You Don't Want to Know*, Adams and Sardiello, eds. Walnut Creek, CA: AltaMira, 2000.
Shenk, David, and Steve Silberman. *Skeleton Key: A Dictionary for Deadheads*. New York: Doubleday, 1994.
Silberman, Steve. "Transformative Mysteries." In *The Grateful Dead Reader*, edited by David G. Dodd and Diana Spaulding. New York: Oxford University Press, 2000.
Trent, James W. *Inventing the Feeble Mind: A History of Mental Retardation in the United States*. Berkeley: University of California Press, 1994.

When "Reason Tatters": Nietzsche and the Grateful Dead on Living a Healthy Life

Stan Spector

That Nietzsche was the first philosopher to speak directly to my experiences with Grateful Dead music is probably not that unusual. Many Deadheads even just cursorily familiar with Nietzsche's discussion of the Dionysian element in art and life have been struck in a similar fashion. Too often, though, the discussion of Nietzsche in relation to the Grateful Dead has not moved beyond that relationship. In this paper, I explore more closely the relationship and affinities linking Nietzsche's thought to the Grateful Dead, first by situating Nietzsche's comments on art and living a healthy life within the wider context of his general critique of Western culture and philosophy, and then by showing how the thoughtful lyricism expressed in so many Grateful Dead songs follows a path similar to Nietzsche's thought.

Nietzsche's first work, *The Birth of Tragedy*, is, as he himself said, the work of a young man; nonetheless, I would argue that certain themes introduced in that work stayed with Nietzsche throughout his active philosophical career. One of these themes is reflected, first in the context of tragedy and then in the context of philosophy, by how Nietzsche identifies the rise of rationality as a dominant operative principle in the post Golden Age of the Greeks. Against the standard literary view of Greek tragedy that placed Euripides at its highest point, Nietzsche argued the exact opposite, namely, that it was Euripides who *destroyed* tragedy precisely by making it rational.

What had distinguished the works of the earlier Greek tragedians, most notably Aeschylus and Sophocles, from the art forms that preceded them, and what set them apart as ultimate expressions of art, was their expression of the perfect tensional balance between the Apollonian and Dionysian tendencies. The tensional tendencies represented by the figures of Apollo and Dionysus had always already been at play in art, whether it was in the more Apollonian epic poetry or in the more Dionysian dithyramb. According to Nietzsche, both principles are necessary for art and, by implication, for a healthy life.

When Euripides did away with the chorus and instructed actors to speak at the beginning of his plays to explain the sequence of events and their causal relationships, he did away with Dionysian elements that speak to the uncertainties and randomness of life. But according to Nietzsche, Euripides did more than just purge the Dionysian element from artistic expression. "Because you had abandoned Dionysus," Nietzsche said to Euripides, "Apollo abandoned you."[1]

Still, it is misleading, on this account, to conclude that by eliminating the Dionysian tendency from his artistic balance, Euripides wrote plays that were wholly Apollonian. In fact, on Nietzsche's analysis, no element of the Apollonian can survive the excision of the Dionysian. In anticipation of the Structuralist move that assigns meaning to terms only in their binary opposition to each other, Nietzsche claimed that the Apollonian is not left over after the Dionysian is eliminated, for neither tendency can sustain itself without the tension of its complement.

Thus, in the plays of Euripides, a new and different principle emerged, effectively killing tragedy. To be fair, Nietzsche noted that when Euripides was old and facing death, he finally recognized what he had done and tried to rectify it. But alas, it was too late, for by the time "the poet recanted, his tendency had already triumphed. Dionysus had already been scared from the tragic stage, by a demonic power speaking through Euripides." But as Nietzsche pointed out, "Even Euripides was in a sense only a mask: the deity that spoke through him was neither Dionysus nor Apollo, but an altogether newborn demon, called *Socrates*" (BT, 82).

So just as Nietzsche inverts our normal understanding of Greek drama by showing that Euripides was not the high point of tragedy but really its assassin, so too has he identified the classical philosophical and cultural icon, Socrates, as an ultimate villain. That is, the villain is the heroic Socrates revered by Plato as the ideal philosophical practitioner who yearns to know how to live the good life; the same Socrates who marks the beginning of our philosophical and cultural tradition, for whom the unexamined life was not worth living; indeed, the same Socrates who introduced the practice of dialectic into the life of reason, thereby establishing a demand for proofs and reasons which has given rise to science (and of course to the invention of the electric guitar). For Nietzsche, Socrates is clearly the one who spoke through Euripides because he had already begun to speak for (and through) all that was to survive the destruction of the Golden Age of Greece. Foreshadowed in the voice of Euripides, the Socratic remedy for all that troubled Greece was to privilege rational knowledge and discourse, over all other forms of understanding.

By eliminating the Dionysian and Apollonian elements from art and substituting reason in their place, Socrates eliminated the immediate and natural impulses and drives and subordinated life to the mediating practices of rational reflection, knowledge and thought. When Socrates said that "the beautiful is intelligible" and that "virtue is knowledge," he claimed that living the good life is living in accord with cool, calm, calculative, deliberative, reflective, theoretical, cognitive, or rational thought, and that art and morality are to be understood and judged solely in terms of knowledge. This notion of "rationality at any cost"[2] has of course led to absurd conclusions, often denying the reality of the very life we are living at the time we engage in reflective, theoretical, or cognitive analysis.

Nietzsche's criticism of Socrates and the Western philosophical tradition is not that we think, but rather that we think *too much,* or over-think. We have allowed thinking and the drive for epistemic certainty to trump the actual living of a life. We have allowed our impulse and drive for reason to become the supreme instinct, which has diminished, or even negated, other impulses and drives that might have come to the forefront; consequently, we have forgotten how to live a natural life. We have forgotten how to recognize the naturalness of an instinct, much less how to know if it is a healthy or unhealthy one, because we have been habituated to mistrust our instincts and to think things out thoroughly before we act. Nietzsche's reintroduction of naturalism into morality and action aims to dismantle reason's project to defeat competing impulses and drives, and to help us understand why reason should be but one drive and impulse among many others that come into play as we live our lives.

Through the rise of Socratic rational discourse and dialectic, the naturalism characteristic of Apollonian-Dionysian relations, once intimately linked to life in our bodies, was replaced by a privilege afforded mental activity. To be sure, ancient Greeks thought things through and exercised rational or cognitive deliberation and computation, but their cognitive thinking and problem solving took place within frameworks established by the tension-filled balance of Apollonian-Dionysian tendencies. As Nietzsche proclaimed at the beginning of *The Birth of Tragedy,* this balance expresses an ontological truth about life precisely insofar as it is reflected in and through physiological states of the body. The Apollonian state was like a dream, while the Dionysian state was a form of intoxication. Whereas the Apollonian dream individuated experience and expressed itself through the visual arts, Dionysian intoxication captured the frenzy and unity of undifferentiated and precognitive experience, and was usually expressed through music.

During the Golden Age of Greece, when tragedy reached its highest fulfillment, rational thought was merely a function of the Apollonian dream experience. Rationality, represented by the god Apollo, occurred within a context marking the interplay between dream and intoxication, and so took place within a fabric of life that was uncertain and random. With the elevation of

Euripides and Socrates, rational thought was abstracted from its somatic and natural setting and allowed to become an independent force, first by negating its Dionysian counterpart, then by abandoning its Apollonian context, and finally by denying altogether the privileged reality of a natural life.

In *The Genealogy of Morals*, Nietzsche described the consequences of this transition, from initially living in accord with our natural, bodily instincts and drives, including thinking, to forsaking the bodily drives and instincts in order to live solely in accord with thinking. In the following passage, he identified some consequences for human beings:

> They felt unable to cope with the simplest undertakings; in this new world they no longer possessed their former guides, their regulating, unconscious and infallible drives: they were reduced to thinking, inferring, reckoning, coordinating cause and effect, these unfortunate creatures; they were reduced to their "consciousness," their weakest and most fallible organ![3]

Having forgotten what it means to live a natural life, *in* our bodies, not *alongside* our bodies, we encounter uncertainties, randomness and disruptions in the flow of existence by trying to think our way through an artificial life we have created in our "mind's eye."

As we turn now to the Grateful Dead, I trust it will become clear that they expressed this view in the lyrics of many of their songs, and that the musical nuances of point/counter-point rhythm and melody provided a rich platform for the delivery of these lyrics to willing accomplices in concert audiences and living rooms saturated with live Grateful Dead music. Like Nietzsche's aphorisms, these lyrics questioned the dominance of rational thought, and, again like Nietzsche, they articulated a "naturalized" morality of action intimately bound up with the worldly existence of the body.[4]

To concentrate the focus of this paper on Grateful Dead philosophy, I have resisted the temptation to discuss songs the Grateful Dead covered, and have concentrated instead on a core collection of their original tunes. Clearly this is not a comprehensive study calling for careful analysis of every song in the Grateful Dead songbook (though if counterpoints to my analysis were exhibited in Grateful Dead lyrics, it would be important to discuss these in relation to my argument).[5] My project here is to delineate philosophical positions embedded in many of their songs, and to show how these lyrics express not only Nietzsche's critique of Western culture, reason and rational philosophies but also his call for a naturalized morality. I do not think it is necessary to look at every song they played: that sort of an analysis is beyond the scope of this paper. Instead, I will look at a core collection of tunes that clearly show this connection. Also, since the songs they wrote did not appear regularly at steady intervals but emerged in clusters of creative outburst, I approach their songs within the context of these clusters.

The first set of original tunes appeared between November 1967 and January 1968, and included "Cryptical Envelopment," "Quadlibet for Tender Feet,"

"Dark Star," "Born Cross-Eyed," "China Cat Sunflower," and "The Eleven." Of these early psychedelic tunes, "Dark Star" stands out as the central composition of that period and has come to be regarded as the signature Grateful Dead tune.[6] While it might be surprising to learn that "Dark Star" is the only song in the Grateful Dead catalogue written collectively by the entire band and lyricist Robert Hunter, this realization soon fades once we recognize "Dark Star" is where we find the first concrete statement of a Grateful Dead philosophy.

As I have argued elsewhere,[7] a case can be made that "Dark Star" captures the precise tensional balance between Apollonian and Dionysian tendencies operative in Greek tragedy, as when Apollo would speak through Dionysus and Dionysius would speak through Apollo. The Dionysian music of "Dark Star" speaks through the Apollonian form of order and structure, and the Apollonian poetry of the lyrics speaks through the nonrational, nonindividuated musical voice of Dionysus. In each singular performance of "Dark Star," the band would first establish a mood instrumentally. After establishing the texture of the song, Garcia would sing the first verse.[8] The first allusions are to a crashing star "pouring its light into ashes." Our first instinct might be to wonder what this means. We might wonder if the ashes are already there, as an end point of the light, or whether the light dims and becomes ash-like, not to mention wondering what a dark star is or what it means for a star to crash. But as soon as these possibilities for understanding surface, the counterpoint arrives on a new wave of lyrical insight: "reason tatters." In the context of the song, this statement is actually quite profound and is, I believe, the cornerstone of a Grateful Dead philosophy that clearly resonates with Nietzsche's genealogical critique of Western philosophy and culture.

In fact, when "reason tatters," the Grateful Dead remind us, "the forces tear loose from the axis." Whether they meant this or not, I cannot help but be reminded of Descartes here. As a seminal thinker in the modern intellectual tradition, Descartes articulated the modernist split of human beings into "minds" and "bodies" and clearly identified the essence of human beings in "thinking," all the while claiming to be able to doubt his body more easily than his mind. But as a major figure in the history of mathematics, Descartes also developed what we now know as the Cartesian coordinates of the "x / y" axis, thereby providing us with a mathematical and rational grid upon which to organize our experience. Just as Nietzsche questioned the exclusive use of a rational grid to organize and make sense of our experience, the Grateful Dead were reminding us that reason is simply an "overlay" on human experience, enabling us to create order and make sense of our experiences in "the clouds of delusion." And when "reason tatters"—that is, when we abandon our comforting reliance on rationality—we will be able to look for the "faults" in those clouds, allowing us to reveal fractures otherwise concealed from view by the gravitational bias of the rational axis.

The Grateful Dead never abandoned these themes, whether pointing to the inadequacy of reason to constrain and affirm human life or to the world of rational order as arbitrary and secondary. Instead, they simply fleshed it out in different songs with different contexts.

In June of 1969, "Dire Wolf," "Casey Jones" and "High Time" appeared, and each song in its own singular way translates the initial impulse of "Dark Star" into a concrete situation. "Dark Star" cautions us against relying solely on reason and the overarching grid of rationality, with its supposed predicative and manipulative power to manage the underlying fabric of life: just where *are* these "clouds of delusion?" Even so, the narrator of "Dire Wolf" begs not to be murdered even though it is his time to go. He tries to bargain with death in a game of chance, cutting to the Queen of Spades; but, as it turns out, "the cards were all the same." The Dead are here reminding us that underneath the grid of rationality, the fabric of life and the clouds of delusion retain their integrity; no matter how we try to reason or scheme our way out of the situation, the natural ebb and flow of the situation prevails. Our trouble comes in trying to recognize this, for, as the narrator of "Casey Jones" tells us, even though we have "two good eyes … we still don't see." The narrator of "High Time" captures succinctly this concrete situation of a human being living a life in the world. First he tells us not to think too hard, for no matter how hard we think about something and try to choreograph a result, "nothing is certain; it could always go wrong." Like our friend in "Dire Wolf," we need to live within the naturalness of the world and "come in when it's raining [and] go on out when it's gone."

The theme of living a life within the naturalness of the world returns in the next rush of songs that appeared six months later, in December 1969. The two salient examples are "Black Peter" and "Uncle John's Band." In the former, as the protagonist lies dying and the wind comes "squalling through the door," he reflects first that no one can manipulate the weather. Then, as he considers his own history, he organizes the events of his life into a flow of experiences that "lead up to this day." What he discovers, though, is that "it's just like / any other day / that's ever been. Sun goin' up / and then the / sun it goin' down." And like every other day, today he "finds" himself alive; but like every other day, he does not know what tomorrow will bring. As we hear in "Uncle John's Band," "it's the same old story … like the morning sun you come, and like the wind you go."

So after making a critical statement about the inadequacy of reason to order and explain our experience of living in the world, the Grateful Dead craft several songs describing our experience of the world prior to its articulation through the axis of reason, which hides the inherent irrationalities found in the faults and fractures of experience. Without the superimposed grid of rationality, the clouds of delusion are simply what they are, faults and all. And instead of explaining why the clouds are delusional, or how to overcome the delusions, the Grateful Dead recognized that the underlying clouds of delusion have their own internal logic and regularities and that human beings are part of that natural world, with its regularities and the irregularities of the faults. But though we are part of that world, we are not simply passively waiting for it to impact us, a point the band made clear in the next rush of tunes, which debuted in August 1970, most notably in "Truckin'" and "Ripple."

With "Truckin'," the Grateful Dead introduced two more features of human experience which I think necessarily follow from the initial insights of "Dark Star." The first of these is that we have to act. After all, we are truckin', "like the doodah man / [who] once told me you got to play your hand / [for] sometime — the cards aren't worth a dime / if you don't lay 'em down." As we live in the natural order facing the regularities and irregularities of the clouds of delusion, we have to engage the world. That is, we have to play our hand, regardless of the fact that sometimes we think we know what we are doing and other times we do not. Or, as the band reminds us twice in the song, sometimes there is a clear path and "the light's all shining on me"; but other times we feel clueless and "can barely see."

Both of these ideas are echoed in "Ripple," which also adds yet another feature to a Grateful Dead philosophy. Of course we have to act in the world because each of us walks a path that "is for your steps alone." And more often than not, the light is not shining on us, and we do not know the way home. But we get an indication of why that is the case; that is, we learn why the emphasis on reason which human beings have used to hide the irregularities and faults in the clouds of delusion ultimately has to fail, and why we are faced with the uncertainty of things going wrong, and our not being able to see. "Ripple" tells us that "there is a fountain that was not made by the hands of men." Perhaps if everything were made by the hands of men, then the imposition of thinking subjects thinking about living could account for all of human experience; but as there is this other fountain, the overlay of the grid of reason is arbitrary and inadequate, and sometimes we must carry on in the dark.

Six months later, in February 1971, the Grateful Dead played "Playing in the Band" and "Deal" for the first time, and in the process reinforced the idea of human action in a world of naturalness and uncertainty. Our friend who is playing in the band trusts neither in reason nor in might, and yet he has faith that in the end it will all "come out right." However, it resolves itself without our needing to think through, choreograph or manipulate the situation. In other words, life is what it is; things work out as they do. In "Deal," we are reminded again that we have to act even though the future is uncertain and "we don't ever know." But we still need to pay attention: "watch each card you play / and play it slow."

So, in a span of just over three years, whether knowingly or not, the Grateful Dead articulated a philosophical position similar to that put forward by Nietzsche. They began by questioning whether reason alone is sufficient to account for a human life — that is, whether we are in fact most essentially things that *think*. They questioned, although not formally, whether we are in the world primarily as thinking beings or whether we are in the world as *living* beings. They saw that thinking can get in the way of recognizing and acknowledging naturalness in the world. As creatures who engage with life's challenges and opportunities, we are drawn into action. Often though, we act without knowing what will transpire from our actions. The uncertainty of this situation in life results from our not being the sole authors of a reality, but mere participants in a mysterious interplay linking ourselves to the world. These themes would continue to unfold as the Grateful Dead produced new music.

For instance, "Box of Rain," written in 1970, added two important pieces to this Grateful Dead philosophical story. The first built on the idea of the naturalness of the world, of one day being like the others; but it mentions, for the first time, an alternative to thinking about the world. The way to live is to "feel your way like the day before," and it is here that the Dead echo Nietzsche's emphasis on the body as the nexus of multiple natural drives and impulses. The mention of feeling in "Box of Rain" anticipates the fuller treatment given in "Crazy Fingers" five years later. The other important feature first mentioned in "Box of Rain" is that our concept of the everyday world we live in might really be just "a dream we dreamed / one afternoon long ago." The dream image receives a fuller treatment in "Stella Blue" just two years later. In each instance, the dream concept parallels the Apollonian dream state Nietzsche identified in *The Birth of Tragedy*.

"The Wheel," first performed in 1972, also revisits two themes. First, it echoes the concept of the "fountain not made by the hands of men" articulated in "Ripple." There are two wheels: "a small wheel turn by the fire and rod," and a "big wheel turn by the grace of God." The second theme it revisits is that we have to act. We may not be able to slow the wheel's turning, nor can we hold on or even let go. We also cannot go back or even stand still. But we still have to "try just a little bit more."

The narrator of "Stella Blue," a song first performed in June 1972, has already lived a life of action, has already played his hand, and has noticed that "when all the cards are down, there's nothing left to see." It appears as though he is coming to the end of his life since he no longer has to pay attention to the cards he plays. He laments that the years of his life have melted "into a dream." That is, his memory of his life has taken on a dream-like quality distinguishing the now dream-like past from the perceived reality of the present life moment. The reality of the present moment of life and our relation to it, the narrator tells us, has three characteristics, all of which remind us of the themes first introduced in "Dark Star." First, he sings that "it all rolls into one." This reflects an ontological claim about the underlying fabric of life, what "Dark Star" calls the clouds of delusion. It is not a statement about the collecting of the events of one's life into a single narrative, for what is most real is the single, unified whole, and not an aggregate composed of many particular and discrete objects. In this reality of the whole, the singer continues, "nothing comes for free," for if we take a stance in regard to the whole by acting in accordance with what we perceive to be particular and discrete objects, events, or concepts—as we inevitably do when we reason—then some possibilities will be open to us while others will be simultaneously closed. Finally, the singer tells us that "there is nothing you can hold for very long."

Again, if we approach the present moment as if life were individuated into many particular and discrete objects, then we are trying to hold onto something that is illusory and cannot be grasped at all. We cannot resonate with these non-things since their existence is as illusive as content in a dream. What we perceive as particulars will eventually melt back into the whole. As human beings, though, we cannot help but find ourselves in that rational stance of a thinking subject relating to objects, and as a consequence will frequently forget these three facets of reality. But there is hope for us, for "when you hear that song / come crying like the wind," we are reminded again of the wholeness and unity of life. We hear the song, but as we forget the endless stream of contents, "it seems like all this life was just a dream."

In 1975, the Grateful Dead performed material comprising the *Blues for Allah* record, and although each of these songs deserves a full reading, I only want to mention two. "Franklin's Tower" introduces the function of the song as a way to redeem falling into understanding the world from the objectifying standpoint of a rational subject who stands apart from objects. As we try to make sense of the world through the grid of rationality, we eventually bump up against reason's limits and inadequacies. Then we hear some advice: "If you get confused, listen to the music play." In other words, let the wholeness and unity of the music clear away the confusion brought on by the conceptual framework that distinguishes everything into subjects and objects.

The second song I want to mention from 1975 is "Crazy Fingers." After singing four haikus, the singer steps back and wonders if "life might be sweeter" for all that has transpired, though he is presently unsure. He decides to "see how it feels in the end." The injunction here does not call on us to deliberate about action, nor even to compare one moment of life with another, as one might do as a thinking subject. Instead, the injunction is to wait and see how it feels; that is, wait to see how your viscera resonate with the situation. Later in the song, the singer emphasizes this difference as he sings "gone are the days we stopped to decide / where we should go." The message is we no longer endeavor to calculate a determination of the future. Now "we just ride." And it turns out this exposure, the ride itself, "feels like it might be alright."

There is certainly more to say about this song, just as there is more to say about other songs, especially "Terrapin" and the set of songs that came towards the end of the Grateful Dead's performing career. There is also more to say about feeling, but that is a topic for a future project relating the sense of feeling-as-living to perception, dancing and the body. The irony here is that my

Winterland, March 24, 1971 (courtesy Michael Parrish, all rights reserved).

saying anything about those songs, even my saying what I have already said, situates me in the Socratic rational mode of propositions and statements. There is some danger in following this temptation any further. If in fact "reason tatters," and Nietzsche is right about the dominance of reason in our culture, then, perhaps in the face of life's confusions our aim should be to strike our own Dionysian-Apollonian balance, heed the narrator's voice in "Franklin's Tower," and "just listen to the music play."

Notes

   1. Nietzsche, *The Birth of Tragedy*, 75. All further references to this book appear in the text as *BT*.
   2. Nietzsche, *Twilight of the Idols*, 44. All further references to this work appear in the text as *TI*.
   3. Nietzsche, *The Genealogy of Morals*, 84. All further references to this work appear in the text as *GM*.
   4. These themes are presented in their most concise form in two places: *The Gay Science* (§§108–117 and 343–347), and *Twilight of the Idols* ("'Reason' in Philosophy" and "Morality as Anti-Nature").
   5. David Dodd and others have been working on a project to annotate all the Grateful Dead lyrics, and have very interesting things to say about the individual tunes in *The Complete Annotated Grateful Dead Lyrics*.
   6. See Graeme Boone's two essays in this volume.

7. Stan Spector, "'It All Rolls Into One': Rapture, Dionysus, Nietzsche and the Grateful Dead," in *All Graceful Instruments: The Contexts of the Grateful Dead Phenomenon*, Nicholas G. Meriwether, ed. (Cambridge: Cambridge Scholars Press, 2007), 196–207.

8. "*Dark star crashes / pouring its light / into ashes. / Reason tatters // the forces tear loose / from the axis / Searchlight casting / for faults in the / clouds of delusion.*" All lyrical references in this paper, both direct and indirect, are taken from Robert Hunter, *Box of Rain* (New York: Viking, 1990). Songs referenced include: "Dark Star," "Dire Wolf," "Casey Jones," "High Time," "Black Peter," "Uncle John's Band," "Truckin'," "Ripple," "Playin' in the Band," "Deal," "Box of Rain," "Stella Blue," "Crazy Fingers" and "Franklin's Tower."

Bibliography

Dodd, David. *The Complete Annotated Grateful Dead Lyrics*. New York: Free Press, 2005.
Hunter, Robert. *A Box of Rain*. New York: Viking, 1990.
Nietzsche, Friedrich. *The Gay Science*. New York: Random House, 1974.
_____. *The Genealogy of Morals*. New York: Random House, 1969.
_____, and R.J. Hollingdale, trans. *Twilight of the Idols: or How to Philosophize with a Hammer*. New York: Penguin, 1990.
_____, and Walter Kaufmann, trans. *The Birth of Tragedy or: Hellenism and Pessimism*. New York: Random House, 1967.
Spector, Stan. "'It All Rolls Into One': Rapture, Dionysus, Nietzsche and the Grateful Dead." In *All Graceful Instruments: The Contexts of the Grateful Dead Phenomenon*, Nicholas G. Meriwether, ed. Cambridge: Cambridge Scholars Press, 2007.

The Other One and the Other: Moral Lessons from a Reluctant Teacher

Steven Gimbel

My transition from "person who likes to listen to the Dead" to "Deadhead" was not a musical experience, but an ethical one. It came at my first show before a single note had been played. I was walking around the lawn at Meriwether Post Pavilion and crossed paths with a scruffy looking tourhead selling shirts.

They weren't tie-dyed exactly; he had taken a white shirt, put a paper doily on top and used spray bottles from a distance to get an effect that was a cross between batik and Georges Seurat's pointillist paintings. They were striking, but they were also shirts that could be cranked out quickly and cheaply so he was only asking five bucks for them, about half of what you'd pay back then for a tie-dyed or silkscreened shirt. It was early in the day and I was likely his first sale, so when I told him all I had was a ten and he didn't have a five to make change, I told him just to keep it. The shirt was worth it to me and it seemed like he could really use the money.

He then didn't shake my hand, he embraced it and said "thank you" in a way that was more sincere than anything I had ever heard. I was brought up with the typical middle class values in which thanking someone was an act of etiquette, a ritualized speech act that is expected of one who is polite. But here was actual gratitude, an authentic connection with another person, not just some artificial, socially constructed, preprogrammed interaction. It was a small thing, but the authentic humanity of it made me weak in the knees.

I realized that this place was special. I was a misfit who intuitively felt that there must be an alternative to the shallow, corporate, facade-laden world I saw all around me, but had no idea there was actually a place where this alternative could be explored, a living laboratory running thousands of concurrent experiments in alternative living. I had found my people.

My circuitous path has led me from that show to the classroom. As a professor of philosophy, I am often called upon to teach courses in ethics. A question I am frequently asked, and which is entirely fair, is, "Can you really teach morality?" If you walk into my class on day one as an asshole, won't you just leave the final exam still an asshole, only one who has now read Kant and Aristotle?

My usual response to this challenge is to get philosophical by arguing that acting morally is a two-step process. First, you need to figure out what is the morally right thing to do in your particular situation. Then, you have actually to do it. Step one is an intellectual endeavor for which ethical theory has been developed. Step two, on the other hand, is what we call a matter of character. My standard answer to the challenge that ethics cannot be taught is that what I *can* do is to make people more thoughtful, organized, structured thinkers about hard moral questions, and this is an important step, but what I cannot do is improve the likelihood that they will do the right thing once they figure out what it is. That last step is about individual choice and character and is simply beyond me as a teacher of ethics.

But reflection upon episodes like the one involving my first show has made me wonder about the soundness of my contention. The Dead, writ large, I will argue, is also a teacher of morality, but one that takes precisely the opposite tack from me. While I am comfortable giving instruction about moral decision-making, but not so when it comes to character and motivating action, the Dead see the first step as one beyond their legitimate claim to influence, but see the second as fair game.

Those Who Choose to Lead Must Follow

The Dead, from its inception, was deeply suspicious of authority. The counter-culture movement as a whole, and the Dead in particular, held it to be axiomatic that there is something worrisome, corrupting, and dangerous when one assumes the position of telling others how to act. This manifests itself in many ways within the band and the organization itself.

From its early shows at the Acid Tests, the concept organically arose that the band would function both as entertainer and entertained, it was not to be the sole focus of the attention of those removed from the band, but rather would serve as a conduit for the group mind. The band was not alienated from those in attendance, but amongst those present, within and reacting to the moment, not creating it from above. In Dennis McNally's words:

> The core of the Grateful Dead philosophy, such as there is, is improvisation. It comes from two places. It comes from John Coltrane and it comes from the

psychedelic experience itself and the Acid Tests. In those Acid Tests, the great paradigm of the Grateful Dead was established which was not the archetypal performer/audience relationship in which the performer is up here and the audience is down there. The Grateful Dead, as a result of those Acid Tests, decided that the audience was their partner. They were part of the band. Everybody was part of the band. It was close to eliminating the dividing line because the band was free to play or not play. It was an experience, not a concert; and that paradigm influenced the Grateful Dead for the rest of their career, even when people were paying a lot of money to get into a stadium and watch them perform. They still felt at heart that the audience was the show, the dancers were the show, they were simply the soundtrack.[1]

This sense of performer/audience equality, of course, became untenable as the venues got larger and larger and the band was more and more physically alienated from the rest of those present, but it gave rise to another feature of Dead shows, the almost complete lack of talk from the stage. With the exception of Bobby's "We'll be back after a quick break" or "Thank you, good night," the band was more than reticent to speak to those who adored them and their music, precisely because such adoration often created an implicit imbalance of power, something they were extremely uneasy with. Again, Dennis McNally:

> One of the reasons Jerry did not talk on stage was that he was very anti-authoritarian and he recognized that as a musician with a loud sound system and people in a room, he had a responsibility. He didn't talk because with that implicit power relationship, he could trip someone out. He felt that music, even harsh, nasty sounding music that the Grateful Dead could play, in "Space," for instance, had no content as such, that it was what people put into it. They didn't make stage announcements or engage in the usual banter you hear from the stage and there was very conscious reasoning behind that.[2]

The Dead were very much aware of the possibility that their words during performances would be taken as authoritative in some fashion, and out of a deep mistrust of authority refrained from providing such words.

But it was not only the band members that held this concern. The fear that their words could be taken as commandments also haunted the lyricists. In a talk from 2007, John Perry Barlow recalled a conversation with fellow lyricist Robert Hunter:

> And we were immediately feeling ourselves beheld in a way that was uneasy-making. And the A-team songwriter — the guy in whose shadow it was my humble task to toil for many years, Bob Hunter — and I were sitting around one night, drinking heavily — this was like '73, '74 — and I said, "This is turning into a cult, or a religion, or something." And he said, "Yeah." And I said, "So far it doesn't have any dogma, which makes it kind of okay as a religion, but it's got ritual, it's got iconography, it's got all these characteristics of religion; it just doesn't seem to have a belief system yet." And he said, "Well, I've been thinking about that. If it's going to get a belief system, it's going to be because of us. We will provide it. I mean, we are the ones that are getting up in the bully pulpit and we'll give it a belief system and we could ride this sucker all the way to some

dark place. But you don't want to do that and I don't want to do that." And I said, "No, no, it's already *in* a dark place, dude. It's scary enough now." [Laughs.] This is post–Altamont; it had already gotten pretty long and strange. And so we agreed that we would never write anything that could be easily taken to form dogma. And we were assiduous about it. And we all screwed up periodically, but you'll find very little preaching in our songs. *Very* little.[3]

Contrary to other contemporaries from the Bay area counter-cultural movement, like Jefferson Airplane and Country Joe and the Fish, the Dead's lyrics began and intentionally remained nonpolitical, intellectually aloof.

There are, of course, many words amongst the lyrics that are deeply evocative in a moral sense, but as Barlow points out, they are all vague, ambiguous, or so open ended as to require significant work to make them applicable to real life contexts.

Whichever way your pleasure tends / if you plant ice, you're gonna harvest wind[4]
Wake now, discover that / you are the song that / the morning brings but the heart has its seasons / its evenings / and songs of its own[5]
But if you fall / you fall alone / If you should stand / then who's to guide you?[6]
Believe it if you need it / if you don't just pass it on[7]

These, and so many other Grateful Dead lyrics, are like aphorisms and allegories from sacred texts, in the sense that they seem to embody deep wisdom that can provide guidance in living a good life, but which you can sift through like sand for years without ever finding a real imperative, something you could nail down as a clear moral truth to guide you. When you have a true moral conundrum, you will still be confused even after you listen to the music play. Perhaps the most explicit lyric in this sense is, of course, the famous line from "Uncle John's Band," "What I want to know is, / are you kind?"[8] While this lyric lacks the grammatical form of an imperative, it surely communicates the rule none of us would hopefully deny, "Be kind." But while this is a nice sentiment, it doesn't really tell us how to deal with seemingly intractable moral dilemmas, exactly the sort of work an ethical system is designed to do.

When I teach my course in ethical theory, I follow the typical path and cover the standard moral systems. A moral system is like a black box with a slot, a button, and three lights, one red, one yellow, and one green. Stick in an action, push the button, and a light comes on. Stick in the option to "save the drowning infant you see in the pool," and the green light comes on—the action is morally necessary, you have to do it. Enter the option "throw infant into the pool in the first place," and the red light comes on—morally forbidden, do not do it. Put in "wear red polka-dotted swim trunks to the pool," and the yellow light comes on—morally permissible: do it if you want; don't do it if you don't want; whatever, but it might have consequences worth considering up front.

There are several famous proposed examples of such systems. Aristotle proposes that a system of virtue, determining what would best benefit the character and development of the actor, is the key to acting rightly. Immanuel Kant contends that moral right and wrong are determined by an inviolable metaphysical rule, which he calls the "categorical imperative." Jeremy Bentham and John Stuart Mill argue that the right action is the one that influences the world in the best possible way. Feminist theorists of the '70s and '80s like Sara Ruddick and Nel Noddings argue that "care" forms a sound basis for moral decision-making. In the end, I argue, robust, real-life moral deliberation at its best comes from trying to balance the results of these irreconcilable approaches.

But even this sort of pluralistic sensibility is far beyond what the Dead are willing to entertain. Any prescriptive proclamation, no matter whether it is treated critically or not, is seen as worrisome. It is seen as an embrace of power that has the potential to corrupt and therefore should not be concentrated.

This is very much similar to the argument that Plato sets out in *Republic* in which he contends that poetic attempts to convey virtue are not only flawed, but deeply dangerous. Poetry or dramatic performance involves what he calls "mimesis" by which he means a sense of imitation or representation. To understand the nature of virtue, Plato argued, we must rationally observe the essential nature of the Form of the Good, something we see at best only obliquely in the world around us. In seeing a performance, we are seeing the impression of nature as perceived by the artist, conveyed in a composition and then interpreted by a performer. Each link in the chain, Plato argues, scrambles the reality we are supposed to be gaining access to, like in the game "telephone" we played as kids where a phrase repeatedly whispered from person to person was slowly transformed into something other than the original. Yet, somehow, it is claimed, we are supposed to find unfiltered truth in the resulting art.

Add to this, Plato argues, the agitation of the passions that accompanies the rhythm and imagery of poetry and the mind is in an intoxicated frenzy that is entirely unfit for rationality. Jonathan Lear, a famous Plato scholar, puts it this way:

> On the one hand, poetry promotes intrapsychic conflict; on the other, it keeps us unconscious of that conflict, for the irrational part of our psyche cannot hear reason's corrections. That is why poetry, with its throbbing rhythms and beating of breasts, appeals equally to the nondescript mob in the theater and to the best among us. But if poetry goes straight to the lower part of the psyche, that is where it must come from.[9]

These two objections are not unlike the reasons the Grateful Dead had for reluctance to address moral questions in any direct manner.

This open-endedness, this embrace of freedom to be and freedom from command is very probably one of the reasons it was the Grateful Dead and not their more political contemporaries that survived as the ongoing emissaries of the era, despite the times having been one of the most politically charged in history.

It's Brother to Brother and It's Man to Man

But although where I feel entirely comfortable as a philosopher charging in is exactly where the Dead fear to tread, it turns out that the converse is also true. That place that I have long considered beyond my purview is one heartily embraced by the band and the lyricists.

Again, acting ethically is a two-step process: step one is determining the morally correct act in the situation and step two is doing it. My job as a philosophy professor in an ethics class is entirely wrapped up in step one. I do not create people who are more moral, but people who are hopefully more thoughtful and careful about being moral. I am not a secular Sunday school teacher. I discuss the rational aspects of ethical discourse, deliberative strategies, and the soundness of the arguments underlying them. I do not try to affect the character of my students, but hopefully make them more sophisticated in the way they weigh their options, whether they decide to act or not.

What makes this second step something I am reticent to approach is that it is not merely a question of rational, abstract logic, but one of psychology. Adam Smith argues that the basic moral impulse that compels us to act as we should is what he called "sympathy," what we now call empathy. It is the ability to put ourselves in someone else's shoes. It may be true that we can never know what another person is experiencing or feeling — this is the old question "How do I know what I see in my head as yellow you don't see in your head as what I would call blue, so that for you the sky *is* yellow, and the sun *is* blue?" But while we don't have direct access to anyone else's feelings, we do have a real sense about what we would be feeling if we were in their shoes.

Hence, humanization, seeing another person in the eyes of the Other is the first step towards taking cold, abstract principles and the judgments that come from them and actualizing them in our treatment of other people. Moral thinking begins with ethical systems. Moral living begins with empathy.

It is a recurring theme in both originals and selected covers by the Dead to look at the stories of those whom we would deem the least appealing members of our society. For a hippie band in the love and peace movement, virtually all you hear about in their songs are murderers, thieves, gamblers, polygamists, adulterers, and felons fleeing justice. Yet, what we see is not glorification of their deeds, but personification of those who committed them.

In songs like "Mississippi Half-Step Toodle-oo," "Brown Eyed Women," and "Mama Tried," we get thoughtful biographical consideration given to the source of agents' penchant for wrongdoing, whether it is predetermined by fate ("had the mark just as plain as day"), because of parenting ("didn't get the lickin's that the other one's had"), or a free choice to ignore "all my Sunday learnin'." In every case what we get is not an excusing of their actions, but an attempt to understand the operative causal factors in their lives. They are neither romanticized nor vilified; they are *humanized*.

And then there are the songs about those who just cannot catch a break. Consider the miners in "Cumberland Blues," who are not only starving, but hoping for nothing more than the chance to work long hours in unsafe conditions; or the eponymous narrator of "Loser," who laments, "All that I am asking for is ten gold dollars, I can pay you back with one good hand."[10] From the very title of the song we know that he is not going to win back the money. Like the junkie in "Victim or the Crime," he is "destruction's loving twin." He is going to lose it again. But in all these instances, we feel a kind of empathy for the characters despite their unwavering flaws and intractable situations.

Plato may have been right that poetry is not the place to go for truth, for propositions that will satisfy the reason concerning the nature of the universe or the nature of the good. And the Grateful Dead steered a wide berth around such claims, worrying about anyone who treads upon such authoritative proclamations.

But while the arts may be a poor vessel upon the seas of truth, they are incredibly influential upon the passions. Art does have the power to affect how we think and what we do. Portrayals of archetypes in art will help determine social attitudes towards them. Think of what comes to mind if one hears the word "blonde," "Irishman," "Jew," or "Polack." Based on nothing more than mere jokes, by their very nature not intended to be taken seriously, we know exactly what is meant when someone of that group is referred to. Art entrenches stereotypes in our minds and these stereotypes function as categories to create the way we interpret people's actions and predilections, and form a part of the basis on which we determine how to act towards them.

This power can be harnessed to help shape people's opinions concerning the morality of actions. Think of American anti–German propaganda posters from World War I by artists like Roger N. Mohovich and Henry Raleigh. The German has a nasty, aggressive expression, a pointed helmet, and usually a bloody knife or bayonette. The U.S. government established the Committee on Public Information with the express mission of changing American minds about joining World War I. In order to get people to support a military engagement against which they harbored deep isolationist objections, the enemy first had to effectively be dehumanized, and for this they chose art in the form of posters and Hollywood films.

Of course, the U.S. government was not the first to realize this power, and Susan Power Bratton, in her article "Luc Ferry's Critique of Deep Ecology, Nazi Nature Laws, and Environmental Anti-Semitism,"[11] examines the ways in which German anti–Semitic attitudes were expressed and entrenched through art of the period, including the films of Fritz Lang, Fritz Hippler, Viet Harlan, and Leni Riefenstahl.

These attitudes, both vilifying and romanticizing, as Bratton points out, often express themselves in value-laden metaphors concerning the natural world. Jews were labeled "vermin" or, as Hitler himself writes in *Mein Kampf*, "a pack of rats." The same sense is maintained in colloquial English. Think "rat fink," "rat bastard," or "you dirty rat."

Even man's best friend is so used. "You dirty dog," "What a bitch," "You ain't nothing but a hound dog." Of course, if you put "rat" and "dog" together, the result is something completely different.

But this very pejorative sense of "rat" is employed in a fascinating inverted way by Robert Hunter. August West is a "wharf rat," indeed, he is the least amongst us, someone cast off and abused. Homeless, blind, and an alcoholic who did a lot of jail time for something he did not do, West is reduced to panhandling. He is exactly the sort of person that most folks cross the road to avoid. He is the American version of India's caste of untouchables.

But what does the narrator do when approached by him? Listen to his story. What does that act do? As Stephen Stern argues in "Blind Hope: Wharf Rat, Levinas, and the Face of August West,"[12] this is an act of humanizing. We hear of West's travails through the lens of a sympathetic portrayal. Hunter has taken the same language used to dehumanize Jewish neighbors and used it to try to rehumanize someone we keep from our nice neighborhoods, relegating him to the area "down by the docks of the city." If the wartime propaganda art was used to dehumanize the Other in order to allow people to fall in line with horribly immoral acts, then surely we can see this rehumanization also as a morally relevant act, one that may just give us pause and slightly change the way we look at the next person who asks us for change on the corner.

This invocation of empathy, the restoring of humanity to those most easily dehumanized in modern society, is indeed an act of moral education. It is a step towards real, living, social justice. It just works a side of the equation I do not touch.

Does this mean that listening to the Grateful Dead will make you a better person? Of course not, but it sure would be nice if only it were that simple. At the same time, it might not be the worst of ideas to make "Three from the Vault" a required text the next time I teach ethics.

Notes

1. Interview with Dennis McNally, December 3, 2006.
2. Ibid.
3. John Perry Barlow, speaking at the annual conference of the Southwest/Texas Society for Popular and American Culture, February 15, 2006. Special thanks to Nicholas Meriwether for transcribing this address.
4. Robert Hunter, "Franklin's Tower," *A Box of Rain* (New York: Viking, 1990), 84.
5. Ibid., "Eyes of the World," 75.
6. Ibid., "Ripple," 185.
7. Ibid., "Box of Rain," 26.
8. Hunter, *A Box of Rain*, 233.

9. Jonathan Lear, *Open Minded* (Cambridge: Harvard University Press, 1999), 240.
10. Hunter, "Loser," in *A Box of Rain*, 138.
11. Susan Power Bratton, "Luc Ferry's Critique of Deep Ecology, Nazi Nature Laws, and Environmental Anti-Semitism," *Ethics and the Environment*, vol. 4, no. 1 (1999), 3–22.
12. Stephen Stern, "Blind Hope: Wharf Rat, Levinas, and the Face of August West," in *The Grateful Dead and Philosophy*, Steven Gimbel, ed. (Chicago: Open Court, 2007), 139–148.

Bibliography

Hunter, Robert. *A Box of Rain.* New York: Viking, 1990.
Lear, Jonathan. *Open Minded.* Cambridge: Harvard University Press, 1999.
Power Bratton, Susan. "Luc Ferry's Critique of Deep Ecology, Nazi Nature Laws, and Environmental Anti-Semitism." *Ethics and the Environment*, vol. 4, no. 1, 1999.
Stern, Stephen. "Blind Hope: Wharf Rat, Levinas, and the Face of August West." In *The Grateful Dead and Philosophy*, Steven Gimbel, ed. Chicago: Open Court, 2007.

Innocence and Experience in the Grateful Dead: A Reading of Stuart Hampshire

Nicholas Meriwether

As the last book British philosopher Sir Stuart Hampshire wrote, *Innocence and Experience* struck many of his peers as an odd way to cap a distinguished scholarly career.[1] After a lifetime of work on traditional subjects in academic philosophy, Hampshire's last book was rooted in a personal explanation of why he was so drawn to his topic, and why such a personal grounding was both valid and important.[2] For those reasons among others, *Innocence and Experience* offers much to scholars and thinkers pondering the Grateful Dead phenomenon, an umbrella term that I intend to encompass the various issues raised by the band, its art and the reception of both.

Famous for his work on ethics in general and Spinoza in particular, Hampshire is also known for his contributions to epistemology, metaphysics, philosophy of mind, and aesthetics. With this last book, he fused many of his eclectic interests into an argument on the nature of morality, and its expression through the two related concepts of innocence and experience. Though he writes simply, the thought behind his studied expression unfolds in a dense and complex series of arguments that build upon each other carefully. Those arguments incorporate and refer to a wide variety of issues familiar to Deadheads and to scholars studying the band and its phenomenon, from the artistic theories the band developed to their relationship with their fans, and the associated issues with mainstream American society and culture. That such broad grounds for comparison should be suggested by a monograph on ethics may seem surprising, but I believe this reflects both Hampshire's own wide-ranging interests as well as the intensely personal cast of his argument. And it is worth mentioning that, to Dead scholars, the fact that he resolutely phrases his very serious thesis in such personal terms is also appealing, a mimic of the high seriousness that underlay the band's own idiosyncratic pursuit of the weird.

Both the seriousness and the personal stakes of the book are explained in his introduction. Proceeding from a recounting of how his childhood and maturation informed his adult proclivities and penchants, Hampshire goes on to explain how his field, philosophy, failed so utterly in the prewar years to recognize its own real-world applicability and ultimately its culpability for the evil that ensued, a point made poignant when he notes that a few of his fellow philosophers were exposed as spies and he himself was questioned. It gives particular weight to the simple remark that opens his penultimate chapter, "We know now, as a lesson of recent history, that those theorists who have in the past represented respect for justice as a necessary and universal requirement of any morality were right" (p. 113). Deadheads targeted by the DEA as adherents of a subversive lifestyle would agree, but that is not my justification for inserting an academic philosopher into the midst of the Dionysian carnival of the Dead world. Though that might appear to be a stretch, as Hampshire states in the opening sentence of the book, "There are a thousand or more themes that might be pursued under the heading of moral or political philosophy" (p. 3). The Dead phenomenon is certainly fair game under that rubric, making up in complexity and color what Hampshire's own personal reference—World War II and the struggle against Fascism—frames in sheer power. (One could argue that the Dead phenomenon is far from insignificant on that basal political level, with thousands of Deadheads serving prison sentences for drug violations, many as the result of targeted police sweeps of concerts and even entire tours. The consequences of openly declaring one's affiliation invited harassment in a number of forms.)[3]

Hampshire's purpose, of course, is quite different from that of Deadhead scholarship: based on certain readings and his own experiences, he crafts an argument about the nature of human society and interaction. My goal here is to use his arguments to illuminate the world of the Dead. But examining his book in the light of our own concerns is an act he would not find illegitimate: in his introduction, he explains that it was in the writings of a non-philosopher, Machiavelli, that he found a crystallization of the issue he sought to address:

> Machiavelli was not interested in philosophy either as it is now conceived or as it was conceived by Plato and Aristotle and by the Stoics. He did not intend to start a deep philosophical discussion about the nature of morality and of its authority.... But by his concreteness and sharpness he forced the question to the surface.[4]

Likewise, in *Innocence and Experience* we can see in its arguments for universal justice and a multiplicity of conceptions of the good a way of getting at many of the questions raised by the Dead, from sociology to history to musicology to poetics. Hampshire's work provides a series of arguments that can serve as a prolegomenon to a unified theory of the Grateful Dead: the nature, role and validity of this vibrant and fascinating art and its surrounding subculture — what it was and what it all meant. His overarching point: that philosophy has tremendous bearing on our understanding of the world — and, therefore, on the way we shape it.

That may seem to justify some tantalizingly absolute generalizations, such as Hampshire would be a Deadhead or that his book justifies the Dead phenomenon on all levels — the former being unlikely (he was a classical music fan), the latter, overstretching. And indeed, there are a number of ways in which Hampshire's book could be said to relate to the Dead phenomenon, but the broadest — and safest — level is suggested by a review Hampshire himself wrote of Elaine Scarry's *On Beauty and Being Just*, which links humanity's instinct for appreciating beauty to our capacity for moral insight.[5] In Scarry's words, "Beauty really is allied with truth," and she finds it deeply connected to our sense of symmetry, fairness, even justice: "It creates, without itself fulfilling, the aspiration for enduring certitude. It comes to us, with no work of our own; then leaves us prepared to undergo a giant labor."[6] Hampshire doubts these connections, calling them analogous, but not directly connected.[7] While the number and levels of connection that I find between *Innocence and Experience* and the Dead phenomenon seem tantalizingly close to direct, I am content to call them merely analogous as well, and if I do my job here, then the connections I draw between my subjects should prove illuminating and vexatious, in the same way that mathematicians see the connections between theory and the real world.

There is a danger here that Hampshire's work will suffer if applied to a phenomenon so removed from his focus, just as he writes in *Innocence and Experience* that he worries about misrepresenting Proust for his own aims (p. 130). But if Hampshire can claim that a core of his philosophical resolution resides only in fiction, in the world of art, then surely the world of art and its scholars should be allowed to borrow from his philosophy.

* * *

The broad philosophical underpinnings of Hampshire's book were not what first attracted me. A friend pursuing a doctorate in Religious Studies posted a quotation on his study wall for inspiration, one that immediately struck me as also describing how the Dead phenomenon worked, on several levels, from the haunting sense of loss described by so many songs to the enduring appeal of the band across generations:

> [I]t is natural to associate a pure and unalloyed happiness with a golden past before we were, if not defeated, at least arrested and encumbered by experience.... It may be worth adding that certain kinds of aesthetic enjoyment are very closely associated with this sense of unalloyed happiness irretrievably lost in

experience. While attending to some perfect achievement in art, such as Mozart's *Figaro* or Casal's playing of Bach or a painting by Vermeer, very great pleasure may often be combined with an elegiac feeling, or sadness that perfect happiness is lost — that it is nowhere again to be found in the unimagined world and that it exists only in the perfect achievements of art.... It is easy to understand that perfection of form, as hoped for, but known now to be unattainable in reality. Beauty has sometimes been interpreted as a promise of happiness, or more exactly, of a lost happiness.[8]

The striking resonances for someone studying the Dead are clear, and an entire paper could be devoted simply to assessing that quotation in the context of the Dead, but a couple of central points merit mention here. First, that sense of "a loss beautifully expressed" describes several of the character songs, such as August West in "Wharf Rat" singing, "I'll get a new start," or even that he's sure his long-lost lover has remained faithful ("'Pearly's been true / True to my dying day,' he said"). Another graphic example is "Jack Straw," as he remonstrates with his partner Shannon, "Hurts my ears to listen," and his John Donne-like line, "Cut down a man in cold blood / Might as well be me," a philosophical point Hampshire himself incorporates directly into one of his tributary arguments.

Even more illustrative are the mood songs, such as "Black Muddy River's" agonized accounting of the bleak results of experience or the catalogue of lost innocence in "Standing on the Moon," with its haunting line, "I hear the cries of children / And the other songs of war." Both of those examples are later compositions, but some of their earliest mood songs such as "Ripple" and "Box of Rain" mapped that territory decades before, with lines like "If I knew the way / I would take you home" and "Maybe you'll find direction, around some corner where it's been waiting to meet you," as if referring to that sense of purpose born in childhood innocence. Perhaps the best evocation of Hampshire's "beauty of a happiness lost" appears in one of the finest Garcia-Hunter songs, "Mission in the Rain," in the verse:

> Ten years ago I walked these streets
> My dreams were riding tall
> Tonight I would be thankful, Lord,
>   For any dream at all.[9]

The reasons for the band's attraction to and felicity with this sentiment lie beyond the bounds of this paper, but a quick sketch would mention Hunter's and Garcia's strong affinity for that strain of feeling in American folk song; in a late interview, they both discuss their abiding fascination with and attraction for "The Mummer's Song," with its mysterious and melancholy line about ten thousand drowning who never were born.[10] It is worth noting that both men lost their fathers as children, too. And there is a tantalizing bit of historical symmetry in the band's experience in the Haight-Ashbury, which went from the innocence of a small, organic, indigenous bohemian community to a bloated, mass-media phenomenon.

The second point suggested by that Hampshire quotation pinned up by my friend is more complex, and it addresses the very slippery issue of how the band remained iconic and yet popular—how they were perceived in later decades as exemplars of an ethos that had otherwise died with the Sixties. And their very longevity—not to mention their constant evolution—indicated the validity and vitality of the Haight-Ashbury ethos they embodied. In that sense, to a fan who first encountered the band in the mid-eighties, the Dead represented the "innocence" of the sixties, a time in which youth culture captivated the attention of the country (and the world), and the question was not whether youth could affect change, but how and when and where. To fans who came of age in the eighties, there was no question of changing or beating the system, only minimizing its immediately pernicious effects, or else escaping—dropping out entirely. And Dead shows were perfect ways of accomplishing both.

This is clearly not the same longing that Hampshire describes, but it is analogous—and at that level, it can fairly be said that fans like me were expressing, and perhaps were even expressions of—a cultural longing for that lost innocence, which had informed the era that witnessed the birth of the Grateful Dead.

The connections between the Dead's art and its appeal over generations immediately suggest even more fundamental applications of Hampshire's concepts of innocence and experience, ones which could even find expression in his book. And it should be mentioned that to some extent, the backgrounds of the band members, particularly Garcia and Lesh, predisposed them to a conscious incorporation of the themes touched on by those philosophical issues. Lesh, for example, credits literary critic Morse Peckham's *Beyond the Tragic Vision* with cementing his determination to pursue a life of art—as band biographer Dennis McNally puts it, for Lesh, Peckham "defined the philosophical underpinnings to his inner certainty that only the arts could be free of the fraud that was society."[11] In an echo of terms that Hampshire would base his argument on, Peckham wrote: "Absorbed in the work of art, we can for a moment experience life as pure value, pure significance, free from the guilt of will and existence. Aesthetic contemplation is our only innocence."[12]

But for all members of the Dead, the ethical implications and political consequences of their artistic philosophy were apparent from the first Acid Test on. In his long interview with Charles Reich, Garcia explained how his concept of "high" informed the band's artistic philosophy in terms that invoke broader conceptions of ethics:

> I'm not talking about unconsciousness or zonked out, I'm talking about being fully conscious. Also I'm not talking about the Grateful Dead as being an end in itself. I don't think of that highness as being an end in itself. I think of the Grateful Dead as being a crossroads, or a pointer sign, and what we're pointing to is that there's a lot of universe available, that there's a whole lot of experience available over there. We're kinda like a signpost and we're also pointing to dan-

ger, to difficulty, we're pointing to bummers. We're pointing to whatever there is, when we're on—when it's really happening.
 REICH: You're a signpost to new space?
 GARCIA: Yes. That's the place we should be—that's the function we should be filling in society. And in our own little society, that's the function we do fill.

When Reich asks where the idea of being a pointer came from, Garcia answers, unhesitatingly, that it arrived with the Acid Tests:

> We never formulated it; it just was what was happening. We were doing the Acid Test, which was our first exposure to formlessness. Formlessness and chaos lead to new forms. And new order. Closer to, probably, what the real order is. When you break down the old orders and the old forms and leave them broken and shattered, you suddenly find yourself a new space with new form and new order which are more like the way it is. More like the flow.[13]

A seamless connection between the band's art and its relationship with its fans—and a connection that carried over into the realm in which Hampshire's focus lies, politics. When the band was arrested for marijuana possession in the fall of 1967—a front-page local news story—the terms they used in their statement emphasized that connection between art and ethics:

> The law [against marijuana] creates a mythical danger and calls it a felony. The individuals who enforce the law use it almost exclusively against individuals who threaten their ideas of the way people should look and act. Behind all the myths is the reality. The Grateful Dead are people engaged in constructive, creative effort in the musical field, and this house is where we work as well as our residence. Because the police fear and misinterpret us, our effort is now interrupted as we deal with the consequences of this harassing arrest.[14]

From ethics to art, in five short sentences. Hampshire would be pleased.

*   *   *

The core of *Innocence and Experience* has even greater implications for Deadhead scholars. The kernel of Hampshire's argument contains a description that expresses perhaps the source of the fascination the Dead hold for academics and other thinkers. Forgive me for the length of this quotation, but it is necessary to frame this final thought:

> Moral innocence and purity are incompatible with the effective exercise of political power on any considerable scale, and two conceptions of virtue and of responsible action, attached to two very different ways of life, have to be recognized; and they have to be recognized as a duality that persists through all periods of history. The opposition between private and public virtue is a philosophical concern just because it does not arise from particular historical circumstances.... The virtues of innocence, which are not necessarily the "monkish virtues," realize conceptions of the good which can inspire strong emotions and great admiration: absolute integrity, gentleness, disposition to sympathy, a fastidious sense of honor, generosity, a disposition to gratitude. The virtues of experience can equally inspire strong emotions and great admiration: tenacity

and resolution, courage in the face of risk, intelligence, largeness of design and purpose, exceptional energy, habits of leadership.... Once again the philosophical point to be recorded is that there is no completeness and no perfection to be found in morality.[15]

Issues of artistic and subcultural legitimacy, of drug use, of occasional lapses in the recording studio or on stage — all of these attacks and more can be assessed in a far broader context, one that does not allow the denigration or dismissal of the real significance and genuine achievement of the band and its subculture, that reflect far more elemental forces. Viewed in that light, those philosophical issues also provide a platform for our own efforts to explain the Dead phenomenon, even at the microcosmic critical level — such as why they were so successful as a business, spectacular missteps notwithstanding. They had to be: the experience of business is what allowed them to pursue the innocence of their artistic vision. Or even more microcosmically, it could explain why Garcia tolerated Deadhead devotion but refused to capitalize on it. In an echo of Hampshire's own experience with fascism, Garcia once remarked that he tried not to think about the influence he had over some of his fans: "I've made an effort not to be aware of it because it's perilously close to fascism. If I started to think about controlling that power or somehow trying to fiddle around with it, then it would become fascism."[16]

The band had the same attitude toward manipulation of fans musically, as Garcia explained in 1981: music is "so close to being perfect fascism" in that "it's so close to being perfectly manipulative. It borders on that, and people who use formula things on the audience are basically manipulating them in the same sense that fascism manipulates people." When his interviewer pressed him, he explained: "...our trip is to learn the tricks and then not use them.... 'Oh, far out, when we do this, look what happens to the audience.' 'Yeah, let's not do that.' We want for the Grateful Dead to be something that isn't the result of tricks."[17]

In one of his closing arguments, Hampshire cites John Stuart Mills' theory that "the progress of mankind, in generating new possibilities of happiness, depends on the diversity of 'experiments in living, and that increases in general happiness depend on the absence of conformity and conventionality. Idiosyncrasy and diversity in conceptions of possible values, contribute to the general advancement'" (p. 118). This offers a perfect summation of a fundamental value of the Dead phenomenon, but Hampshire uses it to make a deeper point, one that suggests an elusive unity I believe underlies and informs the phenomenon and its appeal for critical attempts to explain it. As Hampshire puts it:

> [T]he diversity in conceptions of the good is an irreducible diversity, not only because no sufficient reasons have been given, and could ever be given, for taking one end, such as the general happiness or the exercise of reason, as the single supreme end; but also because the capacity to develop idiosyncrasies of style and

of imagination, and to form specific conceptions of the good, is the salient and peculiar capacity of human beings among other animals. It is their nature ... [p. 118].

The tension between innocence and experience is inevitable; the validity of the Dead phenomenon and the enduring beauty of the band's art can be seen in this primordial philosophical axis, which suggests a way of explaining how the band's music reflects and provides a philosophy that extends to and informs so many of the questions we have about this fascinating, complex phenomenon.

* * *

While it is tempting to let Hampshire end this paper, I think he inspires one additional level of commentary, in keeping with the example he sets in his introduction to *Innocence and Experience*. As a scholar, he went out on a limb with that book, and he did so motivated by an attitude that I believe is strongly in keeping with that espoused by the Dead: that you consciously seek out and learn the highest standards for the activities in which you are engaged, and then measure up to them; and you do so with a fiercely independent, personal motivation. You do not need institutions; you just need dedication. All scholars need such reminders; Deadhead scholars should be especially receptive — and mindful.[18]

Notes

    1. Stuart Hampshire, *Innocence and Experience* (Cambridge: Harvard University Press, 1989). All further references to this work are by page number within the text. Hampshire published a lecture, "Justice Is Strife," which he expanded into a small book after this, but *Innocence and Experience* stands as his last, full-length work.
    2. See especially his "Introduction," 3–19.
    3. Two good discussions of this are Adam M. Kanzer, "Misfit Power, the First Amendment, and the Public Forum: Is there Room in America for the Grateful Dead?" *Columbia Journal of Law and Social Problems* 25.3 (Summer 1992), 521–65; and David Fraser and Vaughan Black, "Legally Dead: The Grateful Dead and American Legal Culture," *Perspectives on the Grateful Dead*, R. G. Weiner, ed. (Westport, CT: Greenwood, 1999), 23–24. The seminal expression of the law-enforcement view can be found in Cynthia Farret, "An LSD Distribution Network," in *LSD: Still With Us After All These Years*, Leigh A. Henderson and William J. Glass, eds. (New York: Lexington Books, 1994), 99–116. Based on interviews with an undercover narcotics agent, she reported, "LSD is characteristically distributed by a person who identifies with the Grateful Dead rock group and assumes a life-style somewhat reminiscent of the 1960s hippies or flower children. Immersion in this lifestyle is currently a common variable in LSD use and sale; becoming known among the Deadheads is often a prerequisite to engaging in any significant distribution of LSD" (p. 109).
    4. Hampshire, *Innocence and Experience*, 13.
    5. Elaine Scarry, *On Beauty and Being Just* (Princeton, NJ: Princeton University Press, 1999). I am not doing justice to Scarry here, and her book has much to offer Dead

scholars, especially her arguments against what she calls the "political critique" of beauty, a charge leveled against the Haight and the Dead in particular by Sixties radicals, especially Berkeley politicos (see especially pp. 58–86).

6. Scarry, *On Beauty and Being Just*, 52 and 53. Scarry is a friend of Hampshire, and anticipates his disagreement in the book, quoting an exchange between them in which she posits, "Beauty assists us in getting to justice...," which he does not believe, "...except, of course, analogically..." (p. 94).

7. Stuart Hampshire, "The Eye of the Beholder," *The New York Review of Books*, vol. 46, no.18 (Nov. 18, 1999), 45.

8. Hampshire, *Innocence and Experience*, 152–153.

9. Robert Hunter, *A Box of Rain* (New York: Viking, 1990), 151.

10. Blair Jackson, *Goin' Down the Road: A Grateful Dead Traveling Companion* (New York: Harmony Books, 1992), 208–9.

11. Dennis McNally, *A Long Strange Trip: The Inside History of the Grateful Dead* (New York: Broadway Books, 2002), 19.

12. Morse Peckham, *Beyond the Tragic Vision: The Quest for Identity in the Nineteenth Century* (New York: George Braziller, 1962), 150.

13. Jerry Garcia, Charles Reich, Jann Wenner, *Garcia: A Signpost to New Space* (San Francisco: Straight Arrow, 1972), reprinted in *Garcia, by the Editors of Rolling Stone* (Boston: Little, Brown, 1995), 95.

14. *San Francisco Chronicle*, Oct. 7, 1967, A1 and A14. The text of their statement appears in Jann Wenner, "Busted: The Dead Did Get It!," *Rolling Stone* 1 (Nov. 1967), reprinted in *Garcia, by the Editors of Rolling Stone* (Boston: Little, Brown, 1995), 52. Manager Danny Rifkin's roommate Harry Shearer cowrote the statement (McNally, *A Long Strange Trip*, 226).

15. Hampshire, *Innocence and Experience*, 177.

16. David Jay and Rebecca McClen Novick, *Voices from the Edge: Conversations with Jerry Garcia, Ram Dass, Annie Sprinkle, Matthew Fox, Jaron Lanier & Others* (Freedom, CA: The Crossing Press, 1995), 73.

17. David Gans, *Conversations with the Dead* (New York: Da Capo, 2002), 53–54.

18. An earlier version of this paper was originally given at the annual meeting of the Southwest Popular Culture Association, Albuquerque, NM, March 7–10, 2001.

Third Set

Experiencing Community Through Grateful Dead Improvisation

Buffalo, July 4, 1989 (© Lloyd Wolf/www.lloydwolf.com).

Modeling Improvisation
Mary Goodenough

The house lights dim. Applause and cheerful delight rise up from the cast of thousands. Shadowy figures move about on stage. Scents of sage, patchouli and cannabis permeate the air. Through smoky hues of violet, magenta and blue, the band members take their places with their instruments. They play a few notes, strike a chord or two, and fuss with their dials. Energy builds to a new crescendo with a short rhythmic drum riff. A look of recognition passes among the musicians, and as they break into their first song, the crowd erupts in a bloom of ecstatic joy. The Grateful Dead experience is again brought to life in mass improvisatory ritual. The show has begun.

The improvisational nature of Grateful Dead music may have been what first caught my ear, but what I had not expected was the ethos of improvisation inherent in the entire Grateful Dead experience. Deadheads from every stratum of the Grateful Dead community regularly improvise to accomplish goals both great and small. I love the story about some friends whose windshield wipers broke on the way to a Grateful Dead concert during a downpour on the Brooklyn Bridge. Show time was in less than an hour. There was no time to call for a tow truck, driving through the torrential rains without wipers would have been too dangerous, and missing the show or arriving late was simply not an option. After a few minutes of brainstorming, they improvised a fix. By removing the shoelaces from a pair of shoes (fortunately someone was wearing shoes with laces — Deadheads usually wear Birkenstocks) and tying an end to the tip of each wiper blade and running the other end of the lace through the open window on each side of the car, passenger and driver were able to manually pull the wipers back and forth, thus allowing their pilgrimage to continue without delay. They made it to the show on time.

Though Deadheads are adept at making do and even thriving with whatever resources are available, many of the innovations discovered within the Grateful Dead community came into being without any particular goal in mind. Rather, they emerged simply because the practice of improvisation — doing

Acid Reign dancers. RFK Stadium, July 1989 (© Lloyd Wolf/www.lloydwolf.com).

something original without an explicit, intended outcome — naturally led the way. In fact, Grateful Dead scholarship has been largely improvised from its inception — each discipline brings its own methodology to the inquiry and sheds light on a different aspect of the phenomenon. In the process, our object of inquiry (which we are viewing from the outside while participating/improvising with it from the inside) has come into view more clearly. But there is still an openness and ambiguity concerning where this inquiry is headed that makes it exciting and interesting.

In a society that favors rational approaches with predictable outcomes, the Grateful Dead became a haven for experiments in improvisation, perhaps unwittingly promoting their methods with wildly unpredictable results. The band itself was the unpredictable outcome of the Acid Tests during the psychedelic '60s. While some of the Acid Tests were no doubt pure chaos, others formed a container around improvisation as a creative form.

Now fast-forward 40 years. The improvisational nature of Grateful Dead music and the community that surrounds it has become the focus of a growing body of research and analysis from a variety of disciplines. The Grateful Dead phenomenon is living proof that improvisation can serve as a model for creativity for a seemingly infinite number of applications. This modeling of the improvisational method, practiced by the Grateful Dead in the performance of their music, and in their approaches to running their business and interacting with their fans, gave rise, however unintentionally, to a broad array of unexpected outcomes.

In *Composing a Life*, cultural anthropologist Mary Catherine Bateson writes:

> The improvised meal will be different from the planned meal, and certainly riskier, but rich with the possibility of delicious surprise. Improvisation can be either a last resort or an established way of evoking creativity. Sometimes a pattern chosen by default can become a path of reference [Bateson, *Composing a Life*, p. 4].

Similarly, an improvised concert will be different from a carefully laid out and staged performance and it was specifically that "possibility of delicious surprise" that kept Grateful Dead fans enthralled and impassioned for more than three decades. The uncertainty of the outcome is what made it both exciting and enticing. The improvisational nature of the Grateful Dead's music may well have been a pattern chosen by default, but in viewing the various ways in which it also became a path of reference for the communities of Deadheads emerging around the band, we can begin to catch a glimpse of the multiplicity, depth and fluidity of improvisation as a model for creativity. Through the prism of a transdisciplinary approach, this collection of essays begins not only to reveal the intrinsic value of what is created by improvising, but also to shed light on the productive potential of the improvisational approach itself.

In a society changing more rapidly than we can grasp, the ability to adapt and improvise becomes not only beneficial for success but also increasingly necessary for survival. Bateson writes further: "The recognition that many people lead lives of creative makeshift and improvisation surely has implications for how the next generation is educated and what we tell our sons and daughters" (p. 16). Indeed, the Grateful Dead phenomenon colorfully illustrates both the practice and proof of the inherent worth of improvisation. The essays in this collection provide a varied yet synchronous set of lenses through which scholars and educators can view the Grateful Dead phenomenon. In a society where the only constant is change itself, perhaps it is fitting that this phenomenon has arranged itself around practices and principles of aleatory improvisation, and that this improvisational collective creation has become an object of transdisciplinary inquiry. The different perspectives presented herein can perhaps begin to form the thousand-petalled lotus blossom through which we may come better to understand the productive relationship between improvisation and community, as exemplified in the midst of Grateful Dead experience and the numerous forms of community engagement spawned by a growing fascination with the phenomenon.

"Mysteries Dark and Vast": Grateful Dead Concerts and Initiation into the Sublime

Eric K. Silverman

Grateful Dead shows could be terrifying.

"When the Dead are playing their best," wrote Robert Hunter, the poetic muse for many of the band's most textually brilliant compositions, "blood drips from the ceiling in great, rich drops" (Hunter, 2000, 11). Hunter continued darkly:

> Together we do a kind of suicide in music which requires from each of us just enough information short of dropping the body to inquire into those spaces from which come our questions. It is partly about how living might occur in the shadow of death: and that death is satisfactory or unsatisfactory according to how we've lived and what we yield. The contemplation of death for the unfulfilled is a nightmare, and it is good that it should be. The vision of life without a great deal of responsibility is hollow.

This was *no* trivial experience.

A Grateful Dead show *at its best* offered a *sublime* experience. And as with any significant encounter with the sublime—like any glimpse of existential mysteries dark and vast, what Boone (1997, 184) dubbed "the sweetness and ephemerality of existence"—these performances were not merely or solely enjoyable, as Hunter so aptly recognized. They were *terrifying*.

My goal in this essay is to explore the (somewhat implicit) terror that animated Grateful Dead shows with experiential force. Writing as a cultural anthropologist with fieldwork experience in Papua New Guinea,[1] I begin polemically by critically engaging scholars who anchor the phenomenology of Grateful Dead shows to primitivist notions of ancient, Asian, and tribal ceremonies.

I then sketch an alternative approach to studying the Grateful Dead, drawing on modernist and postmodern notions of the sublime in order to highlight terror.

A Mildly Distasteful Campbell's Soup

There is little methodological consensus on how best to analyze Grateful Dead concerts. It should not surprise us that analysis of the Grateful Dead phenomenon would gain traction from interfacing paradigms. But one paradigm in particular seems to have acquired a significant degree of popularity: cross-cultural comparison that celebrates *affinities* between the shows and a romanticized conception of premodern religions.

In February 1986, the famous octogenarian mythologist Joseph Campbell attended his first and only Grateful Dead show at the Henry J. Kaiser Convention Center in Oakland. "Rock music had always seemed a bore to me," admitted Campbell (2008, 185). But "at that concert," startlingly, "I found eight thousand people standing in mild rapture."

Several months later, Campbell joined Mickey Hart and Jerry Garcia in a symposium, "Ritual and Rapture: From Dionysus to the Grateful Dead," at the Palace of Fine Arts, San Francisco. A Grateful Dead show, Campbell now observed, "is more than music. It turns something on in here (the heart?). And what it turns on is life energy. This is Dionysus talking ... a wonderful fervent loss of self in the larger self of a homogeneous community. This is what it is all about!"[2]

Comparativist *par excellence*, Campbell summoned not just Ancient Greece but also Russian Easter, the Cathedral of the Virgin of Guadeloupe in Mexico City, and the annual *ratha yatra* (procession of deities) staged at the Hindu temple dedicated to Lord Jagannath in Puri, India. "It doesn't matter what the name of the God is, or whether it's a rock group or a clergy. It's somehow hitting that chord of realization of the unity of God in you all." One night in Oakland, the Grateful Dead crystallized the pan-human essence of religion!

Campbell also tied the Grateful Dead to emancipation from the Cold War. "The Deadheads," he said during the 1986 symposium, "are doing the dance of life and this I would say, is the answer to the atom bomb." Later, Campbell elaborated on this redemptive message (1990/2003, 224–25; 1990/2008, 184–85). Some religious systems unite a community in violent opposition to other societies. By contrast, Grateful Dead concerts recalled "Dionysian" religions that emphasize an "awakening of your nature" and "the common humanity."

To this "world ecumenist" who reduced all myths and rituals everywhere to the same spiritual oneness (Segal, 1990), the devil was indeed in the details! Campbell's vision of religion and the Grateful Dead, however consonant with Western liberalism, always seemed to lead to Christological communion with a dash of Zen, a pinch of tribal magic, and a sprinkling of mysticism.

Campbell notoriously focused only on select, partial incidents from myths—never tales in their entirety. His exegetical method was thoroughly modernist by reducing all local voices, meanings, motivations, and interpretations to a univocal, universal "monomyth" (Dundes, 1980, 231–32; see also Segal, 1978; Dundes, 1997, 17–18). Campbell also neglected to consider what many societies deem fundamental: proprietary and gendered restrictions on who can own, recite, hear, and understand sacred knowledge. And Campbell seemed oddly content to neglect other scholars of myth, religion, and anthropology. Reading Campbell is akin to listening to the Grateful Dead on Top 40 FM radio. The songs are catchy, appealing, and fun. But they don't particularly challenge our expectations or adequately represent the band's repertoire.

However much Campbell is beloved by Deadheads, Grateful Dead scholars and members of the band, he did not seek to understand the Grateful Dead as a locally-constituted, historically-situated social reality. Instead, he cast aside as epiphenomenal all the unique qualities and practices of the Dead—the melodies, improvisations, lyrics, symbolism, set structures, and so forth—in order to reduce the Grateful Dead to the *Ur-religion*.

Deadhead scholars, like any devotees, attribute significance to nuances that might strike casual observers as picayune, neurotic, or simply baffling. Many of us keenly distinguish the Grateful Dead from all other genres and bands. Even categorizing the Dead as "rock and roll" is likely to raise our hackles! Here, difference *makes* a difference. But when Deadhead scholars appeal to other cultures, significant differences can suddenly make *little* difference. The Grateful Dead somehow bears an essential similarity to a whole host of metaphoric exemplars: medieval courts (Shank and Simon, 2000, 68–69), Sufi mystics and Senegalese trances (Sutton, 2000, 112, 188),[3] the Eleusinian mysteries (Smith, 2007), shamans (Reist, 1997, 1999), Taoism (Noonan III, 1999), totemic animals (Goodenough, 1999) and Aboriginal Australians (Norden, 2007, 106–107).[4] These are all of a piece—indistinguishable ingredients in Joseph Campbell's soup.

Anthropologically, these premodern cultural and religious expressions evidence little in common other than a privileged position in the Western imagination as primitivist exemplars of authentic spirituality and celebration supposedly (and woefully) lacking in the industrialized West. From this angle, the Grateful Dead resemble the Noble Savage. Rousseau in concert!

Conjuring Communitas

Many popular and scholarly accounts of the Grateful Dead also find inspiration in Victor Turner's thought. Turner is best known for devising the concept of *communitas* to elaborate on the transitional or liminal stage of Arnold

Van Gennep's (1909/1960) tripartite schema for *rites de passage*. *Communitas* refers to a temporary ritual community united through the antithetical enactment of everyday rules (Turner, 1967, 1969).

In his later years, Turner imbued communitas with a "liberating" quality and also, like Campbell, elided over cultural context in order to posit cultural affinities across vast expanses of time, space, and history. Turner thus likened hippies to mendicant friars, the Vīrasaiva saints of medieval India, and "ritual liminality in tribal societies" (Turner, 1974, 244–46). From Turner's point of entry, Grateful Dead performances appear as carnivalesque renditions of *communitas* that celebrated collectivism, primal truths, and "higher consciousness" rather than individualism, consumerism, and materialism (e.g., Goodenough, 1999; Wilgoren, 1999; Sutton, 2000). The Grateful Dead guided fans into a qualitative, not quantitative, experience by momentarily thwarting the Cartesian rationality that robs our everyday lives of magic.[5]

By drawing on Campbell, Turner, and also Mircea Eliade (e.g., 1965, 1987), scholars construe the Grateful Dead as a grand cipher for a kinder, gentler humanity of romanticized shamans, mystics, and first peoples more generally. These *hyper*-real tribals stand as balms for the angst and alienation of modernity. They are not real tribal people[6] but, rather, personifications of a long-standing Western desire to return to the Garden and restore Paradise Lost.

My concern is *not* with analyses that see the Grateful Dead as an alternative to mainstream American society — although, as others note (e.g., Wood, 2003, 56–61), the music and lyrics are deeply rooted in quintessential American traditions (see also Palm, 1999). Moreover, I seek *not* to deny or invalidate the role of primitivism as a liberal sociopolitical agenda in the Grateful Dead experience. Asian mystics, tribal initiations, Jungian synchronicities, magic, and *communitas* all figure prominently in *local frames of reference* through which Deadheads and the band made sense *to themselves* of the Grateful Dead (e.g., Carr, 1999). Clearly, parallels with other cultures often lent an aura of authenticity to the Grateful Dead experience.

Jerry Garcia himself in various interviews spoke about transcendence, transformation, expanded consciousness, primal energies, and a "seat-of-the-pants shamanism" (Henke, 1991, 37). Garcia and Mickey Hart have each appealed to the "ancients" and a "spiritual existence" accessible only through music (see Meriwether, 2007a, xxxii–xxxiii). "We're not shamans in the classic sense," commented Hart. But "we fulfill some of their function."[7] The Deadhead's on-the-ground *(or in-the-stratosphere!)* phenomenology of a Grateful Dead concert owed much to these primitivist tropes. I seek *not* to question the role of this symbolism in shaping those experiences. Rather, my goal is to challenge scholars of the Grateful Dead who blur distinctions between *local experience* and the *analysis* of that experience in a manner that risks evolving into an uncritical, sometimes Pollyannaish, apologetics.

Deconstructing the Psyche

Communitas typically takes on a joyful sense when applied to analyses of the Grateful Dead. But I suggest that true *communitas* must also include an element of sheer terror and fright. *Communitas* entails a radical, typically traumatic shattering of everyday social and psychological norms—a literal deconstruction of the normative content and categories of thought. *Communitas* thus requires some extraordinary, often brutal, prompting, whether willingly self-induced or forced by others. *Communitas*, especially during tribal initiations, dissolves the basic representations of reality, and splinters the foundational continuities of selfhood. The personality is fundamentally and indelibly fragmented, reorganized, and reintegrated anew. *Communitas* is not an amusing cognitive experience you nonchalantly don, like a concert T-shirt, and then casually doff as you shuffle through the turnstiles a few hours later! *Communitas* is serious ritual violence.

In some Plains Indian societies, wrote Victor Turner (1967, 100), "Boys on their lonely Vision Quest inflicted ordeals and tests on themselves that amounted to tortures." Why call them tortures? Perhaps because the liminal quality of ritual *communitas* requires something on the order of a cognitive breakdown. Only then can the ritual reorient the basic axioms of social and psychic existence. This process most certainly characterized Grateful Dead shows to some, perhaps even most, members of the audience. But we are unable to comprehend this dimension of the Grateful Dead experience by refusing to attend to psychological fright while appealing to a smorgasbord of cross-cultural comparisons.

The symbolic content of *communitas* and initiation ceremonies often resembles Freud's "primary process." Thus ritual sacra, Turner observed (1967, 105), typically assume the appearance of grotesque, monstrous beings. These anthropomorphic and theriomorphic creatures were not aimed, Turner maintained, at "terrorizing or bemusing neophytes into submission or out of their wits." Instead, the imagery intended to startle "neophytes into thinking about objects, persons, relationships ... they have heretofore taken for granted." I agree. But I also think that Turner too quickly dismissed the frightening countenances of these beasts. Moreover, I want to suggest another explanation for this ritual teratology: the grotesque aesthetic, including the visual and lyric iconography of the Grateful Dead, both reflects and contributes to the shattering of normative cognitive categories that makes many rituals powerfully and terrifyingly efficacious.[8]

The psychological terror of *communitas* may be intentionally pursued, and thoroughly enjoyed, but it is terror nonetheless. For corroboration, consider the fate of sojourners who *never* return from *communitas*: they are lost to the world, akin to an ascetic *sadhu* in India who renounces mundane existence to sit, as some do, in the desert staring at the sun.[9]

Initiation Wrongs and Rites

Initiation rites in the romantic imagination involve tribal "wisdom keepers" benevolently escorting the next generation to timeless verities and spiritual rebirth. Let me outline a different portrait based on traditional Melanesia, specifically, the Sepik River region of Papua New Guinea.

Broadly speaking, a pervasive gender dichotomy structures Melanesian social life (see Silverman, 2004). Child-raising is the task of women and female kin. Hence, boys and girls both initially acquire a core feminine identity. Yet boys must eventually enter the world of fathers and men. Male initiation, then, annihilated a boy's originary female identity while dramatically imprinting masculinity onto his psyche. This extraordinary degree of cognitive and emotional transformation does not come easy. It requires a significant, life-altering ordeal. Among the Iatmul people, male initiation traditionally began when men, dressed as spirits, snatched sleeping boys from their mothers. Some shrieking boys soiled themselves. The novices then spent the next six months in the men's house. Henceforth, they would view all relations with women as antithetical to manhood.

The initiation rite "grew" boys into men by emulating female fertility, especially gestation and birth. Melanesian men see female bodies, and especially menstrual blood and birthing fluids, as polluting. Yet these liquids represent the very fertility men desire and express in ritual. The parturient fictions of manhood thus sustain and subvert an ideology of masculine primacy while acknowledging and denying an existential dependence on motherhood (Silverman, 2001).

Neophytes underwent a brutal regimen of privations, humiliations, and outright beatings. A central drama of Iatmul initiation was not the transmission of esoterica but, instead, the horrifically painful process of scarification. Initiators sliced hundreds of small cuts on novices' torsos. This bloodletting expelled from the boys' bodies the last vestiges of maternal blood they acquired at birth so they could fully grow into men. The resulting welts resembled the skin of spirit-crocodiles who govern human fertility. The scars, too, evoked women's breasts and genitals. This way, initiation cut boys *off* from mothers while carving maternal fecundity *into* their bodies and psyches, thus again dramatizing the irreducibly dialogical relationship between manhood and mothering.

Elsewhere in Melanesia, neophytes learned other ways of purging female pollution gained through birth and sexual intercourse that nonetheless mirrored menstrual fertility and purification (see Herdt, ed., 1982).[10] To bleed, men slashed their penises and tongues, jabbed sharp leaves up their nostrils, and yanked thorns in their urethras. Some Aboriginal Australian men practiced subincision, or the slicing open of the underside of the penis to resemble the vulva. Among the Sambia of Papua New Guinea, initiators "grow" boys into men by feeding them semen, the source of masculine potency, through ritualized fellatio (Herdt, 1984; Herdt, ed., 1984). I hazard the guess that writers on the Grateful Dead who appeal to initiation ceremonies have something *else* in mind other than *these* Melanesian practices!

Through costuming, flute music, singing, drumming, screaming, stomping, death threats, and the presence of powerful spirits, the violence of male initiation moved into the experiential realm of "nightmarish horror" (Tuzin, 1982, 337; see also Bateson, 1936, 133). The blood that dripped from the ceiling in Robert Hunter's account of the Grateful Dead "playing at their best" was metaphoric; in Melanesia, the blood is real.[11]

My intention here is not Hobbesian. Rather, I simply wish to challenge a more pervasive, romanticized primitivism in Deadhead social science,[12] one that sees Grateful Dead concerts as fulfilling the same function, and communicating the same message, as "a traditional society's initiation rites" (Goodenough, 1999, 176; see also 2007, 172). I now sketch my own approach to the phenomenological force of a Grateful Dead concert, beginning with the sublime and, ironically, Romanticism.

The Sublime as Crushing Human Experience

During the Romantic era of the mid–18th century, Edmund Burke penned a *Philosophical Enquiry into the Origin of Our Ideas of the Sublime and the Beautiful*. Burke attributed the sublime to pain, danger, terror, fear, horror, vastness, and astonishment. We experience the sublime through multiple sensations: vision, hearing, scent, and especially bodily anguish. But the somewhat macabre, synaesthetic sublime was also "that state of the soul in which all its motions are suspended." The sublime immobilizes the psyche: the "mind is so entirely filled with its object that it cannot entertain any other." We are at one with the enormity of the world—and lost in the experience.

Burke opposed the sublime and the beautiful. While beauty evokes pastoral feelings of tranquility, shelter, and delight, the sublime demands reverential awe and power. In beauty, the self beholds the object of its contemplation. But Burke's masculine sublime, writes the literary theorist Terry Eagleton (1990, 54), *seizes* us in "admiring submission." The sublime "resembles a coercive rather than a consensual power, engaging our respect but not," as in the case of Burke's feminine beauty, "our love."

In *Postmodernism; or, The Cultural Logic of Late Capitalism*, Fredric Jameson (1991, 34) wonderfully defines the Burkean outlook on the sublime as "an experience bordering on terror, the fitful glimpse, in astonishment, stupor, and awe, of what was so enormous as to crush human life altogether." Kant and Schopenhauer similarly tied the sublime to cosmic immensities so diminishing of human existence that the mind reaches the limits of representation. In a sublime experience, we confront emotional and cognitive incapacity — the mental boundaries of our existence. We are crushed.

I propose the sublime as an aesthetic concept for understanding part of the experience of a Grateful Dead concert *at its best*. I am especially interested in the paradigmatic "second set" of a performance — sometime, say, in the 1980s. The opening songs, writes Goodenough (1999, 178), "carried the audience up to the heights." Later, during the improvisational, atonal, and other-worldly "Drums and Space" composition consisting of feedback, electronic wizardry, and unusual percussion, the audience "encountered chaos, disintegration of the ego ... symbolic dismemberment or death ... depths." Eventually, the band moved into a "wild, Dionysian" genre, "followed by a slowly building revelatory type of song, which reached a crescendo and peaked in a moment of epiphany or rebirth.[13] My sense is that most Deadheads would more or less agree with Goodenough's vivid portrayal of a second set. My sense, too, is that many Deadheads would find the topographic contours of this description, and the positioning of audience and band as voyagers, especially relevant to performances enhanced or informed by psychedelic experience.[14]

But what is missing from Goodenough's sketch of a Grateful Dead concert is sufficient consideration of fear. When the mind is unable to "wrap" itself "around" an object of contemplation — when the sublime halts normal mentation and "crushes" experience — the world becomes worryingly strange. From this angle, Grateful Dead shows *do* reveal an affinity with tribal initiation rites and communitas — but in ways not yet fully acknowledged by scholars of the Dead. All three contexts "work" by shattering conventions, thus offering a jarring encounter with the limits of conventional thought.

In "Answering the Question: What Is Postmodernism?" Jean-Francois Lyotard (1993, 43) identifies two modalities of the sublime. The modernist sublime sought to present the uncontainable within a beautiful form. This genre of the sublime would correspond, I suggest, to those Grateful Dead compositions that best correspond to the normal, unambiguous conventions of traditional Americana and rock-and-roll song writing, melody, narrative, and genre — the typically shorter, upbeat, first-set tunes and closers.

Quite different is Lyotard's characterization of the *postmodern* sublime. This sublime forgoes all conventions of taste, beauty, form, and decorum. During Grateful Dead shows, the postmodern sublime surfaced during the longer compositions characterized by lengthy unscripted jams, complex improvisations, extemporaneous sounds, cyclical song cycles, and, of course, Drums and Space. The latter especially presented the audience with an eerie, sonic rendition of uncontained or unrepresentational immensity that refused to abide by singular or simple standards of musical etiquette. Not surprisingly, many Deadheads recall their most intensive, frightening hallucinogenic experiences at Dead concerts occurring during these adventurous, free-form musical experiments.

Other essays call attention to tropes of terror, dread, and darkness in Grateful Dead songs, concerts, and iconography (e.g., Malvinni, 2007, 12; Goodenough, 2007, 164–68; Meriwether, 2007b; Smith, 2007). But few writers on the Grateful Dead theorize this terror as *central* to the Grateful Dead experience or phenomenon. This terror did *not* arise from the sources of fright often attributed to other, especially Heavy Metal, rock bands. The Grateful Dead did *not* glorify or advocate violence. The music, and most fans, did *not* aim to intimidate. The band took great pains *not* to engage in overt moralizing (Gimbel, 2007). And although the band consisted mainly, and sometimes solely, of men, I recall no overt displays of masculine aggression or eroticism. From where, then, did the sublime originate at Grateful Dead shows?

The Dark Vastness of the Grateful Dead

For many Deadheads, the full experience of a show *at its best* necessitated, or at least mirrored, a psychedelic experience. The alteration of normative frames and framing—cognitive, emotional, visual, and sonorous—pushed the Grateful Dead experience, like male initiation, into the sublime. In a wonderful essay in *Poetics Today*, Brent Wood (2003, 41) encapsulates the view of many Deadheads and other "experimentalists" with LSD.

> The psychedelic experience ought not to be seen as a distortion of reality, but rather as an alternative experience of the universe in which the compartmentalization of reality endemic to our rational, everyday mind-set begins to break down and the ability to see connections between one sphere of experience and another is set free.

Three dimensions of the psychedelic experience, I now argue, accounted for the presence of the sublime during a Grateful Dead performance. They are:

- Dissolution or fluidity of ego boundaries, leading to an uncertain sense of self and an instability of personality;
- Absence of semantic stability, promoting a fluid and unstable sense of external reality, especially in regard to the denotative meanings or everyday functions of objects and practices; and
- Entrapment in the hermeneutic circle, leading to an uncertainty in interpersonal communication, as well as unsure definition of the boundaries between self and world.

I further propose that these three phenomenological alterations of everyday perception are not "fun" in any trivial way. They are terrifying, and so explain why many serious Deadheads approached live performances with reverence and trepidation.

The loss of ego-boundaries, or "ego death," explains the sense of "rapture" so often reported by Deadheads as vital to the experience of a show. Deadheads seemingly endorse Tolstoy's famous theory of aesthetics (see also Gettings, 2007).[15] They report a powerful sense of communion, or shared subjective experience, enveloping themselves, the band, the music, and often the world. To be sure, the experience of this oneness can be wonderful, even sacred. At the same time, it can appear frankly terrifying.

The Western idealization of the mystic notwithstanding, secure and stable ego boundaries *are* important. They define the "I" that makes everyday life possible. Too rigid, and the self feels violated at every turn from an expected routine. But if ego boundaries become excessively permeable, as during a hallucinogenic experience, then crucial aspects of the self simply fade. That experience of fading — of losing one's self — contributes to the *frisson* or apprehension many people report at the start of a "trip," shortly after ingesting hallucinogenic substances. And the "warmth" often reported towards the end of a "trip" results, conversely, from the pleasant sense of security associated with the restoration of ego boundaries and hence the self.

Stanley Spector (2003, 2007) offers a similar insight drawing on Nietzsche's opposition between Dionysian and Apollonian aesthetic principles in *The Birth of Tragedy*. The Apollonian voice represents the world of individuation, definition, and structure — the world of dreams. The Dionysian represents non-individuation, unity, and the absence of boundaries — what Nietzsche called "dispossession" (Johnston, 2007, 57). For Spector, the effectiveness of a Grateful Dead performance arose from the experiential *conversation* between these two aesthetic voices.[16] Nietzsche's Dionysian aesthetic might strike us as an exhilarating departure from the staid conventions of everyday social reality. And so they were during Grateful Dead performances! But there was *frightening* risk involved. After all, writes Spector (2007), the Dionysian "shatters both the psychological individuality of a person and the discreteness of objects." In a world of dispossession and nonexistence, the self disappears. You are deconstructed away in an experience that was often said to resemble the imagination of death. Just as Robert Hunter envisioned!

Semantic instability is no less frightening that the loss of self. During a hallucinogenic experience, writes Wood (2003), pragmatic meanings seem trivial. Instead, the "tripper" thinks poetically. Words, images, and things acquire enormous semantic depth and texture. Psychedelic drugs obviate all linguistic signs as conceived by Ferdinand de Saussure in the 19th century. Conventional signifieds are snapped from their signifiers. The world appears irreducibly metaphoric and polysemic — an endless chain of self-deconstructing, free-floating signifiers that offers no stable linguistic anchor on which to tether an understanding of the world. The totality of reality dissolves into a Joycean world of polysemy and "stream of consciousness." We regress to primary process, and primary process alone. This is play at its most frightening seriousness!

The semiosis of Robert Hunter's lyrics enhanced the loss of ego boundaries and semantic instability. The songs, as Wood (2003) discusses, evoke no singular or fixed referents. Lacking "narrative authority," the writerly lyrics, to draw on Roland Barthes, demand the active participation of the listener to achieve resolution. The songs keenly evoke "moods and feelings ... without being limited to any specific context." Members of the audience could thus personally connect the meaning of a song to events within their own lives. In this sense, a full experience of the Grateful Dead entailed the dissolution of the semantic boundary between self and song.

During concerts, Deadheads frequently detached lyrical phrases from the narrative context of songs to serve as aural-conceptual signposts for the psychedelic "trip." These lyrics framed the hallucinogenic experience and also served to halt the endless process of psychedelic signification. In effect, Deadheads "hung onto" lyrics in order not to become totally lost in the "trip." You were not "in" an arena or some physical location, writes Tuedio (2003, 31), drawing on Merleau-Ponty, but "in" the "space" of the song. The Dead, then, offered their audience a musical portal through which to enter a hallucinogenic landscape. As topo-genesis, Dead songs during a concert served as a literal utopia — a real "no place." It was a "place" in which to get lost — but also in which, ideally, to find oneself.

But the music and lyrics, too, represented a window, however barely perceptible, through which the traveler in this imagined landscape could nonetheless glimpse shadows of the pre- and, hopefully, post-hallucinogenic self. The lyrics continued to connect the Deadhead to some vestige of normative perception — allowing, in a sense, a portion of Ego to maintain its grasp on normative space and time — or at least to know, at some level, that it was possible to do so. This accounts for the serious trust so many Deadheads invested in the band. It was axiomatic that the point of the show, in a sense, was to allow the band to guide you to a place of psychic danger and uncertainty — and then to bring you home. The music would take you away to a "space" lacking ego boundaries, selfhood, and semantic continuity. But the music also prevented your worst nightmare from becoming a reality: you would return.

The third and final source of terror I wish to highlight for a Grateful Dead concert of hallucinogenic import concerns the hermeneutic circle. Classically, the hermeneutic circle refers to the idea that all knowledge of the world is first and foremost "grounded" in one's prior experiences. Understanding is ultimately self-referential, thus dashing facile or positivist ideals of objectivity. Indeed, the hermeneutic circle even calls into question the assumption of an objective reality existing "out there" in the world. Even if the external world *does* in some sense exist, we are unable *ever* to access this external reality *directly* since *all* perceptions of the world are mediated by the terms of our own interpretive experiences. Nonetheless, *most* of us are able *most* of the time to ensure that our own private meanings more or less correspond with the external world as seen by others. Humans everywhere live in social realities.

Most of the time, too, we are able to negotiate shared experiences sufficiently to allow for genuine and meaningful communication. We are not, in other words, irredeemably trapped within our own hermeneutic circles. We can talk, empathize, pass judgment, laugh with others, and love. We reach out existentially to connect with others. "Sometimes," as Jerry Garcia reminds us during *Eyes of the World*, "the songs that we sing are just songs of our own." At least we can usually still join others in singing! Hence, the hermeneutic circle does *not* prevent us from ordinarily forging human connections and community. We might need to pause and listen carefully to where others are "coming from," but we generally get there.

Not so for a hallucinogenic experience! If a psychedelic experience becomes sufficiently intensified, "trippers" feel incapable of adjusting their private meanings to the contours of the external world. They also find it difficult, if not impossible, to communicate those private meanings to others. Conversely, "trippers" are unable to understand another person's utterances and communications. In effect, "trippers" are trapped alone in a world of their own unwitting creation, a world nobody else can see or reach, unable to burst free from hermeneutic recursion, and so unable to connect with any other person or object. As in the sublime, they are "crushed." This degree of solipsism is cold and terrifying — like Edvard Munch's *The Scream*.

When the Grateful Dead are playing *at their best*, and *blood* drips from the ceiling "in great, rich drops," you have entered a landscape where far more than mirth is at stake. You have entered the topos of the sublime. Prepare to be existentially *crushed*. Anything less, and it is *just* a concert.

A Final Teratology

I concur with a central thesis shared by Joseph Campbell and others (e.g., Carroll, 2007). Many Deadheads *did* see the wider Grateful Dead community as an aesthetic and ethical alternative to the terrible ravages of war, militarism, alienation, and industrial capitalism that vitiated the latter half of the 20th century.[17] I know I did. Grateful Dead concerts were palpably, wonderfully liberating and rejuvenating. There was, and remains, *nothing* like a Grateful Dead show.

But the overt ethos of peacefulness, compassion, family, collaboration, and kindness that suffused the Grateful Dead experience did *not* preempt the type of existential, or psychological, terror I have tried to identify as central to the concert experience. To focus *only* on the lighter side of the phenomenon is to consider only one aspect of the phenomenological power of the Grateful Dead. And to reduce the Grateful Dead experience to a mere concert phenomenon is unacceptable. Just ask Robert Hunter, or anyone else who saw blood dripping from the ceiling in "great, rich drops."

In *Traces of the Spirit: The Religious Dimensions of Popular Music*, Robin

Lost in the crush of sublime balloons.... Winterland, December 31, 1978 (courtesy Pat and Dena Lee, all rights reserved).

Sylvan (2002, 96–99) draws attention in passing to a powerful vision reported by the journalist Steve Silberman in a 1996 interview. Silberman was discussing the presence of an ethereal, hovering, spiritual "presence" that makes itself known during Grateful Dead shows. This "deity," known by all "serious" Deadheads, Silberman continues, was some sort of inchoate yet animalistic phantasm, "waiting for me inside the experience" of a show, "wrathful and benevolent ... like a beast ... partly lizard, partly mammal ... more than two eyes ... big teeth. And it would just sit there and look out at you." It probably fed off the rich drops of blood described by Robert Hunter. Truly.

What was Silberman's beast? As I see it, along with Sylvan, who draws upon interviews with various Deadheads, this grimacing, smirking monster was none other than a personification of the hallucinogenic experience. Any true psychedelic "trip," any real Grateful Dead show, necessitated an encounter with this or a similar ogre. The monster represented the frightening loss of ego-boundaries, the dissolution of semantic stability, and the entrapment in the hermeneutic circle. This beast was the *terror* of the psychedelic contours of a Grateful Dead experience *at its best*.

You did not play fetch with a beast like this! Quite the opposite: you were the object of its own capricious playfulness. *That* was the difference between a mere rock concert and a Grateful Dead show *at its best*. Only through this beast could one arrive at mysteries dark and vast, and return home. Actually, this is not quite correct: for many Deadheads, the beast *is* home itself.

Notes

1. Support for fieldwork among the Iatmul people, Sepik River, Papua New Guinea (1988–1990, 1994, 2008) was graciously provided by a Fulbright Award, Wenner-Gren Foundation for Anthropological Research, Institute for Intercultural Studies, DePauw University, and Wheelock College. I also attended a numerically significant but indeterminate number of Grateful Dead shows from 1981 to 1993.

2. The many sources for Campbell's comments at this symposium include http://www.sirbacon.org/joseph_campbell.htm, http://www.tekgnostics.com/DEAD2.HTM, and Brandelius (1989), 234. Campbell's show is generally dated February 11, 1986. Returning the favor, several members of the Grateful Dead — Jerry Garcia, Mickey Hart, and Brent Mydland — contributed to the soundtrack of the film *The Heroes Journey: The World of Joseph Campbell*.

3. Hartley (2000) writes about the now-disbanded Church of Unlimited Devotion, a community of ascetic Deadheads, often called the "Spinners," who blended Catholicism with Krishna Consciousness and endlessly twirled during shows to the divine energy channeled through Jerry Garcia's guitar.

4. Equally common are popularized Jungian concepts such as synchronicity, archetypes, and the collective unconscious (e.g., Goodenough, 1999).

5. Of course, only keen attention to physics, quantity, and mundane rationality made it possible to tabulate the number of days between performances of "Dark Star," flip cassette tapes, and hear electric guitars!

6. On this point, however, see Vennum (1999).

7. See Sutton (2000), 118, who cites Jackson (1992), 199.

8. Grotesque imagery during ritual also appeals to folks seeking psychic integration unavailable in everyday experience (see Obeyesekere, 1981).

9. For stunningly beautiful color photographs of sadhus that should swiftly erode any romanticism, see Hartsuiker (1993).

10. I exclude here consideration of a bloody male ritual many readers have personally experienced: Jewish circumcision (see Silverman, 2006).

11. Female initiation ceremonies significantly differ in content, symbolism, and socio-political implication from male rites (see Lincoln, 1991; Lutkehaus and Roscoe, eds., 1995). In future work, I hope to discuss matters of gender, especially masculinity, and the Grateful Dead.

12. For a survey of social science research about the Grateful Dead, see Dollar (2006).

13. Goodenough connects the drumming with the low tones of the bullroarer, as reported by Eliade. In Melanesia and elsewhere, bullroarers figure prominently in myths about the male theft of sacra from ancestresses (see Dundes, 1976). For ritual sounds more generally, see Tuzin (1984).

14. For geographic dimensions of the Grateful Dead and their songs, see Everett (1999), 133–134, and Culli (2004).

15. For Deadheads and ego-extension, see Lehman (2000).

16. Mikhail Bakhtin's literary dialogics (e.g., 1984) offered a similar conversation between the "moral" and the "grotesque." Other references to Bakhtin in connection with the Grateful Dead include Lucas (1999) and Culli (2004). For a Bakhtinian analysis ritual, see Silverman (2001), and Lipset and Silverman (2005).

17. In an earlier paper, I explored how this ethos relates to the themes of violence and desperation that so often punctuate the narratives of Grateful Dead songs (Silverman, 2007).

Bibliography

Bateson, Gregory. (1936). *Naven: A Survey of the Problems Suggested by a Composite Picture of the Culture of a New Guinea Tribe Drawn from Three Points of View.* Cambridge: Cambridge University Press.
Boone, Graeme M. (1997). "Tonal and Expressive Ambiguity in 'Dark Star.'" In *Understanding Rock: Essays in Musical Analysis*, J. Covach and G.M. Boone, eds. Oxford: Oxford University Press.
Brandelius, Jerilyn Lee. (1989). *Grateful Dead Family Album.* New York: Warner.
Campbell, Joseph. (2003). *The Hero's Journey: Joseph Campbell on His Life and Work.* Novato, CA: New World Library.
_____. (2008). "Creativity." In *The Mythic Dimension: Selected Essays 1959–1987*, A.V. Couvering, ed. Novato, CA: New World Library. (Originally published in *C.G. Jung and the Humanities: Towards a Hermeneutics of Culture*, K. Barnaby and P. D'Acierno, eds. Princeton: Princeton University Press, 1990.)
Carr, Revell. (1999). "Deadhead Tales of the Supernatural: A Folkloristic Analysis." In *Perspectives on the Grateful Dead: Critical Writing*, R.G. Weiner, ed. Westport, CT: Greenwood.
Carroll, Elizabeth. (2007). "The Answer to the Atom Bomb: Rhetoric, Identification, and the Grateful Dead." *Americana: The Journal of American Popular Culture,* vol. 6, issue 1. Available online at: http://www.americanpopularculture.com/journal/articles/spring_2007/carroll.htm.
Culli, Daniel R. (2004). "'Never Could Read No Road Map': Geographic Perspectives on the Grateful Dead." MS Thesis, Dept. of Geography and Anthropology, Louisiana State University and Agricultural and Mechanical College.
Dollar, Natalie. (2006). "Mapping the Deadhead Social Science Trip." In *Dead Letters, Vol. III*, Nicholas Meriwether, ed. Columbia, SC: Dead Letters Press.
Dundes, Alan. (1976). "A Psychoanalytic Study of the Bullroarer." *Man,* 11, 220–238.
_____. (1980). "The Hero Pattern and the Life of Jesus." *Interpreting Folklore.* Bloomington: Indiana University Press.
_____. (1997). "The Psychological Study of Folklore in the United States." *From Game to War and Other Psychoanalytic Essays on Folklore.* Lexington: University Press of Kentucky.
Eagleton, Terry. (1990). *The Ideology of the Aesthetic.* London: Blackwell.
Eliade, Mircea. (1965). *Rites and Symbols of Initiation: The Mysteries of Birth and Rebirth.* New York: Harper & Row.
_____. (1987). *The Sacred and the Profane: The Nature of Religion.* New York: Harcourt & Brace.
Everett, Walter. (1999). "'High Time' and Ambiguous Harmonic Function." In *Perspectives on the Grateful Dead: Critical Writings*, Weiner, ed. Westport, CT: Greenwood.
Gettings, Michael. (2007). "Tolstoy's Favorite Choir." In *The Grateful Dead and Philosophy: Getting High Minded About Love and Haight*, Gimbel, ed. Chicago: Open Court.
Gimbel, Steven. (2007). "The Other One and the Other: Moral Lessons from a Reluctant Teacher." Paper delivered at the November conference Unbroken Chain: The Grateful Dead in Music, Culture and Memory. University of Massachusetts at Amherst.

Goodenough, Mary. (1999). "Grateful Dead: Manifestations from the Collective Unconscious." In *Perspectives on the Grateful Dead: Critical Writings*, Weiner, ed. Westport, CT: Greenwood.
Hartley, Jennifer A. (2000). "'We Were Given This Dance': Music and Meaning in the Early Unlimited Devotion Family." In *Deadhead Social Science: You Ain't Gonna Learn What You Don't Want to Know*, Rebecca G. Adams and R. Sardiello, eds. Walnut Creek, CA: AltaMira Press.
Hartsuiker, Dolf. (1993). *Sādhus: India's Holy Men*. Rochester, VT: Inner Traditions International.
Henke, James. (1991). "Jerry Garcia: The Rolling Stone Interview." *Rolling Stone*, October.
Herdt, Gilbert H. (1984). *Guardians of the Flutes: Idioms of Masculinity*. New York: Columbia University Press.
_____. (1984). *Ritualized Homosexuality in New Guinea*. Berkeley: University of California Press.
_____, ed. (1982). *Rituals of Manhood: Male Initiation in Papua New Guinea*. Berkeley: University of California Press.
Hunter, Robert. (2000). "Dark Star." In *The Grateful Dead Reader*, David G. Dodd and Diana Spaulding, eds. Oxford: Oxford University Press.
Jackson, Blair. (1991). *Goin' Down The Road: A Grateful Dead Traveling Companion*. New York: Three Rivers Press.
Jameson, Frederic. (1991). *Postmodernism: or The Cultural Logic of Late Capitalism*. Durham: Duke University Press.
Johnston, David Macgregor. (2007). "The Electric Nietzsche Deadhead Test: *The Birth of Tragedy* and the Psychedelic Experience." In *The Grateful Dead and Philosophy: Getting High Minded About Love and Haight*, Gimbel, ed. Chicago: Open Court.
Lehman, Alan R. (2000). "Self-Concept and Ego-Extension Among Grateful Dead Fans." In *Deadhead Social Science: You Ain't Gonna Learn What You Don't Want to Know*, Adams and Sardiello, eds. Walnut Creek, CA: AltaMira Press.
Lincoln, Bruce. (1991). *Emerging from the Chrysalis: Rituals of Women's Initiation*. 2d ed. New York: Oxford University Press.
Lipset, David, and Eric K. Silverman. (2005). "Dialogics of the Body: The Moral and the Grotesque in Two Sepik River Societies." *Journal of Ritual Studies* 19, 17–52.
Lucas, Brad E. (1999)."Bakhtinian Carnival, Corporate Culture, and the Last Decade of the Dead." In *Perspectives on the Grateful Dead: Critical Writings*, Weiner, ed. Westport, CT: Greenwood.
Lyotard, Jean-Francois. (1993). "Answering the Question: What Is Postmodernism?" In *Postmodernism: A Reader*, T. Docherty, ed. New York: Harvester Wheatsheaf.
Malvinni, David. (2007). "'Now Is the Time Past Believing': Concealment, Ritual, and Death in the Grateful Dead's Approach to Improvisation." In *All Graceful Instruments: The Contexts of the Grateful Dead Phenomenon*, Meriwether, ed. Newcastle: Cambridge Scholars Publishing.
Meriwether, Nicholas. (2007). "Introduction: 'All Graceful Instruments': The Contexts of the Grateful Dead Phenomenon." In *All Graceful Instruments: The Contexts of the Grateful Dead Phenomenon*, Meriwether, ed. Newcastle: Cambridge Scholars Publishing.
_____, Robert Hunter and William Faulkner. (2007). "It Must Have Been the Roses." In *All Graceful Instruments: The Contexts of the Grateful Dead Phenomenon*, Meriwether, ed. Newcastle: Cambridge Scholars Publishing.
Noonan, Joseph P., III. (1999). "The Piping of Heaven: Reckless Musings on Philosophical Taoism and the Grateful Dead Phenomenon." In *Perspectives on the Grateful Dead: Critical Writings*, Weiner, ed. Westport, CT: Greenwood.

Obeyesekere, Gananath. (1981). *Medusa's Hair: An Essay on Personal Symbols and Religious Experience*. Chicago: University of Chicago Press.

Palm, Jason. (1999). "The Grateful Dead vs. The American Dream?" In *Perspectives on the Grateful Dead: Critical Writings*, Weiner, ed. Westport, CT: Greenwood.

Reist, Nancy. (1997). "Counting Stars by Candlelight: An Analysis of the Mythic Appeal of the Grateful Dead." *Journal of Popular Culture* 30, 183–209.

_____. (1999). "Clinging to the Edge of Magic: Shamanic Aspects of the Grateful Dead." In *Perspectives on the Grateful Dead: Critical Writings*, Weiner, ed. Westport, CT: Greenwood.

Segal, Robert A. (1978). "Joseph Campbell's Theory of Myth." *Journal of the American Academy of Religion Supplement* 44, 98–114.

_____. (1990). "The Romantic Appeal of Joseph Campbell." *Christian Century*, April 4, 332–335. Available online at http://www.religion-online.org/showarticle.asp?title=766.

Shank, Gary, and Eric J. Simon. (2000). "The Grammar of the Grateful Dead." In *Deadhead Social Science: You Ain't Gonna Learn What You Don't Want to Know*, Adams and Sardiello, eds. Walnut Creek, CA: Alta Mira Press.

Silverman, Eric Kline. (2001). *Masculinity, Motherhood, and Mockery: Psychoanalyzing Culture and the Iatmul Naven Rite*. Ann Arbor: University of Michigan Press.

_____. (2004). "Iatmul." In *Encyclopedia of Sex and Gender*, C.R. Ember and M. Ember, eds. New York: Kluwer/Plenum.

_____. (2006). *From Abraham to America: A History of Jewish Circumcision*. Lanham: Rowman & Littlefield.

_____. (2007). "From New Guinea to New Minglewood: Notes Towards an Aesthetic Theory of the Grateful Dead." Paper delivered at the November conference Unbroken Chain: The Grateful Dead in Music, Culture and Memory. University of Massachusetts at Amherst.

Smith, Lans. (2007). "An American Nekyia: Terrapin Station and the Descent to the Underworld." In *All Graceful Instruments: The Contexts of the Grateful Dead Phenomenon*, Meriwether, ed. Newcastle: Cambridge Scholars Publishing.

Spector, Stan. (2003). "Who Is Dionysus and Why Does He Keep Following Me Everywhere?" In *Dead Letters, Vol. II*, Meriwether, ed. Columbia, SC: Dead Letters Press.

_____. (2007). "'It All Rolls Into One': Rapture, Dionysus, Nietzsche, and the Grateful Dead." In *All Graceful Instruments: The Contexts of the Grateful Dead Phenomenon*, Meriwether, ed. Newcastle: Cambridge Scholars Publishing.

Sutton, Shan C. (2000). "The Deadhead Community: Popular Religion in Contemporary American Culture." In *Deadhead Social Science: You Ain't Gonna Learn What You Don't Want to Know*, Adams and Sardiello, eds. Walnut Creek, CA: Alta Mira Press.

Sylvan, Robin. (2002). *Traces of the Spirit: The Religious Dimensions of Popular Music*. New York: NYU Press.

Tuedio, Jim. (2003). "The Grateful Dead Parallax." In *Dead Letters, Vol. II*, Meriwether, ed. Columbia, SC: Dead Letters Press.

_____. (2006). "Community Through Excess: Bataille's Festival of Rapture and the Deadhead Concert Experience." In *Dead Letters, Vol. III*, Meriwether, ed. Columbia, SC: Dead Letters Press.

Turner, Victor. (1967). "Betwixt and Between: The Liminal Period in Rites de Passage." *The Forest of Symbols: Aspects of Ndembu Ritual*. Ithaca: Cornell University Press.

_____. (1969). *The Ritual Process: Structure and Anti-Structure*. Chicago: Aldine.

_____. (1974). "Passages, Margins, and Poverty: Religious Symbols of Communitas." In *Dramas, Fields, and Metaphors: Symbolic Action in Human Society*. Ithaca: Cornell University Press.

Tuzin, Donald F. (1982). "Ritual Violence Among the Ilahita Arapesh: The Dynamics of Moral and Religious Uncertainty." *Rituals of Manhood: Male Initiation in Papua New Guinea*, G. Herdt, ed. Berkeley: University of California Press.

_____. (1984). "Miraculous Voices: The Auditory Experience of Numinous Objects." *Current Anthropology* 25, 579–589, and 593–596.

Van Gennep, Arnold. (1960). *The Rites of Passage*. 1909. Rpt. Chicago: University of Chicago Press.

Vennum, Thomas, Jr. (1999). "The Grateful Dead, World Music, and the 'Popular Idiom.'" In *Perspectives on the Grateful Dead: Critical Writings*, Weiner, ed. Westport, CT: Greenwood, 41–54.

Wilgoren, Rachel. (1999). "The Grateful Dead as Community." In *Perspectives on the Grateful Dead: Critical Writings*, Weiner, ed. Westport, CT: Greenwood.

Wood, Brent. (2003). "Robert Hunter's Oral Poetry: Mind, Metaphor, and Community." *Poetics Today* 24, 35–63.

BEARS AND FLAGS: THE GRATEFUL DEAD'S AMERICA AND BOHEMIAN NATIONALISM

Jay Williams

John Prine's anthem "Your Flag Decal Won't Get You into Heaven Anymore" earned its power as an antiwar song because it equated a simple-minded love of flag with love of country and thus with an unthinking support of the Vietnam War. A friend of mine—and I imagine he was one of thousands—used this kind of patriotism for his own nefarious ends. He put flag decals on the bumper of his station wagon and made periodic drives from the University of Kansas to Chicago, carrying hundreds of kilos of marijuana. He never got caught, and that flag decal apparently worked, not as a talisman, but as a kind of identification badge; this was a driver who not only supported the war but also obeyed all laws and was a good citizen. Now consider one of the ways the Grateful Dead used the flag.[1] When they played the 1968 Sky River Festival— and do I need to emphasize the significance of that year?—a large American flag hung behind the stage. Clearly, the combination of band—whose members, it almost goes without saying, had used, were using, and would continue to use illegal drugs—and flag did not signify either the support of America and its war or the satiric use of that signification for the success of the underground drug trade. Deception doesn't work when you are dressed like hippies and play hippie music in front of thousands of hippies smoking weed and high on other drugs. This essay, then, attempts to explain what this alternate use of the flag meant by first locating the Grateful Dead within a long tradition of California bohemianism and then by showing what the Dead risked by employing the flag and how they formulated new ideas through their music and iconography regarding what it could mean to be an American and still retain bohemian values. They sought to replace the nationalist/imperialist conception of homeland with a new national understanding of home.

It is crucial to understanding the nature of the Grateful Dead and the hippie experience as another manifestation of Californian bohemianism not just to locate them geographically — and we will see how important a sense of space is to bohemianism — but also to show how much they are organic Americans (even if some individuals were immigrants or sons and daughters of immigrants; nativism has nothing to do with this definition). That is, they are undeniably, inescapably a part of the nation. Thus, again as we shall see, they were socially and culturally determined to use the American flag and the California state flag as a part of their iconography. But they were politically determined (now used in both senses — unconsciously and consciously) to reinvent it. Just as it is crucial to remind ourselves that the hippies were Americans and that they were quite aware of their geographic, cultural, and social nationality, it is crucial to show how they became a nationalist movement. Such an analysis shows how they existed apart from, but next to, juxtaposed with, America's hegemonic culture. If we did not understand the hippies and bohemians as a nation we would fall into the easy analysis of seeing them as simply a rebellious youth movement, a digression or inconsequential escape from "real life." It would deny, repress, and be unable to explain the long history of American bohemianism.

When Jon Pareles, in his obituary for Jerry Garcia, claimed that the band was an icon of the sixties, he meant that part of the sixties defined by what he calls the counterculture.[2] However, I want to stay away from the term *counterculture*. I prefer to use a related term: *bohemia*. The former term is period-specific whereas the Dead, given the historical circumstances of their origin and growth, need a much broader term to classify it. For example, Dennis McNally begins his "inside history of the Grateful Dead" with the founding of the city of San Francisco in 1776, and though he does so only to contextualize the immigration of Garcia's grandfather, the place of the Dead is crucial to its understanding.[3] San Francisco (or the Bay Area) is almost synonymous with bohemianism because of the multiple waves of antiestablishmentarianism that have manifested themselves there. The Grateful Dead fit into a long line of Californian bohemian thought and life that begins almost immediately with the first years of statehood. Bret Harte, Ambrose Bierce, and others were authors and newspapermen, not musicians, but their art took the form of fiction, and their lives centered around not the concert hall, but magazines entitled *The Overland Monthly* and *The Californian*. These bohemians set themselves against the state boosterism of the industrialists and the middle class and their infatuation with the saintly pioneer and miner. Bohemians of that era were united in a critical appraisal of California in order to distance themselves from widespread boosterism, and one way to do this and to promote their own art and learning was — and this may strike us as odd today — to embrace the French —

the language, the cuisine, the literature. When, in 1864, Harte and Charles Henry Webb discussed the possibility of founding a new journal, *The Californian*, "Harte suggested that it be published entirely in French to give it tone." Here then is an attempt, however comical or wry, to appeal to a foreign culture in order to reform their own. In *The Californian*:

> The editor openly attacked the cult of "the honest miner" and the pioneer, questioning "whether the individual who contributed a find of impious slang to the national vocabulary was peculiarly estimable as a moral teacher...." [The magazine's] sophisticated journalists were trying to destroy the pioneer's confidence in the fundamental principles of the pioneer's credo. Not only did the critics suggest that California might not have the best climate and finest scenery in the world, but they went deeper still; they implicitly hinted that hard work did not always bring success and that virtuous living did not always bring a reward. The institution that suffered the first barrage was the time-honored Sunday-school story. The *Californian* published a series of sketches by Inigo [Webb's pseudonym], Bret, and Mark Twain ridiculing the moral lessons found therein and throwing doubt on the first law of moral economy. Heresy was in the air.[4]

In their effort to set themselves apart from that with which they found fault, heretics seem always to set themselves apart from the world as a whole. These heretics clothed their reforming impulse in humor, satire, and a love of the foreign and thus were mistaken as antisocial. These were tactics that the Grateful Dead, as Californian bohemians, would eschew.

Forty years later, a magazine and its staff still offered a perfect environment for a bohemian way of life, and *The Lark*, a San Francisco periodical of the turn of the century edited by—principally—Gelett Burgess, is a perfect example. Of short duration and youthful, almost hippy temperament, the magazine "was named in a baptism of *vin ordinaire*, ... the common wine of the country.... With all [its] eccentricity, and in spite of it, I know that flavour to be there, and in the two years of LARKS I see the unconscious demonstration of the idea that is native to the earth and air of California — the idea of sloughing old coats of tradition and restraint, and starting unencumbered in the race—and with the face full front ahead, rather than half over the shoulder."[5] It is no accident that Burgess and his fellow writers and editors couched the beginnings of their project in religious, though winey, terms, for a fourth element sustains bohemianism, and that is a certain spirituality and definite sense of higher purpose. As Burgess said, in his own farewell to his folding magazine:

> If [these pages] have been sincere and spontaneous and faithful to an honest motive, played as clearly and as truly as we could flute it,—not without discords and false notes,—for the eye of youth oft wanders from the score,—this phase of life may fall in with the deeper truths and find its place in the Symphony.... It is the Presto movement,—short and gay,—timed to the beating of hearts not yet slowed down to the swing of larger duties and desires, quickened by the joy of life and the beauty of Nature, the mother; pulsing with the hope and promise of

the West, impatient of restraint and convention, yet tempered by the uninsistent accompaniment of a serious purpose that subdues the thoughtlessness of pure abandon.[6]

Burgess' bohemian ideals even determined the magazine's layout — unpaginated, ragged-right margin — and its construction — Hong Kong bamboo paper.

But the turn of the century also saw the rise of a bourgeois, though progressive, anti-imperialist antibohemianism, also centered around a periodical. The second series of *The Overland Monthly* was edited by Milicent Shinn, the first Ph.D. from the University of California, Berkeley. She was dedicated to avoiding the twin pitfalls of conservativism, as represented by the military takeover of Hawaii, and bohemianism, as represented by people like Beirce and Burgess. But giving new life to an institution like *The Overland Monthly* was difficult and she wrote that "I think from the first there was a certain jealous and unpleasant feeling toward us in San Francisco newspaperdom and Bohemia."[7] She attributed the ill will in part to her gender, and, as Chris Gair points out, Diane di Prima and other women in the Beat Generation found that "the rejection of a culture of consumption by male Beats tended not to be accompanied by similar rejection of that culture's patriarchal values."[8] She was a Quaker and believed in Californian exceptionalism — that is, she was not mainstream American in religion or state identity; some, perhaps many, Californians looked East for superior art, at least — but her magazine would have nothing to do with French-flavored fiction or *vin ordinaire*. Given her progressive politics and commitment to art, however, she had more in common with the bohemians — whose writing she actually could admire without promulgating — than with, say, conservative critics of the Beat Generation like Lionel Trilling and Norman Podhoretz. In this way, she was similar to someone like Ben Hecht, who sympathized with but ultimately rejected the bohemianism of Jack Kerouac in favor of Left politics.

Kerouac probably never heard of Milicent Shinn, but he had read Jack London and included his ghost in *On the Road*.[9] London, his closest friend George Sterling, and others exemplified California bohemianism in their time, and certainly it was their lifestyle as much as it was London's seafaring ways that attracted Kerouac to him. In fact, London's spirit lived on into the sixties as Tom Wolfe, in a characterization of Ken Kesey, called him a "Jack London Martin Eden figure."[10] Bohemia in turn-of-the-century California took traditional forms, especially in the Piedmont Heights above the Bay, where Jack London owned a home, or in Carmel, where George Sterling lived, and where artists, poets, newspaper writers, and others played. There was fencing, boxing, music, kite flying, poetry readings, costumes, parties, and woodland masques, all insignia of bohemianism like the beret, goatee, and bongo drum of the fifties. Sterling, whom many thought of as presiding over this subculture, wrote a masque entitled "The Triumph of Bohemia." Performed by members of the San Francisco Bohemian Club in Bohemia Grove in 1907, this play combines the bohemians' love of nature and the natural—which takes shape in this play as a recognizably modern ecological consciousness—with classical sources and drama. The tree-spirits (who open the play with the cry, "Time is our slave") are attacked by their worst enemies: the four wind-spirits, Father Time, and the Spirit of Fire (an especially potent figure given that the San Francisco earthquake had occurred just the year before). Having defeated them, the tree-spirits are attacked by woodsmen, who sing the Care-Song: "Tho' I wander far and wide,/Care, a shadow at my side,/Still shall claim his worship due,/Still shall know me and pursue." Only the Spirit of Bohemia, "a naked youth" (played most likely by Sterling himself), saves the spirits and their trees, persuading the woodsmen that they may have enough lumber for their homes and still preserve the tree-spirits' grove.[11] Bohemia, defeater of Care, must then defeat Mammon, who arrives in the grove to tempt the woodsmen with gold coins. Their battle is decided by the gods above, who send as a sign of their decision a great owl by whose touch Mammon dies. The play ends, and though presumably the woodsmen will go off to log the rest of the state but save Sonoma County, the play intends to sting the consciences of the Bohemian Club's businessmen.

Harte, Beirce, Burgess, London, Sterling, and others all lived beyond the norm, in a bohemian culture. These are men and women who lived their lives fully, in excess of other more conventional lives, but, at least for some amount of time, without excess becoming waste. The spirit of bohemia is notoriously difficult to pin down, but it found perhaps its most poignant, if obscure, expression in a third wave of bohemianism, the Beat Generation. In *On the Road*, one of Dean Moriarty's hallmark sayings is, "Go, go, go"; there is no subject or object to the verb. Or, rather, the subject and object are both IT, in capitals to signify its loudness as sound and its profundity as spiritual concept. When Sal Paradise and Moriarty hear the tenorman in San Francisco blow his choruses, they say that he has IT, he has reached IT. But IT is not the end of a process; IT is the process, and the object is to extend the process as long as possible and, no less important, to transmit IT to others. Paradise describes what lies ahead for all of them as "the ragged and ecstatic joy of pure being."[12] The searching soul—spontaneous, receptive, innovative, improvisational, high on drugs—this is another way to describe bohemianism. Or as John Clellon Holmes' square protagonist in *Go* says, critical of his bohemian friends but accurate in their characterization, they "lacked any caution.... They made none of the moral or political judgments that he thought essential; they did not seem compelled to fit everything into the pigeon holes of a system...; they seemed to have an almost calculated contempt for logical argument. They operated on feelings, sudden reactions, expanding these far out of perspective to see in them profundities which Hobbes was certain they could not define if put to it."[13] How like the hippies at the 2008 Rock the Change concert when asked by Steven Hurlburt, a Deadhead himself, to explain what the phrases from Grateful Dead songs like "box of rain," "roll away the dew," and "eyes of the world" meant.[14]

A large majority knew—they knew!—but they couldn't put it into words. Hobbes thus stands in the middle of a long line of sympathetic but ultimately condemnatory antibohemians, with Milicent Shinn before him and, as we shall see, Abbie Hoffman ahead of him.

From their long-term and meaningful association with Allen Ginsberg, Neal Cassidy, and others, the Dead have rightly been identified as cultural workers in the Beat tradition; the only mistake in such a cultural analysis is the presumption that bohemianism in California started in 1946. In any case, when Jerry Garcia was asked to define the word *hippy*, he did not turn to its denotative meaning, something probably only a square would do, though the *OED*'s definition is helpful in showing how there is some amount of continuity between the Beats and the hippies: "A hipster; a person, usually exotically dressed, who is, or is taken to be, given to the use of hallucinogenic drugs; a beatnik."[15] (Still, squareness has its drawbacks. No beatnik did acid. No acid-head would be called a beatnik. He or she would be called a hippie.) Garcia's ad hoc (spontaneous, bohemian) definition overlaps with both the *OED*'s and with Kerouac's exposition of IT: "Somebody who's turned on ... who's in forward motion, uh, they might have been called progressive at one time."[16] One of the great moments of hippie bohemia came on 14 January, 1967, the day of the Human Be-In on the Polo Fields of Golden Gate Park. Garcia described it this way: "When there was the Be-In up here I'd never seen so many people in my life.... It was a totally underground movement. It was all the people into dope of any sort."[17] Robert Spitz, in his history of the Woodstock music festival, also traces a direct line between the bohemia of one generation and that of another: Sometime before 1967 "Hippies had run the Beatniks off MacDougal Street [in the Village] with unpardonable reproof. They replaced that dark era of black turtleneck sweaters and bongo drums with rainbow gaiety, strobe lights, and a softness of dress and emotion never before exhibited by Village inhabitants. Rock usurped jazz, drugs supplanted alcohol and adolescents swarmed in from parts unknown. Michael [Lang, the main character in Spitz's history because he was the festival's executive producer] plugged himself into the eye of the hurricane with a tireless enthusiasm."[18] Despite that final mixed metaphor, and whether or not we accept the claim that hippies rudely tossed the beatniks out, we see vividly how a locale, whether the Village or North Beach, provides an environment for evolving notions of bohemian life and thought. Though the drugs changed from *vin ordinaire* to LSD, one can thus posit a line of Californian bohemian thought and life that runs from the work of Bret Harte and Ambrose Bierce in the 1860s through Gelett Burgess's *The Lark* to Jack London's autobiography *John Barleycorn* (1912) to Allen Ginsberg's reading of *Howl* (1956) to the Grateful Dead's "Truckin'."[19]

So, even though bohemianism can be treated as it might treat itself — vaguely, careless of boundaries — there are at least four easily identifiable elements: writing, travel, drugs, and communal living/existence, usually centered around a common artistic endeavor, sometimes concrete like a periodical, sometimes more fluid like a shared conception of what art is. Other artistic persona — the romantic genius, the avant-gardist — may overlap with the bohemian to a degree, but whereas the romantic tends toward isolation — we think of the isolated German romantic poet standing on the edge of a cliff, as does the avant-gardist — here we recall Frank Zappa alone in his Laurel Canyon house, composing at night, forcing even his daughter Moon to communicate by notes — the bohemian favors community, and a bohemian's writing, travel, and drug use are characterized by their communality. It is this last element that brings to mind a more theoretical definition of bohemianism and so helps begin the exploration of the Grateful Dead's entanglement with the iconography of Americanism.

If, as Benedict Anderson famously defined it, a nation is "an imagined political community," then bohemia, given its notorious indifference to the affairs of state, can be defined as simply an imagined community.[20] Bohemia, of course, has its material manifestations — the slouched hat, absinthe, the bare foot, and so on — which will figure in important ways later in this essay. But to define bohemia as an imagined community means that it does not exist until a group of people insist on their commonality as outsiders without recourse to what historically binds people together — kin, language, religion of the book, or geographical boundaries. In the sixties, one form that this insistence took was continued participation at musical concerts given by one particular band or form or genre of music. The music of the Grateful Dead and more generally of the San Francisco scene provided people with one way to come together as a community. There were other ways, and the totality of these ways defines an American bohemia. But at the same time the Dead and others insisted on borrowing traditional nation-state iconography to seemingly identify themselves as, not bohemian in the traditional sense, but citizens of a particular nation. The question I want to address is why did the Grateful Dead put the word *political* into the definition of *bohemia* and so transform it into a kind of nationalism. In more general terms, we might ask, When does community become citizenship, and why did the Grateful Dead insist on being citizens of the state of California and of the United States of America?

By 1967 mainstream cultural figures had identified a larger social phenomenon than just a few enclaves of bohemianism in San Francisco and New York City, and they used words like *hippiedom* and *hippieland* to name it. Hippies themselves knew that the creation of a shared identity was taking place across the country (part of the stated mission of the 1964 bus trip by Ken Kesey and the Merry Pranksters was to link up with Timothy Leary and others at Millbrook), and when Woodstock took place in 1969 they discovered only how large their numbers had become; Abbie Hoffman first used the term *Woodstock Nation*, though this act of naming came several years after the fact and was a confused attempt to give a name to an "ethnic," national group. This collectivity of '60s bohemians shares the four elements of the complete definition of *nation* that Anderson uses: "It is an imagined political community — and imagined as both inherently limited and sovereign. The hippie nation was limited, and to paraphrase Anderson, even the most messianic hippie "did not dream of a day when all the members of the human race" would become hippies. It was sovereign, and just as the nation came into being as cultural and socioeconomic forces destroyed "the legitimacy of the divinely-ordained, hierarchical dynastic realm," so too hippiedom found itself as institutionalized hierarchies fell apart. The patriarchal family and society was losing its legitimacy. The justifications for the supposed superiority of one race over another were exposed as fallacious and malicious. And the inherent authority of officials of the federal and state governments was being not only questioned but also challenged and refuted. In the face of these decaying social systems, hippies dreamt of being free.[21]

But I want to focus on how sixties bohemians imagined their community. Perhaps surprisingly, the imagination of their nation came about in similar ways to how first nations came to be realized. According to Anderson, "The novel and the newspaper ... provided the technical means for 're-presenting' the *kind* of imagined community that is the nation."[22] During the sixties in America, the novel did not undergo a significant enough change to be identified as a new nation-forming event. But the newspaper, the broadsheet, the music concert, the rock poster, and the album did. These material events enabled the imagination of a single community by people otherwise unknown to each other. A crucial component in the understanding of the concept of nation is this fact of people not knowing each other. It shows how, despite being strangers, people can be united as a nation. Thus, when Anderson says that just as characters are "embedded" in the society of a novel so too are people embedded in the society of a nation: "These societies are sociological entities of such firm and stable reality that their members can even be described as passing each other on the street, without ever becoming acquainted, and still be connected." Further, in a novel, characters are united through triangulation with "omniscient readers." So, too, in a nation, strangers in a "stable reality" are united by being known by a third person in that society: "An American will never meet, or even know the names of more than a handful of his ... fellow Americans. He has no idea of what they are up to at any one time. But he has complete confidence in their steady, anonymous, simultaneous activity."[23] I'm perhaps belaboring this point of the unification of strangers because I want to focus on how relatively new art forms in sixties bohemia acted in ways that the novel and newspaper did in the early history of nation formation. These art forms created what Anderson calls a "community in anonymity."[24] Hippies knew each other as hippies, and not as persons, through the knowledge that each was simultaneously reading, say, Robert Crumb's latest comic. They knew each other through the knowledge that each was reading the *Berkeley Barb* or the *L.A. Free Press*, in the same way that earlier Californian bohemians knew each other as they all read the latest issue of *The Lark* or *The Overland Monthly*.

More significantly for the specific purpose of an essay focused on a musical group, hippies or Heads or freaks were united by the album they all were listening to or by the music they heard simultaneously within a concert hall. More often than not the shared experience of, say, a Grateful Dead concert is posited, and rightly so, as a joint spiritual enterprise, an elevation of a mass consciousness. But there is this other way that sixties bohemians became identified with each other. Print-capitalism had joined with sonic-capitalism to become vehicles for the imagination of a new bohemian nation. When the audience members left the concert at the Fillmore or the Avalon Ballroom and walked out into the neighborhood, they felt that world inside the concert hall had fused with the world outside. This experience exactly parallels the experience Anderson discusses of readers of José Rizal's *Noli Me Tangere* in 1887 or of José Joaquín Fernández de Lizardi's *El Periquillo Sarniento* (1816): "Here ... we see the 'national imagination' at work in the movement of a solitary hero through a sociological landscape of a fixity that fuses the world inside the novel with the world outside."[25] Consider the experience of listening to "Truckin'," say, in its first incarnation, 18 August 1970 at the Fillmore West. There are two important thematic elements to this song, and both played crucial roles in defining this bohemianism, linking it both to its own historical specificity and to its roots in earlier American bohemianism. As a preliminary note, I want to point out that although the lyrics of the song make no explicit mention of a musical group, let alone one called the Grateful Dead, many listeners take this song as pure autobiography. One of course cannot help do so, given the mention of a bust in New Orleans and the link between the band's constant touring and repeated allusions to travel; I only want to insist that an autobiographical reading taken as fact can obscure other meanings, especially those that posit a different characterization of the protagonist of the song. In any case, the first thematic element is the interplay between home and the road. In classic bohemian fashion, the protagonist in the song is on the move. The word *truckin'* works synonymously with words and phrases such as *The Road, Go*, and *On the Road*, all titles of classic bohemian texts by Jack London, John Clellon Holmes, and Jack Kerouac. At the same time, the protagonist expresses a longing for remaining home, a place to "patch my bones" or "to settle down." Unlike the place one travels, the world outside, home is where "they" aren't. Home is safe from search warrants, where you aren't worn thin, where you simply can be — as opposed to New York, which "just won't let you be." Home, unlike the road, is unnamed; it is not given a specific location. But neither is it simply a state of mind; otherwise one could be at home on the road. No, home is a geographical space, but it could be anywhere, anywhere, that is, where likeminded travelers congregate, read underground comics, and go to concerts to hear music like "Truckin'."[26] The world of the song has fused with the world of bohemian life, of the bohemian nation.

The second thematic element is the unidentified nature of the protagonist. This person — and for a moment let's keep the metaphoric content of his or her life alive — has played his or her cards and now has cashed in his or her chips and is on the move. From one city to the next, exploring and testing environments, our character discovers both how unsatisfactory the outside world is and how necessary and right it is to find this all out; the song is very much of a sonic, modernist *Bildungsroman*. In fact, the song not only relates the protagonist's experiences—the twin bummers of getting busted and of having a friend, "sweet Jane," fall apart, the drawbacks of a number of American cities— but also advises the listener on how to deal with a life so filled with negative experiences. (For an anthem of the "flower generation," it's surprising to rediscover how depressing this song is, despite its up-tempo sound.) And in dealing out this advice, besides illustrating how crucial having a home is, the protagonist, secure in the knowledge that the power of the advice will keep one living a good life, invites the listener to join this life, to join bohemia: "Get out of the door — light out and look all around."[27] Here is the quintessential bohemian call to action. Seize the day! Go! Find IT! Keep truckin'! It's important to keep the universality of this call in the forefront, for, as Anderson points out, one of the hallmarks of nationalism is naturalization. Unlike racism, which disqualifies people by blood, nationalism offers membership even if one is imperfect in a nation's language. Although the Haight suffered because of it, and there were certainly posers among the hippies (the Dead's "Cosmic Charlie" is to some extent about the phenomenon of the weekend hippie), anyone could become a freak. That universalistic call is to a large extent what made "Truckin'" so popular. The unnamed protagonist could be you. "I guess that can't revoke your soul for trying."[28]

The anonymity of membership that "Truckin'" celebrates is crucial in another art form and will take our discussion of bohemian nationalism to another level. Broadsheets, as well as music and comics and newspapers, played an important part in this new independence movement, and the Diggers produced one in particular that bears close examination, for it marked both an end and a beginning in this history of Californian bohemianism. The Diggers, a San Francisco–based collection of social and art activists, in fact embodied the bohemian anonymity and universalism. "Digger activists used made-up names in order to encourage the idea that hippies were new people who, in adapting new identities, were ridding themselves of their past."[29] On 6 October 1967, the year of the Summer of Love and the Monterey Pop Festival, the Diggers (now known as the Free City Collective), held an event called the Death of Hippie Ceremony. By the fall of 1967 the word *hippie* had changed or become threatened so much by interior and exterior forces that its funeral was advised. It was held on the first anniversary of the day LSD became illegal. Although various accounts differ as to what actually happened, and photographs that claim to be of the event show two different coffins and two different groups of people, at the very least a march through the Haight district occurred. People carried a coffin that symbolized the death of the hippie. Candles were burned. Little American flags were held. The crowd dispersed, the coffin disappeared. Given that Woodstock, to name just one event, occurred two years later, it is impossible to say that the hippie movement ended with this funeral.[30] It is possible to say that some kind of pure, uncommercialized version of the hippie ended that fall in San Francisco, but certainly there were many sincere, committed, and unaffected hippies who came later. So, using Anderson's understanding of nationalism given, now, that we can understand the hippies as nationalism, we can see this event as an important nationalistic marker. Perhaps the most crucial characteristic of nationalism, according to Anderson, is that people are willing to die for their country or "country." After the community is imagined it stays in the imagination because "it is this fraternity that makes it possible ... to die for such limited imaginings."[31] The coffin that held the Unknown Hippie—no matter that there actually was no body—is the sixties bohemianism's version of the Tomb of the Unknown Soldier, the "most arresting emblem of the modern culture of nationalism."

> The public ceremonial reverence accorded these monuments precisely *because* they are deliberately empty or no one knows who lies inside them, has no true precedents in earlier times [meaning, for example, ancient Greek culture].... Void as these tombs are of identifiable mortal remains or immortal souls, they are nonetheless saturated with ghostly *national* imaginings.[32]

The broadside that the Diggers printed and circulated to mark this occasion spells out their nationalistic imaginings in an explicit, though, of course, disorganized, fashion. The broadside begins with the announcement that the hippie has become a media creation: "MEDIA CREATED THE HIPPIE WITH YOUR HUNGRY CONSENT. BE SOMEBODY. CAREERS ARE TO BE HAD FOR THE ENTERPRISING HIPPIE. The media cast nets, create bags for the identity-hungry to climb in. Your face on TV, your style immortalized without soul in the captions of the Chronicle. NBC says you exist, ergo I am. Narcissism, plebian vanity. The victim immortalized."[33] The alternative is to become "the FREE MAN [who] vomits his images and laughs in the clouds because he is the great evader, the animal who haunts the jungles of image and sees no shadow, only the hunter's gun and knows sahib is too slow and he flexes his strong loins of FREE and is gone again from the nets. They fall on empty air and waft helplessly to the grass. DEATH OF HIPPY END/FINISHED HIPPYEE GONE GOODBYE HEHPPEEEE DEATH DEATH HHIPPEE."[34] Though there is no difference between the act and being of a hippy and the act and being of a "free man," it was important to jettison the name hippy before its cooptation by the media began to determine how the hippies lived. Of course *free man* just doesn't have the linguistic power of a word like *hippy* and so it never caught on, and perhaps

Peter Coyote and others intended to steer people back to the original meaning of the word and remind their audience of the essential connection between *hippy* and a very traditional understanding of American *freedom*. The broadsheet ended with a beginning, a familiar proclamation of independence and freedom: "WE HOLD THESE TRUTHS TO BE SELF-EVIDENT, THAT ALL MEN ARE CREATED EQUAL, that they are endowed by their Creator with certain unalienable Rights, that among these are Life, Liberty and the pursuit of Happiness. That to secure these rights, Governments are instituted among Men, deriving their just powers from the consent of the governed. That whenever any Form of Government becomes destructive of these ends, it is the Right of the People to alter or to abolish it, and to institute new Government, laying its foundation on such principles and organizing its powers in such form, as to them shall seem most likely to effect their Safety and Happiness."[35] This early art-political action predated by over two years Abbie Hoffman's call in *Woodstock Nation* for the prevention of cultural cooptation by "Pig Nation," but the quotation from the Declaration of Independence indicates that they wanted more. This broadsheet and the funeral helped further define who lived within the new bohemian nation. Just as Venezuelan revolutionaries in 1811 "saw nothing slavish in borrowing verbatim from the Constitution of the United States of America," so too did the Diggers turn to an earlier, successful model of nation formation.[36] One cannot help but link the proliferation of broadsheets and underground press to the early history of the United States and especially to Benjamin Franklin, who as Anderson points out, because of his key role as "printer-journalist" "is indelibly associated with creole nationalism in the northern Americas"[37]; and one only has to think of the Dead's "Franklin's Tower" and Robert Hunter's intentional, though vague (bohemian) association with Franklin in that song, to see how the hippies' nationalism took on aspects of modular nationalism.[38]

The Dead's iconography functioned in the same way as the Diggers' broadsheets, especially their borrowing of the American flag and their use of skeletons. The name of the band itself, so obviously linked to the icons of skeletons, can be seen as an artistic act of nation formation, a shared imaginative bond. Given the importance of the dead to a nation, the Grateful Dead performed a kind of living tomb to the Unknown Hippy. Like the eternal flame of the Unknown Soldier's grave, the Dead, by touring almost constantly throughout their career, kept the memory of bohemian nationalism alive. Like the circulation of the music the circulation of the Dead's skeleton acts as a nationalizing artistic force, especially given how often the skeleton is pictured with an American flag. The cover of *Grateful Dead: The Illustrated Trip* exemplifies this force. It shows the skeleton from the waist up, crowned with American Beauty roses, holding a banner on which the title of the book is written. The red of the roses, the blue of the banner (decorated with white stars), and the white background emphatically place the Dead within the hippie nation-state. Or take the skeleton figure from *The Grateful Dead Movie*. A motorcycle riding, top hat and cane wielding, tripping skeleton, he is dressed in the Captain Trips top hat that Jerry Garcia wore on the cover of the Dead's first album, that Jack Casady and others also wore. This hat shows how the American flag—for which the American Beauty rose is a stand-in—circulated freely among hippies. A large flag hung on Mickey Hart's Marin Country barn in 1970; it adorns the interior art of *Live/Dead*; it of course provides the central form of the Steal Your Face logo; and, as I mentioned before, it hung behind the stage at Big Sky, and hippies carried little flags on sticks at the Death of Hippie parade. There was a prominent flag at the Human Be-In near the stage; Michael Bloomfield and others named their band The Electric Flag and were one of the top sensations at the Monterey Pop Festival. Peter Fonda wears a flag on the back of his leather jacket in *Easy Rider*. Jefferson Airplane used the flag on *After Bathing at Baxter's*. Ken Kesey in 1964 had a fake front tooth colored as a flag.

And the American flag was not the only one so appropriated. The bear from the California flag, perhaps unintentionally, became a modern-day marker of bohemian nationalism. The earliest Californian bohemians, Harte and Beirce and the rest of the crew at the *Overland Monthly*, had borrowed the flag's bear for their masthead, except they had set it free into the wild. The flag's bear, seen in full-body profile walking to some unknown destination, is unthreatening and almost domesticated. Harte's bear is set on railroad tracks, turning and snarling at an unseen approaching train. This is very much a California bear, a state's icon whose independence is crucial. The Dead had their own bear, Augustus Owsley Stanley III, nicknamed Bear, whose circulation of acid, like Franklin's and the Digger's circulation of print, like the music scene's circulation of sound, provided one more kind of technological device to imagine the new nation. Further, the bear became a dancing, laughing bear on stickers, decals, and shirts, multicolored and so obviously stoned. This was New California's new bear.

Mainstream culture rebelled against this wholesale appropriation of the American flag. As Hoffman documents in *Woodstock Nation*, "Last summer [1968] ... [Congress] passed a federal law protecting the flag from 'defacement and defiling.'" So, because the national government wanted their flag back, Hoffman entitled his chapter "Fuck the Flag."[39] But, unlike Hoffman's appropriation of the flag, the Dead and other bohemians never meant to be programmatic, and thus, although Hoffman tried to tie (dye) himself to the Dead (he mentions them uncritically twice in *Woodstock Nation*) and to Woodstock Nation (his pronouncement that, all in all, Woodstock was a good thing is constantly undermined by his doubts about and harangues against the hippies) he was in the end discouraged and frustrated. He was able to name the hippies' nation, but he refused to become a bohemian citizen. Because the hippies' reuse of the flag never became a leftist statement, Hoffman could foresee only the cooptation of hippies by mainstream culture.

Yet bohemians, and especially the Grateful Dead, never became associated with the negative aspects of nationalism. By embracing the flag, the colors of the flag, the thirteen stars, and so on, they only meant, in a broad sense, to play with the flag. Rather than celebrate a ready-made Americanness, they invented their own. Like a standard blues song that provides a basic structure, the stars and stripes gave the Grateful Dead a form to begin from in order to create a new nationalism. They grabbed the American flag away from straight culture, tore it to shreds, and used the shreds to make clothes and blankets. They used it in their emblems. They incorporated it into their music. Their sense of community as bohemians alienated them from the mainstream, and so they constructed their new, alternative American mythology embodied best, perhaps, in the song "U.S. Blues." The song begins, "Red and white, blue suede shoes, I'm Uncle Sam, how do you do." Uncle Sam has been hiding out in a rock and roll band. (And of course it's a blues song!) The Dead can reappropriate Uncle Sam because they recognize that he shares the same iconic status as other pop culture figures, two of whom are mentioned in the song: "Shake the hand / that shook the hand / Of P.T. Barnum / and Charlie Chan."[40] The same appropriation takes place, though more obliquely, in "Ramble on Rose," where the identification of America and rose is implicit. In this song, we get a long list of pop cultural figures, including Jack and Jill, Wolfman Jack, Crazy Otto, Frankenstein, and Billy Sunday. Like bohemianism itself, the song is open-ended ("I know this song it ain't never gonna end"), and like the America the hippies live in the song is "a hundred verses in ragtime," a quintessential American musical form. In fact, in their borrowing of just about every kind of national form of music, the band played their new Americanism on stage.[41]

Further, consider John Perry Barlow's 1992 speech in front of the First International Symposium on National Security and National Competitiveness. In the audience were members of the U.S. intelligence community, and Barlow was invited to give them a different perspective on the culture of the Internet. Barlow pointed out that he and Mitch Kapor were the first to use William Gibson's term *cyberspace* to describe the aphysical reality of computer-aided human interaction. "We saw," said Barlow, "that computers, connected together, had the capacity to create an environment which human beings could and did inhabit."[42] They envisioned it as, specifically, a place where copyright could not exist, where national boundaries would be blurry and perhaps nonfunctional, and where email would decentralize bureaucratic structures. This sensibility is plainly an outgrowth of the sixties Californian bohemian imagining of the virtual world created by drugs: a new, alternative but very workable and livable place that existed side-by-side with straight culture. It was identifiably American, but it did not serve national interests. Both the Haight and cyberspace were meant to be places where bohemian creation could take place, where spontaneity was valued, where a bear could dance high on acid. The flag became an integral part of their art, but it never left their art world. It was always not ironic, not under erasure, but at play.

Even though the later deployment of the flag in the bohemian nation signified, in ways that the Diggers in 1967 wanted their broadsheet to, a return to the purity of American independence, of true revolution, there is no denying that the appropriation of American nationalism may seem to run counter to the careless, unorganized, stoned nature of bohemianism. To appropriate the American flag is to risk being identified with American imperialism, with American consumerism, with American racism. Perhaps Grace Slick meant to counter this association in the song "ReJoyce," on *After Bathing at Baxter's*. There she reversed JFK's dictum, "Ask not what your country can do for you — ask what you can do for your country." She shockingly proclaimed that she would rather her country die for her than that she die for her country. In taking this stand, the Airplane were both following in the bohemian tracks of Stephen Dedalus and rejecting the patriotism of mainstream America, including the liberal wing of the Democratic Party. There is no question that the hippies were never going to go to war for their own nation. That was the stand that left politicos like Hoffman took. In the summer of 1969, while meeting with other underground and counterculture members on a farm in Michigan, he watched the police conduct a raid, and afterwards he thought how "in Chicago [during the 1968 police riot] I felt that I was ready to die over our right to be in Lincoln Park and how defending liberated land meant more than Vietnam. The only way to support a revolution is to make your own."[43] Just as Jerry Rubin was about to go onstage at the Human Be-In in 1967 to deliver a political speech, he told the Dead's road manager Danny Rifkin, "'Now, pay attention. What I'm going to say is very important.'" Garcia reacted negatively: "Like, all that campus confusion seemed laughable too. Why enter this closed society and make an effort to liberalize it when that's never been its function? Why not just leave it and go somewhere else." Earlier, in 1966, Rock Scully, the band's manager, had contrasted the hippie scene in San Francisco with the political scene in Berkeley: "The suit-and-tie Berkeley politicos wanted a political platform and kept busting into our meetings. They wanted to rouse the rabble. Rabble-rousing is their very raison d'être." While his and the Dead's view was, "Let's make it fun, not misery. We've won already, we don't have to confront them [the government and other prowar forces]. Why go on their trip? Why battle? Dissolve. Disappear."[44] To die for one's bohemian nation takes on different meaning from that of the heroic death of soldiers in combat. To be bohemian, one must be willing to "dissolve," to lose one's identity as a bohemian. To travel — one of the defining characteristics of bohemianism — means more than simply taking road trips. It means in its limit sense to actually leave the bohemian nation, never to return. The Tomb of the Unknown Hippie is surrounded by the ghosts of the departed.

What do bohemians become when they leave bohemia? To get at a possible answer to this question, one has to turn to another fundamental commitment of bohemians, that of improvisation. To say that the hippies played with the flag is to say that they improvised on its symbolism, reinventing its symbolism, creating new meanings for it. What I have not addressed is the fact that they did not invent a new flag. Relying on the structure of the stars and bars was much like relying on the twelve-bar blues. Bohemians are not avant-gardists "inventing" new scales. At the same time, we need only look at how Garcia lived as a musician to understand a contradiction at the heart of bohemianism. Garcia spent his days practicing scales and his nights free-associating within given song structures. On the one hand, practice and responsibility; on the other, improvisation and freedom. The bohemian life tends to obscure the former in order to highlight the enlightenment and education one gains from the latter, but a bohemian is neither an anarchist nor a hobo. Bohemians are deeply rooted beings, both in history and in a geographical space. When a bohemian dissolves, he goes back home. He gives up his public identity and removes himself from the public sphere.

This then is the ultimate meaning of American bohemian nationalism. It is the creation of a home that is not a homeland. *Homeland* refers to soil and the people of that particular soil. It easily becomes a term to denote national political objects, and its first use in America pertained to the United States as it was being threatened by outside enemies.[45] *Home* can be both particular and abstract. A house is also a home but never a homeland. *Home* in the abstract means a place of comfort, a place of safety in the sense of being a place one can retreat to. Bohemians can be meaningfully contrasted with avant-gardists to get at the generalized notion of the bohemian home. Both bohemianism and avant-gardism share a similar sense of time. Both are well known for their distaste for calendaric time, for chronos; they favor kairos, the now. But their understanding of place separates them. As I mentioned before, the avant-gardist is an isolated "genius" at work alone. Bohemians, on the other hand, are by nature communal. The avant-gardist works apart from his or her environment. There is nothing identifiably Long Islandish about Jackson Pollack's work. When Zappa produced his most advanced, experimental work, it cannot be located as work produced in Laurel Canyon, let alone Los Angeles. That is, bohemianism is inextricably tied to place, to geography. It must have a home. With the disappearance of the Haight and the Village and other traditional geographies of American bohemianism, the bohemian home still is the site of coffee houses, concerts, and sometimes even academic conferences.

The word *political* as inserted into the definition of *nation*—"an imagined political community"—has the same force for the bohemians that it has for Anderson. It exists apart from constitutions, political theory, and political structures. It is a cultural formation reliant on the circulation of print and sonic capitalism. The risk, then, that the Grateful Dead took as they reappropriated the flag turns out to be no risk at all. It may be legal now to wear a flag bandana, and the flag has reattained its powerful patriotic aura, but the red, white, and blue of the Dead's "Steal Your Face" logo has lost none of its own luster. Bohemian nationalism lives. The freak flag still flies.

Notes

1. The choice of the Grateful Dead as an exemplary sixties bohemian musical group is far from arbitrary. As Nicholas Meriwether shows: "Of all the American bands to emerge from the heady ferment of the 1960s, the Grateful Dead cast the longest cultural shadow" (Nicholas Meriwether, "Grateful Dead," in *American Icons: An Encyclopedia of the People, Places and Things That Have Shaped Our Culture*, Dennis R. Hall and Susan R. Hall, eds., 3 vols. [Westport, CT: Greenwood, 2006], 1:277). Chris Gair has a somewhat different take on the band's legacy, but agrees with Meriwether on their iconic status, using the death of Jerry Garcia as a starting point for the second half of his book: "The '60s had been over for a quarter of a century, but the death of the best-known member of the quintessential countercultural band of the era made the national news and seemed ... ironically to show that nostalgia for the spirit of the decade lived on" (*The American Counterculture* [Edinburgh: Edinburgh University Press, 2007], 120).

2. See Meriwether, "Grateful Dead," 277.
3. See Dennis McNally, *A Long Strange Trip*.
4. Franklin Walker, *San Francisco's Literary Frontier*, 182.
5. Bruce Porter, "My Dear Frank Burgess:–," *The Epi-Lar* (May 1897).
6. Frank Gelett Burgess, "Untitled Memoir," *The Epi-Lar* (May 1897).
7. Quoted in Grant Skelley, *The Overland Monthly*, 65.
8. Gair, *The American Counterculture*, 25. Tom Wolfe, in his *The Electric Kool-Aid Acid Test*, calls Ken Kesey a "Jack London Martin Eden figure."
9. See Jack Kerouac, *On the Road*. Thanks to Gair for pointing this out.
10. Tom Wolfe, *The Electric Kool-Aid Acid Test*. Martin Eden is the semi-autobiographical sailor/writer protagonist of London's novel *Martin Eden*.
11. George Sterling, *The Triumph of Bohemia*.
12. Kerouac, *On the Road*, 161.
13. Quoted in Gair, *The American Counterculture*, 41–42.
14. See Steven Hurlburt, online at: http://www.youtube.com/results?search_query=Roll+away+the+dew&search_type=&aq=f.
15. *Oxford English Dictionary* [online], s.v. "hippy."
16. McNally, *A Long Strange Trip*, 186.
17. Quoted in Meriwether, "1/14/67," *The Deadhead's Taping Compendium*, 1:130.
18. Robert Stephen Spitz, *Barefoot in Babylon: The Creation of the Woodstock Music Festival, 1969*, 36.
19. Gair closely analyzes the transformation from Beat to hippy in terms of a generalized conception of counterculture in his *The American Counterculture*, 139–44. Gair's starting point is crucial for all further studies of the sixties: "There are both ruptures and continuities between the Beat Generation and the countercultural fiction of the 1960s" 139.
20. Benedict Anderson, *Imagined Communities*, rev. ed. (London: Verso, 1991), 6. The literature on nationalism is vast, but plucking Anderson's book out of the mass is not an arbitrary act. Despite the critiques of his book, which mostly center on his misreading of postcolonial states, Anderson's definition is an excellent guide for the study of nongovernmental, cultural-based communities.
21. Anderson, *Imagined Communities*, 6, 7.
22. Ibid., 25.
23. Ibid., 25–26.

24. Ibid., 36.
25. Ibid., 30.
26. Robert Hunter, *A Box of Rain: Lyrics, 1965–1993*, 230, 231.
27. Ibid.
28. Ibid.
29. Marty Jezer, *Abbie Hoffman: American Rebel*, 86.
30. Jezer, in a mean-spirited analysis of the Death of the Hippie, writes that it was simply an event to serve the Diggers' best self-interest: "When the hippie movement in San Francisco became too sordid to defend, they [the Diggers] simply created a ceremony in which they buried the hippie and declared themselves 'free men' (Jezer, *Abbie Hoffman*, 86). And certainly the Diggers did not stop their activities; according to Jezer, they only became more influential, visiting New York in 1967 and transferring many of their ideas and principles to Abbie Hoffman and others (ibid., 87). By "sordid" I am guessing that Jezer is pointing to the increased numbers of people — not just youth — who migrated to the Haight and the coincident increase in hard drug use. But this explanation — overpopulation and "wrong" drug use — is simply another mainstream, hegemonic attempt to dismiss the reality of bohemianism. Somehow the overpopulation of hippies in 1967 in the Haight has become a sign of hippie deterioration whereas the overpopulation at Woodstock has become a sign of hippie viability and vitality, only to be eradicated a few months later with the so-called real death of the hippie at Altamont. Hippies themselves saw the overcrowding in the Haight and at Woodstock and the fisticuffs and death at Altamont as a bummer, a downer, a bad trip — like "sweet Jane" "losing her sparkle" and the bust in "'Truckin'." In "New Speedway Boogie," the Dead sing, "Do we keep on coming or stand and wait?" The answer is to keep trucking (Hunter, *Box of Rain*, 158).
31. Anderson, *Imagined Communities*, 7.
32. Ibid., 9.
33. http://www.diggers.org/free_city_news_sheets.htm.
34. Ibid.
35. Ibid.
36. Anderson, *Imagined Communities*, 192.
37. Ibid., 61.
38. See Andrew Shalit, "Roll Away the Dew: An Exegesis of Robert Hunter's 'Franklin's Tower,'" online at: arts.ucsc.edu/gdead/agdl/shalit.html, which is a bit undisciplined in its analysis, and Hunter, "A Reply to Jurgen Fauth's Essay," online at: arts.ucsc.edu/gdead/agdl/fauthrep.html. Thanks to Steve Hurlburt for bringing these pages to my attention.
39. Hoffman, *Woodstock Nation*, 49.
40. Hunter, *Box of Rain*, 234.
41. Ibid., 174.
42. Quoted in Thomas Streeter, "The Moment of *Wired*," 757.
43. Hoffman, *Woodstock Nation*, 57.
44. McNally, *A Long Strange Trip*, 177, 179.
45. "For the earliest official usage (of "homeland" in America) on record, see Williams S. Cohen, *Report of the Quadrennial Defense Review* (May 1997); Jennifer Bajorek, "The Offices of Homeland Security"; or Hölderlin's "Terrorism," *Critical Inquiry* 31 (Summer 2005), 877, n. 6.

Bibliography

Anderson, Benedict. *Imagined Communities*. Rev. ed. London: Verso, 1991.
Gair, Christopher. *The American Counterculture*. Edinburgh: Edinburgh University Press, 2007.

Gelett Burgess, Frank. "Untitled Memoir." *The Epi-Lark*, 25 May 1897, 7.
Hoffman, *Woodstock Nation*. New York: Vintage Press, 1969.
Hunter, Robert. *A Box of Rain: Lyrics, 1965–1993*. New York: Viking, 1993.
Jezer, Marty. *Abbie Hoffman: American Rebel*. New Brunswick, NJ: Rutgers University Press, 1992.
Keroauc, Jack. *On the Road*. New York: Viking, 1957.
London, Jack. *Martin Eden*. New York: MacMillan, 1915.
McNally, Dennis. *A Long Strange Trip: The Inside History of the Grateful Dead*. New York: Random House, 2002.
Meriwether, Nicholas. "Grateful Dead." In *American Icons: An Encyclopedia of the People, Places and Things That Have Shaped Our Culture*, 3 vols., Dennis R. Hall and Susan R. Hall, eds. Westport, CT: Greenwood Press, 2006.
_____. "1/14/67." In *The Deadhead's Taping Compendium*, 3 vols., Michael M. Getz and John R. Dwork, eds. New York: Henry Holt, 1998.
Porter, Bruce. "My Dear Frank Burgess:-." *The Epi-Lark*, 25 May 1897, 1.
Skelley, Grant. "The *Overland Monthly* under Milicent Washburn Shinn, 1883–1894: A Study in Regional Publishing." Ph.D. dissertation. Berkeley: University of California, 1968.
Spitz, Robert Stephen. *Barefoot in Babylon: The Creation of the Woodstock Music Festival, 1969*. New York: Viking, 1979.
Sterling, George. *The Triumph of Bohemia*. The Thirtieth Annual Midsummer High Jink of the Bohemian Club of San Francisco. July 27, 1907.
Streeter, Thomas. "The Moment of *Wire*." *Critical Inquiry*, 31, summer 2005.
Walker, Franklin. *San Francisco's Literary Frontier*. Seattle: University of Washington Press, 1970 (1939).
Wolfe, Tom. *The Electric Kool-Aid Acid Test*. New York: Farrar, Straus and Giroux, 1968.

IMPROVISING COMMUNITY: A HERMENEUTIC ANALYSIS OF DEADHEADS AND VIRTUAL COMMUNITIES

Gary Burnett

This discussion draws upon the philosophical hermeneutics of Paul Ricoeur together with the cultural hermeneutics of anthropologist Clifford Geertz and information systems scholar Richard Boland to examine one of the many online Deadhead communities that exist in places like the Usenet newsgroup rec.music.gdead, the WELL, archive.org's Live Music Archive Forum, and the Grateful Dead's own dead.net. These communities, some of them in existence since the mid 1980s, are robust environments used by Deadheads to continually redefine and reconceptualize what a "community" might be in the absence of physical proximity.

Whether "real" or virtual, all communities are mediated by interpretive processes. Virtual communities are unique in making such interpretive acts explicit through interaction rooted in textual inscription, reception, and interpretation: participants form their communities through public performances of writing, reading, and interpreting texts. Paul Ricoeur analyzes the ways in which texts use the "mode of 'as-if' ('as if you were there')" in order to bridge the distanciation between writer and reader; this "mode of 'as-if'" provides a framework for analyzing the textual interactions of virtual communities as ongoing improvisational enactments of community. The four "contextual relations" of Geertz and Boland's hermeneutics model (coherence, invention, intention, and reference) provide a structure within which the specific characteristics and "flavor" of online Deadhead communities can be understood.

This paper first provides a very brief overview of online Deadhead communities, followed by a discussion of philosophical and cultural hermeneutics, before turning to an examination, rooted in hermeneutics, of a particular moment in the online Deadhead universe.

Deadheads and Virtual Communities

While most traditional definitions of "community" assume geographic proximity (see, for instance, Malkki, 1997), the sense that the widely distributed audience of the Grateful Dead — an archetypal touring band if there ever was one — might form a community emerged relatively early in the band's career. The famous call of "DEAD FREAKS UNITE," printed in the gatefold of the 1971 live album titled "Grateful Dead" (alternatively known as "Skull & Roses" or "Skull Fuck"), followed by the mail distribution lists for *Dead Heads Newsletter* and the *Grateful Dead Almanac*, simultaneously drew upon and encouraged a sense of interconnection and community among the band's fans across the United States. With the emergence of the Internet, this distributed audience found numerous online venues to adopt as settings for a community that could thrive both apart from concert halls and during periods of time when the band was not touring.

Thus, Deadheads have a very long history of taking up residence online. Such ongoing virtual communities include, most notably, the Usenet newsgroup rec.music.gdead, which began life in the early 1980s as an email-based group variously named "Jerry's Breakfast" or "dead-flames," before moving to Usenet, first as net.music.gdead in 1985 (History, 1996); and the "Deadhead ghetto" of the Grateful Dead conferences on the WELL, an online community founded in 1985 and populated by Deadheads in 1986 (Hafner, 2001; Rheingold, 1993). The connection between Deadheads and online communities is strong enough that deadnet (http://dead.net), the official website of the band, still hosts an active virtual community a full 12 years after the band itself has ceased to exist; strong communities also continue to thrive both in rec.music.gdead and the WELL. This chapter argues that, like other virtual communities, online Deadhead communities function and sustain themselves through an ongoing process rooted in the exchange of texts — they are, that is, predicated on the writing, reading, and interpretation of texts. With its focus precisely on such activities, hermeneutics provides a mechanism for analyzing the ways in which these communities persist. Further, this chapter argues that such ongoing socially situated interpretive activity is an improvisational process.

Philosophical Hermeneutics in the Mode of "As If"

Hermeneutics attempts to theorize the intersection between communication and understanding in textual practice. Deeply rooted in early efforts to codify a set of rules for the "correct" interpretation of biblical texts across both temporal and spatial distance between writer and reader (Hirsch, 1967; Thompson, 1981), modern hermeneutics, growing out of the phenomenology of Edmund Husserl, has been more theoretical in nature, attempting to come to terms with language — and particularly written language — as "the fundamental mode of operation of our being-in-the-world and the all-embracing form of the constitution of the world" (Gadamer, 1976, p. 3). The central figures in this philosophical investigation of language as a constitutive part of the world in which we live are Georg Gadamer and, more recently, Paul Ricoeur. Of the two, Ricoeur's work has the most clearly and strongly emphasized textuality, focusing on the challenges inherent in making temporal and spatial "distanciation" meaningful and productive.

Of his many writings, Ricoeur's 1973 lectures delivered at the Texas Christian University in Fort Worth, Texas, and published in 1976 under the title *Interpretation Theory*, are the most appropriate to the theme of this chapter, which explores the phenomenon of communities emerging through ongoing textual conversations — that is, through the creation, reading, and interpretation of texts in a shared public space (for a full discussion of Ricoeur's hermeneutics as a framework for analyzing virtual communities, see Burnett, 2002). As presented in *Interpretation Theory*, Ricoeur's hermeneutics emphasizes everyday language use in "interlocutory" settings where some degree of a speaker's experience and intended meaning passes to a listener in a communicative act:

> Something passes from me to you. Something is transferred from one sphere of life to another. This something is not the experience as experienced, but its meaning. Here is the miracle. The experience as experienced, as lived, remains private, but its sense, its meaning, becomes public. Communication in this way is the overcoming of the radical non-communicability of the lived experience as lived [Ricoeur, 1976, p. 16].

However, such communication remains, in Riceour's hermeneutics, inherently problematic; as he notes, "My experience cannot directly become your experience" (Ricoeur, 1976, p. 16). Rather, what meaning is created in a "situation of interlocution" (p. 29) — its "semantic content" — is a function of a complex interaction between what the speaker intends to say, what the sentences as they are spoken actually say, and what the listener understands, necessarily inaccurately, of those sentences. Language, as it is projected out into the world toward a listener, escapes the speaker's control and takes on a life of its own. The very act of speaking, that is, inherently introduces a "virtual" distance between the speaker and what has been spoken, and communication takes place within an equally "virtual" distance between speaker and listener.

Written language — the "lingua franca" of virtual communities — literalizes this process of mediation and distanciation: speaker and listener become reader and writer, irreducibly separated by both space and time. The product of writing *literally* becomes an artifact at a remove from the writer, available for the responses of the reader, but no longer subject to the control of the writer. Thus, the inscription of language in writing—producing an artifact that can both move through space and persist through time—fulfills a potentiality that remains merely virtual in speech. Such "intentional exteriorization" (Ricoeur, 1976, p. 27) becomes, for Ricoeur, "the full manifestation of discourse," a way of inscribing or "fixing" the "'said' of speaking" (pp. 25–26), requiring the interpretive act of a reader, through which temporal and spatial distances are potentially made "useful" and meaningful.

In Ricoeur's framework, different kinds of interpretive acts are appropriate for different kinds of text, and the specific mode of reading and interpreting appropriate for a particular text is, to a great extent, a function of the actual makeup of the audience reading the text. Texts exist within specific social contexts, governed by specific economic and social constraints and practices. Texts written according to the norms of certain specific genres—identified by Ricoeur as things like "letters, travel reports, geographical descriptions, diaries, historical monographs," etc., "restructure" the contextual cues of spoken discourse, moving the texts into what he calls the "mode of 'as if' ('as if you were there')" (Ricoeur, 1976, p. 35). This process, drawing upon shared understanding of genre norms, both partially mitigates the distanciation inherent in textual discourse and recasts the situational contingencies of spoken discourse.

The function of discourse, then—which is most fully realized through the mediation of writing—is to project a world, which is available for others to take up and, through the interpretive act, make their own. The active engagement of a reader with a text through the hermeneutic process turns distance into contiguity. This process, which creates connection when there is separation, and community when there is distance, is at the root of text-based virtual community. It is also, because it creates the potential of meaning out of an ongoing process of reinscription and reinterpretation—a cycle consisting of the writing, reading, and interpretation of texts followed by new writing—inherently improvisational. As in much musical improvisation, participants in an online community improvise by drawing upon a shared vocabulary—a set of interests, an agreed-upon framework, genre norms—and create something new that outstrips and transforms what came before. Cultural hermeneutics provides a mechanism for analyzing the specifics of this improvisation.

Cultural Hermeneutics

As the above discussion suggests, the mechanisms of textual interpretation provide the means through which members of online communities are able collectively to improvise, on an ongoing basis, robust cultural environments. Because they exist through the creation and reception of texts, virtual communities depend directly on Ricoeur's "mode of 'as if'"; participants interact through textual conversations "as if" they were actually present within a specific place. Ricoeur's hermeneutics, thus, offers a broad framework for understanding the dynamics of virtual communities in general; his model, however, is limited in its ability to account for the specifics and unique characteristics of individual communities; further, since it explicitly rejects any attempt to establish a hermeneutic methodology, Ricoeur's work cannot provide a specific set of tools for analysis of those communities. Any analysis of these specifics requires a more finely-grained model, and, more to the point, requires a way to operationalize hermeneutics: understanding the shared texts of a community requires uncovering the values and norms embedded in the community's language, as reflected in those texts.

Both the shared improvisation of a community through the creation, reading, and interpretation of texts is necessarily context dependent, and becomes possible through the interactions between the texts themselves, the context in which they are written, and the people who write and read those texts. Cultural hermeneutics offers a specific set of tools for reaching a detailed understanding of both the contexts within which texts are exchanged and the ways in which texts both generate and transform context. These tools come in the guise of four facets through which text and context interact: coherence, reference, invention, and intention (Becker, 1979; Geertz, 1983; see also Burnett, et al., 2003; and Dickey, et al., 2007, for extended discussions of these "contextual relations").

Coherence is the "relations of textual units to each other within the text" (Becker, 1979, p. 212). It describes the normative formal characteristics of texts within a particular context — the set of constraints or rules that govern the creation of texts, making them accessible to readers. Elements of coherence include both the formal norms of grammar and the informal norms of social and textual practices. In online environments, coherence can also include both technically-rooted textual practices (the automated inclusion of "headers" in email messages, for instance, or the fact that "Twitter" posts are limited to 140 characters) and social norms (e.g. community norms for spelling or the practice of using abbreviations such as "ROTFL" ["rolling on the floor laughing"] or "JADP" ["just a data point"] that are instantly understood by community participants but may be opaque to outsiders).

Reference, the relation "of textual units to nonliterary events" (Becker, 1979, p. 212) describes the ways in which events and objects in the world enter into the texts of a community. It is a way of specifying what external *things* are of interest to a community and, thus, of characterizing the scope or subject domain of the community. An analysis of the reference practices of a community — those things in the world outside that individuals within the community commonly talk about, knowing that others will share their interest — is important for understanding the specific makeup of the community;

communities that are similar in other ways will often vary widely in their interests.

Invention, which is the relation "of textual units to other texts" (Becker, 1979, p. 212), is a measure of the status of texts in relation to existing knowledge within the community. Texts can either "speak the past," or reinscribe information that has already entered the community, or "speak the present" through the creation of new knowledge. Routinized turns of phrase — including social niceties such as "have a nice day" or "good to see you" — speak the past almost exclusively. Conversely, statements that completely speak the present are almost unheard of, since even the most novel or radical discourse must, if communication is to take place, remain rooted in existing practice and shared knowledge. However, communities may differ in terms of the degree to which they are willing to accept the introduction of new information; some may prefer to remain on the relatively safe turf of small talk and social niceties, while others are more open to invention.

Intention designates the "relations of the creator to the content of the text, the medium, and to the hearers or readers" (Becker, 1979, p. 212). It describes the purpose for which a text is created by a specific writer. Since, however, a writer's intention is, strictly speaking, an inaccessible internal psychological state which is not accessible to either a reader or to analysis, it functions in practice as a measure of the degree to which intention is overtly signaled in the writing of texts as opposed to simply being assumed. As Ricoeur (1976, p. 30) notes, "The authorial meaning becomes properly a dimension of the text to the extent that the author is not available for questioning." Strictly speaking, then, intention as an element of the hermeneutic process can either be assumed but not analyzed (that is, it is assumed that the writer intended to say something but that intention is not available to analysis because it is purely internal to the writer) or overtly stated in what is written. Communities may differ in terms of how often writers find it necessary explicitly to state their intentions within the texts they create.

These four contextual variables can be viewed in two ways: either as a set of discursive strategies that can be deployed by a writer in the creation of texts or as a set of analytic tools that can be used to explore — and, ultimately, to interpret — the place and meaning of texts within a particular context. In the act of writing, writers can either abide by or sidestep a community's norms of textual coherence, just as they can choose particular references to embed within their texts. Conversely, a reader or analyst, by examining texts with the four variables in mind, obtains a framework for interpreting those texts. In both regards — both as a creative toolbox and as an interpretive toolbox — the variables support the improvisation of community on online settings.

However, the use of the four variables in both the creation and the analysis of texts neither confers stability nor certainty of meaning in textual interactions nor guarantees that interpretations are absolute. Because, as Ricoeur points out, there is an inherent distance between writer and reader (a distance inhabited by the text), there is also always distance between what a writer understands herself to be saying and what a reader takes from the text. Such slippage in meaning between writer and reader is at the core of virtual community, mediated as they are by the exchange of texts. The ongoing process of dealing with these shifts in meaning and understanding — while sharing a set of norms and expected practices related to coherence, reference, invention, and intention — requires improvisation: participants must not only share a set of common tools and expectations, but must also be willing to follow paths suggested by the shifts and slips that occur in the process. To put it simply, community is not a constant, but an improvised thing, finding its way as it goes. The remainder of this chapter examines a particular moment in the ongoing improvisation of an online Deadhead community.

The Case of archive.org and the dead.net "Dead Downloads" Forum

Archive.org, an online "public library" founded by Brewster Kahle in 1995 and devoted to providing access to a wide range of digital materials in the public domain, houses (among many other materials) a collection of recordings of Grateful Dead shows and related performances, ranging from a 1959 recording of bassist Phil Lesh with a 19-piece student band from the College of San Mateo playing his composition "Finnegan's Awake" to the most recent performances of all surviving band members. Initially, this collection included both recordings made by audience members and "soundboard" recordings made either by the band itself or by one of its sound engineers or other road crew members. All of these recordings were available both for "streaming" (that is, for online listening "in real time") and for download, so that users could add them to their own personal collections. However, on November 22, 2005, "brewster" (i.e. Brewster Kahle) issued an announcement that, while audience recordings would still be available for streaming, active downloading of Grateful Dead recordings would no longer be permitted, and that soundboard recordings would be removed entirely. The impetus for this decision was attributed, somewhat vaguely, to "discussions with many involved":

> Following the policies of the Grateful Dead and the Dead communities we have provided non-commercial access to thousands of great concerts. Based on discussions with many involved, the Internet Archive has been asked to change how the Grateful Dead concert recordings are being distributed on the Archive site for the time being. The full collection will remain safe in the Archive for preservation purposes [http://www.archive.org/iathreads/post-view.php?id=47634].

This decision was, as it turned out, partially rescinded nine days later on December 1, with an admission that the archive's "mistaken attempts to move quickly were based on what [they] thought the Grateful Dead wanted" (http://www.archive.org/iathreads/post-view.php?id=49553). At that time, the Grateful Dead recordings were separated from the rest of archive.org's music collections, soundboard recordings were restored for streaming only and audience recordings again became fully downloadable, an arrangement that remains in effect to date. Despite this partial retraction, Deadheads immediately responded with open and vehement complaints, dubbing the decision the "Thanksgiving Day Massacre" because of its timing. The issue was immediately taken up — and discussed at great length — by every online Deadhead community, including the archive's own Grateful Dead Forum, rec.music.gdead, the WELL, and the dead.net forums on the band's own website. Blogs, including both mainstream blogs such as *BoingBoing* (http://www.boingboing.net) and Dead-related blogs such as Christian Crumlish's *Uncle John's Blog* (http://thedeadbeat.com/unclejohn/) and David Gans' Playback (http://playback.trufun.com/), posted items related to the removal of recordings, and an account of the decision and subsequent controversy even hit the pages of the *New York Times* (Pareles, 2005); the initial posting on *BoingBoing* was typical of public response:

> This is pretty disappointing. Deadheads made the Grateful Dead some pretty substantial fortunes over the years by acting as unpaid, volunteer evangelists for their commercial offerings. This is a genuine betrayal of the audience from a couple of greedy people who would line their pockets at the expense of the memory of the generous, mutually beneficial relationship between the band and its supporters [http://www.boingboing.net/2005/11/26/greedy-grateful-dead.html].

Many of the details surrounding the impetus for limiting access to the archive's collection of Grateful Dead recordings remain murky. Not only were there few additional public statements by representatives of the archive, but statements by band members and spokesmen — Phil Lesh, Mickey Hart, and John Perry Barlow decried the decision, while Bob Weir and publicist Dennis McNally supported it (Barlow, 2005; Hart, 2005; Leeds, 2005; Lesh, 2005; Weir, 2005) — contradicted each other and hinted at a divide in the band regarding the wisdom of the free availability of concert recordings in general.

Interestingly, most of these contradictory statements rooted their arguments in an interpretation of the meaning and significance of the Grateful Dead and its history itself. The statements issued by Phil Lesh and Dennis McNally illustrate this interpretive move nicely. Lesh, for his part, cited the value of the archive's collections in the writing of his autobiography, *Searching for the Sound: My Life with the Grateful Dead* (Lesh, 2005a), linking the recordings to the band's "legacy" and a sense of community and open access: "I do feel that the music is the Grateful Dead's legacy and I hope that one way or another all of it is available for those who want it" (Lesh, 2005b). Conversely, McNally, interviewed in the *New York Times*, presented that legacy as something quite different, and as something that had been breached by "massive" accessibility:

"One-to-one community building, tape trading, is something we've always been about," Mr. McNally said. "The idea of a massive one-stop Web site that does not build community is not what we had in mind. Our conclusion has been that it doesn't represent Grateful Dead values" [Leeds, 2005].

What such contradictory positions suggest, I would argue, is not so much that those intimately involved with the band found themselves unable to present a unified front in the face of an unambiguous set of facts so much as they point to the centrality of the hermeneutic process in the creation of meaning out of new information. That is, each step of the process—from whatever precipitated the archive's decision, to the partial retraction of that decision, and on to the responses issued by band members and representatives— begins as (in Ricoeur's words) something "said by someone to someone else about something" (Ricoeur, 1976, p. 30), necessitating an act of interpretation on the part of the "someone" to whom it was said, who then reinitiates the process with a new statement, beginning the cycle anew. This process simultaneously involves both understanding and misunderstanding, as the "distanciation" inherent in discursive interaction facilitates both communication and, as Ricoeur puts it, "radical" noncommunication. Interpretation, thus, is never exact, and "slippage" always occurs, sometimes radically, between the "something" that is said and the "something" that is understood. Each new act of interpretation and reinscription introduces something new into the process; responses, as they occur, are acts of interaction and improvisation, creating something in response to something else.

In the case of the "Thanksgiving Day Massacre," the "official" statements (those made by "brewster," McNally, and band members) are likely not fully "improvised" in a strict sense; one assumes, at least, that they were issued following somewhat careful consideration and were, perhaps, subject to at least some cycles of revision and manipulation before being made public. Nonetheless, in the context at issue in this chapter — the interactive social settings of Deadhead virtual communities—the statements still function as elements in an improvised hermeneutic process through which a community's "meaning" is collaboratively created in a cycle of writing, reading, interpreting, and further writing of texts. And, in those Deadhead communities themselves, the controversy that followed, interwoven with the "official" statements and carried out through often rapid-fire posts made by community members, the meaning of the statements, like the meaning of the event itself, unfolds only over time through the improvised process of interpretation. Each new text, dropped into the community, provides an opportunity for that meaning to be reexamined and made anew.

As noted earlier, the "Thanksgiving Day Massacre" elicited extensive reaction in a number of different online settings, ranging from blogs to several different online communities. As the controversy extended over the period of several weeks in these many forums, literally thousands upon thousands of individual texts were posted by hundreds of individuals. Clearly, a careful analysis of all of this activity is beyond the scope of this chapter; thus, what follows is limited to a small handful of posts from only one community—the "Dead Downloads" forum hosted on the band's own official website.[1] In the discussion that follows, the improvisation of community in this setting is analyzed through the framework of the four "contextual relations" of cultural hermeneutics, outlined above.

The dead.net forums, like many other online communities, are asynchronous—that is, participants do not, as in chat rooms, have to be online at the same time in order to interact, but can read posts and write their own at any time. As in many other forums on the World Wide Web, posts are organized into specific "topics," each of which is devoted to a single group conversation, which is presented linearly and chronologically. While there may be connections between multiple forums—that is, while the participants in one forum likely also participate in and/or refer to others—each one tends to stand alone as a semi-independent unit, with its own particular norms and concerns.

From the point of view of cultural hermeneutics, the use of discrete topics, even without taking the conversation or individual posts into account, links any given forum directly to all four contextual relations. The primary "Reference" focus of each forum is signaled by its topic title, which provides an overall indication of the nominal subject focus of the forum, although "topic drift"—a tendency for the discussion to move to other, tangential, subjects—is common. In addition, the topic title provides a degree of "Coherence" to the exchange of texts that takes place within a particular topic, imparting an automatic, built-in structure to the conversation; participants can only take part in the discussion by posting to a specific forum, and each individual post automatically becomes part of the whole or, to put it another way, is intrinsically structured by the "grammar" and format of the topic as a whole, as well as by the formal characteristics of the forum's design and organization. The topic title also signals the "Intention" of the topic creator that the forum should be viewed as a place with a particular aim —a place where a particular conversation is intended to take place. Further, the organization of discussions into specific named topics can also tend to place constraints around the amount of "Invention" that can take place. A forum, that is, is not (unless labeled as such) a "free fire" zone into which any and all new knowledge may be ported; rather, all subsequent posts within the forum must always already, to a great extent, "speak the past" within the constraints and limitations designated by the title, even if they also partially "speak the present" by bringing new knowledge to the existing topic.

Within this framework, participants collaboratively (and, often, antagonistically) improvise the "Dead Downloads" community, using an ongoing series of individual posts both as elements of the improvisation and as mechanisms for trying to come to terms with the removal of Grateful Dead recordings from archive.org. Over the course of the discussion — which persisted long after the archive's decision to remove the recordings was partially rescinded — very little is actually resolved; the improvisation of community, that is, does not reach closure, but continues to unfold within the ongoing improvisational space of the conversation. Generally speaking, two broadly defined factions of participants emerge in the discussion: those who think that the decision is justifiable in some way or another, and those who do not. These two factions remain in place throughout the entire course of the controversy, with neither being convinced of the rightness of the other. However, despite this unresolved disagreement, the process of improvisation is what is particularly significant to the community itself, as well as the fact that participants share a common vocabulary and set of assumptions — described by the four contextual relations of cultural hermeneutics — that allow them to interact on an ongoing basis. That is, even in disagreement, they are able to keep talking and keep moving toward some kind of shared (if provisional) understanding of the nature of their own community and the event that triggered the particular crisis it feels it is facing.

The specifics of the "Dead Downloads" discussion display aspects of the four contextual variables in varying degrees. At one end of the spectrum, "Coherence" presents relatively few clues as to how meaning and community are improvised in the forum. For the most part, it functions as a relatively stable background to the ongoing interaction — a set of formal characteristics of the posts including such elements as user name (almost always a pseudonym, not linked to an identifiable "real" identity), notation of the date and time of the posts, the arrangement of posts in chronological order, etc. In terms of the expectations and practices of community members, issues related to coherence most often tend to be taken for granted, with relatively few explicit or implicit mentions of the formal characteristics of the texts created by community members. Most such mentions are clustered around posts concerning the distribution of a petition, intended to make it clear to archive.org and the band that many in the Deadhead community have been deeply offended. And, even in these cases, the notion of textual norms and rules is perceived as being appropriate for "formal" documents such as petitions, while implicitly being alien to the more informal practices in the forum itself: "I love petitions with typos. It just wreaks of intelligence. Not that Weir will notice, lysdexia and all...." It is, in part, ironic that a post complaining about "typos" itself contains both intentional and (apparently) unintentional errors. But this irony also points to the fact that the community places little weight on the formal coherence of its textual practices; it is, clearly, highly tolerant of such "errors"; in this improvisation of community, errors simply are part of the heat of ongoing textual production and interaction.

On the surface, in terms of the degree to which it is explicitly stated, "Intention" similarly presents few clues about how community is improvised in the forum; participants tend rarely if ever to articulate explicitly any intention in their posts. However, as an interpretive strategy, Intention is central to the activities of the community and is, thus, a much richer contextual relation than "Coherence." The entire discussion can be seen as an effort, on the part of the community, to gauge or, perhaps more accurately, to reconstruct the intentions behind the removal of the recordings. Explicit claims and attributions of the intentions of others, thus, appear consistently throughout the forum, as in this post by "Mountainboy," the very first post in the forum related to the removal of the recordings, made even before the initial announcement by "brewster":

> Speaking of the live music archive, anyone notice that all the soundboards they used to host have mysteriously disappeared? Think it has anything to do with the download series and GDP's [Grateful Dead Productions] bloated corporate greed of sucking every last penny out of Jerry's corpse? Hope you got the most out of the archive while it was up, cause I have a feeling it's gone and nothing's gonna bring it back.

This post is notable for the immediacy — without any available evidence — of its assumption that, whatever is behind the disappearance of the recordings, the act of removing them reflects the worst possible intentions.

This is a consistent thread throughout the discussion, and claims that the removal of the recordings must be due to greed appear persistently, often linked with an argument that such greed represents a co-option of the Grateful Dead world by the ugliness of mainstream American corporate culture, as in this post by "DooDahDan":

> It's somewhat ironic that this little community of ours, which prided itself on individuality and freedom of expression and choice, has quickly become a microcosm of the greater American society.

Another poster, while imputing more admirable motives for the decision, similarly makes the rhetorical and interpretive move of gauging intentions:

> Any chance that the gelding of LMA is the band's reaction to the faceless, near-automatic nature of downloading from the archive, and that they're merely spurring us to rediscover our mutual interdependence through trading and bit torrent exchange?

What is unswerving through all of this back-and-forth articulation of competing interpretations of intentions is the notion that intention must be explained if the significance of the act is to be understood. In the absence of any adequate or consistent statements of intention from either representatives of archive.org or the band itself, this play of interpretations becomes an improvisational construction of meaning for the community; it is an instantiation of Ricoeur's "mode of 'as if'" — without direct evidence upon which to base the community's understanding, interpretation must be posited "as if" there were evidence, and understanding must be fashioned "as if" it were based on such evidence, in an ongoing cycle of new and conflicting statements and claims.

This is not to suggest, however, that interpretations are constructed entirely out of whole cloth. In the absence of direct evidence, participants rely on "Reference"—a shared set of objects, people, and events to which they can refer—in order to draw inferences and to construct an interpretation "as if" more direct evidence were available. Such a set of references is at the heart of the process of improvising community in the forum. Just as a mix of shared elements—specific structural materials such as verses, along with shared understandings of other musical elements such as particular harmonic centers, sets of tones and timbres, and thematic patterns (and collective disruptions of those elements)—allowed the Grateful Dead to recreate "Dark Star" nearly 200 times while always sustaining the song as a recognizable improvisational space, this shared set of references provides the basic materials for the community's improvisations.

Each community has its own specific set of such materials. In the case of the Dead Downloads forum—and other online Deadhead communities—these materials range from references that are part of the broader culture (both online and off) within which the community is situated, to more Deadhead-centric references that are still accessible to non community members, to more esoteric "insider" references that are part of the arcana of this specific community. A full accounting of this range of shared references is well beyond the scope of this chapter, but one example will suffice to give some of the flavor of "Reference" in this community.

A funny post by "frogman," made early in the controversy, provides a perfect example of this mix, through a community-specific play on the culture-wide phenomenon of the joke asking, "How many ____ does it take to screw in a light bulb?" The answer is "Jerry gave them the light for free then gdp took it away and made them pay for it, but in the transfer the damn thing broke." In a single sentence, this post combines four different types of reference, encompassing: (1) the near-universal joke structure; (2) the community-specific but still recognizable Jerry Garcia (with an embedded acknowledgment of a widely shared perception that he always wanted the music to be "free"); (3) the "insider" reference to "gdp," which would remain opaque to outsiders but is instantly recognizable to community members as "Grateful Dead Productions"; and (4) the history and economics of Deadhead tape trading contrasted with a very different understanding of music as a commercially viable commodity. Through this melding of references, "frogman" not only says something that clearly situates him within the specific frame of reference of the Deadhead community, but also makes a complex point about the core implications of the archive.org decision within that community: it is a decision that is tangled in a maze of Deadhead assumptions about the value of music and the free exchange of recordings, attitudes and beliefs of the band members, capitalist economics, and the sense of loss that has continued unabated since the death of Jerry Garcia in 1995.

This single example provides a good overview of the range of reference at work within the Dead Downloads forum. Not surprisingly, participants refer most often to things most closely related to the forum's name and to the "Thanksgiving Day Massacre": tapes and tape trading; archive.org and its Live Music Archives; the transformation of recording and distribution technologies from analog to digital; the full range of economic and spiritual dimensions of music as art, information, and/or commodity; the Deadhead experience, and the band itself along with other associated individuals and corporate and legal entities. Scattered among such references are another set, linking the specifics of this particular community with the broader cultural world of which it is a part, including references to aspects of western and American history and culture, various pop culture phenomena (at one point the controversy is likened to a wrestling match between a "heel" and a "babyface," with band members cast as the wrestlers), etc.

In this particular community at this particular time in its history, "Invention" is closely linked to both "Intention" and "Reference." As noted above, if there is no evidence upon which to base the community's understanding, then interpretation must be posited "as if" there were such evidence. And, as also noted above, there is in fact only scant (and contradictory) evidence available out of which to craft an understanding of the decision to remove the Grateful Dead recordings from the archive. In this sense, community members must "speak the present" by positing new knowledge that can be used to explain the event, since there is no existing knowledge fully adequate to "speak the past." However, as cultural hermeneutics suggests, it is impossible to "speak the present" completely or to invent knowledge that is entirely new and without roots in prior understanding. Thus, from the beginning of the controversy to the end, participants couch their interpretations and observations in already established terms, whether conjectures about the intentions of absent others or the set of references shared by the community as a whole.

In a sense, such a tension between invention and repetition — between "speaking the present" and "speaking the past" — is the fuel that drives the entire controversy. That is, something new, in the form of the decision to limit access to recordings via archive.org, has entered the world of the community, and community members must struggle to understand this event that no longer allows them to "speak the past." Appropriately, then, arguments abound that are directly linked to issues of invention; participants return again and again to questions and discussions about whether or not transformations in recording and distribution technologies and formats have changed everything, about whether intellectual property rights rooted in an analog world still have meaning in the digital domain, and even about whether or not the idea of a Deadhead "community" can still have meaning in the mediated context of the Internet and in the years after Jerry Garcia's death.

This "tension" — an interplay between existing structures and new understandings, between behaviors and resources rooted in the past and the ongoing need to move in new directions whether in response to new stimuli or simply because things can never just remain static — is precisely the tension of improvisation. Hermeneutics, whether philosophical or cultural, posits such a process as a fundamental element of human communication and understanding. Interpretation (whether of texts in a strict sense, as in biblical texts or the texts of a virtual community, or of other human artifacts and actions) and improvisation are, in this reading, two faces of the same fundamental process. A song like "Dark Star" emerges freshly in each performance even as those who perform it revisit and reinterpret elements drawn from previous performances; in the same way, online community continually unfolds and rediscovers itself through the improvisational revisiting of its own prior texts. In both, the new and the old fold into one another in an ongoing dance, an enduring, ever-changing but always recognizable creation.

Note

1. The dead.net forums that were current at the time of the "Thanksgiving Day Massacre" were replaced in mid–2007, when the entire dead.net Web site was updated and revamped. Unfortunately, it appears that the older content of dead.net was destroyed at that time. All quotations of posts are from the earlier incarnation of dead.net. Because the posts are no longer extant on the web, full citations and URLs cannot be provided. All posts made to the dead.net forums use pseudonyms, and cannot necessarily be linked to participants' actual names or identities. Posts, although they may be truncated in what follows, are presented "as is," without any correction of typographical, grammatical, or other errors.

Bibliography

Barlow, J.P. (2005). "Barlow on Death of Grateful Dead Music Sharing, Fans Protest." In *BoingBoing: A Directory of Wonderful Things*. Available online at: http://www.boingboing.net/2005/11/29/barlow-on-death-of-g.html.

Becker, A.L. (1979). "Text-building, Epistemology, and Aesthetics in Javanese ShadowTheatre." In *The Imagination of Reality: Essays in Southeast Asian Coherence Systems*, Abram Yengoyan, ed. Norwood, NJ: Ablex Publishing Corporation.

Burnett, G. (2002). "The scattered members of an invisible republic: Virtual communities and Paul Ricoeur's Hermeneutics." *Library Quarterly*, 72:2, 155–178.

_____, M. Dickey, M. Kazmer, and K. Chudoba. (2003). "Inscription and Interpretation of Text: A Cultural Hermeneutic Examination of Virtual Community." *Information Research*, 9:1. Available online at: http://informationr.net/ir/9-1/paper162.html.

Dickey, M.H., G. Burnett, K.M. Chudoba, and M.M. Kazmer. (2007). "Do You Read

Me? Perspective Making and Perspective Taking in Call Center Chat Communications." *Journal of the Association of Information* Systems, 8:1, 47–70.

Gadamer, H.G., and David E. Linge, trans. (1976). *Philosophical Hermeneutics*. Berkeley: University of California Press.

Geertz, C. (1983). *Local Knowledge: Further Essays in Interpretive Anthropology*. New York: Basic Books.

Hafner, K. (2001). *The Well: A Story of Love, Death & Real Life in the Seminal Online Community*. New York: Carroll & Graf.

Hart, M. (Statement of 12/02/05). Cited at *Grateful Dead News: Digital Press Clippings on the Grateful Dead*. Available online at: http://deadnews.blogspot.com/2006/01/archive-quotes.html.

Hirsch, E.D. (1967). *Validity in Interpretation*. New Haven: Yale University Press.

"History of Deadheads in Cyberspace." (1996). Available online at: ftp://gdead.berkeley.edu/pub/gdead/miscellaneous/History-of-Deadheads-in-Cyberspace.

Leeds, J. (2005, November 30). "Deadheads Outraged Over Web Crackdown." *New York Times*, Available online at: http://www.nytimes.com/2005/11/30/arts/music/30dead.html?_r=1&scp=2&sq=Dennis+McNally&st=nyt&oref=slogin.

Lesh, P. (2005). An announcement from Phil Lesh. Available online at: http://www.phillesh.net/philzonepages/friends_stuff/hotline-051130.html.

_____. (2005). *Searching for the Sound: My Life with the Grateful Dead*. New York: Little, Brown.

Malkki, L.H. (1997). "News and Culture: Transitory Phenomena and the Fieldwork Tradition." In *Anthropological Locations: Boundaries and Grounds of a Field Science*, Akhil Gupta and James Ferguson, eds. Berkeley: University of California Press.

Pareles, J. (2005, Dec. 3). "The Dead's Gamble: Free Music for Sale." *New York Times*. Available online at: http://www.nytimes.com/2005/12/03/arts/music/03pare.html?_r=1&scp=4&sq= archive.org&st=cse&oref=slogin.

Rheingold, H. (1993). *The Virtual Community: Homesteading on the Electronic Frontier*. Reading, MA: Addison-Wesley.

Ricoeur, P. (1976). *Interpretation Theory: Discourse and the Surplus of Meaning*. Fort Worth: Texas Christian University Press.

Thompson, J.B. (1981). *Critical Hermeneutics: A Study in the Thought of Paul Ricoeur*. Cambridge: Cambridge University Press.

Weir, B. (2005). Radio interview transcription. Cited online at: http://deadnews.blogspot.com/2006/01/archive-quotes.html.

Strategic Improvisation: Management Lessons from the Dead

Barry Barnes

Management expert and quality guru W. Edwards Deming (1981) contended the purpose of business is survival. Yet, increasingly dramatic change is affecting every aspect of contemporary business practice, and survival is no easy challenge. Given today's greater need for flexibility and adaptability for organizational survival, there's an ongoing quest for change formulas and quick fixes. Since the 1980s, business managers and decision makers have been offered a variety of concepts and techniques intended to promote competitiveness and organizational flexibility. These include Total Quality Management, Searching for Excellence, Reengineering the Organization, and Organizational Learning. But despite their best intentions, many of these techniques have lost favor and passed away simply to be replaced by another program du jour. As a result, management continues to look for lasting solutions to the challenge of change and seek a formula for long-term survival and success as exemplified in Jim Collins' (2001) *Good to Great* and Larry Bossidy and Ram Charan's (2002) *Execution: The Discipline of Getting Things Done.*

With continuing uncertainty due to competitive, economic, and political change, one may wonder why strategic plans are even made when the unexpected is so often the norm. While this paper endorses the need for and benefits from strategic planning, it also argues that the turmoil in today's business environment requires an improved, flexible approach to the execution of strategic plans. One such approach — improvisation — has always been with us although it is generally not well known or understood in organizations.

In a world of continually accelerating change and increasing tumult, fixed plans can only take organizations so far. Improvisation, which blends both planning and doing simultaneously, is often how things really get done when unexpected situations arise even if those who improvise are not aware of it. In addition, the process of improvisation can also be done collectively with one's colleagues to solve unexpected problems. This essay proposes that improved knowledge and understanding of improvisation can lead to better spur-of-the-moment actions which in turn can lead to more effective strategy execution and improved organizational results.

This discussion will focus on how best to conceive improvisation in the organizational context, drawing insights from a rich vein of management theory. I will endeavor to explain what is most relevant about improvisation, both individually and collectively; I will also discuss why it is important for organizations to understand this significance; and I will show how improvisational processes can be beneficial when executing strategic and tactical plans. In this paper the strategic improvisation process will be illustrated with examples from an unusual organization, the legendary rock band The Grateful Dead, drawing examples from not only their music but also their business. Both their music and business demonstrate strategic improvisation that is confirmed by their success for 30 years in the extremely volatile music industry.

What Is Improvisation?

In essence, improvisation is doing something unplanned on the spur of the moment using the tools and materials at hand. Karl Weick (1998) suggests improvisation works with the unforeseen and unexpected, and some have described it as the "enactment of quick and unexpected solutions in a sudden crisis" (Ciborra, 1999). Others have suggested improvisation is "situated actions in which the thinking and behavior emerge simultaneously and on the spur of the moment" (Silva, 2002), or that it is "design and execution converging in time" (Moorman & Minor, 1998a). With a refined ability to blend thinking and acting simultaneously or merge design and execution, a case can be made that effective improvisation would allow more flexible strategy execution, and we define this as "strategic improvisation" when it is recognized and the needed skills are developed and encouraged.

Business, Music and Improvisation

Music is one endeavor where risk and spontaneity are frequently embraced and encouraged in order to create an outcome that satisfies all stakeholders. Although this is unlike business where risk is resisted, several management experts have used musical metaphors to characterize effective organizations and leaders. For example, Max De Pree (1992) says, "We have much to learn from jazz-band leaders, for jazz, like leadership, combines the unpredictability of the future with the gifts of the individuals." Peter Drucker (1988) has suggested that organizations in today's Information Age must act like a "symphony orchestra." Given the inherent risk in all change, it is worth considering what lessons improvisation might offer to decision makers and organizations.

Those who are unfamiliar with musical improvisation may think it approaches chaos, but it is *not* chaos. To avoid devolving into chaos, however, improvisation requires a high degree of fundamental musical skills such as playing scales, chords and harmony, which are then combined to provide a common musical vocabulary (Barrett, 1998). In the organizational setting improvisation also requires a high degree of skills such as listening, influencing and effective decision making.

Mintzberg (1987) tells us that crafting strategy requires both formulation and implementation into a fluid process if a strategy is to evolve and adapt, and Crossan (1998) suggests that improvisation offers a technique for the strategic renewal of an organization. If improvisation, both individual and collective, is understood and effectively practiced when unexpected situations arise, organizations will be better able to respond to risk in a spontaneous way that, like effective musicians, provides a more satisfying outcome for all stakeholders.

But how can improvisation be applied in the organizational setting? According to Barrett (1998), when improvising musicians get together they "do what managers find themselves doing: fabricating and inventing novel responses without a pre-scripted plan and without certainty of outcomes; discovering the future that their action creates as it unfolds" (p. 605). Furthermore, managers have some other important things in common with improvisational musicians. Both are "performing" where their actions are seen by their public. The public nature of the performance creates stress for both, tempting them to rely on what has worked well in the past. Finally, there is a pressure for both musicians and managers to appear competent and to avoid risk-taking.

Moorman and Miner (1998a) identified three levels of improvisation: modest adjustment to a preexisting structure; stronger departures from the structure; and discarding all links to the original structure by composing new patterns. Managers and decision makers frequently find themselves making modest adjustments to existing policies and procedures, sometimes making stronger departures from them, and in a few cases tossing out the policies and procedures completely in order to create an entirely new response to radically changing conditions.

Recent articles can be found examining improvisation in new product development (Moorman & Miner, 1998b), innovation (Cohen & Levinthal, 1990), adaptation in the global computer industry (Eisenhardt & Tabrizi, 1995), strategy formulation (Mintzberg & McHugh, 1985), outsourcing (Silva, 2002), and change management (Orlikowski & Hoffman, 1997).

Requirements for Strategic Improvisation

In 1998, Frank Barrett, a management consultant and musician, identified seven requirements for musical improvisation which he contends can also be applied in the business or organizational setting

1. Interrupting habits
2. Embracing errors as a source of learning
3. Allowing maximum flexibility through minimal structures
4. Continually negotiating toward dynamic synchronicity
5. Relying on retrospective sense making
6. Learning informally and developing group norms
7. Alternating between soloing and supporting

These seven requirements provide the foundation for examining strategic improvisation in this chapter. It is important to remember that strategic improvisation is used only when unexpected situations arise for which there is no routine in place, although it is also important to create an environment that encourages improvisation.

The Grateful Dead as an Improvisational Business

In 1995, *Time* magazine referred to the Grateful Dead as "the ragged champs of the art of improvisation" (Corliss, 1995). While *Time* was referring to their musical improvisation, each of Barrett's requirements for organizational improvisation can also be illustrated from the business side of the Grateful Dead. They successfully improvised both musically and organizationally for 30 years in a volatile industry where bands come and go on a daily basis and response to rapid change is a requirement.

The Grateful Dead began playing in a pizza parlor in Palo Alto, California, for $50 a night, and by 1973 they played to the largest crowd in U.S. history (estimated at 600,000) at Watkins Glen, New York. In 1991 total attendance at their concerts was 1.8 million with a 99.4 percent occupancy rate, and ticket sales reached $52.5 million in 1994, their last full year of concerts. Their music was a blend of folk, bluegrass, blues, reggae, country, jazz and rock, and they were strongly influenced by improvisational jazz legends such as John Coltrane and Miles Davis. The improvisational nature of the Dead's music also had a significant impact on their improvisational approach to business, as will be seen in this essay. Thus, by examining the requirements of improvisation with examples from the Dead's musical and organizational history, my aim is to clarify how these requirements apply to organizations and offer valuable lessons to managers and decision makers in today's competitive environment.

Interrupting Habits

Interrupting habits is the first requirement for improvisation and is a requirement for any successful change program. One of the most challenging impediments to any business change is habit both at the individual and organizational level. Habits are routines or unconscious patterns of behavior, and because of their unconscious nature the best intentions for change will have little or no effect without an ongoing reminder to change. By definition, improvisation aims to avoid the routine and usual by seeking something unique and appropriate for each unexpected situation. Musical improvisers encourage each other to take risks and to find spontaneous moments, thus acting as a mutually supportive innovation reminder.

Interrupting habits was a characteristic of the Grateful Dead both as a band and as a business. The band was well known for wanting to "keep things interesting" and preventing their music from becoming stale. In more than 2,300 live performances, the Dead never played play the same set of songs nor did they ever perform the same song the same way twice. In 1981 Bob Weir, rhythm guitarist and vocalist, said, "The whole thing with the Grateful Dead is a challenge to get something new happening, even when you don't feel like doing anything new or feel anything new lurking around the corner" (Jackson, 1999, p. 315).

Organizationally, the Dead were constantly experimenting and changing as well. In 1974 Weir said, "We tend to paint ourselves into a corner from time to time," which created an organizational mindset of being "pirates and scavengers," never taking anything for granted. As the poster children for the sixties, the Dead always maintained an outlaw/outsider mentality, never trusting the "system" or the music industry. Thus, they epitomized former Intel CEO Andy Grove's famous quote, "Only the paranoid survive," which acted as a catalyst for the Dead organization to continually examine their habits and change them when necessary. Quoting Grateful Dead lyricist Robert Hunter, "When life looks like Easy Street there is danger at your door," and routines cause us to be comfortable — like living on Easy Street.

Embracing Errors as a Source of Learning

In musical improvisation, there is an important axiom: If there are no mistakes, we have a mistake. Yet, in most businesses to make a mistake and acknowledge it is often a career-terminating event; errors are not well tolerated in much of Corporate America. Yet imagine an infant learning to walk without falling down or a sports team unable to see the value of practicing to reduce their errors. Thus, we know from personal experience that the best learning often comes from making a mistake and adjusting future actions in response.

Drumming at the edge of chaos. Winterland, October 20, 1974 (courtesy Pat Lee and David Thomson, all rights reserved).

When they officially took the name Grateful Dead in late 1965, all five of the band members were relative novices. Musically the Dead learned much about their music and themselves by simply playing together, learning from their mistakes and practicing for hours and hours to perfect their skills individually and collectively. The Dead worked hard to learn from their errors, certainly as the "ragged champs of improvisation," but also as a business. In a 1991 interview, Dan Healy, their sound man for more than 25 years, described their efforts to create the best concert sound system in the world.

> I have extreme, undivided, unsplintered support from the band, in terms of budgets and stuff like that. I obviously haven't always been successful. There have been times when we've spent large amounts of money to try an idea, and I've fallen right on my face. All they did was pick me up and say "go for it again" [Barnes, 1991].

In the early 1970s, one of Healy's errors cost $15,000 — a considerable sum for the band — but by embracing errors as a source of learning, it was a price they were willing to pay.

Allowing Maximum Flexibility Through Minimal Structures

The purpose of organizational structures and policies is to reduce ambiguity and provide ready-made solutions and communication lines. Yet these can easily become rigid and invisible, inhibiting innovation, flexibility, and improvisation. The Grateful Dead always minimized structure in both their music and their business in order to ensure maximum flexibility. One musical example of this is their song "Dark Star," released as a single in 1968 at less than three minutes long. Yet in concert it could last 45 minutes, demonstrating maximum flexibility from minimal structure.

This same minimalist approach to structure was found in their organization as well. While they were never a large organization, the Grateful Dead did have 70 full-time employees in 1994 when they sold $95 million of concert tickets and merchandise. This small size always made it easier for the Dead to minimize structure and allowed them to operate without job titles or job descriptions. Although they did incorporate in 1976, if there was ever any structure to their business it was family-like, and they frequently referred to themselves as an extended family. As lead guitarist Jerry Garcia said, "What we wanted to do was play music, and we didn't want to have to be businessmen. We didn't even want to decide; we just wanted to play.... We were truly coming from an unstructured space" (Jackson, 1999, p. 162).

Continually Negotiating Toward Dynamic Synchronicity

According to Barrett (1998, p. 613), "What characterizes successful ... improvisation, perhaps more than any other factor ... is the on-going give and take between members. Players are in a continual dialogue and exchange with one another." Continual exchange and dialogue provide the means for an ongoing negotiation between musicians so they can move the music in new directions and cause each other to react and reinterpret the music in real time. As an improvisational band, the Dead sought those special moments when the improvisational "X Factor" appeared — moments when their musical dialogue and exchange would create something between the band and the audience, true moments of dynamic synchronicity and real magic.

Business-wise, the Dead were also in constant negotiation toward synchronicity. Other than the band, personnel were not locked into "jobs" nor was the organization locked into a fixed structure. Instead there was a continual dialogue and exchange focused on meeting the needs of the next concert tour or recording session. In fact, it wasn't until 1976 that Grateful Dead Productions was incorporated, and Grateful Dead Merchandising wasn't formalized until 1993. In many traditional organizations, however, continual exchange and dialogue are the exception rather than the rule with communication often top-down with little dialogue or feedback.

Relying on Retrospective Sense Making

Barrett (1998, p. 615) tells us that "Since one cannot rely on blueprints and can never know for certain where the music is going, one can only make guesses and anticipate possible paths based on what has already happened, meanwhile continue playing under the assumption that whatever happened must amount to something." Thus, improvisation is a process where the music emerges from the interaction of the players rather than from relying on a well-defined song structure where one knows what comes next.

One business decision which embodies retrospective sense making was that of allowing fans to tape their concerts. This went against all business models at the time since this essentially gave away their product for free. Yet the fan recordings offered a more accurate picture of their music than their studio recordings. They were traded widely among fans and quickly became an important means of attracting of new fans as well, something completely unexpected and now a model for many bands today. This demonstrates retrospective sense making and conforms nicely to another Dead lyric, "Some folks trust to reason / Others trust to might / I don't trust to nothing / But I know it come out right."

Learning Informally and Developing Group Norms

In organizations, informal learning is called socialization and is a crucial process where the standards of acceptable behavior are shared and developed in each individual. This process is particularly important as employees learn the organization's values. In an organization that improvises effectively these norms support all the other requirements for improvisation.

According to Barrett, "Learning is much more than receiving abstract, a-contextual, disembodied knowledge. It is a matter of learning how to speak the language of the community of practitioners" (1998, p. 616). To develop improvisational skills, musicians "hang out" together informally, listen to great musicians, discuss it in great detail, memorize the great solos, and jam together after hours. This allows novices to learn the standard tunes, tempos and keys, and even how other musicians dress. Developing these norms in any organization always occurs informally regardless of the existing formal processes.

This process of informal learning was a critical element in the development of the musical vocabulary of the Grateful Dead. All of the band members were from the same part of the San Francisco Bay Area, hung out together from time to time during the early 1960s, occasionally lived together, and played music in various groups before forming the Grateful Dead in late 1965. Also influential in their informal learning together was their involvement in writer Ken Kesey's Acid Tests. During the late 1960s, band members consumed large quantities of LSD together while it was still legal. According to Jerry Garcia, this helped develop an almost psychic musical connection among the band members. Furthermore, it strengthened their social bond throughout the time they enjoyed communal living in the late 1960s.

Due to the strong bond of group norms between band members and their employees, the Dead benefited from minimal turnover both within the band itself and within the Dead's business organization. Most employees maintained their tenure for many years, yet joining the organization was no easy task and generally involved considerable informal learning. One of the early Grateful Dead staffers, Rosie McGee, describes the experience of getting a job in the organization:

> How do you get a job on the Grateful Dead staff? Well, a resume probably won't do you much good, and there's no tried and true path to being hired. Initially, it's who you know. If you just happen to have someone on the inside who will vouch for you ("She's cool!"), if you appear just when a desperate need opens up ("Hey, you sitting in the kitchen—c'mere!"), and show a willingness to take on some lengthy mind-numbing task with the hope of better times ahead—you're in! But once you've done that first assignment, JUST TRY to walk away! If you're good at the job, you may get stuck with it until you scream for release [Jackson, 1999, p. 156].

Dennis McNally, publicist and biographer of the Grateful Dead, confirms the importance of learning informally and developing group norms. He commented that the Dead's approach to hiring someone new was "to test them first as a person" to see if they fit with the style and philosophy of the Dead "family" (Barnes, 1997). Thus, the Grateful Dead used a methodical approach to integrating new associates into their organization by employing an informal learning process.

Alternating Between Soloing and Supporting

Barrett's final requirement for improvisation is alternating between soloing and supporting, which demands each member listen to the others, then fill in and assist where needed without stepping on the other's lead. It requires a receptiveness and ability to see beyond one's own part, to see the bigger whole. According to Barrett:

> One of the most widespread, yet overlooked structures in jazz [improvisation] is the practice of taking turns. Jazz bands usually rotate the "leadership" of the band: that is, they take turns soloing and supporting other soloists by providing rhythmic and harmonic background. Such an egalitarian model assures that each player will get an opportunity to develop a musical idea while others create space for this development to occur [Barrett, 1998, p. 616].

From a musical perspective, the Dead followed a very similar approach, as described in the following comments by David Gans, musician, record producer and host of the nationally syndicated Grateful Dead Hour:

> What made the Dead so great was their willingness to cooperate. Although everyone adored Jerry's solos, the thing that made him such a magical player was

how well he blended in and cooperated with the others ... the glory of Jerry was that for many years he was almost never at a loss for a musical thought, but also never really obsessed with dominating everything [Jackson, 1999, p. 144].

In organizational terms, this requirement closely mirrors the often misunderstood and poorly applied concept of "employee empowerment" so widely touted in businesses beginning in the 1990s. Alternating between soloing and supporting is a critical ingredient for organizations where employees must not only follow but must also lead from time to time by utilizing different skills and abilities from different individuals as they deal with novel and unexpected situations.

Organizationally, the Dead also exhibited soloing and supporting. Even though Garcia was extremely charismatic and typically the focal point of the music and the organization itself, he disdained the role of "leader." Instead, the organization was consensus driven with veto power held by all band members with each a member of the board of directors. Even with the greater degree of formality and structure of a corporation, they continued to alternate between soloing and supporting with the role of president rotated among willing band/board members.

Another indication of the Dead organization's willingness to support as well as solo is their unique and egalitarian approach to compensation. Throughout their history the band shared whatever they earned with everyone involved in the production of the music, including road crew and office staff, including royalties for Dead-written songs. In 1994 the Grateful Dead organization had practically no absenteeism and no employee turn-over. Most of the 70 employees had been with the organization many years and often earned over $100,000 with benefits including profit sharing, retirement, and health care (Brokaw, 1994). This is virtually unheard of in the music industry where bands hire road and lighting crews only for the duration of a concert tour. Throughout their history, the Grateful Dead and their organization have shown examples of alternating between soloing and supporting.

We have now seen examples of each of Barrett's requirements of strategic improvisation, both musically and organizationally, from the Grateful Dead's history. Next we consider what lessons can be learned from their example.

Management Lessons from the Dead

The Grateful Dead survived for 30 years in the turbulent music industry, performed an average of 77 concerts each year, are the most recorded band in history, and were one of the largest concert attractions in the United States, all with little radio airplay and only one Top Ten hit. They had minimal employee turnover and incredibly loyal fans. No other musical group in history has come close to duplicating this remarkable achievement. Much credit can be given to their improvisational approach to both their music and their organization. The band had a clear and compelling vision to play live music, and regardless of circumstances, this vision never varied. Whatever the situation, they would respond and adapt, accept the associated risks and consequences, and continue touring and playing. As a result, their audience grew from 50–100 in the mid-sixties to regularly filling stadiums in the 1990s and selling more than one million tickets annually.

What results can be expected from applying these management lessons from the Dead? Strategic improvisation engages everyone involved, focuses on solving problems immediately, demands open communication, and provides a trusting environment that utilizes the various skills and abilities of the players. Furthermore, strategic improvisation in organizations improves responsiveness to unexpected crises, enhances innovation and adaptability, and provides action when planning takes too long. Finally, strategic improvisation is a requirement for survival in turbulent times because management must always be responsive to changing conditions and will ultimately have to improvise when a crisis arises and no routine or policy applies. Organizations must be innovative, adaptable and able to respond quickly to the unforeseen. Using lessons and examples from the Grateful Dead, this essay identifies and illustrates the requirements for strategic improvisation along with the necessary organizational characteristics.

Conclusion

Creating an organization where Barrett's seven requirements for improvisation are present will allow it to be adaptable, responsive, and innovative and lead to satisfied and committed employees, satisfied and loyal customers, and ultimately to survival in rapidly changing environments. Although the Grateful Dead were far from a traditional model of a business organization, their improvisational approach served them well. As adaptability and change continue to be required for organizational survival, business leaders will want to consider strategic improvisation employed successfully by the Grateful Dead.

Bibliography

Barnes, B. (1991). "An Interview with Dan Healy." *Unbroken Chain*, 6:5, 6–8, 17–18.
Barrett, F. J. (1998). "Creativity and Improvisation in Jazz and Organizations: Implications for Organizational Learning." *Organizational Science*, 9:5, 605–622.
Bossidy, L., R. Charan, and C. Burck. (2002). *Execution: The Discipline of Getting Things Done*. New York: Crown Business.
Ciborra, C.U. (1999). "Notes on Improvisation and Time in Organizations." *Accounting, Management and Information Technologies*, 9:2, 77–94.

Cohen, W.M., and D.A. Levinthal. (1990). "Absorptive Capacity: A New Perspective on Learning and Innovation." *Administrative Science Quarterly*, 35, 128–152.

Collins, Jim. (2001). *Good to Great*. New York: Harper Collins.

Corliss, R. (1995, August 21). "The Dead Trip Ends: Jerry Garcia, the Pied and Tie-dyed Piper of the Grateful Dead." *Time*, 146:8, 60–64.

Crossan, M. (1998). "An Orientation and a Technique to Enhance the Strategic Renewal of the Organization." *Organization Science*, 9:5.

Deming, W.E. (1981). *Out of the Crisis*. Cambridge: MIT Center for Advanced Engineering Study.

De Pree, Max. (1992). *Leadership Jazz*. New York: Dell.

Drucker, Peter F. (1988, January-February). "The Coming of the New Organization." *Harvard Business Review*, 45–53.

Eisenhardt, K., and B. Tabrizi. (1995). "Accelerating Adaptive Processes: Product Innovation in the Global Computer Industry." *Administrative Science Quarterly*.

Jackson, Blair. (1999). *Garcia: An American Life*. New York: Viking.

Mintzberg, H. (1987, July-August). "Crafting Strategy." *Harvard Business Review*.

_____, and A. McHugh. (1985, June 30). "Strategic Formulation in an 'Ad Hocracy.'" *Administrative Science Quarterly*, 160–97.

Moorman, C., and A. Miner. (1998a). "The Convergence of Planning and Execution: Improvisation in New Product Development." *Journal of Marketing*, 62:3, 1–20.

_____, and _____. (1998b). "Organization Improvisation and Organizational Memory." *Academy of Management Journal*, 23:4, 698–723.

Orlikowski, W., and J. Hoffman. (1997, winter). "An improvisational Model for Change Management: the Case of Groupware Technologies." *Sloan Management Review*, 11–21.

Silva, L.O. (2002). "Outsourcing as an Improvisation: A Case Study in Latin America." *The Information Society*, 18, 129–128.

Weick, K. (1993). "The Collapse of Sensemaking in Organizations: The Mann Gulch Disaster." In *Administrative Science Quarterly*, 38:4, 628–46.

_____. (1998). "Improvisation as a Mindset for Organizational Analysis." *Organization Science*, 9:5, 543–555.

Cultural Communication Codes Among Deadheads: A Chronological Account of Communicative Improvisation

Natalie J. Dollar

In this essay, I take a preliminary look at the evolution of the *Deadhead* "*communication landscape*,"[1] exploring *communication scenes* (some enduring, others not) by means of which Deadheads call on *communicative resources—events, forms, sequences of action*, and *symbols*—to enact, inform and shape their cultural identity and community. This focus differs from my previous research by focusing on the larger communication landscape, as opposed to analyses of particular communication situations, such as Dead shows (Dollar, 2002, 1999b), or sequences of communication action, such as show talk and calling the opener (Dollar, 2007, 1999a). My intent in taking this broader approach is to suggest some possibilities for how a communication approach might influence studies of live Grateful Dead music as something essential to the interplay of Deadheads and Grateful Dead fans in general. By treating Deadheads as a *speech community*, and treating *identity* as an interactional accomplishment relying on a *communication code*, one gains insight to how the Deadhead community has responded to changes and challenges, often by seizing the latest communication technology and transforming existing technologies in innovative ways. This essay demonstrates that Deadheads' code has grown in complexity, accessibility, and sophistication, as evident in the metamorphosis from fan clubs and newsletters to the most recently created scene, SIRIUS Satellite Radio's Grateful Dead Channel.

As a preliminary analysis this essay is broadly focused, informed by the ethnographic study of communication (Hymes, 1962, 1972) and cultural communication (Carbaugh, 1988; Philipsen, 2003). This framework differs from approaches that study Deadheads as a subculture or religious community. Instead, I explore Deadheads as a *speech community*, or group of communicators sharing a common language or linguistic variety — English, for most Deadheads — and a set of rules informing the use and interpretation of this linguistic variety in culturally meaningful communication scenes. This *communication code* includes *communication scenes* and *resources* that are deeply felt, commonly intelligible, and widely accessible means for enacting and negotiating their shared identity, what Carbaugh (1988) refers to as *cultural communication*. By examining how Deadheads communicate, we are able to attend to some of the directly observable visible and audible matters being used to construct, enact, and negotiate their identity.

Taken together, these concepts — speech community, communication code, and cultural communication — provide a theoretical framework for conceptualizing identities, relationships and communities as communicative accomplishments, enacted and transformed through cultural communication codes. Significantly, these codes allow for the inclusion of contested and oppositional communication, reflecting the diverse membership of speech communities. This helps to make the framework particularly well-suited to framing responses to the following research questions concerning the Grateful Dead phenomenon: How has the Deadhead cultural communication landscape responded/evolved since its inception at the first Grateful Dead shows (including those performed by the Warlocks)? What are the current here-and-now "means" with which Deadheads converse, and what do these means *mean* for those who use and experience them? By addressing these questions, we can begin to understand how the everyday "lived communication" experiences of Deadheads gain meaning from (all the while shaping) their understanding (and our own) of what it means to *be* a Deadhead.

The specific procedures I use are: (1) to locate communication scenes Deadheads deem cultural, (2) to formulate a brief communication profile of these scenes using Hymes' (1974) SPEAKING heuristic, allowing us to interpret the deeper meaning these resources activate as Deadheads navigate their communicative landscape, and (3) to compare and organize these profiles, suggesting a more holistic view of the Deadhead communication code than currently available. The data set includes interviews and currently available cultural communication resources. My analysis suggests that the SIRIUS Grateful Dead Channel is the latest improvisational response to availability of technology, cultural communicative resources, and the challenges that face a community grounded in a band that no longer exists except in the thousands of hours of recorded music they left. The channel functions as a communicative warehouse combining well-known scenes and resources with innovative new resources.

A Chronological Tour of the Deadhead Communication Landscape

In what follows, I sketch a chronological view of the Deadhead communication landscape, which though incomplete is nevertheless illustrative. To treat all the communicative scenes and resources available would take us well beyond the scope of this essay. Instead, taking my cue from the Deadheads in my data set, I want to explore a sampling of the scenes deemed cultural, giving particular attention to those which have yet to be explored in the growing body of Dead Studies. As such, my analysis may not represent all Deadheads, nor is it likely to reflect any particular Deadhead's use of the communication code. Nevertheless, the analysis presents an interpretation that is deeply felt, commonly intelligible, and widely accessible to many Deadheads.

I organize the essay chronologically, acknowledging that some communicative scenes emerged simultaneously. This tour consists of stops at the following communication scenes along the Deadhead communication landscape: fan clubs and newsletters, Deadhead magazines, show flyers, Grateful Dead radio, virtual music sites, and finally, SIRIUS Satellite Radio's Grateful Dead Channel. Noticeably absent from this list are books, the Grateful Dead hotline and mail order system, and face-to-face interaction at Grateful Dead shows. These omissions should not suggest in any way that these communication scenes are somehow less relevant than those discussed in the essay. Instead, these omissions point to the ominous task of sketching a comprehensive description and interpretation of the Deadhead communication landscape.

Fan Clubs and Newsletters

The Golden Road to Unlimited Devotion, a fan club founded in 1965, signaled the beginning of an enduring communicative collaboration between the Grateful Dead and their fans, soon to be known as Deadheads. Fans became members of the Dead fan club by subscribing to the club:

> A dollar to the club got you posters, buttons, "biographies of each Dead," and the very first issue of *Rolling Stone*. For $2.50 you got one of the first Dead shirts ever made, with Pigpen on it. The club promised personal responses to all fan mail, and promised to divulge "secrets" about the band members' lives [Shenk & Silberman, 1994, p. 114].

The features of this *communication scene*, the fan club, were characteristic of fan clubs at the time. Members subscribed and received "inside" information, responses to their fan mail, and collectables and memorabilia. The interaction was asynchronous and written, components of the communication scene that would not change when the band took ownership of the fan club, dropped the subscription fee, and started a newsletter published and mailed two or three times a year.

This transition was activated in 1971 when the Grateful Dead announced in the band's eponymous live album: "Dead Freaks unite! Who are you? Where are you? Send us your name and we'll keep you informed."[2] Gone were the more traditional fan club communication resources—buttons, stickers, band member biographies and personal life stories—and in their place was a "low-key and astonishingly intimate" newsletter in which "a stoned Hunter would spin a hypnocracy yarn, Alan Trist would add some tour information, and Garcia might be persuaded to contribute a little sketch" (McNally, 2002, p. 454). The outcome was a fan club and newsletter similar to but distinct from the original. First, it was written by members of the Grateful Dead family, including band members themselves, instead of by Deadheads. Second, it employed additional communication resources, such as original artwork, creative writing, and tour reports. Tour reports would become a significant communication resource spawning Deadheads' own tour and show reports. And third, it unintentionally supported the growing taper community by providing tour information which these Deadheads meticulously archived, along with tapes, establishing a network of trading that was unheard of in the music industry.[3]

This "mailing list" driven fan club grew from about 350 in its formative years to over 200,000 as it evolved into the *Grateful Dead Almanac*. This newer version reintroduced band collectables, with a notable emphasis on the music. This time, however, the collectables were not covered by a subscription. Instead, members paid for the merchandise. The *Almanac* would change forms once again when it went digital, becoming the official Grateful Dead website (www.dead.net), which currently functions as an online social network, receiving around 100,000 visits per month by over 50,000 U.S. users (www.quantcast.com Audience Profile[4]).

Significantly, the fan club and newsletter provided Deadheads an additional "communicative scene" in which to be a Deadhead. The only other scene available was the face-to-face encounter, which generally required the concert setting. Access to the "scene" is meaningful on a number of levels, one of the most important being the role of the scene as "a resource in and through which the newcomer can learn about the distinctive local means and meanings of communication" (Philipsen, 2003, p. 43). The newsletter and face-to-face interaction would remain the only two communicative scenes available to Deadheads until 1974.

Deadhead Magazines

In 1974, a new cultural communication scene was introduced by two east coast tapers with the publication of *Dead Relix,* a specialty magazine catering to Deadheads and complementing the Grateful Dead's media coverage in such rock magazine institutions as *Crawdaddy!* and *Rolling Stone*. *Dead Relix* originally served the taping community, as its founders were also the creators of the Grateful Dead Tape Exchange, one of the earlier tape trading networks. As the Grateful Dead's relationship with the "underground" tapers was not yet at the stage Deadheads would come to enjoy, *Dead Relix*, with the encouragement of the Dead, expanded its focus to include culturally meaningful and established communication forms such as show reviews, tour stories, and columns devoted to themes of relevance to the Deadhead community. In time, *Dead Relix* became *Relix* and has over the years veered from its commitment to the Grateful Dead, covering music beyond the interest of many Deadheads (who nonetheless remained their biggest customer base). Of late, *Relix* has returned to featuring the jam band scene, part of the Grateful Dead legacy. *Relix*, like *Crawdaddy!*, continues to exist and is available online.

In 1978 John Dwork and a group of tapers founded The Hampshire College Grateful Dead Historic Society and began publishing the magazine *Dead Beat*. As with *Relix* the impetus for *Dead Beat* was the growing body of mislabeled, unorganized available tapes. In this sense, these magazines are the precursor of *Dead Base* and *The Tapers Compendium* series, two resources Deadheads call on while enacting communication forms organized around show reviews, set lists and show talk. Sensing the growth of the Deadhead community and the desire of Deadheads for informed, reasoned discussion of the music, Blair Jackson and Regan McMahon launched the quarterly, mail-order glossy magazine *The Golden Road* in 1984.[5] Jackson had already begun to build a reputation as one of the most articulate, informed, and scholarly voices on the Grateful Dead. *The Golden Road* was an instant hit with Deadheads.

In 1986 John Dwork and Sally Ansorge Mulvey changed the name of *Dead Beat* to *Duprees Diamond News* (*DDN*). By this time, *DDN* had evolved to a 72-page color magazine with 35,000 subscribers and over 10,000 *DDN* flyers were being passed out by volunteers at Grateful Dead shows (Dwork, 11/16/2007, Unbroken Chain presentation). *DDN*'s particular emphasis in the community was to "articulate the Deadhead experience as a compassionate and socially aware view of the world, supplementing setlists and show reports with articles on environmental action ... interviews with Wavy Gravy and psychedelic theorist Terence McKenna, collections of DEAD DREAMS, and features on myth and spirituality" (Shenk & Silberman, p. 75).

These Grateful Dead-inspired magazines have served as valuable communication scenes, each with common yet distinctive features. All were subscriber-based, indicating the willingness of Deadheads to pay for this asynchronous interaction, which in the Deadhead spirit of sharing is passed on to non-subscribing Deadheads. The organizations required to produce the magazines were significantly larger and more sophisticated in terms of presentation than their precursor, the show flyer (which, significantly, would continue to have a place in the scene, especially for people standing in line to get into shows). The scene now produced and sustained at least three communication resources, as Deadheads used *Relix*, *The Golden Road*, and *DDN* to gain information, and to learn culturally significant symbols (such as show dates and set lists) and patterns of communication (such as show reviews and nuanced interviews). Each had its distinct focus: spirituality and environment (*DDN*), scholarly show reviews (*The Golden Road*), and the East Coast Dead and jam band scene (*Relix*).

These magazines—as with the show flyers, each addressing its own passion within the community—would serve as an important communicative scene with a central locus within the continually evolving Deadhead communication landscape. As with the evolution of fan clubs, these magazines would facilitate the introduction of new communicative resources. For instance, in his "Roots" column, Jackson explored cover tunes and how the Grateful Dead were inspired by these tunes, a theme of communication Deadheads call on when engaging in show talk (Dollar, 1999a & b, 2007). As show flyers and magazines recorded set lists, show reviews and taper columns, Deadheads began to call on these communicative forms in their interaction. More and more non-taper Deadheads began to keep their own set lists at shows, often complimented by unique artwork that would eventually show up on a traded tape cover. These norms and forms of communication are in use to this day, as evidenced in the most recently emergent communication scenes, online and satellite radio.

Magazines allowed Deadhead writers and publishers, with varying degrees of access to the Grateful Dead, and Deadhead readers (with even less access) to celebrate their shared identity, producing a popular and resourceful communication scene within the emerging Deadhead communicative landscape. The act of being able to communicate set lists with abbreviations and notations, for instance, is evidence of one form of *membering*, hearing oneself and being heard by others to be a Deadhead. The act of being able to call on deeply felt and commonly intelligible symbols and forms in face-to-face interactions with other Deadheads is an act of membering with a significant history. These print resources certainly made these ways of communicating more widely accessible while simultaneously enriching their content. This shared identity, however, was not taken to be an agreed upon or static way of being a Deadhead, but reflected instead a diverse yet coherent identity. These magazines encoded this view not only in the different audiences they addressed but also in the diverse opinions and views comprising specific issues arising within the emerging scene. In this way, this communicative scene came to nurture and support the diverse communities taking shape within the Deadhead community, including but not limited to spiritual, taper (Ritzer, 2000) and serious music critic communities.

Flyers Distributed at Shows

With well-established tour schedules and the Grateful Dead Hotline providing information about tickets and schedules, the Deadhead show community had grown quite sizably. Deadheads recognized an opportunity to develop yet another cultural communication scene, flyers distributed at shows, the earliest according to most Deadheads being the *Mikel* flyers, which emerged on the Grateful Dead show scene in August of 1982. John Dwork, who founded another early flyer, also named *Dupree's Diamond News*, described show flyers as a response to "incomplete information that needed to be woven together, mythical and true, accurate [becoming] a log of what's important to Deadheads such as helping members of the Grateful Dead help the Rainforest, tour problems, helping to share a clear light" (Unbroken Chain presentation, my notes, 11/07).

The *Mikel* flyers were the "embodiment of the best aspects of the Deadhead spirit: creative, idiosyncratic, earnest, bigheartedly enthusiastic about the music and the virtues of the tribe — and free" (Shenk & Silberman, p. 193). For three years, *Mikel* offered Deadheads thumbnail essays, press clippings, set lists, letters from Deadheads, crossword puzzles, and statements from founder Michael Linah, who died of cancer in 1985. *Terrapin Flyer* quickly emerged to fill the gap, as by then the show flyer had become a significant contribution to the communicative scene among Deadheads. During this time, *DDN* continued to be distributed by a group of volunteers, eventually merging with *Terrapin Flyer* in 1984. (To this day, Dwork publishes a free eight-page flyer passed out by volunteers in support of the jam band scene, called *In da Groove*.)

These early flyers were both similar and different from the fan club newsletters and Deadhead magazines. The flyers were available at Grateful Dead shows rather than through the mail. Distributed by volunteer Deadheads involving face-to-face interaction, show flyers represented a communicative resource written and published by Deadheads. Although each had its own unique message, the flyers all tended to include set lists, reports on shows, original Deadhead artwork and tour information. There were several important outcomes of these flyers: they offered support for the tape-trading community by providing set lists and show reports; they introduced a new dimension to the Deadhead community — archivists and historians documenting the evolution of the community; they offered the possibility of face-to-face contact with Deadheads one did not know, via the distribution of flyers listing contact information; they provided new information to individuals interested in the Dead and to newer Deadheads learning the scene; and they introduced yet another cultural communicative resource Deadheads would call on in the process of enacting and negotiating their identity.

Grateful Dead Radio

Members of the Dead family used recording equipment in new and creative ways, eventually producing thousands of live soundboard recordings which were not getting airplay (since radio shows tended to play only official record releases of signed bands). Nevertheless, the innovation characteristic of the Deadhead communication landscape facilitated exposure to live Grateful Dead music on commercial radio as early as 1966. Shenk & Silberman describe it this way: "Healy would sneak the Dead into Commercial Recorders at night, and they would record until dawn. Top 40 AM radio wouldn't touch the tapes, because the Dead were an unsigned band, but Healy took them down to KMPX-FM, and played them on his late-night radio show. Word got around that KMPX was playing some interesting music at three in the morning, and Healy's show, and the shows hosted by Tom Donahue and a couple of others, marked the beginning of underground FM radio" (p. 141). Soon the Dead would allow FM broadcasts of entire shows. In time, campus FM stations would begin playing Dead tapes. Thus from the beginning, Deadheads came to rely on commercial and public radio stations for expanded access to their Grateful Dead music.

Many Deadheads consider the "Grateful Dead Hour," introduced on San Francisco's commercial rock station KFOG as the Deadhead Hour, the most significant Grateful Dead radio show on the communication landscape. Today the Grateful Dead Hour, hosted by expert Deadhead, notable music journalist, and talented musician David Gans, is broadcast, simulcast, and streamed online to over 75 stations (see Gans' website—"Truth and Fun"—for his writings, recordings, interviews, bibliography, and extensive list of Grateful Dead radio programs, http://www.trufun.com). The format of his show represents what I call the "original 'head set,'" anticipating a program currently popular on the SIRIUS satellite radio Grateful Dead Channel. Once again, a communicative scene facilitates the development and acceptance of a new communication form, reflected in the growing popularity of Dead radio shows. Recognizing the generative force of the Grateful Dead Hour, some have referred to this communication form as an example of "*'idées fortes'*—ideas of magnitude that shape culture" (http://www.well.com/conf/gdhour/annals.html).

When Gans assumed hosting responsibilities in 1985, after guest hosting to promote his just released book, *Playing in the Band*, he relied on his relationships with members of the Grateful Dead to gain access and permission to air recordings from the Grateful Dead's musical Vault. By 1987, Gans had secured the band's support to syndicate the Grateful Dead Hour. In a move consistent with Deadhead values of grassroots, community-based endeavors, Gans moved the Grateful Dead Hour from commercial to community radio, Berkeley's KPFA, where it celebrated its 24th anniversary January 29, 2009.

In addition to facilitating new communication forms, the Grateful Dead Hour provided yet another scene, privileging a form of communication popularized by Blair Jackson in *Golden Road*, namely critical discussion of musical history and thoughtful conversations about where the Dead fit within this larger scene. Gans describes the focus of his show in this following way: "I see my mission as putting the Grateful Dead's best musical foot forward every week and looking at the roots and branches of their creative tree" (www.nestormedia.com/jazz/019/anniversary_grateful_dead_hour_radio_program.html).

The Grateful Dead Hour and local Grateful Dead radio shows continued to make the music more available to Deadheads, Grateful Dead fans, and new listeners. Ironically, there would come a time when Deadheads actively resisted increasing their community, as growing crowds at shows enacted behavior resulting in harm to the community's image and limiting the places that would allow the Dead to play.[6] That, too, would change when Garcia died and the Dead stopped touring, effectively eliminating the problems caused by growing numbers of concertgoers.

Local Grateful Dead Radio: "Dead Air" and Beyond

Relying on Deadhead interviews and communicative resources has not produced a clear timeline for tracing Grateful Dead radio back before the Grateful Dead Hour. What is clear is that sometime in the early 1980s Dan Healy hosted "Dead Air," playing soundboard tapes on his Garberville, CA, radio station KERB until he asked Deb Trist, who lives in Eugene, OR, to continue the show. Over time, multiple community radio stations would feature Grateful Dead radio programs called "Dead Air," "Live Dead," "Lonestar Dead," and other assorted Dead-based names.

Deb Trist, a member of the Dead family, was able to continue the show format, featuring Grateful Dead soundboards and recordings from the Vault, currently available only through the Grateful Dead Hour and recordings Deadheads made of Grateful Dead Hours and Healy's Dead Air. As with the Grateful Dead Hour, Dead Air would spend time on commercial radio before moving to KLCC, a public radio station, where it continues to air Saturdays, 7–9 PM. Downtown Deb's Dead Air has evolved with technological advances, as did the Grateful Dead Hour, developing a website (www.klcc.org/page.asp?navid=89) and streaming online to national and international audiences.

Recently, I spoke with Kevin Matthews, the current host of Tucson's KXCI "Dead Air" broadcast, with a few interruptions, since December 11, 1983, and he was aware of one or two of these programs but unaware of Downtown Deb's "Dead Air." Further, Matthews reported that his program is not officially related to the others but shares their goal of spreading the music by providing links to local Grateful Dead radio programs on their website (www.kxci.org/deadair). As with each of these local programs, KXCI's "Dead Air" has developed its own identity, both similar to and different from other Grateful Dead radio programs.

Locally designed logos featured on T-shirts, coffee mugs, and other merchandise available from these community radio stations create and rely on communicative symbols distinct to their program and listeners. In most cases these symbols are innovations of culturally recognized symbols such as the Steal Your Face and the Doo-Da Man. This localized Deadhead identity is further created and enacted as most local Grateful Dead radio shows rely on Deadheads, not the Grateful Dead Vault, for music to play. With this comes added insight from the perspective of Deadheads who have collected the music, activating yet another level of meaning for Deadhead listeners experiencing the interactional accomplishment of Deadhead identity.

Over the years, more and more of these Grateful Dead radio programs collaborated with the Grateful Dead, thus extending the availability of rare Grateful Dead music and access to the Deadhead community. Even so, the local programs maintain a distinct identity among Dead radio shows through their websites, using links to Deadhead-relevant sites, histories of their program and hosts, and virtual forums featuring topics of local interest to distinguish their program from others. For instance, KPFT's "Dead Air: Grateful Dead Sets and Diaspora" link to www.dead.net and www.thebear.org. While WESU's "Dead Air" provides a link to the gdradio.net Message Board.

Grateful Dead radio continues to be a vibrant scene in which Deadheads interact about the music, the community, and international, national, and local topics. Participants are listening instead of reading, as with the newsletters and magazines. Participants are engaging one another in synchronous, oral communication which was previously available only in face-to-face scenes. The radio scene continues the improvising pattern of the landscape, offering more and more connections between scenes as hosts and guests cross-reference resources and programs and include links on their websites to additional communicative scenes and resources. The programs call on culturally meaningful communicative resources and develop new resources, thereby increasing both access to the music and the size of the Deadhead community. As would be expected, the programs have been particularly meaningful for tapers. And, as I will briefly explore below, the programs provide a scene that removes the stigma imposed on the Grateful Dead and Deadheads, a communicative predicament addressed in only a few studies (Adams, 2002; Dollar, 2002).

Grateful Dead Online

A growing body of research has developed focusing on virtual Deadhead interaction. Burnett, for instance (this volume), uses a hermeneutic approach to understand these "robust environments continually used by Deadheads to redefine and reconceptualize what a 'community' might be in the absence of physical proximity." Studies of this sort offer insight beyond the scope of my analysis. For the purpose of my discussion, I present a brief examination of two music websites to illustrate the role these virtual communicative scenes have played, and continue to play, in the Deadhead communication landscape.

These communication scenes stream Grateful Dead music, support other meaningful scenes through web links and direct reference, and host forums where listeners interact. For instance, gdradio.net lists the following forums in which their 460 registered users interact: General Discussion, DEAD NEWS, Wharf Rats, Raffles, Vines, CD-R Trading, BitTorrent, and The Dumpster (http://gdradio.net). Gdradio.net users, according to Quantcast Audience Profile, are 58 percent male and 42 percent female, range in age from 3 to 11 (two users) to 50+ (the second largest user group at 137, behind 35 to 49-year-olds at 147 users), are mostly Caucasian (90 percent), tend to make over $60,000 a year (29 percent at $60 to 100K and 28 percent at 100K+), and are college educated (45 percent hold bachelor degrees and 29 percent have completed graduate school), demographics consistent with sociological studies of Deadhead interaction (Adams and Sardiello, 2000; Adams, 2002).

The Grateful Dead Almanac became digitalized with the introduction of www.dead.net, the Grateful Dead's official website. The site, relaunched "as a full blown social network" in 2007 (Gonzalez, 2007) where approximately 54,700 people visit generating 103,941 posts per month. In 2008, September was the busiest month with 72,600 visitors (Quantcast). The progression from the newsletter to social network allow this communication scene to serve as both a music site from which Deadheads can download Dead music and a social site where Deadheads can celebrate and negotiate their identity. Gonzalez (2007) describes the newer version of Dead.net to feature "extensive archives cataloging Grateful Dead history, songs, photos, memorabilia, and shows, indexed and searchable by tags. Dead users will be able to participate in forums, upload their own photo, and bookmark concerts and shows they have attended. Fans will also be treated to exclusive free mp3 show downloads." These forums, archives, and the opportunity to upload photos and bookmark shows allows this scene to function as a heuristic through which interested listeners can observe and learn, as well as experiment with communicating as a Deadhead.

SIRIUS Satellite Radio

The most recently created communicative scene, the SIRIUS Grateful Dead Channel, which launched September 7, 2007, functions as a communication warehouse, supporting widely accessible communication scenes and the communicative symbols, forms, and norms used in these scenes through regular programs such as "Grateful Dead Interviews" and "Grateful Dead Concert Recordings," and introducing new scenes and communicative resources through regular programs such as "Tales from the Golden Road," "'head set," "Today in Grateful Dead History," and "Celebrity Guest DJ Series." This communication scene, as with the scenes discussed above, reflects the continually innovative approach Deadheads have taken in creating a communication landscape responsive to the challenges and opportunities this community has experienced.

One of the most interesting programs, "'head set," relies on a form popularized by Grateful Dead radio (particularly the Grateful Dead Hour, which I call the original "'head set"). This innovative program allows Deadheads to enact a role previously reserved for Grateful Dead radio hosts and experts. As Deadheads assemble their own set, including contextual comments, they add another layer of meaning as they share their individualized account of the "ideal set." Some Deadheads construct their set by combining songs from different shows. Some include musicians covering Dead tunes and Dead-influenced music. Still others improvise the "roots and shoots" form using their "'head set" to continue the ongoing discussion about who influenced the Dead and the influence of the band's legacy.

A number of the channel's regular programs provide Deadheads and other listeners with historical information, exclusive information, and a means for celebrating important dates in the community history. Deadheads use this information to reflect on what it means to be a Deadhead. Consider a recent online response to significance of this scene:

> Personally my favorite part about the channel besides 24/7 access to my favorite rock band of all times is the "Today in Grateful Dead History" segment. This segment will help you think back to your favorite memories of the Dead as David Lemieux, a Grateful Dead archivist, takes you back one day at a time to the events and music that shaped the music world as we know it today [September 11, 2007, http://ezinearticles.com].

As Deadheads hear others engage culturally significant themes, such as one's favorite memories of the Dead, they cannot help but reflect on the theme with regard to self, once again illustrating the interactional accomplishment of shared identity.

This communicative scene also provides Deadheads with a means for celebrating their identity, as listeners participate in specials such as "Jerry Week," consisting of nine days of special programming from August 1, his birthday, through August 9, the anniversary of his death. Another example was the "exclusive premiere of the Dead's upcoming release *Rocking the Cradle: Egypt 1978*" on September 7, 2008, to celebrate the one-year anniversary of the Grateful Dead Channel. Knowing Deadheads anxiously awaited the release of this "historic, never-before heard concert performed at The Great Pyramids of Giza," scheduled to be released in stores on September 30th, SIRIUS and the Grateful Dead used this sought-after cultural resource to symbolize a year of the Grateful Dead Channel (and to increase listener interest in the release).

One cannot discuss the Grateful Dead Channel without including an exploration of "Tales from the Golden Road," a "roundtable discussion/audience participation program" which debuted as a monthly show on January 21, 2008, but in response to listener support was quickly converted to a weekly show by March 2. David Gans and Gary Lambert, both well-known and respected Deadheads with access to the Grateful Dead Vault and family members, have hosted shows with themes such as the 1966 Trips Festival, the release of *Winterland 1973: The Complete Recordings*, Women in the Grateful Dead World, *American Beauty*, and Amazing Taper Tales, to name just a few. Listeners, Deadheads and not, call in to contribute their individualized account of the program's theme. It is in such places that Deadheads often contest one another's interpretation of a show, or of the Deadhead community. Often these discussions continue after the program airs as Deadheads take their communication to Dead.net forums, where the Grateful Dead Channel programs and/or the topic being contested are deemed culturally appropriate. This cross-utilization of the Grateful Dead Channel and Dead.net further facilitates interaction among Deadheads.

"The Golden Road" is also a popular program for curious or new Deadheads. The range of topics explored, the prominence of guests appearing on the program, and the opportunity to listen to rare live music interpreted by Grateful Dead experts and Deadheads contributes to the availability of the Deadhead folk logic necessary for navigating the communicative landscape. For Deadheads who have not attended a Grateful Dead show, particularly those who avoided the concert scene due to the stigma associated with Deadheads, SIRIUS and Grateful Dead radio allow listeners to develop an interest in the music and community without attending a show. In response to the Golden Road's July 27, 2008, show addressing "the ways in which the world is finally coming around to realizing what we've known all along: that loving the Grateful Dead is—dare we say it?—*cool!*" (Dead.net forum), one Deadhead expressed this common struggle with the stigma:

> I've been waiting for a year for this topic to come up. I went to college in '89 and used to go see Widespread Panic and was really into their music but wasn't interested in the Dead scene because I looked at all the drug using hippies as dirty people destined to be second rate citizens many of whom went on to be doctors, lawyers or whatever. And now some 19 years later thanks to this web site [Dead.net], channel 32 on sirius satellite radio and a Bob Wier show I saw last year I'm finally on the Bus and lament grately my narrow minded views of the scene.... Nevertheless, I am in a poker group and play golf with about 8 guys who are completely blown away that a 40-year-old could actually just start to be a serious Dead fan (maybe even a Dead Head) [posted July 28, 2008, Dead.net forum].

As demonstrated in this brief consideration of the Grateful Dead Channel, the scene brings together well-known communicative forms and resources while continuing to extend the Deadhead communication landscape. One benefit of these new forms is that individuals who avoided the Grateful Dead due to a stigma now have a means for accessing the music and exploring the Deadhead community.

Where Do We Go from Here?

This study demonstrates that Deadheads continue to thrive as a speech community, continually utilizing new technologies and opportunities to grow their communication landscape. As this landscape grows, it becomes more and more complex and sophisticated, and increasingly accessible to Deadheads, Grateful Dead fans, and curious participants. The description and interpretation presented in this essay is intended to suggest the possibilities provided when one takes a communication approach to the study of Grateful Dead concerts and Deadheads. The view of the Deadhead communication landscape presented in this chapter is obviously incomplete. Even so, it can be used to suggest many productive directions in which one could take this line of research.

Notes

1. I use the phrase "communication landscape" in place of construct "communication code" to reflect a fundamental Deadhead folk logic grounded in geography (see Dollar, 2007).
2. *Grateful Dead*, Warner Bros, 1971.
3. This collaboration around sharing live GD shows and music has a history and life beyond the scope of this chapter. As documented in other scholarship and DH communication, this relationship has experienced ebbs and flows as the band and their fans have responded to the changing technology and possibilities for access and sharing this afforded.
4. Quantcast is a new breed of audience service, focused on helping buyers and sellers quantify the real-time characteristics of digital media consumers against which they can activate addressable advertising solutions. Quantcast provides publishers, marketers and agencies unmatched capabilities to measure, organize, discover and transact based on directly-measured traffic and inferred audience data. Online at: http://www.quantcast.com/docs/display/info/About+Quantcast.
5. Most Deadheads immediately recognize the reference to either the original Fan Club or the title of the first song on the Grateful Dead's first album, or both.
6. At this time, some scenes promoted the voices of Deadheads, and the Dead, calling for changes in the community in response to the growth. See, for instance, Sutton (2000), who, in his chapter on religion and spirituality with the Deadhead community, writes, "In Deadhead periodicals such as *Dupree's Diamond News* and *Relix*, letters implored people at the concerts to act in the community's best interests" (p. 123). This was in response to "large numbers of people [who] attached themselves to the community without becoming part of it, primarily drug dealers, gatecrashers, and panhandlers who took from the community without giving anything back" (p. 123).

Bibliography

Adams, Rebecca G., and J. Rosen-Grandon. (2002). "Mixed Marriage: Music Community Membership as a Source of Marital Strain." *Inappropriate Relationships*, R. Goodwin and D. Cramer, eds. New York: Routledge.

Adams, Rebecca G., and Rob Sardiello, eds. (2000). *Deadhead Social Science: You Ain't Gonna Learn What You Don't Want to Know*. Walnut Creek, CA: AltaMira Press.

Burnett, G. (2010). "Improvising Community: A Hermeneutic Analysis of Deadheads and Virtual Communities." *The Grateful Dead in Concert: Essays on Live Improvisation*, James A. Tuedio and Stan Spector, eds. Jefferson, NC: McFarland.

Carbaugh, D. (1988). "Comments on 'Culture' in Communication Inquiry." *Communication Reports*, 1, 38–41.

Dollar, N.J. (1999a). "Show Talk: Cultural Communication Within one U.S. American Speech Community, Deadheads." *Journal of the Northwest Communication Association*, 27, 101–120.

———. (1999b). "Understanding 'Show' as a Deadhead Speech Situation." In *Perspectives on the Grateful Dead: Critical Writings*, R. G. Weiner, ed. Westport, CT: Greenwood Press.

———. (2002). "Communicating Deadhead Identity: Exploring Identity from a Cultural Communication Perspective." In *Communicating Cultural and Ethnic Identity* M. Fong, and R. Chueling, eds. Lanham, MD: Rowman & Littlefield.

———. (2007). "'Songs of our Own': The Deadhead Cultural Communication Code." In *All Graceful Instruments: The Contexts of the Grateful Dead Phenomenon*, Nicholas Meriwether, ed. Cambridge: Cambridge Scholars Publishing.

Gans, D. (1990, July/August). "Reporting Live from Deadland." *KPFA Folio*.

Gonzalez, N. (2007, May 29). "Grateful Dead Fan Site Reborn as Social Network." Online at: http://www.techcrunch.com/2007/05/29/greatful-dead-fan-site-reborn-as-social-network/.

Hymes, D. (1962). "The Ethnography of Speaking." In *Anthropology and Human Behavior*, T. Gladwin, and W. Sturtevant, eds. Washington, D.C.: Anthropological Society of Washington.

———. (1972). "Models of the Interaction of Language and Social Life." *Directions in Sociolinguistics: The Ethnography of Communication*, J. Gumperz and D. Hymes, eds. New York: Holt, Rinehart & Winston.

———. (1974). *Foundations in Sociolinguistics: An Ethnographic Approach*. Philadelphia: University of Pennsylvania Press.

McNally, Dennis. (2002). *A Long Strange Trip: The Inside History of the Grateful Dead*. New York: Broadway.

Philipsen, G. (2003). "Cultural Communication." *Cross-cultural and Intercultural Communication* W.B. Gudykunst, ed. Thousand Oaks, CA: Sage Publications.

Quantcast Audience Profiles (www.quantcast.com).

Ritzer, J. (2000). "Deadheads and Dichotomies: Mediated and Negotiated Readings." In *Deadhead Social Science: You Ain't Gonna Learn What You Don't Want to Know*, Rebecca G. Adams and R. Sardiello, eds. Walnut Creek, CA: AltaMira Press.

Scott, J.A., S. Nixon, and M. Dolgushkin, eds. (1987–1994). *DeadBase: The Annual Edition of the Complete Guide to Grateful Dead Songlists*. Hanover, NH: DeadBase.

Shenk, D., and S. Silberman. (1994). *Skeleton Key: Dictionary for Deadheads*. New York: Doubleday.

Simon, R.B. (2005, June). "Radio Head: David Gans Celebrates 20 Years of Dead Air." *Relix*, 101–103.

Examining Grateful Dead Improvisation as a Catalyst for Creating Sustained *Communitas*

Amanda Diederich-Hirsh

In *The Ritual Process: Structure and Anti-Structure* (1969), Victor Turner draws an interesting conclusion: while it is true that "no previous forms of social order have ever been able to maintain *communitas*"; nevertheless, "it is possible that the flexibility and mobility of social relations in modern industrial society provides the best conditions for existential *communitas* to emerge, even if only in countless and transient encounters." And this, he suggests, "is the closest we may ever get to sustained *communitas*" (Turner, 1969, p. 203).

Around the same time Turner was posing this hypothesis, the Grateful Dead were embarking on an experiment that would bring his theory to fruition. During its 30-year ride, the Grateful Dead phenomenon regularly took on characteristics of the ritual process as it revolved through the three stages of *communitas* in a perpetual evolution of contained chaos.

The Grateful Dead played a unique hybrid of jazz, rhythm and blues, gospel, bluegrass, rock and roll, and folk music—forms of music that originated from groups that have occupied weak or antistructural social positions.

What occurs before, during and after a Grateful Dead show closely resembles anthropologist Victor Turner's model of the ritual process with its phases of separation, liminality and reincorporation (Turner, 1969). Deadheads, the following that developed around the Grateful Dead, were a product of this process. The frequent moments of spontaneous *communitas* experienced within the concert setting inspired a loyal following of seekers.

The individual and communal transformations that took place during the Acid Tests echo Turner's idea of participants establishing a total communion with one another and seeking "a transformative experience that goes to the root of each person's being and finds in that root something profoundly communal and shared" (Turner, 1969, p. 138).

Much like Turner's *"dereglement ordonne de tous les sens"* (Turner, 1969, p. 138), participants discovered a new way of relating to one another within this disorder. Once they stepped outside their familiar structural positions, an essential form of human-to-human communication took over, and from this place new windows opened on their world. It was here, amidst the chaos, that the seeds were planted for what the Grateful Dead and their fans would create and nurture for another three decades or more.

"Happenings" Seed Community

Turner claims that hippies differ from classical religions in their pursuit of a particular form of communitas. "For the hippies ... the ecstasy of spontaneous *communitas* is seen as the *end* of human endeavor. In the religion of pre-industrial societies, this state is regarded rather as a means to the end of becoming more fully involved in the rich manifold of structural role-playing" (Turner, 1969, pp. 138–139). This is certainly true of the early Acid Tests. An ecstatic communing of individuals was the original emphasis. However, the original ecstatic transcendence of the Acid Tests as the end product ultimately became the common shared basis for the community that became Deadheads.

Formation of a Floating Community

When the Grateful Dead went out on tour year after year, identifiable utilitarian patterns emerged among their following, generally for the purpose of maximizing resources to prolong their time on the road following the band. In the days and hours prior to and following shows, participants relied primarily on each other for basic needs such as food, drink, shelter, tickets, sacraments (LSD), and medical help. They would forgo "outside" vendors in procuring incidentals such as clothing, jewelry and artwork in favor of patronizing other members of the following. For some, this arrangement even extended to the weeks and months between tours. This created interdependency among the group, more closely resembling Turner's description of the religion of preindustrial society than the hippies. "In this there is perhaps a greater wisdom, for human beings are responsible to one another in the supplying of humble needs, such as food, drink, clothing, and the teaching of material and social techniques" (Turner, 1969, p. 139). Over time, with repetition, this grew into a lifestyle choice for some. Grateful Dead shows and the lifestyle that formed around it resembles Martin Buber's concept of the organic growth of "community." As Turner observes, "Buber's language belongs to the perennial speech of *communitas*—not rejecting the possibility of structure, but conceiving of it merely as an outgrowth of direct and immediate relations between integral individuals" (Turner, 1969, p. 143). Buber's sense of "community" is largely synonymous with both Turner's "*communitas*" and the Grateful Dead's following. "Community is the being no longer side-by-side, but *with* one another of a multitude of persons. And this multitude, though it moves towards one goal, yet experiences everywhere, a turning to, a dynamic facing of, the others, a flowing from *I to Thou*. Community *is* where community *happens*" (Turner, 1969, p. 127).

A Counter Movement to the Counterculture

If the 1960s were a form of rebellion against the existing social climate—the cultural effects of the 1950s—then the Grateful Dead were to some degree a reaction against that rebellion: a *counter-counterculture*. At first glance, the Grateful Dead seem to personify counterculture ideals; however, they were staunchly committed to nonaction, and chose not to confront politics, injustice, or social values like other bands from the 1960s, such as The Doors, Jefferson Airplane, and countless lesser-known groups (Brightman, 1998).

Formlessness as an Anchor in Times of Radical Social Transition

The Grateful Dead and their organization generally refused to pronounce judgment on the values or lifestyles of others, and seldom advocated for their particular way of living. To limit others' actions or expression was the only taboo, and the implicit message was: "live and let live." Hence, committing a judgment would render their non-message rather hypocritical. Criticized (sometimes by their own fans) for being apolitical and even apathetic, the band's reluctance to take a stand on social/cultural issues may in fact have nourished their survival instinct. The inability to reduce the Grateful Dead to a single image or to narrow down their message not only contributed to the longevity of their career, but also allowed them to play largely by their own rules for the duration. Basing their "anti-philosophy" on the improvisational chaos of the Acid Tests, the Grateful Dead organization cloaked itself in mutability, allowing for quick internal and external adaptations depending on circumstances.

When the flower children's political agenda became the new mainstream, the bands that had carried this message forward scrambled for a new identity or dissolved into anonymity. With the exception of a few gifted artists, such as Bob Dylan, who continued to thrive, those whose one-dimensional message revolved entirely around political and social revolution became obsolete. Turner offers an account of how particular groups "rise out of a crack in the established social order ... in times of radical social transition, when society itself seems to be moving from one fixed state to another" (Turner, 1969, p. 133). Somewhere in this transitory space, as the establishment of the 1950s slipped away and the idealism of the counterculture installed itself as the new social order, the Grateful Dead phenomenon found fertile ground in which to grow.

Perhaps the central value of the Grateful Dead phenomenon was that of freedom — freedom to be anything, believe anything, and think anything. It also meant freedom *from* judgment, labels, and social constraints.

From this locus of freedom grew the Grateful Dead's basic belief system, which permeated every aspect of the experience. Freedom of thought, creativity, expression and experimentation had a strong presence. With freedom goes tolerance, which was another salient feature that characterized interactions among the Dead's following. To the casual observer this likely appeared to be a symptom of 1960s popular rhetoric. However, when separated out in subsequent decades, the ideal of "freedom" within the Grateful Dead phenomenon took on some of the sacred qualities described by Émile Durkeim:

> In the general enthusiasm of that time [the French Revolution], things that were by nature purely secular were transformed by public opinion into sacred things: Fatherland, Liberty, Reason. A religion tended to establish itself spontaneously, with its own dogma, symbols, altars, and feast days.... Granted, this religious novelty did not last. The patriotic enthusiasm that originally stirred the masses died away, and the cause having departed, the effect could not hold. But brief though it was, this experiment loses none of its sociological interest. In a specific case, we saw society and its fundamental ideas becoming the object of a genuine cult directly — and without transfiguration of any kind [Durkheim, 1912, pp. 215–216].

This freedom revealed itself to be the very basis of everything that propelled the Grateful Dead movement forward.

Shedding Labels and Deconstructing Stereotypes Within the Scene

The Acid Tests and Grateful Dead concerts facilitated transformative experiences between participants by enabling them to step outside of their structural roles. Participants willingly shed their social labels such as racial, religious, professional, socioeconomic, and political affiliations upon entering the space around a Grateful Dead show. As Turner puts it, "Individuals are not segmentalized into roles and statuses, but confront one another in ... direct, immediate and total confrontation of human identities" (Turner, 1969, pp. 131–132). As Turner recognizes, in contrast to Durkheim's concept of solidarity with its dependence on an "in-group, out-group" contrast, *communitas*-type groups exhibit boundaries that are "ideally coterminous with those of the human species" (Turner, 1969, p. 132). Regardless of the number of shows attended or the time that has passed, identifying oneself as a Deadhead has generally been a matter of personal choice, and Deadheads have certainly emerged from diverse walks of life.

The only reduction that can safely be made is that the population in the Grateful Dead's following bore a strong resemblance to the rest of twentieth-century America's population, and existed within co-terminus boundaries of the general population.

Furthermore, this movement did not demand even a minimum level of commitment, thus creating a constant increasing and abating of participation among individuals, enabling it to maintain an overall steady equilibrium as the years passed. This equilibrium combined with a tolerance for the diverse population, rendered whatever boundaries existed between the Grateful Dead realm and the world of structure that lay beyond nearly transparent. This allowed participants to move back and forth in a dance between the two.

The Metaphoric Language of Communitas as Articulated by Deadheads

Just as Turner was forced to resort to metaphor and analogy in describing *communitas* (Turner, 1968, p. 127), describing what happens in and around a Grateful Dead concert is extremely difficult for participants to articulate. They usually speak in visual or metaphoric terms, describing intense emotions, cognitive revelations, spatial-temporal elasticity, and a connectedness with nature, the universe and mankind. The phrase, "There is *nothing* like a Grateful Dead show" is usually what Deadheads resign themselves to saying after attempting to express that which cannot make sense to the uninitiated.

Grateful Dead "non-leader" Jerry Garcia consistently avoided speaking in terms of the Grateful Dead having any sort of purpose, other than to play music, experiment and have fun. He spoke in much the same metaphoric and visual articulations of *communitas* reflected in the following remark from Turner: "Ideas appeared ... as images. A sequence of thought ... consists of leaping from one picture to the next" (Turner, 1969, p. 141). When *The Greening of America* author and Yale law professor Charles Reich asked Garcia in 1972 about the band's future, he replied, "Everything's kinda hashed out. It stumbles, then it creeps, then it flies with one wing, and it bumps into trees, and shit, you know, we're committed to it by now" (cf. Brightman, 1998, p. 3). Turner suggests that existential *communitas* is concerned with "the direct relation between man and man, and man and nature. Abstractions appear as hostile to live contact" (Turner, 1969, p. 141). Along this vein, Reich asks Garcia how the Acid Tests and LSD changed his life and his music. When Garcia explains that it freed him in several ways, and changed everything (Garcia, Reich, and Wenner, 2003, pp. 17–18), Reich attempts to draw Garcia into translating his experience into a personal philosophy, which Garcia refuses to do. Speaking instead in terms of concrete realities, Garcia seems to eschew the idea of abstractions and explicit philosophical articulations:

> REICH: You mean it taught a religious idea of acceptance or a philosophical idea of...
> GARCIA: No, no, it was the truth; it's the truth just like these flowers are the truth, or the tape recorder there, or us sitting here or that sound we're hearing or the trees. It's the truth so you know it absolutely, you don't have to wonder whether it is. It's not in the form of an idea, it's in the form of a whole complete reality. I'm not saying that it does that for everybody, I don't mean that, I'm just saying that that's what the effect was on me.
> GARCIA: I don't have a personal philosophy ... all I have is an ability to perceive cycles [Garcia, Reich, and Wenner, 2003, pp. 18–19].

Spontaneous Communitas: Generating Art and Religion from a Language of Symbols and Metaphors

According to Turner, under *communitas*, relations between people (or entities) generate symbols, metaphors, and comparisons; art and religion are their products, not legal and political structures. History has shown that art, music and symbol are the principle ways people in these movements connect to spontaneous *communitas* (Turner, 1969, pp. 127–128). Most Deadheads tended to agree that "music + community" was the invocation for transcendence. This belief parallels Turner's observation that artists typically occupy liminal and marginal positions. Within this space they are able to access the "evolutionary life-force," which they pass on through their artistry (Turner, p. 128). Perhaps the greater the artists, the longer they can prop open the window for others.

Turner details the Indian legend of Krishna and the Gopis, or cowherdesses of Vrndavana (Turner, 1969, p. 156). Their dance is remarkably similar in substance to the spacedancing phenomenon performed by Deadheads. In the modern ritual of spacedancing one can see the outward physical manifestation of this ancient act by Krishna and the Gopis. The band and the audience become one in a transcendental figurative lovemaking with all present. Deadheads often express their perceptions of the music in terms of luminous beams of light or tentacles of energy that connect and envelop the space. These beams connect all to each other, and all to it, in a communal yet profoundly personal way.

The artistic products of the Grateful Dead — the music and lyrics — are believed by many fans to be imbued with preternatural powers ("serendipity," some of them might call it). A commonly reported occurrence in the concert setting was what can only be described as hearing the instruments talk. This phenomenon is attributed to all the band members, but most frequently in reference to Garcia's guitar. Most Deadheads will report that at least once, they heard sounds in the music that they processed as a sort of communication eliciting an emotional reaction or cognitive revelation. Interestingly, these sounds could not be described as music *or* as language, but as something in-between the two. This is reminiscent of a famous comment by William James concerning religions: "By their fruits, ye shall know them, not by their roots" (James, 1985 [1902], p. 21).

These passages reflect Turner's language regarding the products of *communitas* having "a multivocal character, having many meanings ... capable of moving people at many psychobiological levels simultaneously" (Turner, 1969, p. 129). Some Deadheads even credit their involvement with the Grateful Dead as a key factor in changing the course of their lives. Here again we see a parallel to Turner. "These cultural forms are ... reclassifications of reality and man's relationship to society, nature, and culture. But they are more than classifications, since they incite men to action as well as to thought" (Turner, pp. 127–128).

The Liminal Condition — Blurring Boundaries and Controlled Chaos

In preliterate society, moments of *communitas* were ensured through "prolonged instants of ritually guarded and stimulated liminality, each with its own core of potential *communitas*" (Turner, 1969, p. 137). In and around the space of Grateful Dead shows, participants often used psychedelics to facilitate a personal and collective mental state where *communitas* could occur. A major effect of hallucinogens is stripping down layers of consciousness to the core of one's essence as a human being. From here it seems a short leap away from communicating with others, or with nature, at a foundational level.

The lack of hierarchy and structure within the Grateful Dead organization necessitated honest interactions among all participants. Psychedelics quickly dissolved boundaries, and unmasked anyone entering this realm.

In Turner's words, "*Communitas* ... transgresses or dissolves the norms that govern structured and institutionalized relationships and is accompanied by experiences of unprecedented potency" (Turner, 1969, p. 128). Just as there was little distinction made between band members and the rest of the organization (the "family"), the line between "fan" and "family" was often a blurry one, as well. Several Deadheads have crossed the invisible threshold in collaborative projects with the Grateful Dead organization.

Replicating the Acid Tests on a Massive Scale

This philosophy extended to the Deadhead following that embraced these ideas about opening up and tuning in. The Acid Tests had dissolved the line between performer and audience. Though it was impossible to recreate the free-flowing interactions of the Acid Tests once the band hit the road to play concerts in larger venues with larger crowds, the Grateful Dead and Deadheads still managed to operate on the same basic model, with significant results. Space was created in a form similar to Turner's "processual" model of *communitas*. A liminal situation was recreated nightly in which preliminal and postliminal attributes were consciously, indeed enthusiastically, stripped away. Within their concerts (and the surrounding area) the Grateful Dead and Deadheads created spatial-temporal moments of permission where it was safe to express these core human instincts and interactions. Here Turner's reference to Erving Goffman's processes of "leveling" and "stripping" finds a home, and Turner observes that this process seems to flood participants with emotion, something to which most Deadheads would certainly attest (Turner, 1969, p. 128).

Mental and Physical Transition as a Permanent State

Turner says the great world religions still contain traces of the "passage" quality of religious life. "The Christian is a stranger to the world, a pilgrim, a traveler, with no place to rest his head. Transition has become a permanent condition" (Turner, 1969, p. 107). The Deadhead manifestation of this is twofold. As previously noted, during the liminal condition, there is a perpetual shifting of consciousness. In a similar vein, drummer Mickey Hart often joked that the Grateful Dead were in the "transportation" business.

However, Deadheads were in a permanent state of locational transition as well. Like the original Franciscan vagabonds, touring Deadheads were committed to a nomadic existence, often eschewing more than the necessary amount of material goods. Unlike the Franciscans, Deadheads were never required to define their doctrine juristically and theologically, thus avoiding any jural-political entanglements. So they did not fall prey to the Franciscans' quandary, who found themselves forced into a structural attitude toward poverty. For the friars, this was the slippery slope into the issues of permanent dwelling place, institutionalizations and dependence on a structural system (Turner, 1969, pp. 147–149). Touring Deadheads seldom stayed in one place for more than one week (the average run at a venue was two or three nights), and while they dealt with the challenges of living on the road, issues generated by our connections to permanent dwellings, property and community institutions seldom became prominent for them, and were typically mediated on an individual basis if they arose. For example, if one wanted to tour with children, the time for this was during summer tour so they would not miss school. Or they might try homeschooling, but regardless, this was not an issue to be solved by the community.

Consistent with their tendency to embrace nuances of the Grateful Dead's evolving lifestyle philosophy, touring Deadheads used the band's musical philosophy to construct a lifestyle around them. The band's formula was to maintain a stable yet open process structure allowing them space to improvise, and plenty of room for conscious meandering or cosmic surprises. Deadheads used the same formula to follow them, setting up and tearing down the environment around the shows, day into night, night into day.

The "Lot" as the Point of Liminal Separation

The parking lot ("Shakedown Street") was a salient feature of the scene, and a sensual delight. It resembled a cross between a primitive marketplace and a New Age bazaar where Deadheads could satisfy their heart's desire. The "lot" was a requisite extended stop before entering the show. In fact, it was physically unavoidable as one had to pass through it on the way into the show. It was here that the communal anticipation would start to build, electricity in the air, the excitement contagious at the prospect of the transcendence awaiting those inside. This is the space "between," the interval linking the world of structure to the place of *communitas*. It is here that the initial separation from structure begins and boundaries start to blur.

Balancing Structure and Anti-Structure in the Reincorporation Phase

The transience of Deadheads was not limited to nomadic cross-country journeys. Another facet of this was their ability to move between the world of structure and the realm of the Grateful Dead. Embracing Deadhead identity generally does not require the individual to reject other social labels. Since Deadheads are free to move back and forth at will, they have the opportunity to strike a comfortable balance between structure and anti-structure. Once outside of the physical concert space — or the temporal space of the tour — they emerged re-energized, fresh with the afterglow of a lightened load after putting things in perspective. This balance is reflected in the following comment by Turner: "There is a dialectic here, for the immediacy of *communitas* gives way to the mediacy of structure. [In rites of passage] men are released from structure into *communitas* only to return to structure revitalized by their experience of *communitas*. It is certain that no society can function without this dialectic" (Turner, 1969, p. 129).

However, this presents some difficulties. Depending on the nature of a

Shakedown Street beckons. Alpine Valley, June 26, 1987 (courtesy Barry Barnes, all rights reserved).

Deadhead's occupation — assuming we disregard the small fringe population who never return to structure between tours — mediating between the two spheres could become a challenge. Experiencing a continuous ebb and flow between the two spheres, Deadheads themselves began to take on a liminal quality. Similar to Francis keeping his friars on the fringes of society, Deadheads tended to strike a precarious balance, as well, secure in the belief that a permanently liminal state offers the optimal conditions for the realization of *communitas* (Turner, 1969, p. 145).

Organic Growth of the Phenomenon

Out of the Grateful Dead's improvisational music spiraled an organization based on the same idea, constantly evolving to accommodate internal and external changes — quite a feat considering the blurred, fluctuating boundaries between "in" and "out" that came to characterize this organization. This pattern extended outward to the community, as well. When outcroppings such as the tapers and vendors emerged on the Grateful Dead landscape, the organization implicitly absorbed them (as a kind of excess), rather than working to eliminate them. As touring intensified, the scene around the band became a logical outgrowth of the Grateful Dead's music. The band's following continued to grow, using improvisation to develop norms for survival on the road and collectively honing a set of behaviors to ensure minimal hassles in order to get to the next show and safely through the tour. This process echoes Turner's reading of Martin Buber's view of *communitas*: "Buber, in short, wishes to preserve the concreteness of *communitas* even in the larger social units, in a process he regards as analogous to organic growth" (Turner, p. 143).

The Deadhead following grew steadily year after year, developing a system of barter, trade, cash, or some combination in exchange for goods. Assistance was provided by the Grateful Dead's own "security force." Medical issues were handled by Rock-Med (also known as Dead-Med), a volunteer team of trained medical professionals who also happened to be Deadheads. Clean and sober Deadheads reached out to the "Wharf Rats," the traveling support group. References to Buber are irresistible here, as Turner says, "Buber's [language] ... belongs to the perennial speech of *communitas*, not rejecting the possibility of structure, but conceiving of it merely as an [organic] outgrowth of direct and immediate relations between integral individuals" (Turner, 1969, p. 143).

Decline of Community

As effortlessly as the band adapted to internal fluctuations, it was harder to manage external forces. The conservative values of the 1980s, reflected in the Reagan era's "War on Drugs," sharply coincided with a surge in the Grateful Dead's popularity. With the influx of new fans, the parking lot scene became a less intimate place. The traveling carnival became an easy target, and undercover DEA agents were dispatched in force. This was the band's "mega-Dead" period, which saw them playing stadiums and arenas to larger and more diverse crowds, the fragile equilibrium of the scene becoming ever more difficult to maintain.

In 1987 the cleavage became very clear. The Grateful Dead's single "Touch of Grey" climbed to number nine on the Billboard 100, the first time in the band's 22-year career they had "made it" on the charts.

Rigid Antistructural Influences on the Implosion of the Grateful Dead

This unanticipated spike in popularity resulted in masses of curiosity seekers hungry not for enlightenment, but for the party promised by sensationalized press reports. The parking lot scene became a destination in itself, as people without tickets and no interest in the music swarmed the parking lots of Grateful Dead shows. Hard drugs such as cocaine and heroin became commonplace alongside the psychedelics. Nicknamed "hippie crack," highly profitable nitrous oxide tanks could be heard hissing all around the parking lot in the later years. Some Deadheads believed that the nitrous business was run by an outsiderhood of east coast mafia types. This created heavy-handed competition, and added to the conflict and violence that was becoming characteristic of the Dead lot. Young runaways made their home in the lot as well. Many of them managed to blend in very well, so Deadheads had to reconstruct boundaries that had long been surrendered, creating a climate of mild suspicion.

As a result of these external pressures, the Grateful Dead felt the threat of creating and imposing rules on their following—antithetical to the value of freedom which it was based upon. Instead, they attempted to use their well-worn approach of adapting to the situation. They broke up their tour route, attempting to discourage people from following them from venue to venue. The band would fly, as the crew tore down, packed up, and drove through the night to the next stop (Parish, 2003). The hotline numbers began announcing mail order ticket request deadlines only one or two days in advance. The band issued repeated pleas that people not come to shows without tickets, and openly discouraged vending. However, by this point, attempts to slow or contain the growth of this scene proved entirely futile. The Grateful Dead became trapped by their own antistructural position: to impose structure would change the very essence of what they were about, but in refusing to impose structure they risked losing what they had built.

The space outside of venues had suffered an irreversible decline by the early 1990s, but the band and Deadheads were still able to muster frequent moments of collective transcendence inside the shared performance space. For Deadheads, it became apparent that regardless of what was occurring outside of the show, once inside, the music still had the ability to suspend it all. In fact, Garcia sometimes spoke about one of his favorite exercises on stage, that he enjoyed stretching the space between notes, triggering a moment of pure silence in the arena.

By 1995, rowdy crowds, violence, and ticketless hangers-on numbering up to 20,000 outside the arenas finally culminated in a gate-crashing incident at Deer Creek Amphitheatre outside of Indianapolis, Indiana. Following this incident, the band distributed a letter to Deadheads in the parking lots outside of the remaining shows in Missouri and Chicago outlining conditions that must be met for the band to continue touring. Most notably, in this letter the Grateful Dead aligned themselves with the authorities: "The security and police whom those people endangered represent us, work for us, think of them as us" (Kruetzman, Garcia, Lesh, Hart, Weir, Welnick, 1995). Back in 1988, the band's concert handout had alluded to the fact that they would stop touring if things did not improve. The 1995 letter was the first formal communication ever from the Grateful Dead to Deadheads addressing their position. The Grateful Dead's chaos had finally given way to form, but it was too late.

Garcia had explained the "Freedom Lie" to Charles Reich in 1972, maintaining that freedom entailed a lot of responsibility and mutual respect. He noted that the Grateful Dead scene operated on that idea, which is why it was able to absorb those who needed a place to sort things out (Garcia, Reich, Wenner, 1972, p. 37). However, by the early 1990s, the scene was too overburdened to support all those who were seeking access to it. Twenty years earlier, Garcia, who had observed the destabilizations responsible for toppling the delicate balance of the Haight-Ashbury experiment, eerily foreshadowed the demise of the Grateful Dead, as well:

> Too many people to take care of and not enough people willing to do something. There were a lot of people there looking for a free ride; that's the death of any scene when you have more drag energy than you have forward-going energy [Garcia, Reich, and Wenner, 1972, p. 36].

Paradoxically, the very freedom that propelled this phenomenon ultimately turned in on itself and self-destructed. Just as the genesis for growth and steady evolution emanated outward from within the core group of band members, so did the demise. One month to the day of the last show, Garcia died of heart failure. Deadheads congregated on the Polo Fields in San Francisco's Golden Gate Park for Garcia's memorial service and it was there that drummer Mickey Hart passed the figurative torch to the community.

Coupled with the letter the Grateful Dead circulated at the last shows of the 1995 tour, this gesture is significant in that the band had never before acknowledged that they perceived this phenomenon as anything other than just playing — with music, spirituality, drugs, and with form and chaos. For Deadheads, it was a transient lifestyle, moving from place to place, leaving venues late at night, with nothing left behind to confirm what had been experienced and shared, and nothing permanent to serve as a point of reference. As a result, Deadheads were sometimes challenged to believe that what they had was real, and that faith alone was required "to keep on keeping on." However, as the Grateful Dead at last acknowledged, they had been consciously building something that must now be passed on and tended to with due care and commitment.

Conclusion

The Dead scene was a logical outgrowth of the Grateful Dead's music, and a loosely structured normative *communitas* grew out of the spontaneous *communitas* that was randomly experienced. By touring continuously year after year with the same basic skeleton, but leaving room for improvisation, Deadheads were able to construct general utilitarian behaviors that would increase their likelihood of getting to the next show in a safe and timely way. This knowledge developed organically into a set of emergent norms that was unofficially enforced within the following. Over time some behaviors were singled out as detrimental to the overall goal, and began affecting large numbers of Deadheads. The following became more diligent about self-policing, while the band adapted their routine.

In most societies, rules and laws are imposed to prevent chaos. However, among the Grateful Dead scene, "rules" were imposed to create or maintain chaos so spontaneous *communitas* can occur. Historically, liminal safeguards are carefully ritualized into some form of structure in the attempt to coax out moments of spontaneous *communitas*. Conversely, the vehicle for the moments of transcendence at Grateful Dead shows was clearly the musical improvisation. In creating and maintaining several pockets of improvisation during a show, the band was able to create optimal conditions for the invocation of *communitas*. Improvisation in this context can be interpreted as freedom. The band exercised freedom to explore, create, and even stumble without selfconsciousness. The same freedom Deadheads afforded the band applied to one another as well, for in Turner's words, "*Communitas* emerges where social structure is not" (Turner, 1969, p. 126). In the dark and light spaces of these explorations, flashes of spontaneous *communitas* would reveal itself, teasing out of the shadows. Freedom was a requisite agent in attaining transformation; indeed, it created a place of permission. Freedom permeated every nook and cranny of the Grateful Dead scene and was cherished and guarded above all else.

In later years, as the scene around Grateful Dead shows declined, the freedom allowing Deadheads to frolic with the muse in fits of spontaneous *communitas* persisted inside the show, since the locus of power was within the music. But when the gatecrashers struck at Deer Creek, the actual physical concert space was violated. It is interesting to reflect on how the flimsy wall (literally and figuratively) separating the Grateful Dead and Deadheads from the dark forces beyond was torn down and trampled. The fact that many gatecrashers considered themselves Deadheads is not insignificant. Boundaries had blurred to the point where one could hardly tell family from foe, inside from outside, or dark from light. Faced with a death threat against Garcia's life, the band left the lights on that night, afraid of what might crawl out of the darkness. True to Garcia's 1972 comment that "formlessness and chaos lead to new forms, and new order, closer to, probably, what the real order is," chaos produced a new form that night. It marked a figurative (if not literal) end to that particular incarnation of the Grateful Dead.

Ultimately the freedom sustaining the Grateful Dead concert scene buckled under its own weight, effectively deterritorializing what Garcia once called "the Grateful Dead Outback," accurately described by author Steve Silberman as "like a wildlife refuge where freedoms thought to be extinct, and species of risk and joy, thrived in secret," and where "to get in on that secret, all you had to do was let the music reach you in whatever ways came naturally" (Gans, Jackson, and Silberman, 1999, p. 44). In later years, the freedom was abused and this place of permission became a free-for-all party for people who largely disregarded the original agent of transformation — the music. By the time the band released the "Deer Creek" letter stating the conditions that must be met for them to continue touring, the scene was effectively collapsing into the realm of jural-political structure. For a "band of outlaws" to associate with the rule of law by effectively incarnating themselves as law enforcement indicated how sharply the boundaries had been reconfigured, and how radically the concept of "freedom" would have to be redefined. Most significantly, to anyone who was still paying attention, the very act of issuing a letter reprimanding the marginal fans for their behavior symbolized the extent to which the social experiment known collectively as the "long strange trip" had become severely challenged by its own irredeemable excesses.

Victor Turner seemed to foreshadow this development when he hypothesized that "the flexibility and mobility of social relations in modern industrial society provides the best conditions for existential *communitas* to emerge, even if only in countless and transient encounters" (Turner, 1969, p. 203). Conditions in contemporary America *were* favorable to the emergence of the Grateful Dead's "long strange trip," and Grateful Dead music certainly seems to have invoked a healthy diet of spontaneous *communitas*. Not only did this experiment seem to validate Turner's hypothesis, but it also managed to create conditions producing 30 years of sustained *communitas*—seemingly beyond the range of Turner's prediction. Jerry Garcia's words strike a prophetic chord:

> The whole thing is making sense on a lotta levels. That's one of the aspects of what we're trying to do. We won't know whether it's successful until we're dead. Until we have some historical place to stand at and look back on it. Get some perspective or something. But that's what we're trying to do [Garcia, Reich, and Wenner, 1972, p. 82].

If the early years of the Grateful Dead were about summoning up spontaneous *communitas*, the rest of their time was spent attempting to balance this force against a few unspoken rules without eroding the basis of its existence. Today, the scene is reflected upon, analyzed, and in another state of mutation. Older and wiser, the surviving members of the band and their legion of followers seem to be working toward fulfilling new visions with the lessons of the past 40 years. Using the old tricks of improvisation and creative freedom, as well as some new moves, it may well be that this community has entered the ideological stage of *communitas*.

Bibliography

Adams, Rebecca G., and Robert Sardiello, eds. (2000). *Deadhead Social Science: You Ain't Gonna Learn What You Don't Want to Know*. Walnut Creek, CA: AltaMira Press.
Brightman, Carol. (1998). *Sweet Chaos: The Grateful Dead's American Adventure*. New York: Clarkson Potter.
Durkheim, Emile, and Karen E. Fields, trans. (1995). *The Elementary Forms of Religious Life*. 1912. New York: Simon and Schuster.
Garcia, Jerry, Charles Reich, and Jann Wenner. (2003). *Garcia: A Signpost to New Space*. 1972. Cambridge, MA: Da Capo Press.

Goffman, Erving. (1967). *Interaction Ritual: Essays on Face-to-Face Behavior.* New York: Pantheon Books.
Grateful Dead online newsgroup at: http://rec.music.gdead.
James, William. (1902/1985). *The Varieties of Religious Experience.* Cambridge: Harvard University Press.
Kruetzman, Bill, Jerry Garcia, Phil Lesh, Mickey Hart, Bob Weir, and Vince Welnick. (1995, July). "Letter to Deadheads."
Parish, Steve. (2003). *Home Before Daylight.* New York: St. Martin's Press.
Shenk, David, and Steve Silberman. (1994). *Skeleton Key: A Dictionary for Deadheads.* New York: Doubleday.
Turner, Victor. (1969). *The Ritual Process: Structure and Anti-structure.* Ithaca, NY: Cornell University Press.

"I Can't Do Anything but Lie": Studying Deadheads While Wearing Simmelian Lenses

Rebecca G. Adams

It was March 20, 1986. The last time my husband and I had attended a Grateful Dead show, at Uptown Theater in Chicago almost exactly eight years earlier, students and hippies had been indistinguishable. Now it was the Reagan era; hippies were all but gone or at least flying under the radar, and most of my students at the University of North Carolina at Greensboro did not resemble them at all. Imagine my amazement when we entered the Coliseum in Hampton, Virginia. It was a sea of tie dye. The air was filled with the smell of marijuana. Dancers in the hallways traced psychedelic trails with their hands. My sociological imagination was aroused.

My presence at the concert did not go unnoticed by the students from my university (see Adams, 2000, for a more detailed account of what follows). During the following week, others who had gone to the concert dropped by my office to share their experiences. One of my department's best majors put considerable pressure on me to study the community. The idea intrigued me, but I was planning to study friendships among college faculty members who attend professional conferences. I was interested in studying friendships of academics because often they form between people who have never lived near each other. I told him studying Deadheads did not fit into my research agenda. He convinced me that I was wrong. Concerts were as good a setting as conferences for the topic I wanted to study.

I decided to have a meeting of students who had been in Virginia for the Dead shows. My colleagues and our students helped me recruit people to attend. I suspect many of the students came mainly because they were interested in meeting each other. I asked those attending the meeting if they would be willing to distribute a questionnaire if I were to develop one. Two of them suggested we form a partnership. They would help me with my research in exchange for learning sociological research methods and receiving credit for an independent study course. I agreed. Four students ended up enrolling. We developed the questionnaire in the spring of 1987, and they distributed it during that summer while they were on tour. Other students provided me with mailing addresses for Deadheads. We collected 286 questionnaires from Deadheads who had attended at least one concert, which constituted more responses to the questionnaire than the number of copies we had distributed. The more than 100 percent response rate perplexed me at first, but then I received a couple of notes from Deadheads telling me they had made copies of the questionnaire to distribute at shows or to their friends.

Despite the wonderful response we had received to the questionnaire, the data were not very revealing. Most of the questions were closed-ended. In other words, the people surveyed were given a set of possible responses and had to select from among them. They were not allowed to answer in ways that my students and I might have failed to anticipate. This type of question limits what you can discover. Furthermore, those Deadheads responding were not given an opportunity to discuss topics we had not perceived as important. As John Barlow (1972/1989) wrote with Bob Weir: "You ain't gonna learn what you don't want to know." We could not expect answers to questions we did not ask. Although we wanted to understand the phenomenon fully, it became obvious that we did not know enough to know what we wanted to know.

I began thinking creatively about my future professional agenda. I wanted to spend more time on teaching than I had been able to do before I received tenure. I hoped to indulge myself by reading the writings of Georg Simmel, my favorite social theorist. I had been trained at the National Opinion Research Center as a survey researcher. I wished to explore different methodological techniques and to develop my skills as a field researcher. With the help of sociologist James "Skip" Skipper, who was then my Department Head, I realized I could accomplish all of these goals by studying Deadhead relationships.

The Director of the Office on Continuing Education and Summer Sessions immediately agreed to sponsor a pair of classes focused on the study of the Deadhead community: Field Research and Applied Social Theory (see Adams, 1991, for a discussion of the class experience). The Board of Grateful Dead Productions agreed to sell a block of tickets to the University for each of eight concerts scheduled as part of the band's 1989 Summer Tour. After 60 hours of classroom instruction, the class boarded a bus and attended concerts all over the Northeastern quarter of the United States. Teaching these courses provided me with the opportunity for full immersion in teaching, an excuse to read Simmel systematically, and entry into the community I wanted to study using field research methods. I initially thought a summer would be enough time for data collection. When we returned from Summer Tour, however, I realized my work had barely begun.

With the intention of learning more about how the contexts in which we live affect our friendships and about how a community without a shared territory could develop and persist, I set out to conduct an in-depth field research project on the Deadhead phenomenon. I was certainly not the first one to deem the community worthy of study. As early as 1977, a book providing a sociological analysis of various "scenes," including the one formed by Grateful Dead fans, appeared in print (Irwin, 1977). In 1989, when I began the field research phase of this project, I was aware of only three articles about Deadheads that had already appeared in scholarly publications (Gay, Elsenbaumer, & Newmeyer, 1972; Krippner, Honoroton, & Ullman, 1973; Pearson, 1987). The most widely-read research about Deadheads, however, had and has been conducted and published by journalists.

Sociology and Journalism: Two Approaches

Journalists have thus shaped the public's image of Deadheads. The media must sell advertisements to survive and, in order to attract advertisers, the media must attract large numbers of consumers. If one is to judge by the nature of coverage, the exotic and disturbing aspects of the community clearly are more interesting to consumers than everyday life among Deadheads. Newspaper articles and television stories about Grateful Dead concerts were usually accompanied by images of tourheads rather than of the professionals and students who outnumbered them at shows (Adams, 2003). When local papers covered Grateful Dead shows, the stories on drug arrests and the influx of drugs into the community, citizens' complaints, litter problems, complaints by city officials, illegal camping, and traffic problems often outnumbered the stories about how peaceful Deadheads were, community projects, and profits (Paterline, 2000). It is not that the negative stories were not accurate; they most likely were. The problem from my perspective as a sociologist is that readers thought they were being told the whole story, but they were not.

I had personal experiences with the press that convinced me that coverage of the Deadhead phenomenon was not balanced (Adams, 1998). Before the class started, the Grateful Dead came to Greensboro as part of their 1989 spring tour. I began my field research project by standing in line at Ticketmaster and at the Coliseum, by spending time in the parking lot before the shows, and by attending all of the shows in the run. I also interviewed police officers who were on duty at the concerts, people cleaning up the parking lot the morning after the run was over, and staff members at nearby hotels and restaurants. The comments I collected were overwhelmingly positive (Adams, 1989a). Our local paper ran an article that quoted only negative statements (Alexander, 1989).

A month later, the same newspaper ran an editorial making disparaging comments about the class, sociology, and the university (DuBuisson, 1989). The author, the deputy editorial page editor, had not bothered to call me or to request a copy of the syllabus before offering his opinion to the public. When I called to complain about his failure to do any background research, he invited me to write an Op Ed piece for a subsequent issue (Adams, 1989b). He succeeded in stirring up controversy.

One of the reasons Grateful Dead Productions was supportive of the notion of the class was because they thought it would bring about some good publicity for the band. Needless to say, I was a bit nervous about agreeing to be interviewed after the experience I had with the media in Greensboro. Before we left for tour, I had been contacted by all three major television networks and numerous newspaper reporters and radio show hosts. The Dean of the College of Arts and Sciences called a meeting to discuss our media strategy. No media representatives would be allowed to travel with us. I was to grant interviews when people requested them, because the courses were rigorous academically and telling this to reporters was deemed better than letting them speculate. I was the only one who was to talk to media representatives until after we returned.

The coverage the class received as we traveled around the country was quite positive, as the band's publicist, Dennis McNally, had predicted it would be. Reporters described the class as an educational innovation and expressed surprise that it was being taught by a university in a state as conservative as North Carolina was perceived to be. This angle was intriguing enough that reporters did not need to denigrate Deadheads or the class to capture the attention of their readers.

A week before the class started, a feature writer for the *Charlotte News and Observer* wrote an article saying that Jerry Garcia had agreed to read the best student papers (Kelley, 1989). Upon our return from tour, another *Charlotte Observer* reporter included this information in a story that went out on the wire services (Haight, 1989). Until it became obvious that Garcia was not going to read the papers after all, I was hounded by media representatives. Reporters still call me occasionally, especially when significant Deadhead community events occur. Fortunately, outside of the Greensboro area, I am considered an expert on something newsworthy rather than as someone who is newsworthy herself. Although I came to the media's attention by teaching the class, most of the reporters who have called me since then have no idea I ever taught it. They merely know I have been interviewed before on the topic of Deadheads.

Not only do sociologists often report different facts from journalists, they report facts for different reasons. As the story of my short-lived fame illustrates, journalists report facts with immediate "news interest." As Robert E. Park (1940) observed: "Once published and its significance recognized, what was news becomes history" (p. 676). News thus has a "transient and ephemeral quality" (p. 676). Sociologists, however, organize facts to support theoretical arguments with longer-lasting legacies than the facts themselves. In my reports on my research on Deadheads, I cite facts to support arguments about how the Deadhead community developed and persisted without a shared territory and about how Deadhead friendships were shaped by the context in which they developed. These arguments are intended to influence scholars interested in the study of relationships and communities. They are equally interesting now that the Dead have stopped playing together and would continue to be useful even if the community were to cease to exist.

Not only are the products of news reporting and sociological research different, so are the processes. Journalists often study a different topic each day or at least each week; in contrast, sociologists sometimes study the same subject for their entire careers. Sociologists are under less pressure than journalists to gather and synthesize information quickly. They consequently have the time to research topics more thoroughly and systematically, are less ready to accept easily available information and initial impressions as representative and factual, and are more likely to have their work rigorously reviewed before it is published.

This is not to say that sociologists are less likely than journalists to have personal and professional attitudes that influence the questions they ask and their interpretations of the information they gather. It is important to note, however, that describing a phenomenon from the perspective of some actors in a setting to the exclusion of the perspectives of others does not necessarily mean that an analysis is biased. In my writing, for example, I usually describe the community from the perspective of Deadheads to the exclusion of the perspectives of outsiders. My description would be biased if I were to misrepresent the outlook Deadheads have on the world they inhabit and help create.

The challenge then was to develop a strategy for ensuring that I would develop an understanding of the Deadhead community that reflected the way its members viewed it themselves. This was a particularly difficult task to accomplish, because the community is large and contains many distinct contingents. It is simply not going to happen that all Deadheads would describe their community in similar terms. One element of my plan was to have Deadheads identify and correct misplaced biases as they interacted with me during the research process, and to have them criticize drafts of my manuscript. This process allowed me to identify subjects on which Deadheads disagreed, and those on which they concurred, and thus to discover some facets reflecting the complexity of the community. This process helped me attain my goal of reducing misplaced bias, but it was not enough.

To guard against bias, sociologists use theory to guide data collection and analyses and carefully craft their studies (Becker, 1967). As the study unfolded, I developed a plan for viewing data through a variety of theoretical lenses, examining the community from a number of different vantage points by filling different roles within the community myself, analyzing data collected from many sources, and recruiting others to help me see the community from their perspectives (Denzin, 1989). In the remainder of this chapter, I describe how I designed the study to ensure that I would use a variety of theoretical lenses to examine the community, which was just one of the strategies I developed to construct as unbiased as possible a description of the Deadhead community.

Sociological Fictions

Every student of introductory social research methods learns that science advances through twin processes, deduction and induction. Sociologists either gather data to test existing theories or develop new theoretical ideas by examining existing data. Although in its pure form, grounded theoretical analysis (Glaser & Strauss, 1967) involves beginning data collection without a theoretical agenda, most field researchers have a conceptual purpose when they enter a setting. As they learn more about their settings, they elaborate on their theoretical interests, narrow their foci, and begin to develop explanations for what they observe. Although field researchers might not consciously look for certain patterns of interaction, their disciplinary training guides them to do so in spite of themselves. Notwithstanding initial intentions to study the entire setting and to understand fully the life world of all of its participants, field researchers often find themselves overwhelmed and thus necessarily limit themselves to examining aspects of the setting which interest them conceptually. So, in practice, study designs typically evolve that are more formal than the grounded theoretical approach would dictate.

Although scholars do not usually read Georg Simmel's work as field research methodology text, at least one other sociologist has. According to Zerubavel (1980), Simmel's theoretical work suggests a deliberately formal approach to field research study design. Such a design would include: an *a priori* theoretical purpose, more interest in the patterns of interaction within the setting than with the setting itself, and an intention to focus on particular aspects of the phenomenon rather than on all of it. The purpose of the remainder of this chapter is to elaborate on Zerubavel's notion of Simmelian field research, drawing heavily on Kaern's (1983, 1990) interpretation of Simmelian theory. The Simmelian approach to field research outlined herein is similar to the process typically used in many ways. The main difference is, however, that it is formal by design rather than by happenstance. The purposeful formality of the study design allows for the systematic development of contextual theory.

So, in addition to using induction and deduction when conducting my research on Deadheads, I also used scientific fictions to improve my understanding of the Deadhead community and to avoid constructing a biased perspective of it. Although this sounds innovative or at least a bit unorthodox, according to Hans Vaihinger (1925) scientists have previously used a variety of types of fictions to advance understanding of phenomena (Vaihinger, 1925). For example, Max Weber's (1922/1964) ideal type of bureaucracy is an example of a "heuristic fiction," a benchmark used to assess reality. Émile Durkheim (1915/1965) used "schematic fictions" when he examined simple cases to understand more complex ones. When doing content analyses, sociologists routinely use "artificial classifications." Statistical analysts use a type of fiction that Vaihinger called "fictions of the mean."

Although fictions are devoid of reality, they are not devoid of utility. Adam Smith (1776/1976), for example, engaged in this type of scientific thinking when he wrote about all human behavior "as if" it were egoistic. He deliberately substituted a fraction of reality, what Vaihinger called a "neglective fiction," for the total range of possible explanations and facts. Without this substitution, Smith would have been unable to construct an ordered interpretation of the political economy. Like Smith, in researching Deadheads, I primarily used "abstractive or neglective" fictions. We use neglective fictions every day to order our world. When we listen to two people talking with one another, we interpret their interaction by using one or more familiar fictions. We characterize the content of their conversation as, for example, domineering or egalitarian and cooperative or conflictive. Without using fiction, the content of their conversation has little or no meaning either to them or to anyone observing them.

Simmel examined various contents (i.e., social interactions) as if different social forms (e.g., conflict, cooperation, exchange, sociability) patterned them. His interest was in understanding the social forms rather than in understanding the content. Simmelian sociologists thus typically select one social form and apply it to a variety of different phenomena in sequence, thereby reaching a better understanding of the particular social form that interests them. For example, Lewis Coser spent much of his career examining various phenomena as if they were conflictive (e.g., 1956, 1967). A strict approach to Simmelian field research would thus be to examine one setting after another, applying the same social form to each and using the observations gathered to enhance knowledge about the social form of interest.

Using neglective fictions to examine social behavior is similar to using color filters to change the image seen through a camera lens. Because each color filter allows the transmission of light of a certain wavelength, using a filter of one color produces a different picture from using a filter of another. Depending on the color of the filter used, different elements of a scene might be focal points. In order to view the world as if it were blue, for example, the photographer uses red and green filters. A photographer seeking to understand the effect of red and green filters would use them in a variety of circumstances and, in the process, reach an understanding of the consequences of viewing the world as if it were blue.

Similarly, different aspects of Deadhead community are highlighted depending on the fiction used to describe it. Viewing the community as if it were experiential, for example, leads to different observations from viewing it as if it were materialistic. In each case, different behaviors, attitudes, and occurrences seem important and each behavior, attitude, and occurrence assumes a different meaning. Taking this logic to the extreme leads to the conclusion that all interpretations of "reality" are fictions.

Deadheads acknowledge that reality is a mental construct or at least is elusive. They were thus particularly receptive to the notion that accounts of reality are incomplete and thus fictitious. In 1990, many Deadheads became familiar with my theoretical perspective when PBS showed a video that had been created as part of the class experience (Adams & Edwards, 1990). In the video, I discussed the approach I was using to study the community. Many Deadheads expressed enthusiasm for my theoretical perspective and asked me for references to related sociological publications.

I considered discovering that Deadheads and I shared this perspective very fortunate, because knowing we had similar views helped me build rapport with Deadheads. Being aware that we shared this perspective also helped me to understand the community more quickly and deeply than I might have otherwise. It did not matter that for Deadheads accepting reality as elusive was a philosophy of life and that for me it was a theoretical perspective and a methodological tool. We had something to learn from each other. All that we initially lacked was a common language. I unintentionally began overcoming this barrier by teaching students who were also Deadheads how to use my approach in studying their community and by learning their language from them.

Later I realized that Jerry Garcia, the most loquacious member of the band, had stated various aspects of this perspective in interviews (see Adams, 1995). He had inadvertently provided a link between my theoretical and methodological approach and Deadhead philosophy. At first I thought this was not as coincidental as it appears. One hippie historian reported that Garcia took sociology classes at the College of San Mateo (Harrison, 1973). Dennis McNally assured me, however, that Garcia never enrolled in college (telephone conversation, February 9, 1997). I nonetheless proceeded to learn something about Deadhead community and about neglective fictions from reading interviews with Garcia.

Jerry Garcia (Gans & Simon, 1985, p. 13) made it clear that he thought that all interpretations of reality were fictitious, even his own: "Verbal communication is open to interpretation, just like songs are. I've prefaced interviews in the past by saying that I can't do anything but lie. All talk is lying, and I'm lying now." Garcia was not admitting that he was a chronic liar. His reputation was quite to the contrary. Dennis McNally told me he considered Garcia to be his most reliable source as he endeavored to reconstruct the history of the band, because McNally had only caught Garcia lying once during their

15-year relationship (telephone and e-mail communications, February 9 and 10, 1997). Rather, with paradoxical humor, Garcia was commenting on the impossibility of using language to describe reality accurately. All things everyone says are lies; they are fictions. When a group of people shares the same opinion, it just seems to them as if they have discovered truth. They are merely simultaneously employing the same fiction.

Let us return to the photographic metaphor again for a bit. Some photographers strive not to understand the effect of the use of a specific combination of filters but to interpret a given scene in a variety of different ways. A photographer with this goal might employ green and red filters to view a scene as if it were blue, employ blue and green filters to produce a red image, and so forth. In the process, the photographer would discover different things about the scene he or she was capturing on film. In each photograph, different aspects of the scene would seem prominent and each element would hold a different significance.

In reference to the phenomenon he helped foster, Jerry Garcia (Gans & Simon, 1985, p. 165) once astutely noted: "There's no central thing which is absolutely true that everybody can know about it." I must say I agree with his analysis. Attempting to discover "the truth" about the Deadhead community would indeed have been a frustrating quest at best; my intention was thus merely to examine this phenomenon consciously using multiple neglective fictions as conceptual "filters." Georg Simmel, whose perspective resonates with that of Deadheads, referred to the neglective fictions that underlie and pattern human interaction (e.g., cooperation, conflict) as "social forms" (see Weingartner, 1959; Kaern, 1983, 1990, for discussions of Simmel's use of social forms). In order to achieve a multidimensional comprehension of the community, I decided to interpret the community as if one social form were its sole basis and then as if another one were and so forth. Norman Denzin (1989, pp. 239–43) referred to this process as "theory triangulation," approaching data from multiple perspectives.

According to Simmel (1907/1986), human beings are multidimensional beings, shaped simultaneously by multiple social forms and able to resist the influence of some of them better than the influence of others depending on circumstances (e.g., community membership). Hence some social forms were more useful than others in distinguishing the community from the mainstream and for understanding its internal dynamics. The process through which researchers select the social forms they use to examine a setting is very important. If they were to select the social forms for *a priori* theoretical reasons, they would learn about how the forms operate in a given setting, not about which forms are most useful to use in interpreting the setting.

Through discussions with Deadheads, I developed an initial understanding of the conceptual filters they use in viewing the community. The young Deadheads I queried seemed to contradict themselves; for example, first they described the community as unified and then they emphasized the importance of individuality to Deadheads. This incongruity does not disturb Deadheads, however, because they are aware that things overflow a single determination and that opposing forces affect each other. As Simmel observed, social forms do not exist in isolation from opposing social forms (Simmel, 1907/1986, p. 15): "...a manifold thing is also uniform, a simple thing is complex, the earthly is divine, the spiritual is material, the material is spiritual, the still is in motion, and whatever is moving is simultaneously at rest." Jerry Garcia expressed the same sentiment (Lyndon, 1969): "See, it's like good and evil.... They exist together in their little game, each with its special place and special humors. I dig 'em both. What is life but being conscious? And good and evil are manifestations of consciousness. If you reject one, you're not getting the whole thing that's there to be had." Although even many literate Deadheads are not familiar with Simmel, they do read interviews with Jerry Garcia. Many of them are also familiar with other texts on this topic. See, for example, Wilhelm's (1960) discussion of "the two fundamental principles" of the *I Ching*. To symbolize their awareness of the duality of human existence, they often sport jewelry and clothing adorned with the symbol for yin and yang.

In order to design my study to avoid misplaced bias in my observations and interpretations, and to help capture the complexity of the phenomenon, I developed a list of pairs of opposing social forms to use as sensitizing concepts, to focus my attention on specific analytical concerns, and to help me note aspects of the community I might have otherwise overlooked. The list eventually included the following social forms: individuality and unity, differentiation and integration, conflict and cooperation, egoism and altruism, hierarchy and equality, materialism and experientialism, and freedom and order. My hypothesis is that to understand how these pairs of social interaction form patterns within a setting helps to reveal both the dynamics of this setting and the nature of some of the more salient relationships that exist within it.

During the research process, I was guided by these concepts but not restricted by them. In some senses, the research process resembled a show experience. Just as Deadheads took mental journeys during improvisational jams and then returned to the reassuring structure of familiar songs, I took conceptual journeys and then returned to the comfort of my research design. No journey leaves the traveler unchanged, however. Just as the songs that followed a jam seemed different to the listener from how they would have before the musical excursion, so did the community seem different to me after my theoretical jaunts. My untamed observations often changed my understanding of my original list of social forms or suggested the utility of additional neglective fictions. When this happened, I modified my working definitions of the social forms or added new pairs of them to my list. Understanding how these pairs of social forms pattern Deadhead interaction helped me discover the dynamics of the community and of Deadhead relationships.

Rebecca Adams and her students on tour. July 1989 (© Lloyd Wolf/www.lloydwolf.com).

Conclusion

This approach to field research is more "formal" or "analytical" than most ethnographic research processes in three ways (Zerubavel, 1980). First, rather than focusing only on the facts, I also concentrated on the perspectives from which they can be viewed. Second, rather than being concerned only with describing the community, I was also interested in the formal patterns that underlie interaction in the community and could be extracted from it. Finally, rather than studying all facets of the community, I examined particular analytical aspects of it.

Although my approach is more formal than that of most field researchers, I did not entirely abandon the more widely used inductive or grounded theoretical techniques (Glaser & Strauss, 1967). Not only did I allow my experiences within the community to change the conceptual filters I used to guide my research endeavors, I began talking to Deadheads before I decided on them. The difference between my modified Simmeilan approach to field research and the more traditional grounded theoretical approach is that rather than each field research study producing a unique ethnography, this method allows for the systematic development of contextual theory. The goal of studies of this type would be to understand the setting in terms of the social forms that pattern the behavior within it. Researchers would use multiple social forms, half derived from their observations of the setting and the other half selected because they were in opposition to the others. These pairs of social forms would guide their observations and ongoing analyses, but not restrict them. Researchers using this approach would study one setting after another, gradually contributing to the development of a typology of settings and thus to the systematic development of contextual theory. Researchers could thus begin to understand settings in terms of the social forms that are useful in understanding interaction within them.

Bibliography

Adams, R.G. (1988). "Inciting Sociological Thought by Studying the Deadhead Community: Engaging Publics in Dialogue. *Social Forces*, 77:1, 1–25.
_____. (1989a, April 10). "Dead Heads: Deadbeats or Nice Folks?" Letter to the editor, *Greensboro News and Record*.
_____. (1989b, May 28). "Second Opinion: 'Dead Heads' Study Is Not a Lark." *Greensboro News and Record*.
_____. (1991). "On the Bus: Teaching about Deadhead Subculture." *Vues of Undergraduate Education in Sociology*, 20:2, 1–5.
_____. (1995). "The Sociology of Jerry Garcia." In *Garcia: Reflections*, 1:1, 16–18.
_____. (2000). "What Goes Around Comes Around: Collaborative Research and Learning." In *Deadhead Social Science: "You Ain't Gonna Learn What You Don't Want to Know,"* R. G. Adams, and R. Sardiello, eds. Walnut Creek, CA: AltaMira.
_____. (2003). "Stigma and the Inappropriately Stereotyped: The Deadhead Professional." *Sociation Today*, 1:1.
_____, and E. Edwards. (1990/1995). *Deadheads: An American Subculture*. Twenty-eight-minute video produced by UNCG Office of Continuing Education in association with R. Adams, narrated by R. Adams, and directed by E. Edwards. Distributed by Films for the Humanities & Sciences, 1990, and broadcast on PBS stations nationally. Re-released by PBS in 1995.
Alexander, L. (1989). "Dead Heads Vex Neighborhood. *Greensboro News and Record*, April 1.
Barlow, J. P., and B. Weir. (1972/1989). "Black-throated Wind." In *Songs for the Dead*. Published and distributed by J.P. Barlow, 1989. (Lyrics written in Cora, Wyoming, and San Anselmo, California, during February 1972, and recorded by the Grateful Dead on the album *Ace*, produced by Warner Brothers in 1972.)
Becker, H.S. (1967). "Whose Side Are We On?" *Social Problems*, 14, 239–247.
Coser, L.A. (1956). *Functions of Social Conflict*. New York: Free Press.
_____. (1967). *Continuities in the Study of Social Conflict*. New York: The Free Press.
Denzin, N.K. (1989). *The Research Act*. Englewood Cliffs, NJ: Prentice-Hall.
DuBuisson, D. (1989, May 10). "The Scholar's Quest is Never-ending." *Greensboro News and Record*.
Durkheim, É. (1965). *The Elementary Forms of the Religious Life*. New York: The Free Press.
Gans, D., and P. Simon. (1985). *Playing in the Band: An Oral and Visual Portrait of the Grateful Dead*. New York: St. Martin's Press.
Gay, G. R., R. Elsenbaumer, and J.A. Newmeyer. (1972). "A Dash of M*A*S*H the Zep and the Dead: Head to Head." *Journal of Psychedelic Drugs*, 5:2, 193–203.
Glaser, Barney G., and A.L. Strauss. (1967). *The Discovery of Grounded Theory*. Chicago: Aldine.

Haight, K. (1989, August 12). "Deadheads as Sociological Phenomenon." *Bridgeport Telegram.*
Harrison, H. (1973). *The Dead Book: A Social History of the Haight-Ashbury Experience (Vol. 1).* San Francisco: The Archives Press.
Irwin, J. (1977). *Scenes.* Newbury Park: Sage.
Kaern, M. (1983). "Understanding Georg Simmel." *Sociological Focus,* 16:3, 169–179.
_____. (1990). "The World as Human Construction." In *Georg Simmel and Contemporary Sociology,* M. Kaern, Bernard S. Phillips, and Robert S. Cohen, eds. Dordrecht, The Netherlands: Kluwer Academic Publishers.
Kelley, P. (1989, June 5). "Grateful for Study of Deadheads." *Charlotte Observer.*
Krippner, S., C. Honorton, and M. Ullman. (1973). "An Experiment in Dream Telepathy with 'The Grateful Dead.'" *Journal of the American Society of Psychosomatic Dentistry & Medicine,* 20:1, 9–17.
Lydon, M. (1969, August 23). "The Grateful Dead." *Rolling Stone,* 15–16, 18, 22–24.
Park, R. E. (1940). "News as a Form of Knowledge." *American Journal of Sociology,* 45, 669–86.
Paterline, B. (2000). "Community Reaction to Deadhead Subculture." In *Deadhead Social Science: "You Ain't Gonna Learn What You Don't Want to Know,"* Adams and Sardiello, eds. Walnut Creek, CA: AltaMira.
Pearson, A. (1987). "The Grateful Dead Phenomenon." *Youth and Society,* 18:4, 418–432.
Simmel, G., and H. Loiskandl, D. Weinstein, and M. Weinstein, trans. (1986). *Schopenhauer and Nietzsche.* Amherst: University of Massachusetts Press.
Smith, A., and R. H. Campbell, A. S. Skinner, and W. B. Todd, eds. (1976). *The Wealth of Nations, Vols. 1 & 2.* Oxford: Clarendon Press.
Vaihinger, Hans. (1925). *The Philosophy of the 'As If.'* New York: Harcourt.
Weber, M., and Talcott Parson, ed. (1964). *The Theory of Social and Economic Organization.* New York: The Free Press. (Original work published in 1922 by J.C.B. Mohr as *Wirtschaft und Gesellschaft*).
Weingartner, R.H. (1959). "Form and Content in Simmel's Philosophy of Life." In *Essays on Sociology, Philosophy, and Aesthetics,* K.H. Wolff, ed. Columbus: Ohio State University Press.
Wilhelm, H., and C. F. Baynes, trans. (1960). *Change: Eight Lectures on the I Ching.* New York: Harper and Row.
Zerubavel, E. (1980). "If Simmel Were a Fieldworker: On Formal Sociological Theory and Analytical Field Research." *Symbolic Interaction,* 3:2, 25–33.

Encore

Jerry Garcia. Summer tour 1989 (© Lloyd Wolf/www.lloydwolf.com).

The Thing Is the Thing Is the Thing Is the Thing Is There Is No Thing

Christian Crumlish

He's gone. Long gone by now. It's been, shit, almost a decade? But these are the sort of shows where word goes out on some ancient Jungian ley line network and the old weird heads come out of the woodwork, back from the land like that time Kimock sat in with Kreutzmann in exile in Hawaii and Sugar said freaks she hadn't even known were living out there in the bush showed up and raised the roof in that tiny bar shack. These were the people for whom northern California turned out to be too rigid, too plastic, too square, too circumscribed.

So liquid refreshment appears easily on the line outside in the San Francisco dusk where many of the same door people are the same door people as before and the homeless in tie dye still blur the line between living outside the law and being honest and my seat is up in the balcony thanks to Calico, although not in the upper-front balcony where the real connecteds get hooked up, but in the front row above the aisle, which is great for peoplewatching, and the guy sitting next to me who knew to come up from Santa Cruz for these December-but-not-New-Year's shows is from my cohort, caught the bug in the mid '80s and has many of the same touchpoints and references and ideas about what was good and what had better be better.

He's got that resiny stuff they scrape off the hairless legs of little boys in Afghanistan or harvest in some shady valley up in Mendocino or farther back into the land of the lost and we talk about what to expect at one of these Now I Can Do It My Way shows Phil's been putting on since they called it quits official. They are hit and miss sometimes, all theory and sounded good on paper, but this time we think it's going to work and we don't know why but we do know.

Cowboy Bob at the wheel. Winterland October 20, 1974 (courtesy Pat Lee and David Thomson, all rights reserved).

Well into the show, when my perceptions are getting cute and no ideas are being discarded or filtered out, it appears as though Phil is a little boy on stilts with arm extenders but that same bowl haircut and '70s aviator nerd glasses but now he is presiding over his chemistry lab and his erector set and conducting the show and winding up the clockwork. He knows how to bring him back. The roof opens and the vandergraaf generator crackles and Phil howls into the night sky: Life!

Or maybe I'm talking to Michaelz during the break and not really positive Michaelz exists, he seems to know everything I've been thinking and he usually posts what I was about to write and he's read all the same sources from Gans to Meriwether, and maybe he's just an idealized projection of myself where I outsource the knowing and can get along with the dancing.

And maybe it's him who mentions it or maybe it's the guy I turn to but he's not there now either, and Michaelz gives me a quizzical look and I seriously wonder, Did I imagine the Santa Cruz dude too?, and I start working up my theory of the rim.

Up at the edge of the balcony the people wear faded festive clothes and they look older, most are gray. Quite a few look to have put on pounds over the years. They wear eyeglasses. I see a lot of bushy white beards.

Out of the corner of my eye for a minute I see him.

Jamaica World Music Festival, Montego Bay, November 1982 (courtesy David Gans, all rights reserved).

But when I look he's not there. He's gone.

The people spread out before me on the rim are a mosaic of nearly Jerry and almost Jerry and sort of Jerry and getting Jerry. I turn to my phantom friend, now real again, or maybe this is earlier in the show, and say how it seems to me that the closer to the edge you get the more you look like Jerry.

"You just don't want to get too close or you could fall in," he says behind inscrutable sunglasses though it's dark in the hall.

And the guitarist, maybe Warren, is standing in Jerry's old spot and hunching over his axe, carrying extra weight, a meaty forearm emerging from his T-shirt sleeve to cradle and scrub his electro-lute. His glasses slip down on his nose, but I don't think he wears glasses.

I saw Wasserman stand there and get more and more Jerry-like, bouncing out variations on the St. Stephen theme on his standup bass.

I've seen Bobby grow a big snuffy smith–style mustache and beard as the morphogenetic field takes hold and the gaze of all of us staring at that spot on the stage causes his cells to mutate and become more Jerry-like.

And now the entire roomful of people are each contributing a cell, a voice, a hint, a memory, a wish, a piece of our Adam Kadmon, a celestial constellation Jerry made of all of us. Our yearnings lift up into void and try to call him back to us.

We've convened. We know how this works. It always worked before. Our need sustained it. We can conjure him back.

I used to stand just so, over this way, and I moved my arms like this and I moved my hips like that and he played and you were over there doing that thing you do and I can almost taste it again, and it's bittersweet.

We can all hear him, his voice runs through all the songs, but he's gone. And nothing's gonna bring him back.

All His Children Grew and Grew (Who Killed Uncle John?)

David Gans

Jerry Garcia had a million dependents, material and/or spiritual. He had his bandmate-partners in the Grateful Dead; his bandmate-employees in the Jerry Garcia Band; he had a wife and an ex or two and several children; he had the support staffs of his two bands and related enterprises; he had Grateful Dead Merchandising and its licensees; the vendors and travel agents and others who supported the Dead and the JGB; the promoters and the stagehands and the caterers and the sound companies that relied upon the income from his gigs; the licensees who made and sold authorized products with the Grateful Dead logo, his likeness, his artwork; he had the unlicensed vendors who sold T-shirts, tie dyes, photos, drawings, veggie burritos, grilled cheese sandwiches, nitrous oxide balloons, psychedelics, drugs, etc., to fans and tourheads in the parking lots and campgrounds along the way; and of course, Jerry had the thousands and thousands of fans who relied on him to deliver the thrills, chills and delicious food for thought for which he was famous. He had relationships with all these people. He didn't know all of our faces, but he felt the pressure of our love, our desire, our need, our greed.

The Dead sprang up in an idealistic neighborhood scene and watched as it became an international cultural crossroads. Clueless hordes destroyed the intimacy of that community; the tragedy of the commons wrecked the social contract; and in 1968, the Grateful Dead left San Francisco and became a touring band. They wound up inheriting the mantle of the entire hippie movement, and a global network of seemingly-anachronistic freaks, by being good at what they did and by allowing their tours to become floating temporary autonomous zones. For the appreciable number who managed to float along with them for months or years at a time, the Dead provided the illusion of escape from normal life. This in turn allowed the Dead to avoid being assimilated into the normal life of the music business with its hit singles and album sales.

Every popular artist, in any medium and genre, begins with an audience that really appreciates what he's doing. It is necessary and inevitable that as the size of the audience grows, so will the proportion of fans who don't really understand the artist's work. They are there for something else. How the artist responds to that situation is a matter of character and destiny. Garcia earned, and rewarded, our attention with earnest, clever, soulful, inventive, and exhilarating music; with his songs and his singing and his guitar, he told a most compelling tale. A Grateful Dead performance was like a great conversation at the hippest of parties, full of jokes and stories and insights and epiphanies; you could be part of it without saying a word. We who loved this thing loved it a lot. We wanted to own it and belong to it; we regarded ourselves as stakeholders.

How Jerry saw himself in all this was almost entirely irrelevant. He was a figurehead to many and a walking cliché to many more. To his fans, he was the crown of creation; to the mainstream, he was the guru to a cult of voluntary outcasts. He was the insanely popular first citizen of a world he helped to create — but in which he never resided.

See, Garcia was a Beat, not a hippie. He passed through a brightly-colored moment in time and drew behind him forevermore a trail of brightly-colored adherents; but after the first year or so, he himself wore black T-shirts and corduroys. He was well-read, thoughtful and philosophical, sharply realistic, and sardonic as hell.

After a certain point — and it was probably earlier in his career than I'd like to admit — the fact of Jerry's performance was sufficient for an uncritical majority of his audience; the quality of the music was lost on and/or of no interest to a large part of his audience. And once the crowd failed to discern between inspired improvisation and phoning-it-in, I think the musicians began to lose their own hunger for exploration and invention. And their motivation to rehearse.

There were plenty of us out in the audience who did care a great deal about the quality of the performance. We, too, had a sense of entitlement, adding yet another layer of expectation and obligation: so many "bring back the old days" factions, each nostalgic for a different milepost on the Long, Strange Trip™. Along with all the sweetness, brotherhood, serendipity and generosity, there was plenty of nasty shit, as well. "Shakedown Street" got its name (courtesy of Robert Hunter) for a reason. There were all sorts of lost souls in the Grateful Dead world, both inside and outside the laminated curtain. I knew some who were lost when they arrived and found that they were able to operate in relative safety there; some who got lost along the way; and some who were broken when they came there and were made whole by their experiences.

Still, fish rots from the head, as a good friend reminded me in a related context not too long ago. In the beginning, I think, the presumption was that everybody would behave responsibly and look out for the group; but it was well known that you could pretty much do what you wanted to do in the Dead world. Those high tribal ideals the family once embodied gave way to the realities of the tour. Power went to the men who put the rubber to the road, the pedal to the metal, and the knife to the throat. The flame burned brightly and the moths attended.

Jerry Garcia was a most reluctant emperor. He was pretty much the only one who could have controlled any of it, from the thugs on his own crew on down, but for the most part he refused to correct anyone's behavior. A longtime associate of the Dead left the tour in 1972, he told me years later, because it had become abundantly clear that "Jerry was never going to control his people." And Jerry was the only one who could have controlled them.

All the good stuff kept happening, too, of course, until the last few years, maybe. As long as the music was compelling, the rest could be dealt with. With decades of living at the center of all this attention — the psychic bombardment by fans, vicious turf wars raging outside his fragile walls, and the inevitable attrition of personal and collective musical energies—the empathy could take a beating and the good will could run out. I think he had been tired of being Jerry Garcia for a very long time.

Garcia's light flickered a lot in those last years.

His commitment to the music seemed to waver and resurge. In January 1993, while we were riding together into San Francisco to record his interview with the composer Elliott Carter, Phil Lesh told me it was his intention to come to every Grateful Dead performance ready to engage with Jerry, should Jerry choose to engage.

I remember one time at the Oakland Coliseum, possibly December 1994, when I burst into tears at the beginning of "Broken Arrow." Jerry was almost inert that night; Bob Weir was putting out a huge amount of energy that seemed to be trapped behind some sort of Gardol shield; and here was Phil Lesh pouring his weak voice and his swelling heart into the song as if it were a matter of life and death. 'Cause it was.

No one who knew anything could have been terribly surprised by Jerry Garcia's death in August of 1995. It had seemed to me to be in the offing for quite some time. At Cal Expo in June 1994, Jerry looked like he was about to fall over dead: his hair and skin were white, and he leaned to one side in a way that could have been seen as dreamy (and doubtless was, by many) but read to me as chillingly mortal.

He was a brilliant musician, a soulful thinker, a profoundly flawed man. His daughter Annabelle, at his memorial in 1995, characterized him as "a great American, but a shitty father." He was the ultimate absent father in this gigantic dysfunctional family. Robert Greenfield, author of *Dark Star: An Oral Biography of Jerry Garcia*, on SIRIUS XM Satellite Radio's Grateful Dead Channel,

May 17, 2009: "What I did not understand at the time [of writing the book] ... was that a lot of the people who spoke to me did so in order to stake their claim to a potential piece of the Garcia estate. They were making a public statement as to the role they played in Jerry's life."

Even now, more than a decade after his demise, we see people speaking for him, speaking to him, and speaking about him. His absence inhabits the musical discourse of his partners.

Lyricist John Perry Barlow told me, long ago, that no one in the Grateful Dead world really understood how they got where they were, and to his mind that bred a kind of conservatism — a reluctance to change anything lest you upset whatever it was that brought this accident about. Everybody was insecure and territorial. That's the nature of scenes like this one: power and status are fleeting and decidedly relative. "We're frequently seen as being privileged somehow," he told Blair Jackson and me in 1981, "but being in the Grateful Dead is in no way privilege. It doesn't exempt you from anything, particularly, and the reward is a fleeting, existential kind of reality where really the most important thing is the gig that just happened. Everything that we've done is culminated in the last note that we played."

Like just about everybody else in that world, I had a weird position and weird relationships. I began as a fan, and then approached the Dead as a journalist; later I lucked into a book deal and then stumbled into Grateful Dead radio; my day job for nearly 25 years has been to put the Grateful Dead's best foot forward. No one knows how many fans first heard of the Dead via my radio show, nor what benefit the band received from the sharing of the music I facilitated; lots of people cite my books *Playing in the Band* and *Conversations with the Dead* as influential and informative sources. I am proud of the records I produced, and I feel that I have contributed to the world's understanding and appreciation of the Dead's unique musical contributions.

Jerry was usually pretty kind to me. I probably took a little too seriously the encouragement he gave me in the early days, but it all worked out okay for me in the long run. As he counseled, I made a place for myself in the Grateful Dead culture. But I spent a good deal of time in a murderous rage, through years of being excluded, rebuffed, fucked with, lied about, lied to, and laid into. Depending on who you asked, I was a scholar, a musicologist, a historian, a promo man, a shill, a pushy fan, a collaborator, a supporter, a parasite, a profiteer, a party crasher, a stalker, a friend.

I learned over the years not to expect any help from even my allies; they had been through this sort of thing a zillion times before, and my problems didn't amount to a hill of beans in this crazy world. There was nothing going on in my daily battles that wasn't also happening to a hundred other people.

I've written quite a few songs about my experiences in the Grateful Dead world. The rest of them aren't quite as obvious as this one, but it must also be said that this one isn't as obvious as it may seem.

All His Children Grew and Grew (Gans) 333

Berkeley Community Theatre, August 1972 (courtesy David Gans, all rights reserved).

Who Killed Uncle John?

Who killed Uncle John
And kept the show from going on?
"Not I," said the nitrous man
Counting money in his van
"The parking lot's my neighborhood
I'm sure the show inside was good"
"Not I," said the tribute band
Playing for nostalgic fans
"It's everybody's flame to keep
Twice as high and half as deep"
It wasn't me who stopped his heart
I served the man who served his art

Who killed Uncle John
And kept the show from going on?
"Not I," said the idiot
Flaming on the Internet
"He owed his wealth to guys like me
I take his work so seriously"
"Not I," said the completist

Fondling his compact discs
"I'm sorry that he's gone away
I'll soon own every note he played"
It wasn't me who stopped his heart
I served the man who served his art

Who killed Uncle John
And kept the show from going on?
"Not I," said the mainstream press
"I found his image ludicrous
His followers were so uncool
I made him out to be a fool"
"Not I," said the publicist
Protecting him from journalists
"I'm writing his biography
I needed him to talk to me"
It wasn't me who stopped his heart
I served the man who served his art

"Not I," said the acid-head
"And I don't think he's really dead
He served his time in hell on earth
Only I know his true worth"
"Not I," said the heroin
Slouching into Terrapin
"I helped him to escape his fame
By letting him forget his name"
It wasn't me who stopped his heart
I served the man who served his art

Who killed Uncle John
And kept the show from going on?
"Not I," said the engineer
Whispering in someone's ear
"I woke up worried every day
And went to bed each night that way"
"Not I," said the kwipment krew
"He loved me and hated you
Guts to open, trips to win
I stayed right in the game with him"
It wasn't me who stopped his heart
I served the man who served his art

Who killed Uncle John
And kept the show from going on?
"Not I," said the dharma bum
Speaking through his talking drum
"Not I," said the entourage
manufacturing mirage
"Not I," said the man from merch
Selling souvenirs in church
"Not I," said the radio host
Refusing to give up the ghost

"Not I," said the DEA
Deploying agents where he played
"Not I," said the troubadour
"Not I"—

"Not I," said the dancing girl
Interrupted in mid-twirl
"I'll show you where the spirit went
I'll meet you at the Incident"

GREENSLEEVES

Bill Graham, October 16, 1984 (courtesy David Gans, all rights reserved).

The Grateful Dead Came to Our House One Day (with 20 People and a Bottle of LSD): A Story About Discovering the Power of Channeling Healing Energy

Jean Millay

> *This is a story about what happened when members of the Grateful Dead, along with Bear, Melissa, Don Douglas and their friends (about 20 people), showed up at our house on the beach with a jar of LSD, and a weird story about having to ditch someone who seemed to be following them — an event that caused me to feel that we were about to get busted.*

My sister Marge and I had rented a house in Venice on the ocean because she had four kids and I had two. She no longer has a job as a literature chemist, because the aerospace company she worked for had lost its government contract. I had been teaching art and English in a rural school in Northern California, and it didn't pay enough to cover basic expenses. Besides, Allen Willis and I had just won an award at the San Francisco International Film Festival for a short 16 mm film about my first (and only) peyote experience. Tim Leary gave us permission to use the name of their book, and he recorded the voice-over introduction for it. Ravi Shankar and Alla Rakha were willing to compose the soundtrack — which they did while watching the film. The realization that

Cow Palace, December 31, 1976 (courtesy David Gans, all rights reserved).

I couldn't show a film entitled "The Psychedelic Experience" and still teach high school in that small town did not occur to me, until the soundtrack was finished. Ooops!

Therefore my sister and I decided that if we combined our households and moved to LA, we might find better paying jobs, as we were the sole support of our children. We also knew that neither we, nor our six country kids, could stay sane if we tried to live in any big city. (In both of the rural areas where we had lived, no one needed to lock their cars or houses, and the kids could ride their bikes anywhere.) So we felt lucky when we found a large house on Ocean Front Walk in Venice. The whole ocean was our front yard, and there were no cars on the Walk to endanger our kids on bikes. Marge got a good job as literature chemist again, and I was hired as a substitute teacher of art and remedial reading at a junior high just north of Watts.[1]

We lived a quiet life on the beach — as quietly as possible with six kids between the ages of 8 to 15 years. The local cops were friendly to our kids and to us — a librarian and a schoolteacher. However, a couple of weeks before, we had placed an advertisement in the LA Free Press about showing "The Psychedelic Experience" movie at the Aeronautics Building auditorium. When Bear found that out, he asked if the Grateful Dead could perform after we showed the movie. We agreed. (However, at that time, the Dead were the weirdest looking people I had ever seen. This was long before they became famous.) After the show, while packing up our gear, I heard (with horror) that Marge had invited them all to come visit us at the beach sometime. And without more warning than a phone call, they all showed up one day.

For me to take LSD, I preferred the expanse of nature, or the quiet of the meditation room with candles and soft music. As a teacher with two children I was always very nervous about the psychedelic scene, unless I could keep it under some kind of control. With 20 or so people at our house taking acid, this was obviously not going to be one of those times. The afternoon was warm and sunny, and most of the group played on the beach. Once I saw Jerry wandering around the parking lot in his wild hair and Day-Glo pink painted boots. He kept saying, "Where are my people? I lost my people?" I guided him to where he and others were happy to connect. As the sunset faded, most began returning to the house. The noise increased. I directed the children to their favorite television show, and suggested strongly that they stay there. At one time, I felt a disturbance on the outside steps. When I went out, two cops were trying to save us from two hippy-looking types who were sitting there. When I assured the cops that these two were my guests, Bob Weir and Phil Lesh both said, "Thanks, Aunt Jeannie," and disappeared into the sanctuary of the house.[2]

After that, I went up to our large flat roof to center myself and, under a vast starry sky, I asked for guidance to keep myself from freaking out under the circumstances. By then the effects of the LSD had taken full hold, and I actually felt the strength of inner light.

Then I heard someone screaming and saw him running around outside. It was a friend of theirs I didn't know. He was a marine just back from Vietnam, and he was screaming and running up and down Ocean Front Walk in front of our house. This had to be dealt with NOW. I went downstairs to find Marge and Owsley in an intense conversation about chemistry, with their radiant auras filling the room. I told them that I was ready to handle the situation, so Bear told his people to bring him in. The marine was wild and out of control, and it took four strong men to carry him into the center room. He screamed for a time until I could look up in the Leary, Metzner, and Alpert book to discover where he was lost, that is, in which "Bardo." He screamed "AIR, AIR, AIR" for a time, and them screamed, "FOOD, FOOD," and then "MOTHER, MOTHER," and then "FUCK, FUCK," and finally, "DIE, DIE." And then he was quieter and said something about "EONS AND EONS OF TIME." At first, we gave him some food when he was screaming for it, but he crammed it into his mouth all at once, letting it spill all over the furniture and floor. Then when he screamed "Fuck" he lunged for me, but Don Douglas intercepted him. The marine was undeterred; he kissed Don instead. (Don's version of this is very funny.)

By then I realized that the man was going through many deaths and rebirths, so when I saw that he was in the part of his cycle in which he could receive a communication, he looked at me and pleaded, "Help me." I looked him straight in the eye and answered, "Trust me." He nodded and before the cycle of screaming started again, two police officers came to the door. The neighbors had called them. The police offered to take him away for us. In those days, the emergency rooms had no idea what to do, so they often gave such people Thorazine to bring them down without resolving the cosmic drama involved. Those who experienced this might remain disturbed for some time. We had no intention of allowing that to happen. Ordinarily, having the police at the door would have been enough to confirm my earlier fears, but I was in a very different state of consciousness now and I could see that Marge would handle it easily.

In any case, so much energy was coursing through me at that time that I felt locked into position with my left hand in the air receiving light and my right hand pressing on the solar plexus of the man lying on the floor. For the first time in my life, I felt that I was channeling energy directly to him, and that he was comforted because he was actually receiving it. The cops left and said we should call them if we couldn't handle it. Marge thanked them and assured them that we would do that if necessary.

Now it was time to exert some control over the nonverbal environment. Anyone who felt anxiety would prevent the completion of trust. I asked everyone to leave except those whom I knew could hold a steady mind and/or loving thoughts. I requested a special record to be played from the other room into our speakers. It was a Bismillah Khan record of North Indian classical music, capable of causing entrainment into a meditative state. Gradually the energy level became more relaxed. Then the screaming cycle started again. When he got to the part where he screamed, "DIE," I was ready for him. I poked my finger into his soft belly, and extemporized the essence of the Bardo instructions for release: "Your blood is flowing into the ocean of all life. You are passing into the place of perfect peace. Use this temporary death to be released from all pain and confusion. Go into the pure light of consciousness." After repeated suggestions that he was actually dying, he became quiet, and after about 15 minutes, he sat up and asked, "What happened?" The two of us went up to the roof, into the fresh ocean air. While we watched the expanse of stars, we gave thanks to the Great Spirit. He had a cigarette and then we went downstairs again to join the others. Finding that such energy could be channeled like that while I was on acid was one of the most important experiences of my life. It was for me, a profound entheogenic lesson that I have used for many other crisis situations or for psychological healing.

Later, whenever I wanted to go backstage at a Dead concert, all I had to do was tell the door guard, "Tell them it's Aunt Jeannie." This worked every time.

Notes

1. The 1965 fall semester started shortly after the riots, and I learned that my students had new school clothes for a change, because many of the stores in their area also

had been looted during that time. I learned which of my students was thrilled to have been chosen "GO-GO GIRL" for the riot club meetings, where they learned to make pipe bombs and all that stuff a rioter needs to know.

2. Phil Lesh included his own version of this event in his book *Searching for the Sound: My Life with the Grateful Dead*.

Bibliography

Leary, T., R. Alpert, and R. Metzner. *The Psychedelic Experience: A Manual Based on the Tibetan Book of the Dead*. New Hyde Park, NY: University Books, 1964.

Lesh, P. *Searching for the Sound: My Life with the Grateful Dead*. New York: Little, Brown, 2005.

Millay, J. *Multidimensional Mind: Remote Viewing in Hyperspace*. A Universal Dialogues Book. Berkeley, CA: North Atlantic Books, 1999.

_____. "Psi and Entheogens." In *The Proceedings of the 21st International Conference on the Study of Shamanism and Alternate Modes of Healing*, R.I. Heinze, ed. Berkeley, CA: Independent Scholars of Asia, 2004.

Willis, A., and J. Millay. *The Psychedelic Experience* (film). San Francisco/Mendocino, CA: 1965. This was originally filmed in 16 mm. It is now available on DVD from the East Bay Media Center, Berkeley, CA.

CONTRIBUTORS

Rebecca G. Adams is a professor of sociology at the University of North Carolina at Greensboro. Her research focuses on adult and older adult friendship, and on friendship formation and community development among fans of the Grateful Dead. Her publications include *Deadhead Social Science* (2000, with Rob Sardiello), *Placing Friendship in Context* (1998, with Graham Allan), *Adult Friendship* (1992, with Rosemary Blieszner), and *Older Adult Friendship: Structure and Process* (1989, with Rosemary Blieszner). A past president of the Southern Sociological Society and fellow of the Gerontological Society of America and of the Association for Gerontology in Higher Education, Rebecca serves as editor of *Personal Relationships* (journal of the International Association for Relationship Research) and is a member-at-large of the Council of the American Sociological Association and advisory editor for George Ritzer's *Encyclopedia of Sociology*.

Cristian Amigo is an award-winning composer and musician, one of a current generation of new music artists concerned with challenging the artistic and social hierarchies between Western art music (classical and jazz) and all music. Known as an acoustic and electric guitarist with an improvising bent, Amigo writes chamber and orchestral music, electronic music, theatre, film, and performance works, fierce riffs, and songs. Cristian's awards include a 2006–2007 Guggenheim Fellowship in music composition, and the Van Lier Fellowship from Meet the Composer. Cristian has a Ph.D. in ethnomusicology from UCLA, currently serves as a music composition advisor for the New York Foundation for the Arts, and is an artist-in-residence at the American Lyric Theater in New York City and Calliope House (Pittsburgh Folk Music Society).

Barry Barnes (Ph.D., University of Kansas) is a professor and the chair of Leadership at Nova Southeastern University, Ft. Lauderdale, Florida, where he was faculty member of the year in 2000. He spent two years teaching at Indiana University–Purdue University, Indianapolis. He teaches executive education clients in South Florida and has taught courses in Germany, China, Brazil, the Bahamas and Jamaica. He spent 20 years in industry with IBM, John Deere, and other companies, and owned three small businesses. He has published in *The International Journal of Business Research*, *Review of Business Research*, *Journal of Applied Management and Entrepreneurship*, and other journals. His recent research and writing is focused on the relationship between leadership, organizational change and strategy, and the innovative and improvisational business practices of the Grateful Dead.

Jerry's marketing side (outside Club Front, 1983) (courtesy David Gans, all rights reserved).

Graeme M. Boone, born and raised in San Francisco, moved to Paris for a few years after finishing his undergraduate degree in music at the University of California–Berkeley, then returned to get a Ph.D. in musicology from Harvard University. Since then he has taught at Haverford College, Harvard, and Ohio State University, where he is currently a professor of music. His specializations include early Renaissance music and 20th-century American music. He has written books and articles on medieval, Renaissance, rock, blues, and jazz music.

Gary Burnett is an associate professor in the College of Information at Florida State University, where he has taught since 1996. He holds a Ph.D. in English from Princeton University and an M.L.S. from Rutgers University. His research has focused on interpretive practices and the relationship between social interaction and information exchange in text-based online communities. Dr. Burnett is the author of a book on the American poet H.D., and his LIS research has appeared in a number of journals, including *Library Quarterly, Journal of the American Society for Information Science and Technology, Library & Information Science Research, First Monday, Information Research,* and the *Journal of Computer Mediated Communication.* With Paul Jaeger of the University of Maryland, he is working on a book titled *Information Worlds: Social Context, Technology, and Information Behavior in the Age of the Internet.*

Revell Carr is a folklorist, ethnomusicologist and Deadhead, who studies American popular music in global contexts. His work focuses on the development of popular music in Hawai'i and the Pacific during the 19th century, and on the American folk music revival of the 20th century. Revell holds a B.A. (creative writing) from Hamilton College, an M.A. (folklore) from the University of Oregon, and a Ph.D. (ethnomusicology) from the University of California–Santa Barbara, and is currently an assistant professor of ethnomusicology at the University of North Carolina at Greensboro. Carr has published essays on the Grateful Dead and popular music in the *Journal of American Folklore, Perspectives On the Grateful Dead: Critical Writings, The Enjoyment of Music, All Graceful Instruments,* and *Dead Letters, Vol. 3.*

Elizabeth Carroll is an associate professor of English and director of the University Writing Center at Appalachian State University in Boone, North Carolina, where she teaches courses on rhetoric, writing, and pedagogy. Her first Grateful Dead show was July 6, 1986, at RFK Stadium in Washington, D.C., and she has been writing scholarly presentations and articles on the Grateful Dead and Deadheads since 2002.

Christian Crumlish has been designing, building and writing about online communities since 1994. He is curator of the Yahoo! Design Pattern Library and author of *The Power of Many: How the Living Web Is Transforming Politics, Business and Everyday Life* (Wiley, 2004). He earned his B.A. in philosophy from Princeton and studied painting at the San Francisco School of Art. He is working on a book about presence and identity in the internetworked age, tentatively titled *Presence of Mind.*

Amanda Diederich-Hirsh earned a master's degree in social science from the University of Chicago pursuing a course of study in anthropology, public policy and sociology, which culminated in a thesis on the creation and maintenance of community. Her thesis examined the Deadhead community through the social science perspective of cultural hermeneutics, as reflected in Victor Turner's book, *The Ritual Process: Structure and Anti-Structure.* Amanda has twice presented papers on the Grateful Dead at the Southwest/Texas Popular Culture Association. She currently divides her time between political consulting work and raising two young Deadheads.

Natalie J. Dollar teaches upper division and graduate courses in intercultural and interpersonal communication, communication theory and youth communication outreach. Before coming to Oregon State University–Cascades in 2002, she was a member of the Corvallis campus faculty (1993–2002) where she was named a College of Liberal Arts Master Teacher. Natalie received her B.A. in communication from Mississippi State University, her M.A. in communication theory from Arizona State University, and her doctorate in cultural communication from the University of Washington. She has published articles and book chapters on "houseless" and street-oriented youth, members of a musical speech community, and ethnographic approaches for studying group interaction. Her current interests focus on dialogue as a means of forming relationships among individuals or groups in conflict and teaching community dialogue. In March 2003, she founded the Community Dialogue Project (CDP) to provide educational opportunities for Central Oregonians. Working with her Oregon State students, she offers an annual Community Dialogue Workshop.

David Gans is a musician, writer, journalist, record producer, photographer and radio host who has written on the Grateful Dead for more than three decades. He has been the producer of *The Grateful Dead Hour* and is author of *Playing in the Band* (St. Martin's, 1996) and *Conversations with the Dead* (Da Capo, 2002).

Steven Gimbel is an associate professor of philosophy at Gettysburg College. He is the editor of *The Grateful Dead and Philosophy*; *Defending Einstein: Hans Reichenbach's Early Writings on Space, Time, and Motion*; and *Methods and Models: A Historical Introduction to the Philosophy of Science.* His articles have appeared in *Philosophy of Science, The British Journal for the Philosophy of Science, Studies in the History and Philosophy of Modern Physics, The Journal of Applied Ethics, Erkenntnis,* and *Pragmatics and Cognition.*

Mary Goodenough received an M.A. in Slavic languages and literature from the University of California–Berkeley in 1989, and has taught and translated Russian for nonprofits in the United States and Russia. Her article "Grateful Dead: Manifestations from the Collective Unconscious" appears in *Perspectives on the Grateful Dead* (Greenwood, 1999), and her "Grateful Rites, Dead Initiation" appears in *All Graceful Instruments* (Cambridge Scholars Press, 2007). She has presented papers on the ritual significance of rock performances at the Southwest/Texas Popular Culture Association.

Stanley Krippner is a professor of psychology at Saybrook Graduate School in San Francisco, distinguished adjunct professor at the California Institute of Human Science, and distinguished professor of psychology at the California Institute of Integral Studies. The author of many books and more than 700 articles and chapters, he has served as president of the American Psychological Association's divisions of Psychological Hypnosis and Humanistic Psychology, the Association for the Study of Dreams, and the Association for Humanistic Psychology.

David Malvinni is the director of music education for a Santa Barbara nonprofit called CAMA, and is an adjunct professor in music and American ethnic studies at Santa Barbara City College. He completed his Ph.D. in musicology at the University of California–Santa Barbara, and also holds a master's degree in music from the University of Massachusetts–Amherst, and a B.A. in philosophy from Rice University. He wrote *The Gypsy Caravan: From Real Roma to Imaginary Gypsies in Western Music and Film* (Routledge, 2004). He has published on a wide variety of musicological topics, including the Grateful Dead, and maintains a full schedule as a performer and teacher of classical guitar and violin.

Erin McCoy is pursuing her doctorate in humanities at the University of Louisville. Her research concentrates on the rhetoric of war-based music in America, but she also writes about music as social rhetoric whenever she can. McCoy is currently working on a feminist critique of *Workingman's Dead* and *American Beauty,* and her short story "All the Good Things You Are" appeared in *InterCulture* magazine (spring/summer 2008).

Nicholas Meriwether is the oral historian at the South Caroliniana Library at the University of South Carolina. His work on the Grateful Dead and Beat culture has appeared in a variety of popular and scholarly periodicals, and he is editor of *All Graceful Instruments: The Contexts of the Grateful Dead Phenomenon* (2007) and the scholarly series *Dead Letters*. He has also published scholarly essays on rock music, Southern history, and American literature, and several short stories.

Jean Millay received her Ph.D. in 1978 in human science from Saybrook Graduate School and Research Institute. For six years she was president of the Parapsychology Research Group in San Francisco. Her latest book about her years of research is *Multidimensional Mind: Remote Viewing in Hyperspace* (North Atlantic Books). In 1971, Dr. Millay co-invented (with Tim Scully) the stereo brain wave biofeedback light sculpture, a device that compares brain waves between two persons or between one's own cerebral hemispheres and feeds that information back as patterns of light and sound.

Shaugn O'Donnell is the director of graduate studies in music at the City College of New York, and also serves on the music theory faculty at the CUNY Graduate Center. His research interests include set theory and analysis, metaphor theory, and rock music, particularly psychedelia.

Eric K. Silverman is an associate professor in American studies and human development at Wheelock College in Boston. He has conducted several years of ethnographic research in Papua New Guinea and is the author of *From Abraham to America: A History of Jewish Circumcision* (Rowman & Littlefield, 2006) and *Masculinity, Motherhood, and Mockery: Psychoanalyzing Culture and the Iatmal Naven Rite* (University of Michigan, 2001).

Stan Spector received his Ph.D. in philosophy from the University of Colorado, and specializes in 20th century European thought, including phenomenology, transcendental philosophy, existential philosophy and hermeneutics. In addition to "Coleridge's Misreading of Spinoza" in *The Jews and British Romanticism: Politics, Religion, Culture,* he has published a number of articles on the interface between the Grateful Dead phenomenon and the philosophies of Nietzsche, Heidegger, and Merleau-Ponty. He is a certified Rolfer and a professor of philosophy at Modesto Junior College. He is currently writing *Nietzsche and the Grateful Dead*, a theory of art phrased in terms of the body and its application to the Grateful Dead experience.

Alan Trist has been the Grateful Dead's music publisher since 1970. In the 1980s he was a member and editor at the Hulogosi book publishing cooperative. He is the author of *The Water of Life: A Tale of the Grateful Dead*, a retelling of the classic folk tale from which the band takes its name, and a contributor to and editor of various books on the Grateful Dead. He divides his time between Eugene, Oregon, and the San Francisco Bay Area.

Jim Tuedio is a professor of philosophy and the director of the University Honors Program at California State University–Stanislaus. The co-editor of *Perspectives on Mind* (D. Reidel, 1988), he has published numerous articles discussing key themes in phenomenology, developing applications for Continental ideas in philosophical counseling, and drawing on relevant dimensions of Continental/postmodern thought to discuss Grateful Dead musical experience. His latest project is a book on Nietzsche, Bataille, Deleuze, and the Grateful Dead (Mellen Press).

Jay Williams is senior managing editor of *Critical Inquiry* and the publisher and editor of the *Jack London Journal*. He is completing a study of the complete works of Jack London entitled *Author Under Sail: The Imagination of Jack London*.

Jason Kemp Winfree is an associate professor of philosophy at California State University–Stanislaus. He is the co-editor of *The Obsessions of Georges Bataille: Community and Communication* (with Andrew Mitchell) and the author of numerous articles on Continental philosophy. He is currently writing a book on community under the influence of late 20th century French thought.

Brent Wood is a lecturer in the Department of English and Drama at the University of Toronto at Mississauga and is a specialist in the interfaces between poetry, music, and cultural evolution. His previously published criticism has focused on the oral poetry of Robert Hunter, rhythmic patterns in hip-hop lyrics, and the role of chaos in the work of William S. Burroughs. His first Grateful Dead concert was at Niagara Falls, 1984.

INDEX

Acid tests 25, 32, 35, 37n23, 71, 75, 79, 86, 88, 102, 107, 153, 167, 169, 173, 192–193, 204, 205, 212
Adorno, Theodor 21
Aeschylus 180
After Bathing at Baxter's 246
"Alabama Getaway" 80
aleatory 21, 140, 143
Alla Rakha 3, 4, 33, 339
"Alligator" 77, 79
American Beauty 49, 77, 141, 291
"And I Know You Rider" 49
Anderson, Benedict 238–243, 247
Anthem of the Sun 3, 33, 46, 87
Aoxomoxoa 33
Apollo 180–184, 223
Appadurai, Arjun 107–108
Aristotle 194
Armstrong, Louis 21

Bach, Johann Sebastian 20, 52
The Band 76
Barrett, Frank 269, 270, 273, 274, 275, 277
Barthes, Roland 44, 169, 224
Bateson, Mary Catherine 213
Beatles 21, 43, 76
Beats 19, 29, 45, 66, 235
Beck, Jeff 21
Beethoven, Ludwig van 20, 60; Fifth Symphony 63; Ninth Symphony 63
Benjamin, Walter 111
Benson, Bruce Ellis 12
Bentham, Jeremy 295
Berio, Luciano 59
Berkeley Barb 239
Berlin, Irving 66
Berry, Chuck 43
Besseler, Heinrich 73
Bierce, Ambrose 233, 225–237, 244
"Big Boss Man" 79
"Big Railroad Blues" 79
"Black Muddy River" 65, 114, 203
"Black Peter" 110, 114, 123, 185

Bloomfield, Michael 74, 244
Blues for Allah 188
Boland, Richard 251
Boone, Graeme 214
"Born Cross-Eyed" 63, 184
Bossidy, Larry 267
"Box of Rain" 187, 203
Bratton, Susan Power 197
Brelet, Gisèle 137
"Brokedown Palace" 115
"Brown-Eyed Women" 115, 196
Browne, Earle 21
Buber, Martin 295–296
Burke, Edmund 220
Burkholder, Peter 63–64
Burnett, Gary 288

Cage, John 21, 46
California Free Press 240
The Californian 233–234
Calvino, Italo 141
Campbell, Joseph 215–216, 225
Carbough, D. 280
Carroll, Beth 225
Carter, Forrest 129
"Casey Jones" 124, 185
Cassidy, Neal 237
"Caution (Do Not Stop on the Tracks)" 79
Charan, Ram 267
Child, Francis James 111
"China Cat Sunflower" 38n35
"China Doll" 144
Christian Science 28
Cilliers, Paul 45
Clapton, Eric 21, 74
Cohan, George M. 66
Cohen, Allen 29–30, 31
"Cold Rain and Snow" 110, 160
Coleman, Ornette 21
Collins, Jim 267
Coltrane, John 21, 32, 43, 48, 51, 59, 61, 270
"Cosmic Charlie" 241
Cowell, Henry 21

351

Cowell, Sydney 59
Coyote, Peter 243
Crassan, M. 269
Crawdaddy 283
"Crazy Fingers" 187, 188
Crumb, Robert 239
"Cryptical Envelopment" 183
"Cumberland Blues" 119, 123, 161, 197

"Dancin' in the Streets" 79
"Dark Star" 24, 38n35, 46, 77, 85–105, 140, 159, 184, 263, 265, 273
Davis, Miles 21, 48, 270
"Days Between" 160
Dead Beat 283
Dead Relix 282–283
"Deal" 112, 186
"Death Don't Have No Mercy" 140
Death of Hippie Ceremony 241
Dedalus, Stephen 246
"Deep Elem Blues" 79
Deleuze, Gilles 44, 148–149
Denning, W. Edwards 267
De Pree, Max 268
Derrida, Jacques 43, 54, 165–166, 174, 176
Descartes, René 184
The Dharma Bums 29
Diggers 241–243, 246
Dionysus 7, 149, 180–184, 201, 215, 221
"Dire Wolf" 121–122, 185
Dolphy, Eric 48
Doors 296
Dorsey, Lee 65
Drucker, Peter 269
Duprees Diamond News 283–285
Durkheim, Émile 297, 316
Dwork, John 283, 285
Dylan, Bob 61, 76

Eagleton, Terry 220
"Easy Wind" 124
"The Eleven" 184
Eliade, Mircea 217
Eliot, T.S. 28, 87
Ellington, Ter 27
Emerson, Ralph Waldo 28, 66
Enlightenment 20
"Estimated Prophet" 112
Euripides 180–181
Europe 72 49, 141
An Experiment in Dream Telepathy with the Grateful Dead 4
"Eyes of the World" 49, 50, 77, 225

Fallout from the Phil Zone 77
"Feel Like a Stranger" 113
Feldman, Morton 21
"Fire on the Mountain" 110
First International Symposium on National Security and National Competitiveness 245
"Foolish Heart" 112

"Franklin's Tower" 112, 188, 243
"Friend of the Devil" 49, 159, 161
From the Mars Hotel 115

Gadamer, Hans-Georg 153, 157, 158, 160, 253
Gair, Chris 235
Gans, David 275, 286–287, 291
Garcia, Jerry 4, 13, 43, 50, 60, 61, 66, 71, 77, 78, 79–80, 85–87, 89, 115, 133, 157, 160, 204–205, 313, 317–318, 331, 329–332; acid tests 86–89, 167, 148, 298–300; aleatory music 143–144; beats 29, 240–242, 330; being alive in precious moments 88–89; Bohemianism 233, 246–247, 330; chaos 135–155; conditions of music making 157–158, 160; Eastern/spiritual influences 32, 143; folk tradition 160, 203; freedom 299, 306; the Grateful Dead *pharmakon* 165–177, 299; Lesh's style of playing 48–52, 88, 157–158; lyrical ambiguity 115; metaphysics 32; musical center 50–52; received views 32, 246; seeing the weird 86, 122; and surprise 32, 143
Garcia, Sara Ruppenthal 32
Geertz, Clifford 251
Gillespie, Dizzy 21
Ginsberg, Allan 29, 32, 237
Glass, Philip 46
Go 236, 240
Goethe, Johann von 12
Goffman, Erving 301
"Goin' Down the Road" 63, 64
"Golden Road" 65, 114
Golden Road 283, 284, 287
Golden Road to Unlimited Devotion 281
"Good Morning Little Schoolgirl" 78, 79
Goodenough, Mary 54, 221
The Grateful Dead 33, 61, 252
Grateful Dead Almanac 289
Grateful Dead live performances: February 23, 1966 78; November 19, 1966 78; November 1966, Zenefit 32; January 14, 1967, First Human Be-In 3, 32, 237; January 1967, Krishna Consciousness Show 32; February 27, 1969 89, 99; March 2, 1969 140; April 4, 1969 100; August 18, 1970 Fillmore West 240; February 1971, Capitol Theater 4; 1973 Watkins Glen 270; February 1986, Kaiser Auditorium 215; March 20, 1986, Uptown Theater, Chicago 310; June 25, 1995, RFK Stadium 115; July 5, 1995, St. Louis 115; July 9, 1995 115
"Greatest Story Ever Told" 160
The Greening of America 298
Griffin, Rick 33
Grove, Andy 271
Guattari, Félix 47, 134–140, 146
Guy, Buddy 22

Harlan, Viet 197
Hart, Mickey 4, 32, 63, 156, 157, 301

Harte, Bret 233–237, 244
Hecht, Ben 235
Heidegger, Martin 71–84, 155–156
"Help on the Way" 112
Hendrix, Jimi 21
"Here Comes Sunshine" 49, 110
"He's Gone" 110
"High Time" 121, 124, 185
Hippler, Fritz 197
His Holiness the Fourteenth Dalai Lama 26, 29, 88
Hoffman, Abbie 237, 238, 243, 244, 246
Holmes, John Clellon 236, 240
Howlin' Wolf 22, 78
Hunter, Robert 8, 43, 44, 45, 54, 63, 85, 87–88, 107, 109, 110–113, 118, 120, 184–188, 225
Hurlburt, Stephen 236
Husserl, Edmund 253
Huxley, Aldous 23
Hymes, D. 280

"I Can't Come Down " 114
I Ching 32, 129, 131, 319
"I Need a Miracle" 109
"Iko Iko" 110
improvisation: *Afrological* 21; associative 11; conversational 12; definition 11; *Eurological* 21; hierarchical 11–12; Hindustani 22; *Improvisar* (Sp) 22; Javanese and Balinese gamelan 22; jazz 21–22; Karnatic 22; mind/body binary 20; transformational 13
"In the Midnight Hour" 77
"It Hurts Me Too" 79
Ives, Charles 32, 43, 45, 48, 58–70

"Jack-a-Roe" 160
"Jack Straw" 203
Jackson, Blair 287
Jameson, Fredric 46, 220
Jefferson Airplane 296
Johnson, Bunk 21
Joplin, Janis 122
Joyce, James 45
Jung, Carl 30–31

Kahle, Brewster 257
Kalachakra mandala 27
Kant, Immanuel 195, 220
"Katie Mae" 79
Kelley, Alton 33
Kerouac, Jack 29, 66, 235, 237, 240
Kesey, Ken 25, 43, 75, 109, 240, 274
King, B.B. 22

Lambert, Gary 291
Lang 197
The Lark 234, 237, 240
"Lazy River Road" 160
Lear, Jonathan 195
Leary, Timothy 238, 339

Led Zeppelin 21
Lesh, Phil 4, 13, 32, 43–56, 58, 60–61, 65, 77, 101, 129, 143, 156, 258, 331, 341; and improvisation 45–47, 79–80, 85–87, 88–89; and postmodern multiplicity 43–47
Lévi-Strauss, Claude 54
Lewis, George 21
Lieber, Francis 130
Linah, Micheal 285
Live Dead 3, 89, 96, 99, 140
Lizardi, José Joaquín Fernández de 240
Lomax, Alan 113
London, Jack 235–237, 240
"Looks Like Rain" 110
"Loose Lucy" 112
"Loser" 197
"Lovelight" 79
Luhmann, Niklas 44
Lyotard, Jean-François 44

Machiavelli, Niccolò 201
Maimonides Medical Center 4
"Main Ten" 100
Malvinni, David 13
"Mama Tried" 196
Mathews, Kevin 287
McCartney, Paul 52
McGee, Rosie 275
McKenna, Terence 175
McMahon, Regan 283
McNally, Dennis 5, 31, 67, 164, 192, 204, 233, 275, 313, 317
Meier, Barbara 32
Meizel, Katherine 113
Merleau-Ponty, Maurice 224
Merry Pranksters 45, 109, 274, 283
Mikel 285
Mill, John Stuart 195, 206
"Mindbender" 113
Miner, A. 269
"Minglewood Blues" 79
Mingus, Charles 61
Mintzberg, H. 269
"Mission in the Rain" 110, 203
"Mississippi Uptown Half-Step Toodleloo" 196
"Mr. Charlie" 80
modernism 43–45
Mohovich, Roger N. 197
Monk, Thelonious 21
Monson, Ingrid 12
Moorman, C. 269
Mouse, Stanley 33
Mozart, Wolfgang Amadeus 20
Mulvey, Sally Ansorge 283
The Mummer's Song 203
Mussorgsky, Modest 43

"New Speedway Boogie" 122–123
Nietzsche, Friedrich 8, 139, 153, 180–183, 223

Noddings, Neil 195
"Not Fade Away" 64
Noli Me Tangere 240

Old and in the Way 153
On the Road 29, 236, 240
"Operator" 79
Oswald, John 46
"Other One" 109
The Overland Monthly 233, 235–237, 244

Park, Robert E. 313
Parker, Charlie 21, 23
Peckham, Morse 204
El Periquillo Sarniento 240
Plato 166, 195, 192
"Playin' in the Band" 77, 159, 186
Podhoretz, Norman 235
Pollack, Jackson 247
postmodernism 5, 7, 11, 54, 59, 215: and modernism 43–45; and psychedelia 45–47
Prima, Diane di 235
Psychedelia 45–47
The Psychedelic Experience 29, 32, 340
Psychedelic Shop 29

"Quadlibet for Tenderfeet" 183

Raleigh, Henry 197
"Ramble on Rose" 245
Reich, Charles 298, 305
Relix 283–284
Richards, I.A. 172
Ricoeur, Paul 251, 253–254, 255, 256
Riefenstahl, Leni 197
"Ripple" 186, 203
Ritzer, Jeremy 165
Rizal, José 240
Rocking the Cradle: Egypt 1978 290
"Rollin' and Tumblin'" 81
Rolling Stone 283
Rolling Stones 21, 48
Rollins, Sonny 21
Rorty, Richard 8
"Rosa Lee McFall" 159
Rubin, Jerry 246
Ruddick, Sara 195

"St. Stephen" 112
"Samba in the Rain" 110
"Same Thing" 79, 81
San Francisco Bohemian Club 235
San Francisco Oracle 29, 31
Santana, Carlos 21
Saussure, Ferdinand de 223
"Scarlet Begonias" 112
Scarry, Elaine 202
Schopenhauer, Arthur 220
Scully, Rock 34–35
"Shakedown Street" 109
Shankar, Ravi 32, 33, 339

Shinn, Milicent 235
Shorter, Wayne 21
Simmell, Georg 315–321
Skipper, James "Skip" 311
Slick, Grace 246
Smith, Adam 196
"Smokestack Lightnin'" 78, 79, 80, 81
Snyder, Gary 29
Socrates 181–183
Sophocles 180
Spector, Stanley 223
Spitz, Robert 237
"Spoonful" 78
"Stagger Lee" 65–66
"Standing on the Moon" 203
Stanley, Owlsey (Bear) 244, 340, 341
"Stella Blue" 153, 187
Sterling, George 235–236
Stokowski, Leopold 63
Stoneman, Scotty 43
"Sugar Magnolia" 110
"Sugaree" 64
Suzuki, D.T. 29
Sylvan Robin 226

Taylor, Cecil 21
"Terrapin" 161, 188
Terrapin Flyer 285
Thelin brothers 29
Theosophy 28
Thomas, Michael Tilson 62
Thoreau, Henry David 28
"Throwing Stones" 63
Tibetan Book of the Dead 28, 29, 32
Tolstoy, Leo 223
"Touch of Grey" 114
Transdisciplinary 5, 7, 213
Trilling, Lionel 235
Trist, Alan 282
Trist, Deb 287
The Triumph of Bohemia 235–236
"Truckin'" 112, 186, 240–241
Tucci, Giuseppe 26, 88
Tuedio, Jim 224
Turner, Victor 216–217, 218, 294–303, 307
"Two Soldiers" 160

"Unbroken Chain" 115
"Uncle John's Band" 119–121, 185, 194
"U.S. Blues" 80, 161, 245

Vaihinger, Hans 316
Van Genne, Arnold 217
"Victim or the Crime" 171, 197
"Viola Lee Blues" 65, 77, 79, 80, 141

Wake of the Flood 49
Walker, Bill 33, 99
"Walkin' Blues" 81
"Wang Dang Doodle" 81
Waters, Muddy 22, 74

"We Bid You Goodnight" 63, 64
Webb, Charles Henry 234
Weber, Max 316
Weick, Karl 268
Weir, Bob 4, 50, 66, 78, 109, 115, 157, 331
Weir, Tom 33
West, August 198
"West L.A. Fadeaway" 80
Whalen, Philip 29
"Wharf Rat" 198, 203
Wharf Rats 173
"The Wheel" 112, 144, 187

Whitman, Walt 28
Willis, Allen 339
Winterland 1973: The Complete Recordings 291
Wolfe, Tom 235
Wood, Brent 222, 223
Workingman's Dead 77, 118–126

Yardbirds 21

Zappa, Frank 46, 247
Zen Buddhism 19, 29

www.ingramcontent.com/pod-product-compliance
Ingram Content Group UK Ltd.
Pitfield, Milton Keynes, MK11 3LW, UK
UKHW021843140426
5217IPUK00022B/1569